The Postgraduate's Companion

The Postgraduate's Companion

**Edited by Gerard Hall
and
Jo Longman**

Los Angeles • London • New Delhi • Singapore

Editorial arrangement © Gerard Hall and Jo Longman 2008
Chapters 1–27 © SAGE Publications, 2008

First published 2008

SAGE Publications Ltd
1 Oliver's Yard
55 City Road
London EC1Y 1SP

SAGE Publications Inc.
2455 Teller Road
Thousand Oaks, California 91320

SAGE Publications India Pvt Ltd
B 1/I 1 Mohan Cooperative Industrial Area
Mathura Road
New Delhi 110 044

SAGE Publications Asia-Pacific Pte Ltd
33 Pekin Street #02-01
Far East Square
Singapore 048763

Library of Congress Control Number: 2007939950

British Library Cataloguing in Publication data

A catalogue record for this book is available from the British Library

ISBN 978–1–4129–3025–3
ISBN 978–1–4129–3026–0 (pbk)

Typeset by Newgen Imaging Systems (P) Ltd, Chennai, India
Printed in India at Replika Press Pvt Ltd
Printed on paper from sustainable resources

Contents

List of Figures

List of Tables

List of Contributors

Laurence Bebbington is Team Leader for Social Sciences, Law and Education in Information Services at the University of Nottingham. He is also the University's Copyright Officer. He has worked at the universities of Glasgow, Strathclyde, Cambridge and Birmingham. He has lectured in information science and librarianship, published various papers on legal issues in information work, and regularly presents papers or takes seminars on copyright in research, teaching and learning.

Dr Lucinda Becker works as a lecturer at the University of Reading, based in the Department of English; she is also the Deputy Director of the Graduate School for the Social Sciences. She is Fellow of the Higher Education Academy and the university's Centre for Career Management Skills.

Professor Mary Bownes is Vice Principal for research training at the University of Edinburgh and Chair of the BBSRC Studentships and Fellowships Strategy Panel. As Professor of Developmental Biology she has supervised many PhD students. She has published over 100 research papers in international journals.

Jude Carroll is Deputy Director of the Assessment Standards Knowledge Exchange (ASKe) Centre for Excellence in Teaching and Learning at Oxford Brookes University. She has researched, published and spoken on managing student plagiarism and on teaching international students within the UK and internationally. She holds a teaching Fellowship at Oxford Brookes University.

Dr Joanna Channell is a specialist in the study of written communication, with a long track record of helping specialist and technical writers to communicate their ideas. After 10 years' experience in the Higher Education Sector, she set up her consulting business to provide research and training to government departments, local authorities, businesses and universities. This included design and delivery of research training programmes to eight universities. Her publications include *The Words You Need* and *More Words You Need* (Macmillan 1980 and 1985), and *Vague Language* (Oxford University Press, 1994). She contributed to the new edition of the Macmillan English Dictionary (2007).

Professor Pam Denicolo, University of Reading, is the Director of the Graduate School for the Social Sciences, the Director of Post Graduate and Professional Studies in the School of Pharmacy and an active member of the University Committee for PGRS. Her passion for supporting and developing graduate students is also demonstrated through her contributions to the UKCGE Executive Committee, the SRHE Postgraduate Network and UKGRAD activities including the RUGBY Group, which reviews and evaluates the national implementation of the Roberts-Funded generic skills training, and the RCUK/UUK working group on the European Code and Charter. As a psychologist working particularly in the fields of Higher and Professional Education, she has supervised around forty-five successful doctoral students, examined many more. She is also a visiting professor at three Higher Education Institutes abroad, with a particular remit to develop their research student support and training.

Dr Fiona Denney is Senior Graduate Skills Development Officer at King's College London, where she is in charge of implementing the Roberts skills agenda for postgraduate research students and research staff. Fiona has been a senior lecturer in Marketing and also provides training and consultancy for academia, industry and the not-for-profit sector.

Dr Roberto Di Napoli is Senior Lecturer in Educational Development at Imperial College London. He has co-edited the following books: *Fuzzy Boundaries? Reflecting on Modern Languages and the Humanities* (CILT, 2001) and (with Ron Barnett) *Changing Identities in Higher Education: Voicing Perspectives* (Routledge, 2007). He acts as a consultant for the University of Barcelona, Spain.

Dr Kate Exley is Senior Staff Development Officer at Leeds University and Consultant in HE. A former geneticist, she has worked in Educational Development for 15 years, led workshops at 60 institutions and is editor and author of the book, *Key Guides for Effective Teaching in HE*, Routledge (2004). Kate contributes to several accredited teaching programmes for researchers and academics and is external evaluator for the Integrative Learning Centre for Excellence at Nottingham University.

Simon P. Felton was the general secretary of the National Postgraduate Committee (NPC) during 2005–2007, a representative and campaigning charity aimed at enhancing the postgraduate experience. His academic background is in the social sciences where he undertook an MSc in Urban Regeneration, Research and Policy at the University of Birmingham.

Helen Foster is a university manager and her current role is Head of Transnational Education at the University of Nottingham. Her role supports and co-ordinates activities around the operation of the overseas campuses in China and Malaysia. Helen has held a number of roles within Higher Education managements including, Head of Postgraduate Admissions,

Postgraduate Funding Manager and had previously worked in a University Planning Department.

Dr John R. Gibbins was the Director of Postgraduate Skills Development at the University of Newcastle following an appointment as Principal Lecturer in Research Management at the University of Teesside. In both he helped develop University Research Ethics Policy and Procedures, and became Chair of the University Research Ethics Committee at Teesside. He has published extensively the latest of which is entitled 'John Grote, Cambridge University and the Development of Victorian Thought', *Imprint Academic*, 2007. Dr Gibbins was Chair of a Hub of UK GRAD, is a member of the Executive of UKCGE and was a member of the 'Rugby Team' advisory group. John has retired from full-time work to write and provide consultancy in the fields of researcher development and ethics.

Professor Wyn Grant is Professor of Politics at the University of Warwick and President of the UK Political Studies Association. He is co-author (with Philippa Sherrington) of *Managing Your Academic Career* (Palgrave, 2006).

Professor Howard Green was until recently Senior Adviser to the Vice-Chancellor at Staffordshire University, Professor of Urban Planning and Chair of the UK Council for Graduate Education. He is now Senior Partner in the Higher Education consultancy, Postgraduate Directions (www.postgrdauatedirections.org.uk) which specialises in postgraduate development.

Dr Ged Hall has been involved in training and development activities for research students since 1997 when he worked in the gas, oil and utility industries. Since 2003, he has been working at the University of Nottingham where he is Research Training and Roberts Money Manager.

Dr Chris Hart is author of *Doing a Literature Review* (Sage, 1998), *Doing Your Literature Search* (Sage, 2001) and *Doing Your Masters Dissertation* (Sage, 2003). Chris has successfully supervised many masters and doctoral projects and been research director on numerous, public and commercially funded, national and international research projects.

Dr Steve Hutchinson is a zoologist by training who turned to staff development and worked for several years for the universities of York and Leeds where he was also a regional hub coordinator for the UK GRAD programme. He is now an independent training consultant (see www.hutchinsontraining. com) and writer and leads programmes and courses for universities throughout the UK.

Dr Carolyn Jackson is Senior Lecturer in the Department of Educational Research, Lancaster University. She has published widely with Penny Tinkler on the doctoral examination process. She has also published extensively on gender issues in education; her most recent book *'Lads' and 'Ladettes' in School: Gender and a Fear of Failure* was published in 2006 by Open University Press.

Clare Jones has worked in the Higher Education sector since 1998 initially as a skills and employability specialist and later as the careers adviser for research staff and students at Nottingham University. Prior to that Clare had worked in a number of public sector and charity organisations building her career around a strong skills portfolio.

Dr Martyn Kingsbury is Lecturer in Educational Development at the Centre for Educational Development Imperial College London. Following a degree in Applied Biology, a PhD in Pharmacology and postdoctoral research in Japan, Bath and Imperial College, investigating various aspects of heart disease, he became increasingly involved in education.

Dr Helen Lawrence completed a PhD and three years post-doctoral research in sociolinguistics before her current role in skills development where she focuses on facilitating transferable skills workshops for postgraduate researchers. Helen currently works in Professional and Organisational Development at the University of York.

Robert Lawrie is Head of Scholarships and Student Finance at University of Edinburgh. He has a bachelor's degree in Divinity from Glasgow, and a masters degree in Business from Strathclyde. He has been working in the area of student funding since 2000, including three years at UCL where he managed the Scholarships Office.

Dr Richard Lilley escaped from academia in 1999 to become a behavioural research consultant with Tracksys Ltd., which was set-up by a fellow escapee. He also runs workshops and training days on postgraduate survival skills.

Dr Jo Longman has worked at the University of Nottingham for the past 11 years with numerous research students and research staff. She established Nottingham's highly regarded Research Training Programme in 1996 when the idea of centrally offered support and training for research students was still in its infancy.

Chris Luton is Head of Intellectual Property at the University of Nottingham. After qualifying in Law in 1982 he was employed by Commercial Trademark Services in the Far East. He then ran a successful hi-tech company for 15 years before periods working as a consultant to a patent firm in London, running the European Business Innovation Centre in Kent, working (formerly) at the University of Kent, then at the University of Nottingham where he is presently Head of Intellectual Property.

Professor Sharon Monteith is Professor of American Studies and Postgraduate Dean (Arts) at the University of Nottingham. She has supervised and examined many PhD students. She is a General Editor of *Scope: Journal of Film Studies* that is run by postgraduate students at Nottingham and is the author of a number of books.

Dr Rowena Murray has an MA from Glasgow University and PhD from Pennsylvania State University. Formerly she worked in staff development at

Strathclyde University (Glasgow). Currently she is Reader in the Faculty of Education at Strathclyde. She has published books and articles about academic writing for students, researchers and academics.

Sarah Musson is Manager of the Staff Career Coaching Service at the University of Bristol, where she has been working since 2003. Before this post she was a self-employed careers consultant in the private sector. She is also a qualified counsellor, and works at the university's staff counselling service.

Ellen Pearce has a bachelors degree in History from Cambridge. In 2003, she established the new Centre for Excellence (CfE) for the UK GRAD Programme. As Manager of the CfE Ellen has overseen the development of UK GRAD. She has been an ambassador for UK GRAD and a champion for the needs of postgraduate researchers, speaking at national and European events discussing graduate education and training.

Professor Stuart Powell is Professor of Educational Psychology at the University of Hertfordshire and is also Honorary Secretary of the UK Council for Graduate Education (UKCGE). He and Howard Green co-authored the book *Doctoral Study in Contemporary Higher Education* (Open University Press/ SRHE) and has also authored the work *Doctorate Worldwide* which was published in June 2007. He was for some years the Director of Research Degrees at the University of Hertfordshire.

Dr Seema Sharma currently works as a marketing coordinator and an independent science careers consultant. Seema completed a PhD in Molecular neuroscience at the School of Pharmacy, University of London. She has since worked as a technical specialist, a journalist and has gained considerable experience in providing career advice to scientists as a careers event programme manager.

Dr Sara Shinton works with a range of organisations in a variety of ways, but with a common theme of improving the career management and effectiveness of researchers. To know more, see www.shintonconsulting.com

Dr Penny Tinkler is Senior Lecturer in Sociology at the University of Manchester. Alongside her work with Carolyn Jackson on the doctoral examination process, Penny has published widely on twentieth-century girlhood and, more recently, the history of women and smoking. Her most recent book, *Smoke Signals: Women, Smoking and Visual Culture in Britain*, was published by Berg in 2006.

Foreword

Dr Janet Metcalfe
Director, UK GRAD Programme

Ellen Pearce
Manager, Centre for Excellence, UK GRAD Programme

This book is written at a time of significant and exciting change in the world of doctoral education. In recent years, there has been an increased focus on the contribution of researchers, evidenced by a plethora of European and national policy developments which highlight the importance of research and researchers to the growing knowledge- and innovation-centred economies of the future.

With this backdrop, research degree programmes themselves are undergoing significant changes. In the past few years, we have seen a huge diversification in terms of the range of qualifications available, an increasing international research student base, substantive quality assurance developments and impressive government commitment to raising the skills levels of research students.

There is a common misconception that all research students work in academic lecturing or research positions on graduation. This is not the case. In fact, less than half of research students (from the UK) are working in the education sector immediately after their research studies, and only 22% are working as post-doctoral researchers. It is, therefore, important that research degree programmes are aligned with preparing researchers for their potential future careers. Non-academic employers recruit postgraduate researchers for their high-level skills – the ability to work independently, to communicate complex models and theories to a range of audiences, to problem solve, and to 'hit the ground running'.

In response to these changes, this book brings together a growing number of academics and other professionals interested and involved in all the issues related to postgraduate research degrees. It is written for research students, and those considering registering for a research degree. The book provides the first comprehensive guide for research students: a 'one-stop-shop' that will be relevant from the very beginning of the process to having finished a degree and beyond. The book offers clear practical advice, positive yet realistic, along with signposts to a variety of other sources of support and reference points.

For you as a research student, this book is about the importance of making the most of your research degree – it's about making the right choices for you, and how to make the experience of being a research student work for you and those around you. It aims to help you understand the broader context of research degree programmes, what you can expect from your institution, and what you yourself need to take responsibility for.

Much has been done in the UK to support the careers of research students; this book is part of that increasing support. The UK GRAD Programme is committed to supporting research students in reaching their full potential – we wish you every success in both completing your research degree, and in your future careers, wherever and whatever they may be.

Acknowledgements

Our thanks go to the many individuals who have generously given their time and expertise to help with this book along the way. We want to take this opportunity to thank the researchers from whom we have all learned over the years, and specifically to thank those who have contributed directly to this book with case studies and examples.

Thirty-two people wrote contributions to the book in addition to us and we wish to acknowledge the hard work and commitment shown by all those people to making this book a reality. In addition, many others helped us by reviewing chapters and providing invaluable advice and guidance; our editorial board (Dr Tim Brown, Professor Alistair McCulloch, Professor Pam Denicolo, Jan Perrett, Dr Steve Ketteridge and Dr Sara Shinton) and also Barbara Graham, Robin Dollery, Jason Campbell, Will Archer, Dr Jon Turner, Dr Mike Davidson and Dr Sue Scarborough.

Thanks should also go to our families and friends for providing both support and fun distractions; both were needed and appreciated.

Every effort has been made to trace all the copyright holders, but if any have been inadvertently overlooked the publishers will be pleased to make the necessary arrangement at the first opportunity.

1 Introduction and How to Use This Book

Dr Ged Hall and Dr Jo Longman

This book provides support, guidance and ideas for anyone contemplating starting the fascinating, challenging and rewarding journey of undertaking a research degree in any of its many guises, whether they are doing this direct from undergraduate study or returning to education after a break. It is also written for those who are already undertaking a research degree, whether that be part-time, full-time, funded or self-funded, living close to their institution or studying remotely. The book also provides help for those who are looking at the next phase of their lives once their research degree is complete.

The uniqueness of this book therefore lies in its coverage of the entire process, from key considerations around choosing to undertake a research degree, through the process of getting the degree, to what you might do when you have completed your degree. Our intention is to provide a 'one-stop-shop' companion text that will support you throughout the process. The book is also different in its determination to signpost other sources of support, throughout and at the end of each chapter and to remain positive and encouraging about the benefits of undertaking a research degree.

In 2005/06 the Higher Education Statistics Agency (HESA) reported that 16,515 doctorates were awarded in the UK;[1] 12,950 full-time and 3565 part-time. This number has been steadily rising over the last decade, illustrating the increasing popularity of gaining such a qualification. But what exactly is a doctorate and more broadly what is a research degree and what makes individuals study for one? Where is the best place to undertake a research degree, how can you improve your chances of securing a place and how much will it cost you to get one? What will the process of getting your research degree be like, how can you improve your chances of completing successfully and what will you do once you have your degree?

We put this book together in an attempt to directly answer these essential questions in an accessible and engaging way, and also in a way that will provide maximum support to the individual reader. Having completed our own research degrees at a time when there was precious little help available other than our supervisors, we appreciate that our journey would have been smoother at various points had we had access to this information and advice, as well as something to provide some inspiration! Having enjoyed working closely with research students over the last decade, we understand that sometimes it isn't easy to either ask these questions or to get clear answers.

As a brief note on terminology, throughout the book we use the term 'research degree' and 'research student'. What we mean by research degree is a qualification whose process is predominantly based around research. Some of these degrees can lead to a doctoral-level award and some to a masters-level award. When the term doctorate is used this refers to all varieties of PhDs, the Doctor of Medicine qualification, Practice-based doctorates, European Doctorates, Taught Doctorates and Professional Doctorates. We have tried to ensure the information in the book is relevant to all such qualifications. The term 'research student', which is used throughout the book, relates to a student studying for a research degree. To understand more about different research degrees see the discussions in Chapter 2 of this volume.

The book contains contributions from academics and professionals with considerable experience of the following three stages of research student life in the UK:

1   Considering becoming a postgraduate research student in the UK
2   Being a postgraduate research student in the UK
3   Careers following a postgraduate research degree in the UK.

We specifically sought contributions from those not only with specific expertise in the above, but also a variety of contributors reflecting the wide range of Higher Education Institutions in the UK. Chapters are therefore written by those with experience of old universities as well as new ones, and from various locations in the UK for example.

Before we go any further it might be helpful to clarify exactly what we mean by the UK, as this book is all about research degrees in the UK (which are in some cases different from research degrees elsewhere). The UK is made up of the countries of England, Scotland, Northern Ireland and Wales. The management of funding for universities in each is via different organisations. In England it is the Higher Education Funding Council for England (HEFCE), in Scotland it is the Scottish Funding Council (SFC), in Northern Ireland it is the Department of Employment and Learning (DELNI) and in Wales it is the Higher Education Funding Council for Wales (HEFCW). The source of the funds is the same but the way those funds are distributed differs in each country.

Throughout the process of compiling this book we have been conscious that our readers will have a varied experience and understanding of the UK system of education, and that many of our readers may be considering studying in the UK for the first time. We have found the British Council website (www.britishcouncil.org/ and click on *Study in the UK*) a very helpful resource in this regard.

The book explores the three stages of postgraduate research student life as outlined earlier, and it does so for all the disciplines. Getting this view across the disciplines has been one of the central challenges we have faced; to make it general enough to be applicable across the disciplines, but specific enough to be useful and informative. We hope we have managed to get that balance right.

How Is the Book Organised?

Chapter 2

Although we have already given you a flavour of the definition of a research degree the difficult question of what a research degree actually is, is tackled much more completely here. The postgraduate research degree marketplace is a complex one and is difficult to understand for those who are not familiar with it. There are increasing numbers of research degrees available (some of which lead to the doctoral qualification) – offered in increasingly diverse ways, by a huge range of Higher Education Institutions. The question of definition is so central to the whole book that this chapter stands alone before the sections begin.

Section 1 of the Book (Chapters 3 to 7)

For prospective research students, this section gives clear advice on deciding if a research degree meets your own personal needs and motivations. It then helps you to understand how much it may cost and where you may be able to find funding to meet those costs. It also helps you to choose which university is right for you before helping you through the application process.

Section 2 of the Book (Chapters 8 to 21)

For research students currently working towards a research degree, the book covers the major aspects of getting going with research; research training, communicating research, teaching, writing-up and successful completion.

It also covers what might loosely be termed 'academic integrity', that is, what being a professional researcher is all about. This includes plagiarism, copyright and intellectual property rights, confidentiality, and adopting a professional approach to working with colleagues.

Importantly, this section also includes a chapter exploring what to do if things don't quite go according to plan.

Section 3 (Chapters 22 to 27)

The final section of the book covers the interesting topic of what you could do after completing your research degree. The section begins with a detailed look at some recent research about what PhD students do, and then looks at identifying and valuing your skills. The other chapters each looks in depth at one possible career path frequently taken by those with a research degree.

We have concluded with a Glossary of Terms to help our readers navigate through the somewhat murky waters of the world of Higher Education, and offer two appendices:

- The first containing the Quality Assurance Agency's (QAA) *Precepts* which all Higher Education Institutions in the UK must adopt in order to offer research degree programmes
- The second containing the Research Councils' *Joint Skills Statement* which highlights the skills that a research degree helps research students to develop
- The information within these appendices are referenced often throughout the book.

What the Book Doesn't Do

The book does not cover discipline-specific material, including the methodological aspects of research (study design, data collection, data analysis etc.). The book does not explore postgraduate taught degrees (MAs or MScs) in any detail.

How to Use This Book

Once you have read Chapter 2 and have a clearer idea of what a research degree actually is, then use the whole of the first section of the book to help to navigate through the decision-making processes you face (deciding whether to undertake a research degree, where and why and working out how much it might cost you and how you'll find the funds). There is also some detailed, valuable and practical advice in Chapter 7 about the application process itself.

Once you have started your life as a research student try to at least dip into all the chapters in Section 2. There is good advice on prevention of problems, for example, in Chapter 18 titled 'Beating the Research Blues', so don't wait until problems arise before you read that chapter. Similarly, the chapter on the Viva (Chapter 21) gives sound advice about general preparation as part of the journey of the research degree that will stand you in very good stead when it comes to your viva, so don't wait until two months before your viva to read that chapter!

When you are nearing completion of your degree the final section of the book should come into its own, but again it will be helpful if you read some of this section before that point. For example, read the chapter which most immediately appeals to you in terms of your career plans, long before you actually start applying for jobs. This will give you the chance to think about your career in advance of actually applying for posts, as you need to be clear that the path you choose is the one you really want to take.

You will find interactive material in each chapter in the form of questions, exercises and case studies. We encourage you to seriously engage with the material in each chapter by working through the interactive content, as it will help you to make more personal sense of the material and will also make the information, advice and guidance more memorable in the longer term.

Most of the chapters in this book look at processes of one sort or another, and aim to provide support for your own thinking throughout those various processes, for example, working out if undertaking a research degree is in fact the right thing for you to do, or working through the process of writing your thesis. It is helpful to accept from the outset that there are no rights or wrongs in approaching these processes and that the guidance provided may not always seem helpful to you. We encourage you to make full use of the ideas, advice and guidance that feel right for you, and to simply leave those that do not.

We hope you find this book an invaluable tool in supporting you at every stage of your journey through your research degree and on into whatever you choose to do next. Furthermore, it should help towards making sure your research degree is rewarding and successful. Undertaking research at the postgraduate level is a great challenge, and the doctorate of course is the pinnacle of the education process. The rewards therefore, personally, professionally and intellectually can be immense. May we wish you the very best of fortune along the way.

Note

1 See www.hesa.ac.uk/holisdocs/pubinfo/student/quals0506.htm. The data is entitled 'HE qualifications obtained in the UK by level, mode of study, domicile, gender, class of first degree and subject area 2005/06'.

2 What is a Postgraduate Research Degree?

Professor Stuart Powell and
Professor Howard Green

Introduction

This chapter sets the scene for those following by describing the current situation in the UK with regard to research degree study. That situation is not straightforward and the chapter seeks to explain some of the complexities as well as summarise what potential and existing students need to know. In order to contextualise some of the rather idiosyncratic aspects of the UK postgraduate research scene – reference is made to the UK in its European and worldwide contexts.

Having read this chapter you should have a better understanding of what the various kinds of research degree programme on offer in UK universities are likely to afford in terms of learning experiences and levels of achievement. Your place as a student within university systems should be clearer – though the complexities will of course persist. Finally, you will be aware that while you may be experienced as a university student – the step-up to research degree level requires that you take much more of an ownership role than is likely to have been the case in your past studies. For the first time in any university student's career the curriculum is not pre-determined (though some aspects may be so, as is discussed later) it is not a matter of studying what is laid out before you but rather of doing that and then adding to the sum of knowledge and understanding.

This chapter seeks to explore this essential difference between 'taught' and 'research' degrees by describing and analysing the nature of what it means to undertake, and succeed in gaining, a research degree award.

Background to the Education System in the UK

The UK has a large and, for the most part, well-regarded system of universities which gives it a world-class position in both Higher Education generally and in research and research education in particular. Originally dating back to the thirteenth century, the system has changed and developed as opportunities and imperatives have arisen. Currently there are well over one-hundred universities, colleges and other institutions able to award research degrees in the UK.

The grouping of institutions very much reflects the dynamics of change and their specialisations. In broad terms we can recognise three broad groupings:

1   The 'Russell Group' made up of 19 research-intensive universities, each of which claims to be working at world-class level. In 2003/04 this group accounted for over 60% of UK Universities in terms of research grant and contract income and awarded about 55% of doctorates in the UK. This group is characterised by universities such as Oxford, Cambridge, University College London and some of the provincial universities such as Manchester, Leeds and Bristol University.
2   A second grouping, the 1994 Group, is made up of 16 of the smaller, yet nevertheless, research-led universities. This group includes institutions such as Lancaster, Durham, St Andrews and the University of East Anglia. Several of these were the new universities of the 1960s.
3   Finally there is the so-called post-1992 Universities (sometimes referred to as Modern Universities) which were designated by the re-branding of the former polytechnics following the 1992 Education act.

Recently, several institutions that are not part of these three groups have formed the Alliance of Non-aligned Universities.

Change is continuing however and we have seen in the last year the creation of another batch of universities by the renaming of, for example, the Bolton Institute (now Bolton University) and University College Worcester (now the University of Worcester). Also, following the merger of the Victoria University Manchester with UMIST (University of Manchester Institute of Science and Technology) there has been the creation of the University of Manchester.

There is considerable, and perhaps inevitable, rivalry and snobbery around the university structure as each institution seeks to establish its credentials particularly as far as research and research degrees are concerned. The latter are often seen to be a significant factor in terms of status because provision of postgraduate research (PGR) indicates the highest level of study (i.e. the doctorate) and the highest level of intellectual activity (research leading to the creation of new knowledge). In essence, doing research and providing research degree study lie at the heart of the role of universities as knowledge changers and producers – that is rather than 'merely' as the conveyors of existing knowledge (i.e. to the 'taught' student population). This connection between research degrees and perceived status is mirrored across the world, indeed many countries (e.g. Japan, France, Mexico) restrict to an 'elite' group of universities the right to award research degrees. But at this stage, and for our purposes in this chapter, it is important to note that all institutions in the UK with university status are able to award research degrees. For many however it is a minor, if important element of their business. We should also note that in the current climate as it is described throughout this book – some universities may choose in the future not to offer research degrees – seeing them as simply not cost-effective. At the time of writing however, UK universities offer research degrees and each will have a different approach and ethos that will be of importance for the student choosing the institution to attend.

In world-ranking terms only the universities of Cambridge and Oxford regularly appear in the top 10 and for those of you who are striving to research at the very best you may like to consider the opportunities offered by these other world leaders (see Table 2.1).

As already noted, UK universities have what we refer to as research-awarding powers – that is the right to award research degrees. There are in addition other institutions which are able, directly or indirectly, to award research degrees. These institutions include, for example, some research institutions and colleges of higher education. In these cases, the awards are made jointly with a collaborating university.

We should note here that there are some, at times significant, differences in the way research degrees are managed and funded between the nations of the United Kingdom. In this chapter we are unable to describe these in detail. The model of research pooling, in which institutions collaborate in the management of research degrees is of particular interest and is one which may ultimately lead to discipline-based graduate schools as have been developed successfully in Finland for example.

Who Are the Principal Players?

Although we have suggested that there is a large number of institutions with the power to award research degrees, Table 2.2 highlights the fact that the market is dominated by a small number of players.

TABLE 2.1 World ranking of UK universities in the first 50

Institution	World ranking	
	2005	2004
Cambridge	3	6
Oxford	4	5
London School of Economics	11	11
Imperial	13	14
University College London	28	34
Manchester University and UMIST	35	43
Bristol	49	91

Source: THES, 2005.

TABLE 2.2   The distribution of doctorates awarded by institution (2000)

Quartile	Number of universities
Upper	5
Second	9
Third	18
Lower	97

Source: Millichope, 2001.

TABLE 2.3   Doctorates awarded in the top ten Universities (2004/05)

Institution	Total
Cambridge	920
Oxford	705
UCL	655
Birmingham	570
Imperial	515
Manchester	515
Leeds	465
Nottingham	460
Sheffield	455
Bristol	410
Total	5,670
UK	15,255

Source: HESA, 2006.

In 2003/04 the top 10 institutions in terms of the number of doctorates awarded were as indicated in Table 2.3.

It is noteworthy that none of these institutions in the top 10 are located in Scotland, Wales or Northern Ireland. This raises a note of some significance with regard to the evolving pattern of higher education in the UK. Following the devolution of power to Scotland and to a lesser extent Wales, higher education policy has shown some divergence, in addition to that already observed in Scotland, particularly with reference to funding organisation and the involvement and role of both the Scottish Funding Council and Scottish Parliament.

Finally in this section, we should acknowledge that the opportunities for research degree study are not confined to any one country. For many students, the lure of studying in faraway places offer real attraction not only intellectually but also in terms of broadening their life experiences, for example, the Universities of Washington, Vancouver and Grenoble offer sporting challenges for the keen skier as well significant intellectual learning environments. Importantly, however, you should be aware of the different characteristics and programmes which universities can offer and the regard with which their degrees are held. It is most definitely not the case that research degree study is a uniform business across the world or indeed across Europe. Indeed, it is perhaps fairer to typify the UK research degree process as being atypical of the rest of Europe and the world – certainly in terms of its examination processes and its development of differently labelled professional doctorates.

Of course, there are international commonalities in terms of what is meant by doctoral study; for example, the need for doctoral candidates to make a 'contribution to knowledge' and to indicate the ability [in a self-supporting and independent way] to continue to make such a contribution, are common markers for a doctoral-level qualification. But you need to be aware that the kinds of experience related by existing UK-based doctoral students will not necessarily be replicated elsewhere. This is of course not necessarily a bad thing; we merely alert you here to differences.

We should also note here that there is an increasing number of opportunities for periods of research study to be undertaken overseas in collaborating institutions abroad – particularly though not exclusively – in other parts of Europe. The use of English as an international language of study and of research, particularly in many northern European countries, is a key advantage for English speakers wishing to study outside the UK. In our own view, international collaborations are potentially advantageous, in a range of dimensions, for all concerned. We return to this topic, and in particular to the 'European Doctorate', later in this chapter.

Definitions of Postgraduate Degrees – Taught as well as Research

There are several ways in which we can define postgraduate awards.

Whether they are taught or researched. Hence we speak of postgraduate taught (PGT) or postgraduate research (as already indicated: PGR). It is perhaps worth noting that whilst this dichotomy is still observed, most PGT programmes involve a research-based dissertation, often referred to as research masters, and most PGR programmes have an increasing amount of taught input. Indeed, degrees such as the MRes may have significant taught components (see later in this chapter).

The level at which they are delivered. The level of delivery is now specified in the Quality Assurance Agency's (QAA's) typology, which refers to masters-level (level 4) and doctoral-level deliveries (level 5). We note the descriptor for masters level in Appendix A.

Within the masters level, there are three components: the Postgraduate Certificate (PG Cert.), the Postgraduate Diploma (PG Dip.) and the masters itself. These awards are defined by quantity of learning at masters level (even though their nomenclature may not mention 'Masters'. In the case of the PG Cert., this is awarded for 60 credits, the PG Dip. for 120 credits and the masters for 180 credits, all at level M or 4.

In the UK at least, postgraduate awards are sometimes classified in terms of time. The 'in-time' awards are often professional courses such as those in Town Planning, Health Education, Business and Education. In these cases, the award is a so-called conversion, or addition, to an existing award to give professional recognition and accreditation. The Post Graduate Certificate in Education (PGCE) and Master of Business Administration (MBA), for example, are clearly conversion programmes.

Although we have dealt with masters awards as a distinct category they are closely linked to doctoral work, either through institutional entry requirements or in a more structured manner through the funding policies of the research councils. Indeed, in some instances a masters qualification in a relevant discipline is a preferred or necessary prerequisite for entry onto a doctoral programme. This use of the masters as a precursor to doctoral study varies across institutions and, perhaps more significantly, across disciplines. For example, the need to have a masters before embarking on a doctoral programme is more common in the Humanities than it is in some of the Natural Sciences. (We return to the Masters as an entry requirement when we cite the QAA's Precept 7.)

Finally, we should make reference here to the Master of Philosophy (MPhil) degree. This award is employed differently across the sector. In many institutions it is an award that marks the end of a first phase of research degree study (it may well be that the programme of study is defined for registration purposes as the MPhil/PhD) though it is rarely taken as such (i.e. you simply transfer registration from the MPhil to the PhD stage). In this way it may be used as an 'exit award' or 'step-off award', that is an award that a student might apply to be examined for, if for whatever reason it is not possible for him/her to continue to do a PhD submission. In this same way it may be one of the awards available to examiners on final examination. In some institutions it is a self-standing research degree award. However it is used, it falls between the masters programmes (taught or research) and the PhD. It is usually a research degree (i.e. not taught). Given the inconsistencies of the above it would be wise for you to consider this award within the specific context in any given university.

Research Awards: The Doctorate

The Range of Doctorates

The doctoral award as employed within the UK Higher Education sector is varied in its manifestations. Indeed, this diversity and our understanding of diverse structures and their purpose represent one of the major current concerns for doctoral education in the UK. Students can work towards doctoral awards with different nomenclatures – involving different levels of entry qualification, modes and kinds of study. The broad categories of doctoral study in the UK are described below.

There is a formal definition of a doctorate provided by 'The Framework for Higher Education Qualifications' (FHEQ) in England, Wales and Northern Ireland – January 2001 (QAA) and we cite it in Appendix B.

The Doctor of Philosophy (PhD)

The PhD is perhaps the award normally recognised as a doctorate; sometimes referred to as the D.Phil, it is usually exemplified by the development of a thesis or intellectual argument and its presentation in written form as a dissertation (often described simply as 'the thesis'). Universities in the UK have been awarding PhDs since the thirteenth century. Since that time the award has commonly been accepted as the highest level of academic achievement attained by university students. This acceptance is universal except in countries such as France where there is more than one level within the concept of a PhD.

The nature of the PhD, and the nomenclature attached to it, has been subject to a variety of changes since the thirteenth century with accelerated changes over the past 20 years. In its earliest manifestations, the PhD was undertaken within specific disciplines and the award reflected its subject specificity with titles such as Doctor of Theology and Doctor of Law. In Germany the notion of a Doctor of Philosophy held sway and this was introduced into the UK system too where, despite initial resistance, it became the standard with the title of PhD or DPhil. This resistance related in part to debates about the role of universities and more particularly the role of research in the mission of those institutions. In the second half of the twentieth century the view of universities as institutions, necessarily engaging in research and of academics therefore as necessarily being researchers, became predominant. This view accommodated the notion of the PhD as a minimum requirement for academic tenure and in one sense the award became a kind of qualification for academic employment within the university sector.

As we have already noted, the view of the essential nature of a university and hence of the PhD as a key part in its structures and practices (as indicated in the previous paragraph) is open to question in the current debate about the future of Higher Education in Europe, in the current climate of changes to the funding regimes and in terms of the rapid expansion of the university sector in the UK.

QUESTIONS TO CONSIDER

Key question to consider if you are contemplating a PhD. Will my interest in the specific topic to be researched sustain me through a lengthy programme of study?

Taught Doctorate

By definition a so-called Taught Doctorate contains a significant element of taught work. This work is set out in agreed curriculum statements with specified learning outcomes that are subject to formal assessment. To distinguish a Taught Doctorate from a conventional PhD the taught content would need to include more than just research methodology and here the boundaries between the two forms of doctoral study are blurred. Many universities in the UK now offer taught elements in their PhD programmes even though they would not describe those overall programmes as 'taught'.

Typically the curriculum of a Taught Doctorate will include the production of a substantial research project and this will be examined by viva voce. Students in Taught Doctorate programmes are typically taught in cohorts but examined individually.

The so-called New Route PhD may be seen as an example of a Taught Doctorate though here again there is fuzziness around the relationship between taught elements and the overall research programme. This New Route was originally known as the 'Enhanced PhD' and this title gives the flavour of the intentions of its originators. It revolves around a consortium of 34 UK universities (see newroutephd.ac.uk). It arose along with the concerns about the PhD being too narrowly focused and sought to address some of the perceived needs of the international market for doctoral study. In its partial emphasis on front-loaded, taught, enhancing elements it is similar to the model of the PhD found in North America. However, it differs from that model in distributing taught elements throughout the course rather than focusing them entirely in the early stages of the programme.

It has to be said that for many academics in the UK the notion of a 'Taught Doctorate' is a contradiction in terms. Many would argue that the making of a contribution to knowledge cannot be taught in the conventional sense of the term in as much as it is not possible to predetermine a curriculum that will lead to such a contribution (necessarily one could not know what the 'new knowledge' was until it was achieved). This is not to say of course that a doctoral programme might not legitimately contain taught elements – that would prepare candidates for their research in terms of enhancing their knowledge and skills base.

QUESTIONS TO CONSIDER

Key question to consider if you are contemplating a taught doctorate. Will the taught elements add to my experience of studying at doctoral level?

Doctor of Medicine

The Doctor of Medicine is distinct within doctoral qualifications in that it is awarded by thesis written by qualified medical practitioner who may already have the title 'Doctor'. Again, criteria for the award are variable across universities, as are the kinds of supervision involved. According to Phillips and Pugh (2000) the title of doctor as used by general medical practitioners is an honorary one. Such 'doctors' do not in fact have a doctorate from their universities but rather are credited with [two] bachelor's degrees that jointly encompass the (Masters) notion of being licensed to practise [medicine].

PhD by Published Work

In the UK Higher Education sector the use of publications in doctoral submissions has been a practice marked by lack of consistency and ill-defined borders. This is in direct contrast to many other European partners, for whom a PhD submission typically comprises a written dissertation supported by number of publications. In such countries there is no award demarcated as a PhD by Published Work – it is simply accepted that a doctoral submission will contain such work.

In the UK however, for some institutions, publication as part of a doctoral submission is highly desirable while for others it has until recently been discouraged or simply banned. Many institutions offer the specific award of 'PhD by Published Work' but only to members of staff, some extend the privilege to alumni. There are different notions of what counts as a publication and different notions of how a submission containing publications can be constructed and assessed. The evidence for this can be found in the two national surveys of this award undertaken by the UK Council for Graduate Education (UKCGE, 1996; Powell, 2004) and which indicate a persisting trend of variation. If you have prior publications and envisage including them as part or all of a doctoral submission then we advise that, in the first instance, you read the Powell, 2004 publication – not least because it contains an Appendix giving detail of the situation in most UK universities with regard to avail-ability of the award, restrictions on who may apply, place of publications in relation to the development of a thesis and so on. We also suggest that if you do have publications and are interested in the possibilities of employing them, then your first port of call ought to be the university from which you are a graduate simply because many UK universities (though not all) restrict the award to graduates and/or members of staff.

The important non-pragmatic issue for anyone with prior publications is to consider those publications in terms of their relationship to 'contribution to knowledge'. Remembering that this is the essential (though not only) marker for doctoral level it is important in the first instance to reflect on the coherence of the publications in terms of any such contribution as well as the originality and continuing significance of the work. The fact of publication is no necessary indicator in the matter of contributing to knowledge – though clearly the place of publication (i.e. respected, peer-reviewed academic journal) might be such. Many successful candidates for the award of PhD by Published Work select judiciously from their list of publications those that contribute in a coherent way to a central thesis (meaning here 'intellectual position defensible by argument') – even if that thesis has various strands.

Broadly then the award is open to candidates who have already undertaken and published a portfolio of research – their registration and their supervision become matters of making sense of those works in a summarising and integrating way and indicating, usually in a discursive, linking commentary/dissertation the contribution to knowledge that has been made.

QUESTIONS TO CONSIDER

Key questions to consider if you are contemplating a PhD by Published Work. Do I have a number and quality of publications that may be seen as significant in my field and do they form a coherent whole? What more may I need to do to develop my works into a 'contribution to knowledge'?

Professional Doctorates

Perhaps the most clearly differentiated of the doctorates other than the PhD is the Professional Doctorate (UKCGE, 2002), characterised by a significant taught element and delivered in cohorts. Examples of professional doctorates include the doctorates in Education (EdD), Engineering (EngD) and Business Administration (DBA). For a brief history of the professional doctorates see Powell and Long, (2005). In terms of professional doctoral awards, the diversification seems to be greater in the UK than in most if not all countries in the world (see Powell and Green, 2007).

In one sense the professional doctorate may be described as a development of the notion of a taught doctorate. It is one where the field of study is a professional discipline and where the student is supervised within a professional context or supervised within a university setting but in relation to that context. The 'contribution' that the successful candidate makes will necessarily be within the defined professional area – so someone studying for an Education Doctorate (EdD or DEd) would expect to contribute to some aspect of the theory and/or practice of education.

There are currently well over 150 professional doctorate programmes in the UK in a range of subjects including education, engineering, business administration and a clutch of health-related subjects (see Powell and Long, 2005 for detail and an analysis of the range of titles on offer).

The professional doctorate has its origins in dissatisfaction with the PhD as a qualification appropriate for advanced professional work outside of academia and a perceived need for more relevant and appropriate doctoral level of study within the professions. All professions tend to be marked by a growing complexity and an increasing interrelatedness with other linked professions. Professional workers are increasingly in need of the kinds of research-based, analytical approaches to problem solving that are the hallmarks of doctoral-level study. More pragmatically, holding a first (undergraduate level) or indeed second degree (masters level) no longer gives a professional worker an advantage over colleagues and hence, perhaps, the need for more a more professionally oriented research doctorate. It is also the case of course that the professions in themselves need advancement in the current knowledge-driven society – doctoral candidates should, in theory, increase the knowledge base of those professions through the contributions that are the outcomes of their research.

For those readers who may consider studying for a professional doctorate outside the UK, it should be noted that the situation across the world differs in relation to these awards. For example, according to Allen et al. (2002), the EdD was developed in Canada in the late nineteenth century as a response to a perceived need for teachers and lecturers to further their professional education at the highest level. An EdD programme was established at the University of Toronto in 1894. However, Allen et al. (2002) also note that the professional doctorates have never established a firm popularity in Canada and the end of the twentieth century has seen a decline in numbers of programmes, with more faculties redesigning the PhD award rather than developing separate professional doctoral awards. Many parts of the rest of Europe simply do not have any award that compares with the UK professional doctorate – certainly not in terms of nomenclature and style of delivery. Indeed it is probably fair to say that the UK professional doctorate is viewed with some suspicion by many European partners, though such suspicion is often based on misunderstandings about 'taught' content and level of contribution.

One significant difference between the PhD and the professional doctorate is the criteria for entry to the programme and success in terms of the outcome. Entry to PhD programmes is usually determined on the basis of academic qualifications, but in the case of the professional doctorate a candidate may need to have professional qualifications in addition to those of an academic kind – particular kinds and levels of professional experience may also be required.

In a professional doctorate the field of study is a professional discipline which may, of course, subsume different academic disciplines, for example, education may subsume some aspects of psychology and sociology. The professional doctorate will be closely related to the development of practice within the profession and may indeed be accredited by a professional body and result in a professional qualification. It follows that, typically, the professions concerned are those where there is a strong practice element that, in turn, is mediated by intellectual understanding and reflection. UKCGE (UKCGE, 2002) noted that the main disciplines that had developed professional doctorate programmes were as follows:

- Engineering where the EngD was seen as a way of fast tracking talented engineers – deemed to be in need of training in high-level problem-solving skills allied with sophisticated technical expertise and the ability to collaborate effectively in team-based industrial situations.
- Education where a dissatisfaction with a contribution to the field by researchers that was felt by many to be too remote from the actual needs of teachers practising at the 'chalkface'. The EdD typically seeks to constantly bring evidence-based research tools to bear on practical issues within teaching and learning and within the management of the educational system.
- Clinical Psychology where the kinds of masters-level courses, accredited by the British Psychological Society, for those with a first degree in psychology wishing to specialise in clinical work have been extended to take in doctoral-level study. The DClinPsych is now accepted as the entry-level qualification to engage in clinical practice. It is worth noting here that the DClinPsych is unique in the range of doctoral study in the UK in being the only doctorate that is deemed to be at the level of an entry requirement to a profession (Clinical Psychology). In this sense it is an anomaly which only serves to further confuse the situation in the sector. It also raises questions about whether or not it is a realistic expectation to require a candidate who is seeking to enter a specific profession to gain entry by contributing to knowledge about it.

QUESTIONS TO CONSIDER

Key questions to consider if you are contemplating a professional doctorate. If you are contemplating registering for a professional doctorate the primary issues you need to consider are as follows: (a) Is the qualification recognised and valued in my profession? and (b) Is my professional work related closely enough to the parameters of any 'taught' components for a useful synergy to develop between what I learn and the progress of my own professional practice?

Practice-based Doctorate

The concept of the Practice-based Doctorate has existed in the UK and subsequently in some other parts of Europe since the early 1990s (Durling et al., 2002; Frayling, 1993) though the award, and in particular the PhD by Musical Composition as an example of it, predates this. Since 1990 there has been a trend in the UK towards integrating independent Art and

Design Schools into universities. This process brought with it an increasing emphasis on research training in areas where previously studio skills were valued 'rather than analytical or intellectual skills' (Durling et al., 2002: 8).

To many across the sector the practice-based doctorate is distinguishable from both the PhD and the professional doctorates in that, typically, it involves production of creative works as a direct way of contributing to knowledge. There are clearly some problematic issues arising from this view. Primary among these is the question of whether or not a practice-based doctorate can be awarded solely on the basis of the production of a creative work(s) – assessed by knowledgeable peers who are experienced in the field and who can therefore pass judgement on whether or not the work(s) is worthy of note as excellent in respect of the criteria operating in that field and as contributing to knowledge in itself. An alternative position is to suggest that however much critical acclaim can be agreed upon in these respects, the work(s) require an intellectual contextualisation and critical interpretation if it is to be deemed worthy of a doctoral award. Both of these views are manifest in particular institutional regulations in the UK – there is no national consensus.

We suggest here that, if you are considering undertaking a programme that leads to an award that is described in the particular university regulations and advertising material as a 'Practice-based PhD', you should read carefully the stated criteria for the award. These criteria may well be couched in terms of 'a successful candidate for the award will need to demonstrate x and y.' We suggest such careful checking for two main reasons. First, a university that is not clear in its own regulations about what needs to be achieved to indicate to examiners that the required doctoral level has been reached is best avoided. Second, you need to be clear in your own mind that what is going to be required of you (in order for you to demonstrate this doctoral level) is achievable in terms of your own creative practice. In short, it is not a good idea to embark on a project that leads to outcomes that may satisfy your own creative needs but not a set of judgement criteria that is seeking something else or something in addition to the creative outputs. You need to be aware of what is being expected of you and your creative practice.

QUESTIONS TO CONSIDER

Key question to consider if you are contemplating a practice-based doctorate. Similar to the note made earlier in relation to the professional doctorates, it may be important (depending on your personal circumstances) for you to consider the recognition and standing of the award within the creative domain in which you work.

European Doctorate

The European Doctorate is an award of an individual European university, made in accordance with the criteria set out by the Confederation of European Union Rectors' Conferences. It is a variation of the existing PhD, under which the following conditions have been met:

1   The thesis must be prepared as a result of a period of registration at a UK university that includes a period of research in another European country normally of not less than ten weeks.
2   Part of the viva voce examination must be conducted in a European language other than English, normally an official language of a European country. The examiners conducting the viva voce must include at least one from a university in a European country other than the UK.
3   The thesis examiners must include at least two from universities in two separate European countries other than the UK.

Several UK universities offer the European Doctorate, usually in defined areas of study between groups of partner universities such as the European Doctorate in Sound and Vibration Studies at the University of Southampton. Others such as the University of Sussex offer the award in all subjects. Yet other UK universities team up with mainland European universities and are involved in programmes that differ significantly from the UK doctoral model – of any description. The University of Warwick, for example, is a partner in a programme led by the University of Barcelona's Department of Business Economics and Management, entitled 'European Doctoral Programme in Entrepreneurship and Small Business Management'.

QUESTIONS TO CONSIDER

Key questions to consider if you are contemplating a European doctorate. Is it important to me to have this European dimension to my studies and to my award? Will I be able to sustain the pragmatic elements of this kind of doctorate?

The 'Product' of Doctoral Study

The tangible 'product' of a doctoral programme is referred to, in commonplace usage, as a thesis or dissertation. The terms dissertation and thesis are often used synonymously in the UK Higher Education sector in that both may be taken to mean the submission made by a doctoral candidate. There is, however, a distinction between the two terms that is more than merely pedantic and one that identifies the outcome of a programme of doctoral research. A thesis is an intellectual position adopted by the candidate and then defended in both a written submission and subsequently in an oral examination. The submission, which may take more than one physical form, is then a disquisition (which might be referred to as a dissertation) – an elaborate treatise or discourse in which that intellectual position is defended. To use the terms thesis and dissertation synonymously is therefore to conflate two quite distinct meanings; nevertheless this is what, as we have noted above, traditionally happens in the UK and indeed overseas.

By stressing the real meanings of the terms commonly used interchangeably we seek to emphasise that a doctoral candidate needs to develop and then present his/her thesis in one of several potential physical forms; typically, the dissertation is the permanent record of that thesis.

The form and length of the dissertation will reflect the nature of the thesis. For most universities, regulations for the dissertation are specified in terms of length or size. We note below the typical specification for a traditional doctorate. The degree to which individual universities enforce these word limits varies significantly. Table 2.4 shows average maximum dissertation lengths (excluding ancillary data).

Other doctorate submissions can be in quite different formats. For practice-based doctorates: artefacts, scores, portfolios of original workshop performances or exhibitions form part or even the whole of the submission. In the case of a doctorate in music the submission *may* be a substantial composition written specifically for the award together with an appropriate commentary or a performance with associated recording (individual university regulations apply).

More recently there has been growing interest in the submission being in electronic format. This offers particular opportunity for work which is not naturally in written form as the potential of multimedia allows candidates to provide the permanent record of the work in a way which better reflects the particular discipline. Again, individual institutions operate differing regulations in relation to 'e-theses' and 'e-submission of theses' (these two things are not necessarily the same).

Examination

Readers may wish to refer here to Chapter 21 of this book, which deals with the viva. The final examination is a traditional element of the British doctorate

TABLE 2.4   Average maximum dissertation lengths, based on an analysis of the regulations of ten institutions from across the UK sector

	Subjects	Maximum dissertation length
PhD	Science and engineering	40,000 words
	Other areas	80,000 words
Professional research Doctorate		60,000 words
MPhil	Science and engineering	20,000 words
	Other areas	40,000 words

and is made up of two elements: the examination of the dissertation (whatever form that takes and however it is described by the particular university) by at least one external examiner of the dissertation, whatever form that takes, and the viva voce or oral defence of the dissertation.

Unlike in most other countries, the viva is an intimate affair generally held in private in which the candidate is questioned on context, general content and detail of the submission. Increasingly there is move to open the viva to be a more transparent process. The QAA Code of Practice (QAA, 2004), for example, suggests:

> some institutions now appoint an independent, non-examining chair: this is thought to be good practice, not least in ensuring consistency between different vivas and in providing an additional viewpoint if the conduct of the viva should become the subject of a student appeal. Where the appointment of an independent chair is not feasible, institutions should find alternative ways of assuring fairness and consistency, acceptable to the student, that enable them to know the viva is conducted in an appropriate manner.

Which of the Doctorates to Research for?

In selecting which specific doctorate you might consider researching, there is the more general issue of doctorate or not? Subsequent chapters examine in more detail the pros and cons of undertaking postgraduate work. At this stage we simply note that some jobs require a doctorate while others do not; some pay significantly more for those with doctorates while others do not and relatively few doctorates go on to become academics.

Some elements of the decision about which doctorate to follow will be made for you by the entry requirements and delivery modes for the awards themselves. We might summarise some of these to give you an indication of the kinds of issues involved. The precise details will depend on individual institutions and their specific regulations, and sponsors if you are seeking financial support.

PhD Open to All Has the Following Features:

- Normally requires masters or good honours degree in a relevant subject
- Is single research project based
- No age constraints
- Available full- or part-time.

PhD by Published Works Has the Following Features:

- Requires significant published outputs

- Often availability is restricted to academic members of staff
- Usually part-time.

Professional doctorate Has the Following Features:

- Generally requires a period of work experience at a senior level and sometimes current professional engagement
- Is usually part-time.

It is worth noting here that the QAA Code of Practice (revised, 2004) in its Precept 7 (see Appendix 1) introduced a broadly based set of entry requirements for all doctorates (though ultimately decisions rest with the particular institution). Precept 7 sets out the expectation that, for doctoral research, students will have one or more of the following:

- A degree, normally with class 2(i) or equivalent in a relevant subject
- A relevant master's qualification or equivalent
- Evidence of prior professional practice or learning that meets the institution's criteria and good practice guidelines for the accreditation of prior experiential and/or certificated learning (AP[E/C]L).

The UK PhD in the International Context

Comparison between the UK and Elsewhere

We have already noted the possibilities of studying abroad for some or all of a PhD programme. In order to help you understand the situation better we include here some brief comparisons between the UK and overseas in terms of postgraduate study. It is all too easy to assume that doctoral education is the same worldwide and that practices are similar country to country. Whilst this may be true in broad terms, the detail tells a different story. The doctorate we recognise originated in Germany in late nineteenth century, from where it was exported to the USA and then to the UK and subsequently to Australia and Canada and finally globally. In this process it was modified to suit local requirements and interests. In a short paragraph it is difficult to summarise all the differences (see for example, Powell and Green, 2007. In Table 2.5 we identify some key features.

Bologna and the Higher Education Area

The UK doctorate is still a world leader as far as the international market is concerned. There are, however, changes that are taking place both in Europe

TABLE 2.5   Key features of the PhD from different international contexts

Type of Programme	
USA	Significant taught programmes prior to major research project
Canada	Research project supported by some research training
Europe	Magnum opus
Nature of Submission	
USA	Credits plus thesis
Europe	Some thesis (France, Germany, Nordic countries); some publications (bound together with a commentary) (Netherlands)
Type of Examination	
Australia	Internationally based (i.e. involving examiners from outside of the country) but no viva
Nordic countries	Viva – public affair with international external
France	Public presentation and defence

and at a global level that will influence the future, particularly in view of the Bologna declaration, which set out a framework for a European Higher Education Area by 2010 (Reichert and Tauch, 2003). The original declaration covers six areas of activity to which four more were added recently in the communiqué, *Realising the European Higher Education Area* following the Berlin Conference in 2003. These are noted below.

1   Adoption of a system of easily readable and comparable degrees
2   Adoption of a system essentially based on two main cycles: undergraduate/postgraduate (masters)
3   A common system of credits (ECTS)
4   Increased mobility of students, teachers, researchers etc.
5   European co-operation in quality assurance
6   Promotion of the European dimension in higher education
7   Lifelong learning
8   Higher Education universities and students
9   Promoting the attractiveness of the European Higher Education Area
10 Doctoral studies as a third cycle.

Each of these elements is seen to be interdependent, so a common system of credits will enhance the mobility of students within a common two-cycle (now three-cycle) system. The recent addition of the doctorate is of particular interest here because it is arguably the area of European education that displays the greatest diversity. The doctorate programme is an essential link between the Higher Education Area and the emerging research area. If Europe is to increase the number of researchers by 700,000 as the Commission outlined in its action plan 'More research for Europe – towards the 3% objective' (European Commission Research, 2003) then research training will be vital.

For those of you considering embarking on a research degree this then is a time of increasing possibilities for engaging in your studies across national boundaries within the European Union particularly and to a lesser extent worldwide. Increased harmonisation, and the deliberate encouragement of mobility of researchers, across the European higher education sector should bring increased possibilities for such study.

Where to Do Your Research?

Readers may wish to refer here to Chapter 7 of this book. We noted above that the market for postgraduate study is now global: this is particularly so for British students as the language of postgraduate work in an increasing number of universities worldwide is English. However, if you are to study in the UK, you should think of those factors which will be important to your decision. You may of course have little choice either for personal reasons, mode of attendance reasons and straightforward availability of programme reasons. Your decision making may be influenced by the following criteria.

Subject-related Matters

Does the institution offer what I want (and here the devil is in the detail)? Particularly for taught programmes, check that the specific curriculum of the awards is what you are looking for. There is often significant variation in curriculum even in programmes with identical names. Ask for lecture lists and reading lists and check that the options you are interested in will be offered when you are there.

Status-related Issues

Does the institution have a reputation for the programme you want to follow or the research area you are interested in?

Staffing-related Issues

Do you want to study with a particular person or research group? However, take care because there are several instances where the person you particularly wanted to supervise your work has left or is on sabbatical leave (universities may be reluctant to guarantee any particular supervisor).

Financial Issues

Is funding available from the research councils, the institutions or external sponsor?

What is the level of the funding and what does it cover?

Will you be able to earn additional income from teaching or other university-related work?

What funding is available for additional activities such as field work and conference attendance?

Issues of Success Rates and Time to Completion

The time taken to complete a doctorate depends on many factors – some academic relating to the complexity of the problem, some organisational relating to the management and supervision of the work, some financial relating to the level of support and hence time that the student is diverted away from the research. The UK has adopted 'time to submission' as a key indicator of success for programmes, and from very low levels in the 1980s, rates have improved in research council and Wellcome Trust-funded programmes hover around the 80% level after four years. However, recent analysis has demonstrated that for doctoral programme other than these, rates are much lower.

Different Methods of Studying for a Research Degree

Readers may wish to refer here to Chapter 21 where matters of completion and submission rates are considered in more detail. The methods of studying for doctorates have been changing quite rapidly as institutions are adapting to market conditions to fill their places. More and more students are approaching doctorate study in what we might regard as non-traditional modes. These include part-time, distance or by e-learning (or by a combination of these). Whilst we can differentiate in this way – what we are really discussing is a mode other than full-time mode. It is also possible to combine full-time and these modes during the course of study. After all, most full-time students spend their final period before submission in some form of part-time, at-a- distance, study.

Again, which method you adopt will, in part, depend on your own circumstances and what institutions have available? You will find that many institutions and some disciplines find it difficult to accommodate part-time study. For others it is the main thrust of their research degree delivery.

For you as the purchaser of this service you need to consider the advantages and disadvantages of each approach. Set out your own table of pros and cons. But you will want to consider the following shown in Table 2.6.

Whilst the funding of PGR study, particularly by the research councils, is becoming more responsive to needs; as we will see below, very few students complete their doctoral work within 3 years and hence you can expect to spend at least some part of even a full-time programme studying part-time.

TABLE 2.6   Pros and cons of different methods of studying for a research degree

	Full time	Part time
Pros	Complete quickly	Maintain salary and employment rights
	Engage fully in research environment	Keep feet on ground (i.e. remain realistic)
Cons	Live on limited income	May take long time to complete
	Loss of three plus years of pension rights	Is additional to normal work
	Lose touch with the 'real' world	Personal stress

Universities tend to adopt the euphemism 'writing-up' for this period of essentially non-funded, part-time study.

Different Styles and Approaches

Given the variety of awards now available with the general title of doctorate, it is not surprising that there are a variety of styles and approaches to their delivery. Whilst the QAA Code of Practice has identified some common features of delivery which are recognised as good practice, there remain significant differences at both institutional and disciplinary levels. We can perhaps identify the two extremes of a continuum of approaches with the laboratory-based team at one extreme and the lone scholar at the other.

In the physical sciences the doctoral student normally works with a laboratory team, led by a senior member of staff, with other staff, 'post-docs' and one or more research students. The research student is seen as one of the team, frequently working on a project decided by the team leader and funded as part of a project research grant. Contact with other researchers in the team and supervisor is frequent (if not continuous). As the research work for the PhD contributes to the overall project there is often little scope for personal inputs. Some would suggest that the student is fulfilling the role of research assistance.

At the other extreme, and often experienced by research students in the Humanities and Social Sciences, students work on their own project which they will have devised and developed (though the theme may of course reflect the research work of the department or supervisor). In such cases the student will frequently work in isolation, sometimes with extensive periods away from the department undertaking field investigation or working in specialist libraries.

Departments offering the professional doctorates will adopt totally different approaches to delivery. Dealing as they do largely with part-time professionals, many will adopt a block-release or long weekend timetable. Additionally, most professional doctorates are run with groups of students and hence might be seen to combine the two extremes we noted above – with intensive periods of team working and long periods as the lone scholar, the latter being increasingly mediated by the use of e-based discussion groups.

Quality Assurance of Doctoral Awards

The quality of the postgraduate award and student experience is taken very seriously in the UK and is one of the key factors which give UK postgraduate education a significant competitive advantage. Quality assurance is monitored by the Quality Assurance Agencies (QAAs) (one in Scotland, one in England and one in Wales). Quality assurance is achieved through two principle approaches: (1) the provision of a Code of Practice to which institutions must adhere, and (2) regular audits of all universities' provision.

Historically, the major emphasis of the QAA audit process has been on undergraduate provision. However, recently, more emphasis has been placed on postgraduate and particularly PGR provision. The Code of Practice for Postgraduate Research Programmes was initially produced in 1999 as the first of many QAA codes. Revised in 2004, it is now a comprehensive document giving a clear framework and guidelines for the effective delivery of doctoral programmes. The code covers a range of activities in the research degree process under the headings of 27 precepts (see Appendix 1).

Whatever UK university you enrol in, it will be seeking to adhere to these precepts; given their importance, included are in Appendix 1 to this book. The Code, whilst placing an obligation on both institution and student, provides a clear statement of what research students are entitled to expect during the course of their studies.

The Changing Nature of the Postgraduate Research Degree: Current Developments in the UK

Postgraduate research provision is never static and we have already noted some of the changes which have taken place over the past years. In this section we address some of the notable changes in the last 10 years or so and those which may challenge UK universities in the future.

Funding and the Level of Student Stipends

Readers may wish to refer here to Chapters 4 and 5 of this book. Individual funding of doctorate studies comes from a variety of sources; universities, research councils, industry sponsors, employers and personal self-funding, and so on. Although there is still some variability in the level of funding that each of these agencies will provide there has been a general and substantial upward drift in the level of support. This trend was the result of the Roberts' Review of science and technology recruitment (see later) following the increasingly difficult recruitment of students to science, engineering and technology.

The resulting changes led to research council stipends rising significantly to a figure more comparable with the net salary of the average new graduate. In order to be competitive, most other funders followed this lead. Some sponsors such as the Wellcome Trust pay substantially above the research council level.

In addition to the basic stipend, there are additional payments for London-based study, attendance at conferences and field work. But, the stipend is not a salary and consequently employment rights normal to salaried positions such as national insurance and superannuation are absent. Losing a few of 'pensionable years' may not seem to be important at age 25 but when reaching retirement it can represent a substantial pension loss.

Institutional Organisation and the Growth of Graduate Schools

Readers may wish to refer here to Chapter 6 of this book. There is a range of models of what constitutes a graduate school and what role it performs. The model adopted depends, in part at least, on the size of the university and the number of doctoral students it has. In cases where there is large number of doctoral students, graduate schools tend to be at faculty or departmental level. In universities with relatively few doctoral students the graduate school will tend to be at university level. The resources, facilities and responsibilities of graduate schools vary widely between the different models adopted; many have dedicated accommodation for their staff with associated teaching and learning space for other staff and students. Many are responsible for research training programmes and in some cases for the training of supervisors. Particularly in the university-wide graduate school, quality assurance and student monitoring, the management and support for higher degree committees and institutional returns to the various agencies are often vested in the graduate school.

Graduate Schools are therefore a potential plus point for those considering different universities for their postgraduate study; we should also note that there is no necessary correlation between the quality of provision and the existence of a graduate school in any particular university. Here, as in so many other aspects of the postgraduate scene, there is more difference in practice than commonality and in some universities the graduate school may be little more than a virtual concept with little or no impact on you as a student.

Research Training both Generic and Specific

The 1993 White Paper, 'Realising Our Potential' formalised the debate about research and research training arguing that 'the Government welcomes the growth in postgraduate courses. It is concerned, however, that the traditional PhD does not always match up to the needs of a career outside research in academia or an industrial research laboratory' (HMSO, 1993: 57).

The Paper highlighted the perceived nature of the concerns about the PhD, as it states that 'a period spent in PhD training represents a substantial investment of public funds and it is important to ensure that it represents good value for money for the taxpayer as well as the individual concerned' (HMSO, 1993: 57).

It went on to argue that there is a role for preparatory matters in research training when it suggests that 'for most students who have undertaken a first degree, the Master's qualification will provide an opportunity to acquire extra knowledge and skills, either in preparation for a period of research training leading to a PhD or for employment' (HMSO, 1993: 61).

Subsequently the Office of Science and Technology (OST) outlined a recommended structure for a new one-year Research Masters (MRes) degree, which would include both taught and research components. This degree was intended as a foundation either for a doctorate or for a research career in industry or the public sector.

The OST proposed the following:

- A significant research component (60% of the 42-week postgraduate year)
- The provision of a grounding in research techniques relevant to a range of disciplines as well as the development of specialist knowledge
- The inclusion of modules intended to broaden the students' experience and to equip them with transferable skills in management, communication, commercial understanding, the exploitation of research and team working.

The need for training to satisfy the requirements of industry and the professions was well established by the end of the 1990s. The changes had gathered momentum during the 1990s to be accepted without question. There was, however, little if any research evidence to suggest that this shift was appropriate and little to support its efficacy. Nevertheless other agencies noted these shifts in policy and interpreted them in different ways – but with the same purpose in mind. Readers may wish here to refer to Chapter 14 where transferable skills training is considered in more detail.

The Economic and Social Research Council (ESRC) introduced guidelines on research training for those departments which were in receipt of ESRC studentships. These guidelines provide comprehensive and detailed information on ESRC's expectations both generic and subject specific.

In addition the Research Councils and Arts and Humanities Research Board (now a council – 'AHRC') made explicit a clutch of capabilities which they expect all research students to possess. These include the following:

- Research Skills and Techniques
- Research Environment
- Research Management
- Personal Effectiveness
- Communication Skills
- Networking and Team working
- Career Management.

(see Appendix 2 of this volume).

The setting up of the UK GRAD Programme and the recommendations by Roberts to fund generic training for research council sponsored students underlined the commitment to ensure students are adequately provided with generic research training.

Following the Roberts Review of the supply of people with science, technology, engineering and mathematics skills in the UK, which culminated in the so-called Roberts Report, *SET for success in* April 2002, institutions with research council students were allocated additional funding of approximately £800 per student to deliver the Roberts recommendation of two additional weeks of generic skills training each year per student.

Research Degree Supervision

A key element of doctoral research is the provision of a supervisor who will oversee and advise on the development of the individual research programme. The supervisor is therefore a key payer in the doctorate production process. Major changes have taken place in the recent past in terms of supervision, the provision of supervisors and their training, much of which is now enshrined in the QAA Code of Practice (QAA, 2004).

For some time many institutions have adopted a team approach to research degree supervision, motivated by a wish to ensure students have good access to supervisors and are not dominated by the thinking or style of a single supervisor. This is now recommended for all institutions in Precept 12 of the QAA Code of Practice.

> Each student will have a minimum of one main supervisor. He or she will normally be part of a supervisory team. There must always be one clearly identified point of contact for the student.

In addition, the Code requires new supervisors to undergo a compulsory training programme, while more experienced supervisors should continue to update and refresh their knowledge and skills. The supervisory system is central to the way in which postgraduate study is conducted in the UK and you should look to it as a significant support that you can access. Despite some anecdotal comment to the contrary, a majority of students confirm in surveys that they are happy with the support that they receive from their supervisors.

Changes in HEFCE Funding

We have noted that there are growing differences in the practices adopted by the various nations of the UK. This is particularly true in terms of funding; the Higher Education Funding Council for England (HEFCE) has been the first to indicate a concentration of resources in universities in England. From 2006 it simplified its funding model to provide explicit funds for the supervision of research degrees (as determined in JM Consulting Ltd, 2005) but only to those departments which were rated 4 and above in the 2001 Research Assessment Exercise (RAE). In addition, HEFCE has allocated what it calls Capability Funds to support the development of research in particular subjects. This funding stream applies to seven Units of Assessment (UoAs): Nursing, Professions Allied to Medicine, Social Work, Art and Design, Communications, Cultural and Media Studies, Dance, Drama and Performing Arts, and Sports-related Studies. Funds for research students will continue for departments rated 3a and 3b in these UoAs until the next RAE in 2008.

These changes to funding may have a significant impact on the capability (and indeed inclination) of institutions to continue to support research degrees in particular subjects. From a student's perspective, this means that while a department will be able to recruit students, it will not necessarily be funded, unless of course the individual institution chooses to cross-subsidise. This may lead to a two-tier system – well-funded departments and not-so-well-funded departments. From your own point of view, therefore, it will be important to ask about the level of funding at the institution or department of your choice.

The Future – Concentration and Collaboration

The 2004 Higher Education White Paper said relatively little about postgraduate education. It did, however, point to government thinking about the future concentration of research students in a smaller number of research universities. It did not at the time carry through the discussion into explicit policy. It did not, however, discourage the funding councils from implementing funding policies which encourage concentration as we have seen. This produced an interesting paradox: all universities retain the powers to award doctorates (note that some of the most recently designated universities do not at present have such powers but are in the process of applying for them) but many will not be funded by the funding councils to so do.

As yet the implications of this paradox are still being realised and discussed. However, it seems inevitable the next few years will see the development of consortia of universities operating on the 'Wisconsin model' – that is some feeding the central research institution with potential research students.

Conclusion

In this chapter we have tried to set the scene for much of what follows in the rest of this book. Many of the topics discussed here will be revisited in more detail later. We have taken a cautious view of what is required of you as a potential research degree student and we have not tried to hide any of the difficulties that you may face nor any of the inconsistencies that permeate research degree study. It is, perhaps necessarily, a complex business. However, we would recommend you to take the challenge. Undertaking a research degree is, for many people, the highest academic challenge of their lives and it can be an uplifting, positive and life-changing experience.

Acknowledgements

Appendix A is reproduced with permission from *The Framework for Higher Education Qualifications in England, Wales and Northern Ireland* © The Quality Assurance Agency for Higher Education, 2001.

Appendix A

Descriptor for a qualification at Masters (M) level: Masters degree.

Masters degrees are awarded to students who have demonstrated:

i A systematic understanding of knowledge, and a critical awareness of current problems and/or new insights, much of which is at, or informed by, the forefront of their academic discipline, field of study, or area of professional practice;

ii A comprehensive understanding of techniques applicable to their own research or advanced scholarship;

iii Originality in the application of knowledge, together with a practical understanding of how established techniques of research and enquiry are used to create and interpret knowledge in the discipline;

iv conceptual understanding that enables the student:

- to evaluate critically current research and advanced scholarship in the discipline; and
- to evaluate methodologies and develop critiques of them and, where appropriate, to propose new hypotheses.

Typically, holders of the qualification will be able to:

a Deal with complex issues both systematically and creatively, make sound judgements in the absence of complete data, and communicate their conclusions clearly to specialist and non-specialist audiences;

b   Demonstrate self-direction and originality in tackling and solving problems, and act autonomously in planning and implementing tasks at a professional or equivalent level;

c   Continue to advance their knowledge and understanding, and to develop new skills to a high level; and Will have:

d   the qualities and transferable skills necessary for employment requiring:

- the exercise of initiative and personal responsibility;
- decision-making in complex and unpredictable situations; and
- the independent learning ability required for continuing professional development.'

Appendix B

QAA Doctoral Descriptor (National Qualifications Framework) Doctorates are awarded to students who have demonstrated:

i   The creation and interpretation of new knowledge, through original research or other advanced scholarship, of a quality to satisfy peer review, extend the forefront of the discipline, and merit publication;

ii   A systematic acquisition and understanding of a substantial body of knowledge which is at the forefront of an academic discipline or area of professional practice;

iii The general ability to conceptualise, design and implement a project for the generation of new knowledge, applications or understanding at the forefront of the discipline, and to adjust the project design in the light of unforeseen problems;

iv   A detailed understanding of applicable techniques for research and advanced academic enquiry.

Typically, holders of the qualification will be able to:

a   Make informed judgements on complex issues in specialist fields, often in the absence of complete data, and be able to communicate their ideas and conclusions clearly and effectively to specialist and non-specialist audiences;

b   Continue to undertake pure and/or applied research and development at an advanced level, contributing substantially to the development of new techniques, ideas, or approaches; and will have:

c   the qualities and transferable skills necessary for employment requiring the exercise of personal responsibility and largely autonomous initiative in complex and unpredictable situations, in professional or equivalent environments.'

References

Allen, C., Smyth, E. and Wahlstrom, M. (2002) 'Responding to the field and to the academy: Ontario's evolving PhD', *Higher Education Research and Development*, 21(2): 203–214.

Durling, D., Friedman, K. and Gutherson, P. (2002) 'Debating the practice-based PhD', *International Journal of Design Sciences and Technology*, 10(2): 7–18.

European Commission Research (2003), *European Research Area, More Research for Europe – Towards 3% of the GDP*. European Commission, Brussels.

Frayling, C. (1993) 'Research in art and design', *Royal College of Art Research Papers*, 1(1). Royal College of Art, London.

HESA (2006) *Students in Higher Education Imitations, 2004/05*. Higher Education Statistics Agency, Cheltenham.

JM Consulting Ltd (2005) *Costs of Training and Supervising Postgraduate Research Students*. A report to HEFCE by JM Consulting Ltd, February 2005. Available at: www.hefce. ac.uk/pubs/rdreports/2005/ (accessed 4 February 2005).

Millichope, R. (2001) 'Doctorates awarded from United Kingdom Higher Education Institutions', *Statistics Focus*, 3(2): 23–30.

Powell, S.D. (2004) *The Award of PhD by Published Work in the UK*. UK Council for Graduate Education, Lichfield.

Powell, S.D. and Green, H. (eds) (2007) *The Doctorate Worldwide*. Buckingham, Open University Press.

Powell, S.D. and Long, E. (2005) *Professional Doctorate Awards in the UK*. Lichfield, UK Council for Graduate Education.

Quality Assurance Agency (QAA) (2001) *National Qualifications Framework*. Available at: www.qaa.ac.uk/academicinfrastructure/FHEQ/EWNI/default.asp (accessed 7 October 2007).

Quality Assurance Agency (QAA) (2004) *Code of Practice for the Assurance of Academic Quality and Standards in Higher Education: Section 1: Postgraduate Research Programmes* (2nd Edition). Gloucester: Quality Assurance Agency.

Reichert, S. and Tauch, C. (2003) 'Trends 2003. Progress towards the European Higher Education Area', *Bologna Fours Years After: Steps towards Sustainable Reform of Higher Education in Europe, July 2004*. European University Association.

UK Council for Graduate Education (UKCGE) (1996) *The Award of the Degree of PhD on the Basis of Published Work in the UK*. Lichfield: UKCGE. Available at: www.ukcge. ac.uk/publications/reports.htm. (accessed 7 October 2006).

UK Council for Graduate Education (UKCGE) (2002) *Professional Doctorates*. Dudley: UKCGE. ISBN: 02952–5751283. Available at: www.ukcge.ac.uk/publications/ reports.htm (accessed 7 October 2006).

Section I

Considering Becoming a Postgraduate Research Student in the UK and Securing an Offer

3 Why Do a Postgraduate Research Degree?
Simon P. Felton

Introduction

This chapter will look at the potential benefits and also the possible drawbacks of a postgraduate research degree enabling you to clarify your expectations and make an informed decision about whether this is the correct path for you. Spending time considering the challenges you may face and gauging the benefits you will accrue will contribute to your motivation to pursue this exciting course of action. This motivation will then contribute to a successful outcome and the realisation of those benefits.

Specifically, this chapter includes the following:

- Common reasons why people choose to do a research degree and what may lie beneath them
- Potential benefits to be gained from a postgraduate research degree
- Possible drawbacks of doing a postgraduate research degree
- Advice on how to clarify your own reasons and decide if this is the right course of action for you.

This chapter prompts you with questions throughout the text to help you to clarify your reasons, what benefits you expect and what drawbacks you anticipate. This will enable you to make a positive decision to pursue a research degree or not and be happy with whatever choice you make.

Common Reasons for Pursuing a Postgraduate Research Degree

I really loved my subject and wanted to continue researching as I enjoyed research, I didn't have clear career aspirations so I chose based on my enthusiasm for the subject.

(Research student, Cardiff University)

The reasons for individuals undertaking a postgraduate research degree are diverse because they are driven by personal needs and desires.

Two surveys published in the last few years have looked at the reasons why people pursue a research degree. One survey, by the National Postgraduate Committee (NPC 2002), that targeted all UK-domiciled postgraduate students found that nearly half (46%) of full-time students who were asked 'why they chose further study?' said their primary reason was to improve their career prospects. The next most popular primary reason was to continue studying (35%). The values for part-time students were similar; career prospects 41% and continuing study 34%. Part-time students were more likely to list personal development as a reason for pursuing postgraduate study (18% putting this as their primary reason compared to 9% of full-timers). A small proportion of both full- (2.8%) and part-time (3.8%) students listed the fact that they had secured funding as their primary reason for continuing to study.

A second survey conducted on behalf of the UK GRAD Programme called 'What Do PhDs Do?' (UK Grad, 2004), which is explored in depth in Chapter 22, found that the common reasons for pursuing a research degree were the following:

- Subject interest
- Desire for career progression
- Broader career choice or career change
- Personal benefit defined broadly in terms of a sense of achievement, a boost to self-confidence etc.

The key reasons deduced from both surveys therefore are as follows:

- Interest in a particular field of study
- Career motivations (better job, career change, necessary for chosen career etc.)
- Personal development and intellectual challenge
- Secured funding.

As well as these reasons, anecdotal evidence from talking to research students suggests that there are some other common reasons:

- To benefit some aspect of human life, for example, contribute to a cure for some disease, help to deal with global warming, etc.
- It was suggested to them as an option for their next step by a university lecturer
- To avoid entry into the job market
- Did not know what else to do.

I really enjoyed research and was encouraged by my tutor to continue onto a PhD. I wanted to continue my research and the opportunity to shape developments in biochemistry really appealed to me. It broadens the horizons, allows one to reach the peak of study and it can bring great intellectual reward and open many horizons. (Research student, University of Birmingham)

QUESTIONS TO CONSIDER

1 Do you share any of these reasons?
2 What other reasons do you have?

What Benefits May Be Gained by Studying for a Research Degree?

One of the significant benefits of a postgraduate research degree and the purpose of research is the generation of an original contribution to knowledge and the enormous personal and intellectual satisfaction this can afford you.

The research degree is an internationally recognised qualification. Additionally, the UK's positive reputation for research will add to that recognition. The UK remains second to the US on most measures of quality of research in an international context (such as citations and discipline strength by cited work) and benefits from younger research graduates as compared to other countries (King, 2004; UK Grad, 2004). You will share in that positive recognition.

The employment potential of a research degree lies in the research student having demonstrated the capability and tenacity in undertaking an extended piece of investigative work as well as in specific technical skills acquired. A research degree also develops important transferable 'life skills' and employability skills such as public speaking, presentations, writing proposals, specialist knowledge, self-reliance and responsibility. Research students having organised their own studies can be excellent project managers, experts at analysis, and capable of working through complex processes with confidence and autonomy; skills recognised by the Quality Assurance Agency (QAA) as those gained by masters and doctoral qualifications (see Chapters 14 and 23 and Appendix 2 for further information on skills).

My research was focussed on the developments in genetics and pushing the boundaries of knowledge while contributing to a wider project. The sponsorship by the company provided the means to complete the PhD and the route to a research career with the company. I was glad that the company was involved as the research was focussed for work in the sector and the company itself. (Research student, Imperial College, London)

What Are the Possible Drawbacks of Studying for a Research Degree?

> I'd got the academic 'buzz' during my Bachelors, the dissertation was the key factor, and I decided to go further than just my Masters where the 'buzz' got stronger. Some people thought it was just a continuation of being an undergraduate but it is not like that. There was a lot of work to do in a limited timeframe for my Masters and the PhD is really demanding, with not much time for relaxing – you need to be clear you really want to do this as it's costly in time, money and relationships.
>
> (Research student, Queen Mary College, London)

While there may be considerable benefits from pursuing a research degree there are also drawbacks, as Ben points out, such as the financial cost, the time commitment required and the possible impact on your personal life from taking on such a lengthy commitment. It is important these 'costs' are considered alongside the benefits before undertaking a research degree. The financial costs of undertaking a research degree maybe considerable, this is explored in detail in Chapter 4. This section highlights some of the other drawbacks.

The time required to complete a research degree, especially a PhD or equivalent, can cause a number of issues:

- Employers who are seeking young graduates may see a graduate with three-year work experience as more valuable than a student with research degree experience. You may have to work hard to convince them otherwise, although we believe you can.
- Maintaining the motivation to complete and therefore be successful in your studies can be very problematic over a number of years, especially if you are studying part-time. It is also very difficult to predict what any changes in your personal circumstances over this timescale may be and what impact any changes may have, either positive or negative.

The nature of a research degree may not suit you as an individual for the following reasons:

- Research students often experience loneliness or isolation in the process of conducting research. Remember that the uniqueness of the work you are doing may also mean there are few people around who may understand it.
- The autonomy that research gives may also be a burden to those who prefer structure in their working environments.

Although many research students suggested that a deep interest in the work was one of the reasons for undertaking the research degree, it may also become a drawback if your interest becomes an obsession that diverts your attention from other priorities in your life to the detriment of those priorities. You should be aware of this and those around should also be aware of this before you embark on a research degree.

Finally, others may not 'see' the benefits of a research degree that are obvious to you. For instance, employers may exhibit a stereotypical reaction that you maybe over-qualified. You may ultimately need to work hard to convince those around you (family, partners, friends etc.) as well as those who may employ you of why undertaking a research degree has been so beneficial.

Factors for Success

There have been a number of studies that have looked at the factors that affect the successful completion of research degrees, which have been discussed in a very interesting paper by Wright and Cochrane (2000). From their reading of this literature the factors break down into three broad categories:

1 Institutional and structural issues associated with research degrees themselves
2 Non-psychological individual issues such as availability of financial support
3 Individual resilience reasons such as motivation, self-confidence etc.

The study described in the paper focused on the second category and found that successful completion within four years of starting a PhD (full-time or equivalent timescale part-time) was more likely if a research student was:

- from a science, engineering or medical-based subject
- the holder of a first or upper second-class bachelors degree
- funded by a UK research council
- studying part-time
- an international research student.

The factors differed slightly for successful completion within 10 years (full-time only; the study did not extend to the equivalent part-time timescales). They were found to be:

- in science, engineering or medical-based subjects
- funded by a UK research council
- under 27 years of age
- international research students.

In their discussion of the results, Wright and Cochrane suggested that the inclusion of part-time and international students, in this 'ideal' mix of factors for success was perhaps attributable to the third category of reasons, that is individual resilience reasons. They go on to propose that these groups may have invested more in the process, in terms of money, time and effort, and were perhaps therefore clearer of what they would lose if they were unsuccessful.

Although this hypothesis was not tested in the research, it does sound logical from the way they present it. It is for this reason that we strongly suggest you be clear why you want to do a research degree which will give you a similar level of 'investment' in its outcome. It is this investment which will enable you to develop the perseverance and tenacity that are crucial attributes for any research student. Clarity of your motivations to undertake a research degree is explored in more detail in the next section.

What Lies beneath These Common Reasons?

If we were to ask a person who was considering undertaking a research degree why and were told one of the common reasons listed earlier in the chapter, we would probably follow up any of those answers with 'Tell me more' or 'Explain that in more detail'. In this section, we will try to delve deeper into the possible answers that this may elicit and present you with some questions to consider.

Interest in a Particular Field of Study

This is a highly motivating reason and is certainly a common one as we have seen. However, someone who does not share this interest would surely ask you to be more specific and to say exactly what is it about this subject that really warrants your attention. If this is your current reason for considering a research degree, it maybe worth examining this to understand what initially caused this interest to develop. For instance, was it an event in your personal life or the experience of being taught by a charismatic lecturer who was passionately interested in this subject or another similar event? If it is an external event, you do need to be clear that they have really led to a deep personal interest in the topic and are not the actual reason themselves.

QUESTIONS TO CONSIDER

1. Has your interest in this topic been stimulated by another event or person?
2. Is your interest in this subject strong enough to see you through what may be quite an extended period of study?
3. Can you study further in your field of interest through other routes without undertaking a research degree?

Career Motivations

> I couldn't have secured an academic post without a PhD. If you are starting a career in academia you MUST have a PhD.
>
> (Academic, University of Manchester)

> A research degree gives me a good grounding for the commercial and academic world. It has given me the confidence to discuss projects and I feel that I can achieve anything. I chose to do my research degree for career progression reasons – to develop myself and add value to me in the employment market.
>
> (Marketing Director)

If this is your reason then you should replace the title of this chapter with 'Why Do This Particular Career?' because that would be the nature of the follow-up questions to understand the reasoning in more detail. It is important to research the career you are interested in to understand how potential employers would view applicants with a research degree (start by talking to people who actually work in the field you're interested in). You therefore need to determine if you are really committed to this career choice and are sure that holding a research degree will help you to get that ideal job.

QUESTIONS TO CONSIDER

1 Have you researched this career fully to determine if it is right for you?
2 Have you looked at how the prospects for this career path will look like in one, three or more years?
3 Will a research degree really give you a competitive advantage over other job seekers in this area who do not have a research degree?

Personal Development and Intellectual Challenge

The personal development reason is again complex. It may elicit follow-up questions regarding the exact nature of the development you want to undertake. You may also then be asked why you feel it is necessary.

Initially the intellectual challenge reason is much easier to grasp, but doing original research is definitely challenging. However, follow-up questions along the lines of 'why test your intellect in this particular research area?' could produce some interesting observations.

QUESTIONS TO CONSIDER

1 Will a research degree provide you with the appropriate ways to develop yourself in the areas you have identified?
2 Why do you want to develop yourself in this way?
3 Why do you want to test your intellect in *this particular* research area?

Secured Funding for the Degree

The obvious follow up question with this reason is 'why did you look for funding to do this research?'; this is because this reason is not really a reason but a means by which you can undertake this research without undue financial hardship. If you are currently in this situation it would be wise to think clearly about your motivations to undertake your particular area of enquiry and not any other project that has funding attached to it.

QUESTIONS TO CONSIDER

1 What other areas of research also attract funding?
2 Would you be more interested in these areas?
3 What other reasons do you have for choosing to do this particular research project?

To Benefit Humankind

It is easy to see why this reason is extremely compelling and motivating. However, there are issues to consider here too. Is the impact or benefit of the research you will be undertaking achievable within the usual timescales of a research degree? Even though we have said that a research degree may take a significant investment of time it may still not be long enough to achieve the benefit you desire and it is likely to be only a small step in that process.

QUESTIONS TO CONSIDER

1 Will your passion to benefit humankind survive the disappointments if your research does not progress as quickly as you would like or the 'solution' to this problem is not as you had hoped?
2 Will you be satisfied with the contribution you can make within the timescales of a research degree?
3 Have you talked to other researchers about this?

Suggested as an Option

This reason is very likely to raise questions such as 'do you always follow the suggestions of others?', as it does suggest that you may not have thought long or hard about what you would like to do with the next few years of your life. If this suggestion has come from an academic, you may be seduced by the compliment. However, a research degree requires you to be an independent researcher; a person who thinks through issues and takes responsibility for a course of action. Therefore, you should look for your own reasons if you are currently in this situation.

QUESTIONS TO CONSIDER
1 What are your reasons for considering this option? 2 What other options are there that may interest you?

Avoid Entry into the Job Market

This reason again sounds as if you have not positively decided a research degree is for you. It implies that you know what you do not want to do. If eliminating all the things you do not want to do with the next few years of your life leaves you only with a research degree as the last option, have you really considered and explored all your options?

QUESTIONS TO CONSIDER
1 What other options have you considered other than a 'traditional' job and a research degree? 2 What really does interest you and make you excited in life?

Wright and Cochrane (2000) described reasons such as the last two as 'bandwagon' reasons, which implies that if these reasons apply to you then you are being taken through life rather than driving its direction for yourself. This could be viewed as a worrying trait for a person who is endeavouring to demonstrate that she or he is an independent, resourceful and professional researcher who can operate with a high degree of autonomy.

How Could You Go about Deciding Whether a Research Degree Is for You?

Before you commit to enrolling on a research degree, it would be useful for you to delve into your personal situation; what are your reasons?, what benefits do you expect to gain?, and which of the drawbacks may affect you?, is the research degree you are considering the right one for you? and so on (see Chapter 2 for more information relating to this final question). One useful way to do this is to be challenged to articulate these answers in a conversation with a friend. This person should be someone you trust and someone who is capable of asking those awkward questions that your initial answers may raise. This may also help you to see things that you had not thought of, which may either reinforce or reduce your commitment to this course of action.

QUESTIONS TO CONSIDER

Here are four key questions for you to answer in your conversation with your friend:

1 Why you are choosing this course of action?
2 What will you gain from pursuing your research degree?
3 What might you miss out on by pursuing a research degree?
4 What would happen if you were unsuccessful in your research degree?

This section attempts to draw all of the information presented so far together to help you prepare for this conversation. Remember that just like the viva neither you nor I will have predicted all the questions that you could be asked in this conversation, and this is the very reason why it is such a useful exercise to clarify your hopes, doubts and expectations of what lies ahead.

1   Why you are choosing this course of action?

　　a   List your motivations for doing a research degree.
　　b   Explain these motivations to someone you trust who will objectively and constructively challenge you to explain the detailed reasons beneath them with questions such as:

　　　　i   Do you know what academic research is?
　　　　ii   What previous experience of research do you have, did you enjoy the research?
　　　　iii Why will doing a research degree fulfil your ambition?

    iv Could you do something else to fulfil your ambition?

    v Can you maintain your passion and enthusiasm over the course of the research degree?

    vi Are you doing it for personal, financial, career gains?

Capture the results of this conversation; it may produce information and reasons you have not considered before.

2 What will you gain from pursuing your research degree?

    a List all the possible benefits that you believe you will gain from pursuing a research degree.

    b Do some research to determine if the benefits you have listed are likely to be realised.

    c Quantify the benefits you believe are realisable.

    d Work out your order of priority for these benefits. This will give you your minimum level of benefit that must be gained from your research degree to call it a success.

3 What might you miss out on by pursuing a research degree?

    a List all the other education/career/life directions you could take.

    b What benefits would you gain from each scenario and quantify them all?

    c Prioritise these benefits against those you are likely to gain from doing your research degree.

4 What would happen if you were unsuccessful in your research degree?

    a What is the most important thing you will have lost if you don't obtain your research degree?

    b Will you be able to take any of the other education/career directions you listed above?

    c At what point in your research degree would you be unable to take each alternative course?

Once you have done this are you convinced that a research degree is for you? Do the benefits outweigh the drawbacks? Whatever the answer, you will have given yourself the best chance for success no matter what you decide to do.

The clear message is that you should understand in detail your motivations for choosing to do a research degree. This is especially important for part-time study where you will need to maintain this motivation over a considerable length of time.

> [D]o not ignore or underestimate the commitment balancing part-time research with a full-time job. (Part-time research masters student)

A research student from the University of Leeds encourages you to think all this through:

> postgraduate study demands focus and determination, there are more dangers and potential areas for failure. You need to plan your studies and get support from fellow academics, colleagues and family if you are to succeed and enjoy it.

Conclusion

This chapter aimed to help you to answer the question 'Why do a post-graduate research degree?' You should now be clearer about your personal motivations for enrolling on a research degree and the benefits you are expecting from it.

It is crucial to consider why you want to undertake a research degree. It will help you to continue to generate the passion that will see you through the whole process. It will also be easier to see how doing the research degree is helping you to meet your goals. This will help you to shape the direction of the research and to develop into an independent researcher.

If you are confident about your reasons and the expected benefits and you are fully aware of the potential drawbacks, it will be easier to maintain your enthusiasm for your research degree and see it through to a successful outcome. From the growth in the numbers of people undertaking research degrees over the last few years it is clear that pursuing a research degree is an attractive and potentially, hugely beneficial course of action.

Hopefully, after this careful consideration you will make the positive decision to take a research degree (and therefore benefit from the rest of the chapters in this book!). If this is the case then you may also find it useful to periodically review and reflect on your initial reasons for your choice, the benefits you are accruing, especially those you had not foreseen and to understand how you are dealing with any drawbacks. This type of activity will make your research degree the true educational and developmental process it can be. Expect it to be challenging, but remember the most challenging situations are often those which generate the most significant benefits.

Acknowledgements

I would like to thank all the postgraduate students and graduates who shared their experiences to ensure that when you think about undertaking a research degree it is a success and that you don't repeat their mistakes and achieve what you want.

SOURCES OF SUPPORT

Bentley, P.J. (2006) *The PhD Application Handbook*, Maidenhead: Open University Press – The first chapter of this book explores the issues raised in this chapter in an accessible and lively way.

www.careerweb.leeds.ac.uk/downloads/Empress_LR_000.pdf – Employers' Perceptions of Recruiting Research Staff and Students. This research report provides useful background to what employers value when recruiting research staff and provides ideas on how to increase your employability if career issues motivate you to do a research degree.

www.cse.ucsd.edu/users/mihir/phd.html – This URL has been created by a US supervisor of research students to help his current and prospective students to understand the PhD process. It also includes some questions you need to ask yourself before choosing to do a research degree.

www.dartmouth.edu/~csrc/students/gradschool/artsci/ – The Careers Service of Dartmouth College (one of the 8 Ivy League colleges that also include Harvard and Yale) has some similar questions to help you to consider your options.

www.phd-survey.org/advice/advice.htm – This URL is again compiled for potential research students in the US. It contains questions to ask of yourself as well as sections with questions to ask of potential universities and supervisors.

www.prospects.ac.uk – Comprehensive website providing career advice and information on postgraduate study with sections on why do postgraduate study, choosing where to do it and advice on funding. For information relating to this chapter go to the home page, click on Postgrad Study and select 'About postgrad study' from the menu.

www.grad.ac.uk – Useful website giving guidance for researchers on completing a doctorate, skills training and national and regional events to support researchers.

References

King, D.A. (2004) 'The Scientific Impact of Nations', *Nature*, 430: 311–316, available at: www.dti.gov.uk/files/file11959.pdf (accessed 2 January 2008) – Nature journal article which explores the scientific impact of various nations to establish national research productivity comparisons such as citations and discipline strength by citation.

NPC (2002) *National Survey of Postgraduate Funding and Priorities*, Troon: The National Postgraduate Committee of the UK, available at: www.npc.org.uk/page/1083342227.pdf (accessed 5 October 2007).

The UK GRAD Programme (2004, 2006, 2007) *What Do PhDs Do?*, available at: www.grad.ac.uk/wdpd/ (accessed 5 October 2007) – Provides a useful introduction to why do a PhD, where PhDs work and on disciplinary differences.

Wright, T. and Cochrane, R. (2000) 'Factors Influencing Successful Submission of PhD Theses', *Studies in Higher Education*, 25(2): 181–195.

4 How Much Will It Cost?
Dr Ged Hall and Dr Jo Longman

Introduction

This chapter covers the difficult subject of how much a postgraduate research degree may cost you. The difficulty involved in giving an answer is that it very much depends on what type of research student you are; UK-domiciled or resident of the European Union (EU), or from outside the EU. It also depends on your individual preferences and needs – how expensive you are! There is also some variation from institution to institution regarding the fees you will pay, and then to complicate the picture even further there are significant 'cost-of-living' variations across the UK.

Our aim in this chapter is to help you think through the detail of how to calculate what it will cost you. In addition to the direct costs of doing a research degree, you should also consider the 'opportunity costs', that is what you might have been doing with your life (including what you might have been earning) if you decided to do something other than a research degree for the next few years of your life. These are what we have called the hidden costs of studying for a research degree.

To help you to consider these various aspects the chapter is divided into five main sections:

1   University and research degree-specific costs
2   Living costs
3   Hidden costs
4   How you can pay for all of this
5   Other sources of information.

The chapter includes examples and case studies to show the costs for different types of research students and different modes of study.

Once you have read this chapter you will have a clearer understanding of the obvious and hidden costs of choosing to pursue a research degree. Our estimates are that a doctoral degree in the UK may cost you between £600 and

£700 per month *plus* fees, which probably seems like an enormous amount. We will try to help you to think through the costs associated with undertaking a research degree so that you can come to a balanced decision regarding how these costs are offset by the possible benefits of this course of study.

Many of the practical, emotional and psychological difficulties experienced by research students are debt related and this may be due in part to prospective research students not fully thinking through the issues around how much it costs to undertake a research degree. A really interesting piece of research (a PhD thesis) by Dr Toni Wright explores in some depth PhD study outcomes and the student experience (Wright, 2006). Her research, from a longitudinal study, suggests that as many as 43% of initial respondents and 38% of those who remained in the study four years later reported difficulties with money. This produced a strong correlation with PhD outcome of $p = 0.02$, making this by far the most commonly reported non-academic study related issue in that research study. Add to that the figure that 63% of international research students (out of 4044 who answered the question) agreed with the statement 'I have had to endure financial hardship during my studies'[1] and you can see that financial issues are common amongst research students.

The next chapter of this book looks at ways you can get funding to meet these costs (although of course 41% of research students are self-funded through various means[2]).

University and Research Degree-specific Costs

Tuition Fees

The largest single university-specific cost item is the tuition fees that are payable to the institution. Fees are usually payable at the start of each academic year as a requirement for registration for that year of the course. Some institutions do offer slight discounts if you are fully responsible for the fee and you pay the fee in full, whilst some offer an instalment option.

The level of fees is dependent on two main factors:

1 The classification of your residence status
2 Variations from one discipline to another, for example, lab-based science subjects compared to desk-based subjects.

Residence Status

There are three residence classifications; they are Home, International and Island. The definitions of those categories are outlined in a piece of legislation[3] passed by the UK parliament. Simplistically Home students are defined as people who are normally resident in the UK and the EU (which may include certain European countries who are not members of the EU). International students are broadly defined as those whose normal residence is outside of this area. The final exception is the Island classification, which relates to those whose normal residence is the Isle of Man or one of the Channel Islands.

Generally speaking the Home student tuition fee is set by the UK government and for the 2006/07 academic year this figure was £3160 per year for an MPhil or PhD degree and £4130 for a research masters degree. It is expected that these figures will increase in line with inflation for the 2007/08 academic year.

For those of you who are classified as International students the fee will vary from institution to institution as there is freedom to set a fee figure that more closely reflects the costs of providing you with the various facilities the institution offers. In addition to reflecting the costs of the course, the level at which the fee is set is driven by competition between institutions for your registration. For instance the fee payable, for a desk-based subject, at four different universities in 2006/07 was £10,360, £9210, £8900 and £8220.

For research students classified as Island, the fee varies from university to university, with some charging the same fee as per International students, while others charge the Home fee.

Discipline Variations

You will have noticed in the previous section that when we compared the fee paid by international students at four institutions we specified that the subject was a desk-based discipline. This is because different fees may be applied to subjects that require more facilities and consumable resources such as laboratory-based subjects. This variation only applies to international students due to the Home rate being set centrally by the UK government as discussed above.

At one UK institution the highest fee charged in 2006/07 was £21,700 for an International student pursuing research in one of the medical sciences – this is for one year of the course. The lowest (at the same institution) was £5180 in subjects such as Archaeology and English.

Our advice, therefore, is to explore the websites of (or talk to) the institutions you are considering attending to find out how much the fees are per year for the discipline area you want to study in.

Other University Charges

In this section we will look at the other charges that are common across most universities. These charges arise from the process of administering your research degree or from the process of conducting your research itself. We will also consider the college fees that arise if you choose to study at Oxford or Cambridge universities.

Administration Charges

Most of the charges and fees in this section can be avoided if you are aware of the timing and deadlines involved in the process of your research degree from first registration (or enrolment) through to graduation. However, you should be aware of them in order to allow some leeway in your budget for them. Here we try to highlight the key ones and to quantify them.

One additional fee that we hope you will never need to pay is the re-examination fee, which is around £140.

Another fee that should be avoided, if at all possible, is that which is levied when an extension to the registration period is requested. This fee is likely to be around £130.

There are also avoidable penalty fees for late registration, often around £60–70 depending on how late you register.

If you are undertaking laboratory-based research you may also have to pay a deposit or lab bench fee in order to use the university's equipment. This is likely to vary dependent on the academic discipline in which you are studying as well as the regulations in force at your institution. It is difficult to give you an average value for the bench fee as this can be dependent on the exact nature of your project not just the discipline in which it is located. You should be notified of this in your offer letter but if you are in any doubt ask.

Penalty charges for cheques that are not honoured by your bank or when direct debit mandates have not been fulfilled are also common. Again, charges of this type can be avoided with prudent financial management.

Finally, the happy event of attending your graduation ceremony after all your hard work can quite easily cost over £100, when the costs of hiring your academic gown, paying for guest tickets, official photographs and other souvenirs are taken into account.

Oxbridge College Fees

At Oxford and Cambridge universities each research student must be registered via a specific college of the university. Each college charges fees in addition to the university fee, which is known as the *composition fee*. These fees cover the facilities that the college provides which include library facilities, study space, common rooms and pastoral care; the fees do not cover accommodation. In 2006/07, this fee was around £2000 per annum; the exact amount being dependent on the college you choose.

Library Costs

Although the costs for individual items in this category may seem small, they could well mount up over the course of a year. For instance, have you considered if the institution's library contains all the material you will require? If not then you will need to pay for this material to be sourced from other libraries. Then when you receive it, you will definitely want to copy the key parts of it. All of this adds up and may soon exhaust any allowance you may receive from your institution (see Chapter 6). Even if your library contains all the reference material you will ever need in your studies, which is very unlikely, you will need your own copies of most of the journal papers that you will reference so that they are at hand when you are working away from the library.

To try to quantify this cost we have estimated how much photocopying and printing might take place for a science-based research degree below.

This fictitious thesis references nearly 200 journal papers, many of which cover a number of pages of text, a rough average being five pages. This gives 1000 pages of journal papers.

Then there is the production of the thesis itself; 200 pages x 5 copies. This gives another 1000 pages.

It is difficult to estimate how much printing a research degree student might do throughout the course of their studies; even if only two pages were printed per day during the course of 4 years of a research degree (3 years of research plus 1 year of writing up) this comes to another 2000 pages.

This gives 4000 pages as the total amount of printing and photocopying. At 12p a sheet, this gives a grand total of £480.

Our advice to you here is to speak to the subject librarian for the discipline in which you will be studying at each university you are considering to inquire if the material (archives, journals, etc.) you will need for your research is held. To supplement the information they provide, we also suggest you speak to other research students in your discipline at each university to get a feel for the costs they have incurred in sourcing material for their projects.

If the university you are registered with stocks most of the material you need for your research, then the costs of inter-library loans can be kept to a minimum. As an example, the Table 4.1 presents the different costs for inter-library loans published on the websites of four universities, and it is easy to see how costs like these could easily mount up if the university does not stock most of the material you are going to need to access.

Supporting Your Research

Other costs that you should consider when working out your budget are those that arise from the research itself. These costs are normally travel-related or related to fieldwork that you may have to undertake. For instance, you may need to visit an archive regularly that is some distance from your home or attend meetings with collaborators. Fieldwork may also involve accommodation costs or the purchase of technical clothing that you do not already own. If your project is financed via a research grant, then these costs may have been

TABLE 4.1 Comparison of inter-library loan fees at four UK universities

	Inter-library loan	Renewal of loan	Urgent copy or loans	Overseas copy or loans
University 1	£3.50	£3	£8–11	£11 (worldwide search)
University 2	40 requests per academic year @ £1 then £4.47 above that	£1	Not listed	£6 and £8
University 3	First 150 £4 then £16 each	Same as loan fee	£12	N/A
University 4	Free cost is borne by department in which you are registered	Free	Free	Free

considered in the bid and therefore you may be reimbursed. However, if this was not the case or you are self-financing then you will have to consider how you could cover these costs.

Financial Statements

As part of its application process, the University of Cambridge requires any applicant to sign a financial guarantee undertaking form. The guidance says that you should not sign this form if you are in any doubt about your ability to pay the required fees and living expenses for the duration of your research degree.

International research students who are required to apply for clearance to enter the UK as a student, will need to provide information that demonstrates that they can meet the fees and costs of studying in the UK. This can be a letter of support from your funding source or even your personal bank statements.

Living Costs

Living costs are defined here as the day-to-day expenses incurred living in the UK such as the costs of accommodation, utility bills, food, clothing, travel etc. Living costs in the UK, like in most countries, vary considerably from place to place, see Table 4.2.

The national average cost is 100%, so a figure of 109.7% means prices in this area are 9.7% higher than the national average. Unison's use of the Office of National Statistics (ONS) data, as discussed above, shows significant regional variation, for example, the cost of living in Wales is 17% lower than the cost of living in London.

TABLE 4.2   Regional price variation for the 12 government office regions of the UK

Government office region	Regional variation in comparison to the national average = 100%
East	101.1
East Midlands	97.4
London (Greater London)	109.7
Northern Ireland	95.8
North (North East)	94.2
North West	96.9
Scotland	94.5
South East	105.3
South West	101.3
Wales	93.1
West Midlands	97.8
Yorkshire/Humberside	94.2

Note
Reproduced with the kind permission of the Bargaining Support Group of UNISON.

Calculating your own individual cost of living is a complex undertaking with many variables. Our intention here is to provide some key considerations you should make when thinking through the cost of undertaking a research degree, rather than to explore all the variables in detail.

Key Variables

Some of the key aspects of cost of living for a research student are as follows:

- Accommodation – university, private renting or buying a property (generally students are exempt from paying Council Tax charges, although the Council Tax does not apply in Northern Ireland where there is a different local tax which students may have to pay – check with the university you are considering[4])
- Necessities (food and clothing)
- Utility bills (heating, hot water, lighting, telephone etc.)
- Dependants (including costs of childcare, or caring for dependent adults)
- Travel (international, national and local if living away from your main campus location)
- Leisure activities/socialising.

Remember also that the cost of living is subject to annual inflation and exchange rates and there may be considerable variability over the three or more years that you will be studying for your research degree. Any accurate financial plan has to take such increases into account. In May 2007, the rate of inflation in the UK was 2.5%.[5]

Clearly, the cost of living will be entirely influenced by the kind of lifestyle you choose as well as where in the UK you live. You will need to consider accommodation, but the cost of that accommodation will be very different depending on where and how you live, for example, cheap, shared university accommodation or private, rented accommodation, in comparison to buying an exclusive property in an expensive part of town and living alone. Similarly the clothes you buy and the food you choose to eat, and how much you person-ally consider it acceptable to spend on socialising, all impact entirely on the overall cost of undertaking a research degree.

If you are entering the UK as an International student you need to be able to demonstrate to the immigration authorities that you have sufficient funds to meet all of your expenses (including fees). UKCISA, the Council for international student affairs, publishes a range of guidance documents for international students. (See www.ukcisa.org.uk/student/information_sheets.php, which covers entry requirements.)

Case Studies

In the tables below, two simplified scenarios are offered. One of a part-time EdD student from South Africa, and in the second table a full-time science PhD student from the UK. These scenarios are explored across a number of regions of the UK to compare locations. These figures support the British Council's suggestion that students require around £700 a month (exclusive of fees) to be able to live in the UK.

Part-time EdD: The scenario presented in Table 4.3 is that of a 43-year-old, part-time overseas (Cape Town, South Africa) student registered for an EdD

TABLE 4.3 Cost* comparison for a part-time EdD research student in three different regions of the UK per year

	An HEI in Wales	An HEI in London	An HEI in the South West
Course fees	£4128	£6048	£4836
Flights from S. Africa to UK (KLM) twice	To Cardiff £667 (includes transport from airport) x 2 = £1334	To Heathrow £522 (includes tube fare) x 2 = £1044	To Bristol £745 (includes transport from airport) x 2 = £1490
Local bed and breakfast accommodation for 4 weeks	£840	£1400	£980
Books/stationery	£252	£252	£252
TOTAL†	£6554	£8744	£7558

Notes
* Costs based on the 2006/07 academic year.
† Full-year costs.

in their second year, living in his/her home country but coming to the UK to his/her university twice for a two-week visit in that year. It will take him/her five years to finish the EdD and graduate.

Note: Clearly this student will also need to pay for the cost of living in South Africa for the duration of the EdD; the student may quite possibly be working as a head teacher at the time. We have not attempted to cost this here; we have simply provided the *additional* costs associated with completing the EdD at three different locations in the UK.

Full-time PhD: The scenario presented in Table 4.4 is based on a 24-year old, full-time home (UK) student registered for a PhD in a bench science such as Pharmacy or Biomedical Sciences in their first year, living in postgraduate halls of residence on campus (minimal travel costs incurred, travel costs include UK travel to visit family/friends), who plays squash twice a week with another student, using the university's sports facilities.

Tables 4.3 and 4.4 are based on the *Education UK* (part of the British Council website) Budget Planner.[6]

TABLE 4.4   Cost* comparison for a full-time science research student in three different regions of the UK per month

	An HEI in Scotland	An HEI in the East Midlands	An HEI in Northern Ireland
Course fees	£264	£264	£264
PG halls of residence fees	£325	Single study bedroom (shared kitchen/diner and bathroom with up to 6 others) £335	Single study bedroom (shared kitchen/diner and bathroom with up to 6 others) £227
Utilities costs (electricity, gas and water)	£31	Included in hall fees	Included in hall fees
Phone	£21	£21	£21
Travel[†]	£49	£51	£50
Food/sundries[†]	£49	£51	£50
Clothes[†]	£29	£30	£30
Leisure/sport	£14	£20	£14
Books/stationery	£21	£21	£21
Socialising[†]	£97	£100	£99
Insurance[††]	Included in hall fees	Included in hall fees	£7
Other expenses/luxuries[†]	£20	£20	£20
TOTAL[†††]	£921	£913	£802

Notes
  * Costs based on the 2006/07 academic year.
  † Figures are derived from the figures in the British Council's Budget Planner but adjusted for regional variation using the data from Table 4.2.
 †† Insurance covers: contents of your room @ £3000.00, accidental damage and key cover, vacation cover, legal expenses, mobile phone cover. Insurance does not cover: items you regularly take out of your room, portable computer cover, course fees cover.
††† Monthly costs.

There are some caveats to the approach of adjusting the figures in Table 4.4 for regional variation:

- The ONS data (that Table 4.2 is derived from) is from 2004 and it is therefore out of date. Regional economies and therefore the cost of living are likely to be different now. Unfortunately, ONS have only produced this analysis once.
- The figures are based on a UK average which has been adjusted by region. This analysis is very likely to under-predict the cost of living in large cosmopolitan cities where most universities are located.

However, this analysis does show that you should look closely at the costs you are likely to pay in the geographic location of the universities you are considering. We advise that you use these headings and attempt to get more accurate data via direct contact with the university and research students who are already studying there to compare the universities you are considering.

Hidden Costs

The figures presented and discussed above are the clearly visible costs of undertaking a research degree in the UK, but there are also costs that may be less immediately obvious to you. If you are serious about working out the real financial costs to you, you should also consider the following.

Time out of a Career

For younger researchers, the result of undertaking a research degree could include some hidden costs as listed below:

- Missing out on accelerated earnings early on in a career – entering a profession with a research degree behind you may not recoup this lack of initial earnings, that is, it may be that others you graduated with from your undergraduate degree are currently earning beyond the national average[7]
- Delay in starting to pay off any student loans from a previous degree
- A reduction in pension entitlement based on fewer working years to contribute to a pension scheme.

Other Employment-related Benefits

Securing other employment-related benefits whilst a student such as healthcare, travel, loans, dental care, insurance etc. may be something research students have to be highly proactive about (exploring these options with your students' union for example), whereas in the workplace these additional benefits may automatically constitute part of your employment package.

Part-time Students

When exploring the relevance of these hidden costs for your own specific circumstances, it is important to factor in changes over time. This has been discussed above with reference to inflationary pressures and fluctuations in exchange rates, but for part-time students an additional difficulty is in predicting individual circumstances over an extended time period of five or more years. It may be worth discussing this with existing part-time research students as well as financial support staff at the university you are considering registering with.

How You Can Pay for This?

Once you have calculated the real cost to you of undertaking a research degree you may be somewhat shocked. However, consider that if you had done the same exercise for your undergraduate degree you may have had a similar shock. However, you now need to take some time to consider your motivations for pursuing this research degree (go back to Chapter 3), and to consider the central question of how you can meet these costs. Chapter 5 in this volume helps with some ideas of where to look for funding to meet the costs of a research degree.

To pay for fees and a contribution to your living costs you could explore the following possibilities:

- A studentship from the university
- Funding from an external sponsor (research council, charity, government, industry etc.)
- Funding your own research (remember 41% of research postgraduates do this), possibly using a Career Development Loan[8]
- Working to supplement your income. Teaching (mainly at undergraduate level) is common – see Chapter 17 on this. Your institution may well put a limit on the amount of time you spend working or teaching – check the regulations at your own institution. Overseas research students will be able to work a maximum of 20 hours a week during term-time to fulfil the obligations relating to their visa.[9]

Conclusion

This chapter aimed to give you a clearer idea of the complexity of calculating how much your research degree might cost you. Having a realistic idea about this is important, as difficulties with finances are one of the most common causes of anxiety for research students. We hope that by using the information above, particularly the headings in the example tables, you will have a framework for beginning a costing exercise specific to your own circumstances. The costs of a research degree must be appraised in the context of your motivations for undertaking research at this level. In this assessment, we hope that you feel that the immediate costs are easily offset by the longer-term benefits of undertaking and completing your research degree.

Acknowledgements

Table 4.2 was drawn from data originally published in 'Relative regional consumer price levels in 2004', *Economic Trends*, 615, February 2005, Office of National Statistics, www.statistics.gov.uk/articles/economic_trends/ET615Wingfield.pdf. The table was published by UNISON Bargaining Support in Bargaining Support Fact sheet: Local Statistics – August 2006, www.unison.org.uk/bargaining.

Notes

1 Figures from the *International Student Barometer* May 2007 a survey tool used by a UK consultancy company called IGraduate (www.i-graduate.org/). The survey is not available on the website as it is only available on subscription.
2 Higher Education Statistics Agency 2005/06 data. This data is for Postgraduate research where the qualification aim is a research–based higher degree. These programmes of study include doctorates, masters, postgraduate bachelors degrees and postgraduate diplomas or certificates (not PGCE) studied mainly by research students.
3 Education (Fees and Awards) Regulations 1997 (as amended).
4 See Guidance Notes for Students (July 2006) www.UKCOSA.org.uk/images/tax.pdf (accessed 24 April 2007).
5 www.statistics.gov.uk/cci/nugget.asp?id=19 (accessed 2 July 2007).
6 With kind thanks to the British Council (see www.educationuk.org/budgetplanner/) (accessed 10 September 2007).
7 There is some interesting information on salaries at www.prospects.ac.uk (search for salaries) (accessed 10 September 2007).
8 See www.direct.gov.uk/en/EducationAndLearning/AdultLearning/CareerDevelopmentLoans/ index.htm for further information (accessed 15 September 2007).
9 www.educationuk.org/downloads/sources_of_funding.pdf (accessed 30 June 2007).

SOURCES OF SUPPORT

Look at the websites for the institutions you are considering for local cost estimates, for example, Oxford University indicate minimum amounts they feel are needed, even for dependants.

If you are an international student, ask if the university offers a pre-arrival guide for international students.

British Council websites and publications available at:

www.educationuk.org (Guidance for overseas students on funding sources – www. educationuk.org/downloads/sources_of_funding.pdf) and www.educationuk.org/ budgetplanner/ This gives general guidance on living in the UK.

www.educationuk.org/downloads/study_live_uk.pdf (information on studying and living in the UK)

UKCOSA (the council for international education) guidance notes – www.ukcosa.org. uk/student/living_costs.php This site provides guidance on preparing for study in the UK and fees and student-support facilities.

UpMyStreet.com for buying and general guidance about an area (schools, crime rates etc.) including costs

Reference

Wright, T. (2006) 'PhD Study Outcomes and the Student Experience', PhD Thesis, University of Birmingham.

5 Where Can I Get Funding?

Professor Mary Bownes and
Robert Lawrie

Introduction

There are two sides to every coin, and studying for a postgraduate research degree is certainly no exception. If you have already started to investigate the options open to you in your chosen field, you will probably have discovered by now that gaining the offer of a research place at a suitable university (see Chapter 7) in the area you are interested in is a relatively straightforward matter compared to sourcing and securing the necessary funding you'll need to see you through your course. This chapter is therefore dedicated to providing information and advice for all postgraduate research students, wherever they come from, on the various funding opportunities available – not only as a guide to where to look for the most appropriate form of financial support but also, most important of all, the steps you should take to give your search the best chance of success.

First things first. Research funding is extremely competitive and due to the limited resources available many research students will find it difficult to secure funding. In view of this, you are strongly advised to start your search for financial support at the earliest opportunity as, in many cases, funding bodies may require you to make an application at least one year before you are due to start your research degree programme.

You should also remember that while universities may indicate that there are no deadline dates for you to meet with regards to your application for postgraduate research; this is not true for students seeking a scholarship or sponsorship support. Overseas students in particular need to start their search for funding at least 14–18 months before they intend to start their research and all students, regardless of nationality, should be prepared to spend a considerable amount of time researching all potential sources of funding available to them. You will often need to have secured the offer of a place to study before you can apply for support. In some institutions, the awards are applied for by the host university and in others you need to apply for them yourself with the support of your host.

It is very unlikely that a university or sponsor will simply contact you and offer you an award. Although some students may be luckier than others, there are no shortcuts to success in securing research funding and it is never enough to rely on the quality of your academic grades to propel you to the top of the list (and you will often need excellent grades just to get on the list in the first place). If you are intending to eventually follow an academic career path as a postdoctoral researcher then the experience gained in applying for research funding will be extremely useful as grant applications are very much part of the life of an academic. The best advice we can offer is to do your homework thoroughly and be prepared to put in whatever time it might take to gain a full picture of the different awards and grants that may be available to you, whether through the university or from an external funding body – especially those with a particular interest in your line of research. Remember also that you may be able to raise smaller amounts of funding from more than one source which, added together, will provide the financial support you need to pursue your studies as planned.

Always bear in mind that each funding body has its own rules and criteria for making awards. So you'll find it well worth your while familiarising yourself with these to make sure your application fully addresses the funding body's specific requirements. Remember that your application is the first and only picture the funding body will have of you. As you don't want it to be the last, make sure you give it the time and thought it deserves. The benefits of submitting a well-presented and complete application together with all supporting documentation cannot be stressed enough. Before submitting a funding application you may wish to consider the following 10 tips:

1 Read the application form carefully and complete it in full
2 Always type or neatly print information in black ink
3 Don't trust your computer spell checker – many panel members may be unimpressed by poor communication skills
4 Don't use jargon or obscure language as your application may be considered by people who are not specialists in your field
5 Be succinct and keep to the required word limit
6 Have at least one other person review your application and supporting documents, including your personal statement
7 Remember to sign your funding application and date it where requested. Incomplete and unsigned applications may be disqualified
8 Give your referees as much advance notice and information as possible. It is useful to provide your referee with an up-to-date CV as well as detailed instructions of what is required, the deadline for submission and details of where they should send your application or reference
9 Keep a copy of all completed forms and applications

10   Pay close attention to funding application closing deadlines. Applications submitted after the deadline are usually not considered.

Often, your host university will have experience and will offer you guidance. Listen to them, as they will have seen lots of applications and have a good idea of what will contribute to success. So read on – and good luck!

Sources of Funding for UK Students

Research Councils

The primary source of financial support for most UK research students takes the form of studentships offered by 7 different research councils. Awards given to 'Home' students are normally on a full studentship for three to four years to cover tuition fees and provide a tax-free maintenance allowance (known as a 'stipend'; £12,600 p.a. from October 2007) to help with other expenses. In addition, EU students who have been ordinarily resident in the UK during the three-year period immediately prior to their degree programme start date; EU migrant workers and their children are also eligible to receive a maintenance grant. Other EU students are eligible for a fees-only award. The rules concerning eligibility for full research council studentships or fees-only studentships are complex and potential applicants are encouraged to confirm their eligibility with the relevant university office.

Competition for these awards is always intense and, inevitably, only a small percentage of candidates in each study area will be successful. Each of the research councils is dedicated to research and training in specific disciplines as listed below. These are correct at the time of publication but they can change at any time, so it is important to check their current websites.

- *The Arts and Humanities Research Council (AHRC)* has eight submission panels, indicating the wide range of arts and humanities subject areas covered. Panel 1: Classics, Ancient History and Archaeology; Panel 2: Visual Arts and Media – practice, history and theory; Panel 3: English Language and Literature; Panel 4: Medieval and Modern History; Panel 5: Modern Languages and Linguistics; Panel 6: Librarianship, Information and Museum Studies; Panel 7: Music and Performing Arts; and Panel 8: Philosophy, Law and Religious Studies.
  Website: www.ahrc.ac.uk
- *The Biotechnology and Biological Sciences Research Council (BBSRC)* covers seven key areas within biosciences. These are as follows: (1) Agri-Food; (2) Animal Sciences; (3) Biochemistry and Cell Biology; (4) Biomolecular Sciences; (5) Engineering and Biological Systems; (6) Genes and Developmental Biology; (7) Plant and Microbial Sciences.
  Website: www.bbsrc.ac.uk

- *The Economic and Social Research Council (ESRC)* offers awards for research degree programmes in the Social Sciences which may cover the following disciplines: Area Studies and Development Studies; Economics; Economic and Social History; Education; Human Geography; Linguistics; Management and Business Studies; Planning, Environmental Studies and Housing Studies; Political Science, International Studies and International Relations; Psychology and Cognitive Science; Interdisciplinary Studies in Science, Technology and Innovation; Social Anthropology; Social Policy, Social Work and Health Studies; Socio-legal Studies and Criminology; Sociology; and Social Statistics, Research Methods and Computing. Website: www.esrcsocietytoday.ac.uk
- *The Engineering and Physical Sciences Research Council (EPSRC)* provides funding for research and training in Engineering and the Physical Sciences. Study areas include: Chemistry, Engineering, Information Technology, Manufacturing Technology, Materials Science, Mathematics and Physics. Website: www.epsrc.ac.uk
- *The Medical Research Council (MRC)* covers five broad subject areas: (1) Health Services and Public Health Research; (2) Infections and Immunity; (3) Molecular and Cellular Medicine; (4) Neurosciences and Mental Health; and (5) Physiological Systems and Clinical Sciences. Website: www.mrc.ac.uk
- *The Natural Environment Research Council (NERC)* covers a range of areas under the broad heading of Environmental Sciences, including Atmospheric, Earth, Biological, Terrestrial and Aquatic Sciences. Website: www.nerc.ac.uk
- The Science and Technology Facilities Council (STFC) covers four main areas – (1) Astronomy, (2) Particle Physics, (3) Space Science and (4) Nuclear Physics. Website: www.scitech.ac.uk

In most cases, you will be required to apply through the university department where you intend to carry out your research rather than making your application directly to the relevant research council. Most universities usually have strict deadlines for AHRC and ESRC applications submitted to the relevant university department for initial consideration. Details of deadline dates can normally be found on university departmental websites.

One particular type of award funded by the research councils is called CASE (Co-operative Award in Science and Industry) which offers full three-year studentships with an enhanced stipend. These awards are topped up with funding from UK industrial, public or governmental bodies and provide research students with the opportunity to work in an industrial or commercial environment on a project of interest to the company. Most CASE awards are made via EPSRC, but they are also available from other research councils including BBSRC, ESRC, NERC and STFC. Further information can be found on the various research council websites.

Research students studying at a Northern Ireland university may also consider applying for a Department for Employment and Learning (DELNI) award which covers most fields apart from Biology and Biotechnology, Natural Environment, Particle Physics and Astronomy (available at: www.delni.gov. uk/index.htm).

Research councils and research charities will also offer funding for researchers who choose to carry out their research within a research institute rather than at a university. Research institutes have no power to award a degree of any kind, and so are required to partner with a university. As a research student you will be physically located within the research institute and be supervised there. It is also likely that you will have a university supervisor and so you will be required to comply with the rules and regulations for doing a PhD that are in place at the university at which you are registered. Many institutes will offer PhD studentships with some being advertised as funded posts available in a particular topic. If you decide to be based within an institute, you will still be required to register with a university as well.

University Funding

Many universities offer scholarships of their own which may cover tuition fees, either at the home or overseas rate, as well as a generous stipend. Stipend levels range from institution to institution, with the University of Bristol for example currently offering some research scholarships with a maintenance stipend of £5000; the University of Leeds between £8400 and £12,600; while UCL offers a stipend of £14,600 to scholars in receipt of their Graduate School Research Scholarships. Some universities may offer partial awards. You can usually find details on available awards on university websites or by contacting the department in which you intend to carry out your research. Drawing on their past experience, supervisors are often a good source of information about alternative funding opportunities within your area of research. Closing dates for applications tend to be sometime during March or April, but you should always check with the university for details.

Some UK universities have a central Scholarships Office with responsibility for promoting scholarships and other funding opportunities through dedicated scholarships websites and postgraduate funding publications – University College London, Leeds and Edinburgh, for example. Many other universities publicise their awards on a number of different locations within their university website, often requiring a lot of patience and perseverance on your part as you search through the site to find relevant information on appropriate avenues of funding that may be open to you. You should also bear in mind that the terms and conditions, eligibility requirements and value of each scholarship will differ from university to university. Also remember that these requirements may well be related to legacies and terms as stated by the sponsor, and so they tend not to be very flexible. Be careful that you read the eligibility criteria to ensure that you match these before applying.

As with research council funding, you should remember that university scholarships are highly competitive with many more applicants than there are awards available. For example, one particular university recorded an average of over 1200 applications a year for only 20 research scholarships. With that in mind, you should not rely on one particular scholarship to fund your research but investigate all possible sources of funding and apply for as many as you are eligible for. It is better to be in a position of being offered two scholarships and having to turn one down, rather than to find that you have been unsuccessful in the one application you put forward.

In addition to scholarships, some universities offer research assistantships which provide research students the opportunity to carry out their research at the same time as being in paid employment as part of a relevant research team. These positions are often advertised in publications such as *The Times Higher Education Supplement*, *The Guardian* (Tuesday) and *Prospects*. Please look at these carefully as only some of these will enable you to register for a PhD at the same time, while others may require you to study for your PhD on a part-time basis which will obviously take longer. You will also find that some universities have schemes which waive fees or provide a scholarship to cover fees for their staff. So it is worth investigating if this applies to you if you are offered a job within a university.

Other universities also provide full or partial demonstratorships and teaching assistantships in some of their departments, offering a stipend and tuition fees (usually at the UK/EU rate) in return for teaching or demonstrating for a certain number of hours per year. Further details on these can be obtained from department websites.

Hardship Funds

Universities receive funds which they administer on behalf of the government to assist enrolled UK students in financial need. The funds are limited and are only intended to provide safety-net support for students experiencing unforeseen financial difficulties.

You will therefore be expected to have exhausted all other possible sources of financial support, such as a bank overdraft or a Career Development Loan (CDL), before applying for assistance from this so-called Hardship Fund. The amount of money which postgraduate students receive from Hardship Funds tends to be much less than undergraduate students and will vary from one university to another. Some institutions may also offer financial assistance, from their own funds, to some EU and overseas students who are not eligible to receive an award from government funds. These funds will probably be limited and, again, are not designed to be a student's main source of income but to provide emergency help in the event of unexpected financial circumstances.

Other Sources of Funding

If you are unable to secure a scholarship or research council funding, you may wish to consider taking out a loan. There is a loan scheme which is particularly relevant to this situation – a Career Development Loan. Research students from the UK who are disabled may also be eligible for a Disable Students' Allowance.

Career Development Loan

If you are ordinarily resident in England, Scotland or Wales with an unlimited right to remain in the UK, you may be eligible to apply for a Career Development Loan which is a deferred repayment bank loan. Three banks offer these loans – Barclays, The Co-Operative and the Royal Bank of Scotland. You can borrow anything between £300 and £8,000 to help you fund up to two years of study (or even up to three years if the programme of study includes work experience). The Learning and Skills Council pays the interest on your loan while you are still at university and for up to one month afterwards. You are then required to repay the loan to the bank over an agreed period at a fixed rate of interest. For information on financial assistance to support your learning, including Career Development Loans, please visit www.direct.gov.uk/adultlearning or contact 0800 100900.

Some banks offer other types of loan specifically designed for postgraduate study. Information can be found on these banks' websites.

Disabled Students' Allowance

If you are from the UK and disabled, you may be eligible to receive assistance from the Disabled Students' Allowance to help with the additional costs incurred in attending your programme of study as a result of your disability. Depending on your needs, extra support from the Allowance could include specialist equipment; a non-medical helper's allowance; help towards the additional costs of travelling to your place of study; and a general allowance. You will not, however, be eligible for this allowance if you are already receiving research council funding intended to provide this kind of support. Further details on the allowance can be obtained from the Disability Office within your university, or from SKILL – The National Bureau for Students with Disabilities. Visit their website at www.skill.org.uk or telephone 020 7450 0620.

Sources of Funding for EU Students

EU citizens who do not meet the three-year UK residence criteria may qualify for a fees-only research council award but will not receive assistance for living costs.

The EU provides grants to promote the exchange of students and academic staff within Europe, such as the SOCRATES-ERASMUS (The European Community Action Scheme for the Mobility of University Students) programme. This programme was set up to assist EU students in pursuing their university studies in another EU country. In order to benefit from this mobility scheme, a bilateral agreement will need to exist between your home institution and the university which you wish to visit to carry out research. If you are fortunate enough to benefit from this scheme, then it is unlikely that you will have to pay any tuition fees to the host university for the period that you are studying there. Instead, you will normally be required to continue to pay your tuition fees at your home institution at the usual rate. Further details on the ERASMUS programme will be available from your university's International Office and from the UK SOCRATES-ERASMUS Council.

Funding is also available from the Marie Curie Fellowships Scheme. The Marie Curie Host Fellowships for Early Stage Research Training (EST) are aimed at offering scientific and/or technological training as well as providing complementary skills for researchers in the early stage of their career. Universities or research organisations make an application for funding and then seek to appoint suitable researchers for periods from three months to three years. Details on this scheme can be found at www.cordis.lu/improving or from the European Communities Commission, Marie Curie Fellowships, 200 rue de la Loi, B-1049, Brussels, Belgium.

Sources of Funding for Overseas Students

If you are classified as an overseas student for fee-paying purposes, you will be required to pay the full cost of the fees – sometimes three to four times more than the normal home rate of fees applied to UK national students (see Chapter 4 for more information on the costs of doing a research degree). The reason for this is that the funds for university buildings and infrastructure are from the UK Government and home students benefit from paying subsidised fees below the economic costs of the research training provided. On top of your tuition fees, you will also need to have enough money already in place to cover living costs such as accommodation, travel, food and all your other day-to-day expenses. Therefore, you are strongly advised NOT to travel to the UK or begin your research degree unless you have sufficient funds to pay for both your tuition fees and living expenses.

As a starting point, you should visit your local Ministry of Education and British Council offices, both of which will be able to offer useful advice as well as details on the various funding opportunities available to postgraduate students from your own particular country. If there is no British Council office near where you live in your home country, then you should contact the nearest British Embassy or High Commission.

There are a number of prestigious scholarship schemes open to overseas students intending to undertake postgraduate research in the UK. The number of awards available is limited and, inevitably, competition for these scholarships is always intense. These schemes include the following:

- *The Overseas Research Students Awards Scheme (ORSAS)* which provides awards to overseas research students on the basis of outstanding merit and research potential. These awards are now administered by every UK university and are intended to cover the difference between the home rate and overseas level of tuition fee.
- *Commonwealth Scholarships* offer full scholarships for study or research for postgraduate degrees covering travel, tuition fees and living expenses. These awards are open to Commonwealth students who wish to study in another Commonwealth country and normally provide funding for one to three years of study. Candidates, who should be resident in their own country at the time of application, should apply through the Commonwealth Scholarship Agency in their home country. A list of Commonwealth countries can be found on the Commonwealth Secretariat website at www.thecommonwealth.org/Internal/142227/members/
- *Dorothy Hodgkin Postgraduate Awards* offer full tuition fees and a maintenance allowance in a number of UK universities to students from India, China, Hong Kong, South Africa, Brazil, Russia and certain other developing countries. These awards, which are funded by the UK research councils and industrial sponsors, are open to top-quality science, engineering, medicine, social sciences and technology students wishing to undertake PhD research in top-rated UK research environments. Each award covers the overseas rate of tuition fees and a standard maintenance allowance. At present, 26 UK universities participate in this scheme and further information can be obtained at www. rcuk.ac.uk/hodgkin

In addition to the above scholarship schemes, many universities offer scholarships specifically for overseas research students. The value of these awards can vary greatly from one university to another. Some awards cover the full amount of tuition fees and offer a maintenance grant for a period of up to three years, while other awards may cover tuition fees only or just the home rate of fee, or some kind of partial scholarship. You will also discover that some universities, who wish to target particular countries for their recruitment purposes, will offer country-specific PhD awards. As eligibility conditions vary so much from institution to institution, you should read all the details on available scholarships very carefully to make sure that you do indeed meet all the eligibility criteria before making your application. Remember that it is entirely reasonable to obtain support for funding by piecing together support from a number of sources.

Sources of Funding for US Students

Fulbright Scholarships

Students from the US may also consider applying to the Fulbright Commission who offer around 11 scholarships each year to US graduate students wishing to study in the UK. The aim of the Fulbright Scholarships scheme is to promote mutual understanding between the US and the UK, and the awards are designed to cover tuition fees as well as providing a maintenance grant for housing, travel, food and other living expenses over an academic year period of 10 months. The application deadline for these awards is usually mid-October the year before your programme start date in the UK. Further details can be obtained from the Institute of International Education in the US or from the Fulbright Commission.

Marshall Scholarships

Also available for young US citizens of high ability wishing to pursue postgraduate study in the UK, these scholarships are designed to cover two academic years (22 months) in respect of tuition fees, a living allowance and some study expenses, fares to and from the US and, where applicable, a contribution toward the support of a dependent spouse. At least 40 scholarships are awarded annually. Once again, applications are required a year in advance of you starting your postgraduate degree, normally in early October. Further information can be obtained from the Marshall Aid Commemoration Commission.

US Federal Stafford/Graduate plus Loans

Many US students who fail to secure full funding from a university scholarship or other sources rely on US Federal Stafford/Graduate Plus Loans. These loans are operated by the US Government and offer US citizens affordable loans to assist with the costs of studying. Loan funds are provided by private lenders (banks), then guaranteed by a guarantor. You will often find that Federal Loans are administered by a specialist organisation (such as IEFC) who work with a number of lenders and guarantors. Eligible postgraduate students can presently receive a maximum Stafford loan of $20,500 per year, topped up if necessary by a Federal Graduate Plus loan up to the cost of university attendance per academic year. In addition to a Stafford loan, postgraduates can alternatively apply for a US Private Loan – loans run specifically through lenders who each offer their own loan product. Once again, eligible students can receive loans up to their cost of attendance as approved by their university. Further details will be available from either the Scholarships Office or International Office at the university where you intend to study.

Other Sources of Funding

You will also find that some educational trusts and charities may be willing to offer a measure of financial assistance towards fees, books and living costs. Many grants from trusts and charities offer only limited funding with more applications received every year than funds available, so you should never rely on this source alone as the answer to funding your university costs. You will be expected to have exhausted all other sources of funding before applying for a grant, and may well be asked to provide documentary evidence to prove it. Many trusts have specific criteria as to the group of people they most wish to benefit from their grants – for example, students living in a certain area of the country, or those who are studying a particular subject area. Two useful publications are *The Grants Register* (published by Palgrave MacMillan, Houndmills, Basingstoke, Hampshire RG21 6XS, 1982) and *The Directory of Grant Making Trusts* (published by the Charities Aid Foundation, Kings Hill, West Malling, Kent ME19 4TA, 1987–88). You will also be able to find details on some of the major research charities, who offer considerable financial support for research, from the Association of Medical Research Charities (AMRC), Leverhulme Trust and Wellcome Trust.

Further Information

Opening a UK Bank Account

Whatever form of funding you receive, you will need a suitable UK bank or building society account in place as it is normal practice for funding providers to make payment by direct transfer into your nominated account, whether as a one-off payment or released in stages over your study period.

The most common type of bank account is a 'current account' which offers the convenience of immediate access to your money, both over the counter at your bank and at cash machines (ATMs). This is in contrast to an 'interest-bearing deposit account' which normally requires you to give the bank a period of notice before you can make any withdrawals.

To open a bank account, you will normally need to provide the following identification:

- An official document containing a photo ID – for example, your passport or driving licence, an EU national identity card or National Union of Students card
- Proof of address, such as your formal letter of acceptance from the university or a funding award letter from the university or other funding body
- If you are an overseas student, you may also be required to produce a letter of introduction from your university department.

If you are an international or EU student, you will not normally be allowed to open a bank account until you arrive in the UK to take up your studies. You should also bear in mind that, unlike UK students, your account will not offer an overdraft facility. As well as providing the identification outlined above, you may also be asked for proof of both your home address in your country of origin and your new address in the UK. Some banks may also require a letter of reference from the bank you are registered with in your home country, written in English, providing details of your credit status.

Conclusion: Student Stories

I was extremely passionate about doing a research degree in Mathematics at UCL. However, I didn't think about applying for funding until it was too late and so my parents had to fund my first year which was very difficult for them. As an international student, I was determined to find funding for the remaining years of my PhD and, after browsing the university website, I applied to three scholarships schemes. I was successful in obtaining an ORSAS Award and my supervisor also arranged a Teaching Assistantship in the department. Between these two awards, my fees are covered and I also receive a maintenance allowance.

(Hiral Patel, PhD Mathematics, University College London)

When I was applying for PhD funding, I first looked at the Scholarships Office websites of each of my preferred universities. My funding has been of great benefit to me and has covered my tuition fees and living expenses. I was extremely fortunate in receiving three scholarships – an ORSAS Award, University of Leeds Tetley and Lupton Scholarship, and University of Leeds International Research Scholarship – which have allowed me to dedicate myself fully to the research projects I have been involved in, even enabling me to attend national and international conferences.

(Pan Li, PhD Biological Sciences, University of Leeds)

Finding funding was very challenging as, not being from the UK or EU, many scholarships were closed to me. I started with a year of a self-paid. MSc course, during which I investigated all possible sources of funding for my future studies. Starting with The British Council website and the websites of universities offering PhD study in my field, I gradually built up a picture of all the funding opportunities available to me and was greatly helped in this by my College office and supervisor. Eventually, I was successful in securing a Wellcome Trust scholarship for a 4-Year PhD programme in cardiovascular disease. This award gives me a stipend and covers my tuition fees up to home fee status, showing what can be achieved if you are prepared to put in the time and hard work necessary to find the funding you need to realise your study ambitions.

(Tali Pechenick Jowers, PhD Medicine and Veterinary Medicine,
University of Edinburgh)

Acknowledgements

The authors would like to thank Dr Ian Lyne at the BBSRC for his helpful comments particularly regarding research council funding.

Appendix

Research Councils

Arts and Humanities Research Council (AHRC)

Address: Postgraduate Programmes
               Whitefriars
               Lewins Mead
               Bristol
               BS1 2AE
Telephone: 0117 987 6543
Email: pgenquiries@ahrc.ac.uk
Internet: www.ahrc.ac.uk

Biotechnology and Biological Sciences Research Council (BBSRC)

Address: Polaris House
               North Star Avenue
               Swindon
               SN2 1UH
Telephone: 01793 413200
Email: Postgrad.studentships@bbsrc.ac.uk
Internet: www.bbsrc.ac.uk

Economic and Social Research Council (ESRC)

Address: Polaris House
               North Star Avenue
               Swindon
               SN2 1UJ
Telephone: 01793 413150
Email: ptdenquiries@esrc.ac.uk
Internet: www.esrcsocietytoday.ac.uk

Engineering and Physical Sciences Research Council (EPSRC)

Address: Polaris House
               North Star Avenue

                      Swindon
                      SN2 1ET
Telephone: 01793 444000
Email: studentships@epsrc.ac.uk
Internet: www.epsrc.ac.uk

Medical Research Council (MRC)
Address: 20 Park Crescent
              London
              W1B 1AL
Telephone: 020 7636 5422
Email: students@headoffice.mrc.ac.uk
Internet: www.mrc.ac.uk

Natural Environment Research Council (NERC)
Address: Polaris House
              North Star Avenue
              Swindon
              SN2 1EU
Telephone: 01793 411500
Internet: www.nerc.ac.uk

Science and Technology Facilities Council (STFC)
Address: Polaris House
              North Star Avenue
              Swindon
              SN2 1SZ
Telephone: 01793 442002
Email: studentships@stfc.ac.uk
Internet: www.scitech.ac.uk

Scholarship Schemes

Commonwealth Scholarship and Fellowship Plan
Address: The Commonwealth Scholarship Commission
              Woburn House
              20-24 Tavistock Square
              London
              WC1H 9HF
Telephone: 020 7380 6700
Internet: www.csfp-online.org

Fulbright Scholarships

US Contact Details

Address: Institute of International Education (IIE)
809 United Nations Plaza
New York
NY 10017 3580
USA

Internet: www.iie.org/fulbright

UK Contact Details

Address: US Educational Advisory Service
The Fulbright Commission
62 Doughty Street
London
WC1N 2JZ

Telephone: 020 7404 6994

Internet: www.fulbright.co.uk

Marshall Scholarships

Address: Marshall Aid Commemoration Commission
c/o ACU
Woburn House
20-24 Tavistock Square
London
WC1H 9HF

Internet: www.marshallscholaship.org

UK SOCRATES-ERASMUS Council

Address: Research and Development Building
The University
Canterbury
Kent CT2 7PD

Telephone: 01223 762712

Email: info@erasmus.ac.uk

Internet: www.erasmus.ac.uk

Sources of Information

The British Council

Address: Bridgewater House
58 Whitworth Street
Manchester
M1 6BB

Telephone: 0161 957 7755
Email: general.enquiries@britishcouncil.org
Internet: www.britishcouncil.org

SKILL – The National Bureau for Students with Disabilities

Address: Chapter House
             18-20 Crucifix Lane
             London
             SE1 3JW
Telephone: 0800 328 5050
Email: info@skill.org.uk
Internet: www.skill.org.uk

UKCISA – The UK Council for International Student Affairs

Address: 9-17 St Alban's Place
             London
             N1 0NX
Telephone: 020 7107 9922 (Open between 1 pm and 4 pm Monday
             to Friday)
Internet: www.ukisa.org.uk

SOURCES OF SUPPORT

Association of Medical Research Charities (AMRC) provides support and guidance to medical and health research charities in the UK.
www.amrc.org.uk
The British Academy is the national academy for the humanities and the social sciences which provides support through research grants for individual and joint projects and assistance for conferences.
www.britac.ac.uk
EuroDoc is the European Council of doctoral candidates and young researchers.
www.eurodoc.net/index.php?lng=en.
European Science Foundation (ESF) promotes high-quality science at a European level.
www.esf.org
FindAPhD.com is a comprehensive guide to current research and PhD studentships.
www.findaphd.com/firstmain.asp
Leverhulme Trust makes awards for the support of research and education. The Trust emphasises individuals and encompasses all subject areas.
www.leverhulme.org.uk
New Scientist provides the latest news on every field of science from around the world, including the very latest science and technology job vacancies.
www.newscientistjobs.com

Postgraduatestudentships.co.uk identifies different types of funding opportunities open to potential postgraduates.
www.postgraduatestudentships.co.uk/

Prospects provides details on postgraduate study opportunities and funding information available from universities, public funding bodies, and charities and trusts.
www.prospects.ac.uk

Research Fortnight offers a funding-alert service for researchers across all disciplines.
www.researchresearch.com

Royal Society of Edinburgh (RSE) is an educational charity, registered in Scotland.
www.royalsoced.org.uk

The Royal Academy of Engineering which promotes excellence in science, art and practice of engineering.
www.raeng.org.uk/research/researcher/default.htm

The Royal Society which supports top young scientists, engineers and technologists.
www.royalsoc.ac.uk

United Kingdom Research Office (UKRO) is a subscriber-based organisation providing information and advice primarily to UK organisations on EU-funded opportunities for research and higher education.
www.ukro.ac.uk

Wellcome Trust is the world's largest medical research charity funding research into human and animal health.
www.wellcome.ac.uk

Sources of Information about Where to Do a Postgraduate Research Degree and How to Choose the Best Institution

6

Simon P. Felton

I chose the university because I had studied here for my undergraduate degree and the experience of that put me in contact with research that was taking place in the department and world class supervisors. I also loved my time here because the campus had a real learning and research feel and I knew the facilities and support available plus the reputation of the university is excellent.

(Research student, University of Birmingham)

Introduction

This chapter will look at sources of information about where to do a postgraduate research degree and how to choose the best institution. It will guide you through a process based on what successful students have done previously and show you the stages to go through in making your decision and, hopefully, making the right choice. Specifically, this chapter describes a decision-making process that includes the following:

- Guidance on establishing your own personal decision-making criteria
- Advice on where to look for information, including the advantages and disadvantages of each source
- Common information you could obtain from a prospective institution including questions to ask potential supervisors.

Having decided to pursue a postgraduate research degree (see Chapter 3) it is important to decide where to study and how to compare institutions in this decision. Choosing the best institution for you is important to ensure that your decision to do a research degree is a successful one. You should ensure a considerable investment of time and effort is involved in making these important decisions.

It took me a long time to decide on my MSc. I looked at course research ratings and spoke to course admission tutors together with a consideration of the reputation of the university. The research paid off as I'm now doing my PhD at the same university and really enjoying it. (Research student, University of Surrey)

This research student's commitment to this process has ensured that their time at university has been an enjoyable and successful experience. You should also be aware that in addition to investing time and effort in the decision process you might also have to invest financially in this process to pay for visits to universities you are considering and the cost of postage, telephone calls and even application fees.

Although not covered in this chapter, the specific type of research programme you want to pursue is also important to consider. Chapter 2 has a more detailed analysis of the different types of research degrees that are available in the UK to aid your decision.

The Decision-making Process

The key element in any decision-making process is the individual making the decision, as such the process presented here should be used as a guide and you should modify, add or delete stages from it as you see fit. The processes explored in this chapter are as follows:

1 Use Chapter 3 to help you to understand your individual reasons and motivations, including the benefits and drawbacks you envisage, for pursuing a research degree
2 Develop and prioritise a list of questions that are important for you to make your decision. Use the Quality Assurance Agency's (QAA) precepts in Appendix 1 and the common questions presented later in this chapter to help you to formulate this list
3 Use easily accessible sources of information, such as the university websites, prospectuses, league tables, independent websites, etc. to determine an initial list of possible universities that may be able to satisfy your objectives for your research degree and appear to address your key decision factors. Begin to work out who could be your potential supervisors at each university. Remember to be clear regarding your research interests and to select potential supervisors whose research interests are similar
4 For each university on the initial list produce a set of questions that you need answering that the easily accessible information has not answered
5 Contact each university on your list (email is probably the best route here) to try to obtain the answers

6   Assess the quality and timeliness of the responses you receive
7   Narrow down your list to determine which universities you would like to visit, if it is possible, or investigate further if visits are not possible
8   Work out if you could build a successful working relationship with the potential supervisors you have contacted and met during the decision-making process.

This process will obviously take time. You should also be aware of the timescales and constraints involved in the process as much of it will be set out for you by the academic timetable and your existing commitments. Open days for instance often take place between October and March and prospectuses will often be written well in advance of your planned year of entry. If you are currently a student, it is advisable to consider potential research programmes at the start of your final year to ensure you make an informed decision. If you are not a student, this should be considered at least a year ahead. This will also help in your searching for any potential funding.

After going through this process, with any changes you feel you need to make to it, you will feel that you have done all you can to ensure that the decision you make is the correct one for you. The rest of the chapter will look at this process in more detail.

Your Reasons for Pursuing a Research Degree

As mentioned in Chapter 3 it is extremely important that you understand your motivations for choosing to pursue a research degree. If you know your motivations, the benefits you are looking for, and the drawbacks you are aiming to avoid, you will be clearer about the key factors that will shape your decision. In fact, it is this information that you really should know before you begin to study the information provided by universities to determine which is the right one for you and your long-term objectives for pursuing a research degree.

Defining Your Decision-making Criteria

Now that you are certain of your reasons for choosing to pursue a research degree you should look at how research degrees are structured to begin to develop your decision-making criteria in more detail. As mentioned in Chapter 2, all research degree programmes in the UK are expected to follow the QAA's Code of Practice (see Appendix 1 or the QAA's website for more detail). As you look at this information, ask yourself the question 'how would I prefer this to be implemented to help me to be successful and to achieve my objectives?'

To help you to think this through the common decision-making criteria are presented here in the following sub-sections.

Academic Excellence

This criterion is fundamental to the process of deciding where and with which supervisor you should study for your research degree. There are a number of ways to assess this criterion, none of which is perfect therefore you should make use of all of them and come to your own decision. They include the following:

- QAA's reports of the audits of universities
- The Research Assessment Exercise (RAE)
- Higher Education Statistics Agency's (HESA) performance indicators
- League tables.

The QAA safeguards academic standards and quality of awards across the UK by auditing universities and colleges. Reports of these audits are available on its website, www.qaa.ac.uk.

The higher education funding councils review the quality of research through RAE. The RAE looks at research quality and the output from individual departments and academics, to give an indication of quality and help make comparisons between departments and institutions. The last RAE in 2001 gave departments a ranking of increasing excellence from '1' to '5', with a 5*-rated department being of international importance in its field and providing the very best research practice.

The RAE can be useful for choosing institutions, as it highlights universities in each subject area where the quality of research conducted is considered excellent. Departments that have excelled in research and demonstrated this in the RAE have also benefited from greater funding by higher education funding bodies and it is likely the environment will be focused on good research. This is not to say that good research does not happen in lower-rated departments. The RAE is undergoing changes, with a new methodology being used in the next assessment in 2008. However, until the results of the new RAE are available past RAE scores are still a useful way to assess research quality. The results of RAE 2001 can be found at: www.hero.ac.uk/rae

The quality of the postgraduate experience may vary substantially from different graded departments. The experience in a 5*-rated department with lots of postgraduates where you are one of a number of students may contrast to a developing research community in a lower-rated department with fewer postgraduates which may offer more staff for supervision and may provide a student experience closer to staff in respect and privileges.

> I had a difficult decision to make as there were two excellent departments, one graded 5* and another in a similar field of research which

was 4 rated. Having visited both departments and meeting students and potential supervisors I felt that although the 5* department was world class the 4 rated department offered opportunities to develop my research and considered students as closer to staff as there were fewer of them. I was given more responsibilities to develop myself including teaching and was supported as a junior staff member whereas I felt that I would be just another PhD student in the better-rated department. (Current research student)

The National Postgraduate Committee (NPC) believes that the RAE is a useful tool to determine research excellence but also notes that the RAE is crude in its boundaries and concentrates research funding away from potentially pioneering or new research in less-highly rated departments. As the currently available (summer 2007) department ratings are based on the RAE conducted in 2001, they should be viewed with caution as academic staff, whose work the rating is based on, may well have moved to another university. This movement of staff tends to increase as the subsequent RAE becomes more imminent.

HESA publishes performance indicators for universities in the UK. One such measurement is research output compared to the funding that is provided to a particular university. This provides additional information to the RAE, including the numbers of PhDs awarded. This information can be found at: www.hesa.ac.uk

Several newspapers, websites and other organisations also produce league tables which rank universities with regards to a number of criteria. For instance, the World University Rankings Top 200 was published in October 2005 in the *Times Higher Education Supplement* (THES). The table was created based on the criteria that were specified and weighted by the THES. In this league table the overall score of institutions was made up of peer review, recruiter review, international faculty score, international students score, and faculty/student and citations/faculty score.

Although league tables can be useful in comparing institutions, there is no agreement on which data to use for a comparison. Different league tables use different criteria and an institution can shift from year to year with very subtle changes in individual criteria or even in which criteria are used. You should therefore view them as guides and use your own judgement in determining whether an institution is right for you. You should decide what factors are important to you in choosing between departments and use league tables and rankings cautiously.

Sources of league tables and rankings are listed below:

www.education.guardian.co.uk/universityguide/
www.timesonline.co.uk/uniguide/
www.thes.co.uk/worldrankings/
www.topgraduate.com/

Another useful way for you to check academic quality is to look at academic journals, books and media articles to see which academics are publishing work in your area of research. Read this literature and assess for yourself which is higher or lower in quality. This is a key skill you will need during the course of your research degree so it is worthwhile beginning to practise it now. It is also useful to see which academics are invited to deliver keynote addresses at conferences in your field.

Research Programme Success Rates

As noted in Chapter 2, UK institutions consider 'time to submission' as an indicator of research programme success. Therefore if you are able to find success rates and times for each department you are considering, they will give an indication of past research student experiences. However, the time to submit will depend on a number of factors both personal to the research student and specific to the department and institution at which they were studying.

Facilities

A key aspect of your experience as a research student are the facilities that will be provided in study space and desk space, IT facilities and access, library resources and inter-institution loans. It is important to consider what facilities are promised or highlighted in prospectuses and how those promises are actually delivered. The NPC recognises the importance of facilities and has produced guidelines on the provision of exclusive postgraduate facilities (www.npc.org.uk/postgraduatefactsandissues/postgraduatepublications/ npcguidelinesontheprovisionofexclusivepostgraduatefacilities2003).

Undertaking postgraduate research means making a substantial commitment to your studies in time and money and it is important that facilities are available to support your progress. The institution can be likened to a workplace, one which would be expected to be equipped in a suitable manner. It is important to ensure that facilities are available throughout the year and extended hours for access to facilities if studying part time.

> I decided to do a research degree after working for 15 years and expected that I would have access to personal computers, email, internet access together with a desk and phone. I chose the department for its research opportunities and experience and also the facilities. These all matched my expectations and needs and I received an induction into other facilities and opportunities for researching here. (Current research student)

If you are studying part time these facilities will be particularly important in supporting your research programme. Further issues will include transport, parking and personal security.

Location and Accommodation

Location often plays a part in choosing where to study. Certain locations or regions may present obstacles because of their distance from home, commitments or contacts.

> When I was looking for my Masters, the combination of subjects I wanted to do (digital signal processing and communication systems) only seemed to be available at Bristol and Surrey. I applied and was accepted at both and since both had good teaching and research ratings, I chose Bristol because I thought it was a bigger city and would have a better social scene. After the Masters, my supervisor encouraged me to stay on for a PhD. Since I liked working for him and had my friends in Bristol, I didn't look anywhere else. (Research student, University of Bristol)

Factors in choosing the location include the atmosphere of the campus, department or town or city. It is important to consider whether travelling will be required between campuses and facilities such as libraries.

For part-time students, location will often be the most pressing constraint to minimise the time taken to commute between the university and your other commitments such as your family and employment.

An important but sometimes overlooked concern in choosing an institution is the role of accommodation. For those of you who are able to choose a university close to where you live currently this will not be a major concern, as you may be able to continue living where you do currently. However, for those of you who will need to move, you will need to consider accommodation on campus or in private, rented accommodation. It is likely that living with fellow postgraduates will be preferable for social and networking reasons and this will impact on choices of accommodation; in postgraduate-only halls of residence or private accommodation for postgraduate or mature students. Accommodation will be needed all year round in contrast to the undergraduate year and it is important that when choosing institutions, a consideration of what type of accommodation is desired and how to seek this is considered.

QUESTIONS TO CONSIDER

- Is the institution close to friends or family for support?
- Can you afford to live in the town or city, as some areas are more expensive than others? (See Chapter 4)
- Is there support to find accommodation?
- If you want to live on campus are you able to do so, for instance, are there post-graduate-only halls of residence?
- Will you have to travel to get access to the facilities and resources you need for your research?
- How to find people to live with?
- When to look for accommodation?

Employability

One reason for undertaking a postgraduate research degree is to enhance your career prospects. Looking at the employability of graduates from an institution can be useful in considering the value of its research degree programmes. It is also useful to consider what potential employers think of someone who completed a research degree at that institution.

One of the reasons to undertake a research degree is to take an academic career path. It is therefore sensible to talk to the research staff in the early stages of their career to get as much information and advice of what this entails and how best to build your career in this direction.

Refer to Section 3 of this book for more information on this area.

QUESTIONS TO CONSIDER

- What are the employment destinations of graduates of the institution or department?
- What is the nature and availability of skills training and extracurricular activity – through the department, institution or student-led activity?
- What are employers' perceptions of the value of the institution's degrees?

The Postgraduate Community

One of the key decisions affecting your choice should be the postgraduate community into which you will become a member. Individual students often feel they are alone and it can be lonely and depressing when you hit stumbling blocks or find a part of your research hasn't delivered what you had hoped for, especially when you are engaged in a unique research project. It is important to ask if there are opportunities within the department, and the university more widely, for other activities and networking that help reduce the possibility of feeling isolated.

The nature of the community into which you will become a member will differ from department to department and institution to institution. Often, due to the nature of research, the postgraduate experience is very department based and it is important to look at the departmental social support alongside institutional support. This may be supported by institution-wide or faculty-based 'Graduate Schools' but these vary between institutions with some of them offering social and welfare provision, and study and social space, which may not be so with other institutions, as they may be solely administrative.

QUESTIONS TO CONSIDER

If an institution has a Graduate School, you need to consider the following before you apply:

- Does it provide a central administrative point for research students?
- Does it provide working space, where you can meet research students from other areas?
- Does it offer pastoral and educational support?
- What other support does it offer? For example, funds to support conference attendance.

When choosing between departments and institutions, it is easy to overlook support networks and any postgraduate community against other factors such as facilities and league tables but the postgraduate community will be vital to your experience during the various stages of your research programme. Although some institutions will have developed postgraduate or graduate associations, and research seminars, most others will not. However, the ability to create your own networks can overcome the lack of organised schemes. Often students with similar feelings will precede the creation of informal networks and subsequent associations and societies. There is a more detailed consideration of establishing support mechanisms in Chapter 8.

The National Postgraduate Committee was established as a network to support postgraduate representation and support both in local institutions and nationally and to ensure that institutions were aware of how critical peer support is to the successful completion of postgraduate programmes. The postgraduate community or its potential for development should be a key supporting factor in your final decision on which university to choose for your research degree.

QUESTIONS TO CONSIDER

- What peer-support mechanisms are offered at the institution, faculty and department levels?
- What support is available for research students from the university student unions?
- Does the institution have a Graduate School and what facilities and support does it offer?
- What is the culture of the department you are considering and would this type of culture suit you?

Availability of Professional Development Opportunities

Over the last few years there has been considerable investment in the professional development opportunities available to research students. One such activity that research students have long appreciated is the opportunity to teach.

The NPC in partnership with the University and College Union (UCU) has created an employment charter for research students who teach, which provides some basic expectations you should have.

Some of these expectations include the following:

- A letter of appointment, definitive job description and written statement of terms and conditions – setting out responsibilities, hours of work, rate or rates of pay
- Ensuring that your teaching commitments still give you adequate study time – recognising your main aim will be obtaining the qualification you are studying for
- Full induction training – receiving the same induction and orientation training as other academic and related staff
- Fair rate of pay.

See: www.npc.org.uk/postgraduatefactsandissues/postgraduatepublications/Employmentcharter.pdf

For a more detailed discussion of teaching opportunities read Chapter 17.

These opportunities may be extremely useful for any career you are considering after your research degree.

QUESTIONS TO CONSIDER

- What opportunities are there for professional development?
- How much support is there for this sort of activity?

In this section, various decision-making criteria have been suggested. This list cannot be exhaustive for every reader of this book, as the questions you have will be influenced by your motivations for pursuing a research degree. In addition, what priority and importance you attach to these criteria is for you to decide with the proviso that any university you consider must have some research capability in the area you want to work in, without which a successful outcome is unlikely.

Hopefully you have now developed some criteria or mechanism by which you will assess which university is the correct choice for you; we will now look at how you may go about answering those questions.

Accessible Sources of Information

University prospectuses are the commonest form of easily accessible information on which to base some of your decision making. Universities will mail out copies of their prospectus which are increasingly online. A prospectus offers useful information about the types of research programmes available at a particular university as well as information about the student-support services and accommodation it offers. Although such information is useful, it is less likely that specific information is provided about programmes, departments or academic culture which you require to make your decision. However, prospectuses are useful for you to produce a list of universities to help you investigate in greater detail.

In addition to the prospectus, university websites also provide specific and often detailed information that will be useful to you in making your decision. Explore the website of universities you are considering; not just the section aimed at prospective students. The key reason for looking more closely at the website is to determine whether the university provides opportunities to research in the area you are interested in. Collect as much information as you can; specifically you should seek information on the staff in the department and the research they are involved in, copies of any research papers and information on existing departmental research, information on the research programme, administrative processes and fees information.

The internet also provides other accessible sources of information that can play a very useful part in making your decision. Non-university websites such as those listed later provide a useful method of comparing institutions objectively and seeing how alumni value the degrees they have been awarded together with their views on the experience of the institution. Some websites also assess how employers rate different universities.

Websites however are not always factually correct and their ease of creation should give rise to caution when using them to choose institutions, particularly if their publication date is not recent. It is also worth cautioning that the rise of personal homepages can highlight extremes of dissatisfaction and satisfaction with an institution and these personal views of institutions should be judged objectively.

Useful websites:

www.education.guardian.co.uk/higher/research/ – *Guardian's* education section specifically focusing on research. Provides useful news about what is happening in research and research performance indicators based on the number of PhDs awarded and amount of research grants and contracts obtained in each institution in comparison to the money given for quality-related research. This can be useful for keeping informed about developments in research. Although performance indicators highlight research-intensive institutions, they are crude statistics ignoring other measures of research.

www.guardian.uk.studylink.com/index.html – *Guardian*-hosted StudyLink website provides a searchable database of courses with institution profiles some of which also contain student testimonials.

www.hero.ac.uk/uk/research/index.cfm – *Higher Education Research Opportunities* aims to be the primary internet portal for academic research and higher education in the UK providing an entry point for enquiries about higher education in UK.

www.postgraduatestudentships.co.uk/ – This is a website dedicated to bringing all the different types of funding opportunities open to potential postgraduates together in one place. It is a new site but one that is comprehensive in the research opportunities listed.

www.prospects.ac.uk – This provides comprehensive information on postgraduate study, postgraduate funding opportunities and postgraduate course opportunities. This website is a good start when considering where to undertake a research programme and how to fund the programme.

www.thes.co.uk – *The Times Higher Education Supplement* is a UK-based newspaper that reports specifically on issues related to higher education. It is useful for finding out about developments in postgraduate research and for listing studentships. The website provides limited free access to articles and league tables, which limits its usefulness.

www.topgraduate.com/ – A commercial site aimed at linking graduates and their community with recruiters and education providers. It has a comprehensive list of the world's top universities with a review of each institution. It is useful for comparing institutions and considering their global competitiveness but the review of the institution is written by the institution itself.

You should use your internet search and prospectus research to produce a list of universities that you believe offer research opportunities closely aligned to your interests and that you believe are able to support you effectively during the process of conducting your prospectus research. You should also begin to develop a list of potential supervisors at each university you are considering.

Specific Questions That You Would Like Answered

Your analysis of these various sources of information will no doubt still leave you with some unanswered questions:

QUESTIONS TO CONSIDER

- 'Who is best placed to supervise me?' – You should have a few names from your internet research.
- 'What is the culture of the university and the department?' – Does it suit your personality and working practices?
- 'What do other research students have to say about their experience?' – You may have uncovered one or two comments about universities on your list. How accurate are they and have they come from research students in the department you are considering?

You will no doubt have more questions than those discussed here and in fact your reading of prospectuses and websites may generate other questions you had not considered before you started this process. Therefore, you should begin to formulate a set of questions for each university on your list that will reveal the detail you need to narrow down your list.

As you put the questions together try to categorise them based on who in the university is best placed to answer them. For instance, one of your questions may be about the payment of fees that would best be answered by the university's central administration, whereas you may also have another question regarding the office space you expect which may be best answered through a combination of talking to potential supervisors and their current research students.

Information that would also be helpful in narrowing down your list of possible universities could include the following:

- Copies of the current postgraduate handbook for each department you are considering
- The number of enrolments in the last five years and the number of research degrees (of the type you are considering) awarded
- Supervisors who received supervisor training and their personal success rates
- The time allowed for supervising a student and publications produced by research students.

Contact Each University on Your List with Your Questions

Send the categorised questions to the most appropriate person or part of the university you feel would be best placed to answer them. This may be dictated to you as some universities prefer you to use a central applications contact who would then collate the answers to the questions. However, by this stage you should begin contacting potential supervisors to be clear that they would be happy to supervise your research project. Chapter 7 goes into more detail on how best to do this.

When applying for this information you may get different responses such as a general letter explaining the application process and how to apply, a departmental brochure (if there is one), a list of research interests of academic staff, recent publications, a list of research active staff, an application form, fee information or a research degrees brochure. It is important to remember that there is unlikely to be consistency across the board on what you might receive but a response with lots of useful information suggests a university that is keen to sell itself and attract potential students such as yourself.

Assess the Quality and Timeliness of the Responses You Receive

Both the quality of the answers you receive and the timeliness of the response will help you to formulate a view of the university. Have the questions been answered to your satisfaction or are the answers not what you hoped they would be? Do the answers show a consideration and understanding of the questions you have asked or are they rather superficial? Has the time taken to put the answers together been quicker or slower than you would have expected? Were you updated on the progress of putting the answers together or did you wait to hear from the university for sometime before eventually getting the answers? All of this will help you to develop an understanding of how efficient a particular university is and how it deals with research students queries, which may indicate how you are likely to perceive being a research student at that institution.

Narrow Down Your List to Determine Which Universities You Would Like to Visit or Investigate Further If Visits Are Not Possible

If you are able to visit a university before committing yourself to an application you will be able to clarify whether the impression you have begun to develop about that university is correct or not.

Open days, which often take place between October and March, are a useful way to really delve beneath the university's marketing material and offer you an opportunity to get a sense of what it will be like to study there. For this research student it was an invaluable part of the decision making process:

> I had studied the research area and the universities expertise and was fairly sure it was the right place to do my PhD. What clinched it for me was

visiting the campus and having that intuitive feeling that it was perfect, from library facilities and department facilities to the environment and social setting. I'm glad I visited; it confirmed that my research had picked a good university to do my PhD and I'm now coming to the end of my second year. (Research student, Warwick University)

Open days also allow you to speak in person with potential supervisors to ensure the programme on offer is right for you. As you will be spending a long period of intense study influenced by the people around you, it is important to know if they can deliver what they promise and if they are in tune with your views. The open day also allows prospective students the opportunity to compare facilities such as library facilities, the academic atmosphere and department research interests. Things to remember when undertaking an open day visit include the following:

- Go armed with as many questions as you can and be prepared to 'interview' potential supervisors; remember they will want to make sure you are the right person to offer a place to and you should be sure you will want to accept an offer from this university
- If you have spoken with or visited other academic departments at other institutions, compare the organisation of the respective departments and the particular interests of the staff running it
- Try and speak to research students in the department and ask them to relate their experience of being a research student there. Speak to as many research students as you can to gain a balanced view of the department.

Education fairs provide another opportunity to find out about an institution and meet its representatives. They can be extremely useful if you cannot visit each university you are considering. Fairs take place throughout the year and can be solely for one institution or may include many institutions. Fairs will include representatives of institutions who can register your interest in doing postgraduate study at their institution. They may also include other representatives such as academics and career advisors.

It would help to do the following to make your visit to an education fair more successful:

- Find out who is attending from each institution represented
- Use the Fair Guide. It will list the exhibitors and background information about the postgraduate experience. It should also provide a plan of the stands and details of any talks that are taking place
- Have some questions ready. This seems obvious as this whole process is aimed at answering the questions you have about the experience of being a research student at a particular university
- Make a note of the people you speak to in case you want to contact them later.

If none of these options is possible for you, then you should make use of email and telephone contact with people at the university to develop your view of the institution. However, you should remember not to bombard any one individual, keep your communication focused and professional because they are also developing their view of you.

Contact Possible Supervisors and Their Research Students

Having experienced a good and bad supervision experience I would suggest that anyone considering doing a PhD researches the academic credentials of the university and research group but most importantly researches the personalities you may be working with and whether you will fit into that environment. I spoke with current research students of my potential supervisor and asked staff in the department I had spoken with about the supervisor.

(Research student, Glasgow University)

Contact academics whose research interests are closely related to your own. You should be attempting to find out if you they could be a potential supervisor and also if you could form a successful working relationship with them. This decision should be a personal one based on whether you would respond well to each others working style. Chapters 8 and 9 give more information on this important relationship, the quality of this relationship can contribute to the success or failure of a research programme.

A good working relationship between you and the supervisor is essential, as postgraduate research study is often about working alone. It is useful when choosing an institution to meet your prospective supervisor(s) from which you can consider whether you felt comfortable, did you understand each other and could you follow their ideas?

The relationship between the supervisor and a student can be likened to that of an adolescent and parents where the adolescent is developing their role in society while the parents can misunderstand and sometimes block this progress. It is crucial that in considering a potential supervisor you also consider whether you are comfortable communicating with the supervisor and able to manage expectations and solutions. The NPC suggests that you develop an agreement with a supervisor that explains the expectations and responsibilities in the relationship to aid this process.

If you could, ask to speak to the potential supervisor's current research students and find out about any research networks and support groups you may join. Talking to other research students is extremely valuable as they are currently going through the research experience and are a ready source of information. Talking to other students will also remove some of the apprehension about the experience of a research programme and choosing successfully.

Even after asking these questions of someone you consider to be a potential supervisor, there is no guarantee that the person is available to supervise your project; the person may have plans to go on a long research sabbatical ahead of your project start or any time in the middle of it. The department may also not guarantee any specific supervisor and you may find a supervisor delegates his job to a junior colleague. It is important to check with the potential supervisors (or the academic with responsibility for research students across the department) what the procedure is for allocating supervisors.

QUESTIONS TO CONSIDER

- Who would your supervisor/s be and how well would you work with them?
- How are supervisors allocated to research students?
- What are the supervisory arrangements (sole supervisor, supervisory team etc)?
- Will you be working alone or as part of a research group?
- Is funding available and does it include responsibilities such as teaching?
- What is the individual success rate of supervisors for research students' completion?
- What are their current career plans for instance? Do they anticipate any research sabbatical or taking on significant administrative roles such as head of department that would impact their availability to offer supervision?

Conclusion

The decision on choosing where to do a postgraduate research programme, while seeming potentially time consuming, should be seen as a valuable opportunity to ensure you choose the best institution for you. You will be investing time, effort and money into a programme and your institution and department should develop your research skills, career development and personal development to enable you to achieve the aims for which you undertook the programme as discussed in Chapter 3.

The decision on where to complete your research programme cannot be made easy for you, but by using the example decision-making process to guide you through collecting information from the internet, prospectuses, open days and academics you should be able to make an informed decision on the right institution for your research programme.

To summarise, the following are the key steps in this process:

- Establish your research interests and your motivations for undertaking a research degree
- Develop a list of questions and prioritise them

- Use quality assessment tools to highlight the strengths of universities you are considering
- Gather as much information as early as possible from websites, brochures and institutional visits
- Find out about facilities you will have access to on your programme such as desk space and social space
- Find out the postgraduate community and the peer support you will have access to in the different stages of your research programme
- Contact academics and potential supervisors and consider if you could work with them for a long period of time.

Acknowledgements

I would like to thank all the postgraduate students and graduates who shared their experiences with me to help to frame and enhance the advice contained in this chapter.

SOURCES OF SUPPORT

www.npc.org.uk/essentials
www.prospects.ac.uk
www.thes.co.uk
www.topgraduate.com
www.education.guardian.co.uk/higher/research
www.postgraduatestudentships.co.uk
www.education.guardian.co.uk/higher/research
www.hero.ac.uk/research.

References

Graves, N. and Varma, V. (eds) (1997) *Working for a Doctorate: A Guide for the Humanities and Social Sciences*, London: Routledge.

Phillips, E. and Pugh, D. (1989) *How to Get a PhD*, Milton Keynes: Open University Press.

UK GRAD Programme (2004) *What do PhDs do? 2004 Analysis of First Destinations for PhD Graduates*, Cambridge: UK GRAD Programme.

7 Writing a Research Proposal, Securing an Offer and Applying for Funding

Professor Sharon Monteith and Helen Foster

Introduction

This chapter is intended to provide an understanding of the essential preparation needed for your application to a university to undertake doctoral study. It will define a key document that prospective students, irrespective of discipline, will find of vital importance – the *Research Proposal*. This document has a number of uses which are outlined in the chapter and will be important for securing an offer at a university as well as applying for funding.

The chapter is set out in several sections:

- The definition of a research proposal
- The inspiration that leads to a research proposal
- Who is a research proposal for
- Putting the research proposal together with a step-by-step guide
- Choosing a university including timing and funding advice
- The formal application process and completing your application form.

The sections point to examples we have included in the appendices of research proposals that have resulted in successful applications for funding and secured students offers of university places. The chapter also includes basic advice about how to approach writing your research proposal and your application for study.

The Definition of a Research Proposal

Whatever your discipline, the benefits of writing a research proposal for your individual project are basically the same; even if you join an ongoing research team, with a project that is up and running, you will be expected to be able to distinguish your own contribution. Even if you have not been required to write the original proposal to which your work contributes, producing such a document for your element of the overall project will enable you to distinguish your contribution clearly.

The research proposal is the beginning of your studies whether you apply for a Masters by Research (MRes), a Masters of Philosophy (MPhil) or any doctoral programme. The research proposal is a written document that initiates your intellectual engagement with a university of your choice.

The proposal you send to a university is a position paper in which you set out the parameters of the research that will coalesce in a lengthy written dissertation for any Humanities or Social Sciences student and/or a distillation of the work undertaken as part of a laboratory-based exploration if you are in the Sciences or Medicine, or a dissertation that emphasises the professional and vocational grounding of your study in Nursing or Business, for example.

Your research should excite you and you should not be frightened of where it will take you. You should look on your research proposal not as a static set of principles or a constraining set of objectives, but as an evolving, developing summary and introduction to your investigation. A research proposal is essentially a template for your doctorate.

Who Is a Research Proposal for?

A proposal has a number of purposes and is useful for a variety of audiences. First, it is the document that will prove to different agencies that you are an astute, inquisitive and incisive researcher and that you have found a niche within a field of enquiry where you will locate your study. Second, it is the document that will be used to evaluate you when you apply to a university, a funding body or a sponsor. Third, you will need to hone the proposal, returning to it often within the process of annual review once you begin your studies, to ensure that your research questions are emerging in clear and concise ways as your research progresses. The proposal is your main plan, a working document and a touchstone to which you will return in order to measure your progress. Once you begin your studies, for example, you will probably be asked to provide a snapshot of your project to be included on a department's website so that other researchers in other institutions will be able to contact you if they work in similar areas. Your proposal will be the working document from which you will provide the breakdown of your project for other interested parties. These may include the organisers of conferences where you may be advised by supervisors to present your work. There will be opportunities to submit a poster or a conference paper as part of your professionalisation as a student and it will be important to describe your work in sharp and effective prose. You will have begun to refine your style and approach in writing your proposal for a range of different audiences (see Figure 7.1).

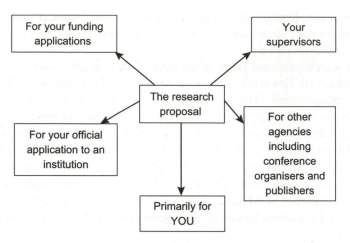

FIGURE 7.1 Who is a research proposal for?

Finally, the research proposal is primarily for you. It will evolve into the abstract which will form the first section of your final thesis. As your original research proposal was the first communication with an external audience, so your abstract will become your first communication with the examiners who will determine whether your study has been successful. If you are working within a discipline where you may attempt to turn your research into a book following the successful completion of your research, this proposal, and later abstract, will evolve into the book proposal you may send to prospective publishers. In this way, the initial research proposal is a catalyst for everything that follows.

The Inspiration That Leads to a Research Proposal

You may have been inspired by a topic or an idea in your professional life or a previous study that has motivated you to undertake a research degree. It may also be the case that the ideas about the specific research that you have elected to pursue have been evolving throughout your undergraduate studies. A particular taught module may have excited your interest in a field of enquiry or a particular intellectual methodology, and this may form the basis of an investigation that you would like to carry out as a postgraduate researcher. More specifically, your final year undergraduate dissertation may well have whetted your appetite for a more profound way of engaging with your subject.

Whichever point you enter the research process, you will be supported in gaining the skills and training required in order to undertake research effectively, that is, to organise and write a project and to present your findings to an academic audience. Research training encourages us all to be reflective about the theories and practices that underpin our research at any and all stages of our careers.

Your supervisors will support you in selecting the appropriate methodologies for your research, and in developing those analytical and practical skills which are required for the effective written and oral presentation of research. While supervisors focus on discipline- and project-specific intellectual support, you will be encouraged to improve your ability to think critically and conceptually by attending generic training sessions too. Training will help you to recognise that research requires you to engage with complex and often ambiguous, even contradictory, materials and conditions.

While you will have opportunities to discuss the typical characteristics of a research project as it develops, your research proposal is the initial test that you have the ability to develop a sceptical or critical view about sources of information and that you will be able to weigh the significance of specific facts, perceptions and interpretations. From the very first, you should begin to work with the concepts and ideas that shape your project and demonstrate their significance in the context of your study.

Putting the Research Proposal Together

Your research proposal is the first written material you will send to the academics who may become your supervisors for the next few years. For them it is a test of your intellectual rigour. Your response to their comments will be a test of your ability to work with constructive criticism and to build on that criticism. As you begin to think about your subject, you may have several ideas or areas you wish to pursue in more detail. A way of distinguishing between these in settling on your proposal will be to test the parameters of each potential thesis (by thesis we mean the key idea(s) that underpin your potential study and its intellectual trajectory). Even at the beginning of your research you should be able to test the distinctiveness of your project. You do this by reading around the research that has already been carried out in your chosen area. At this stage you can start to locate yourself with and against different critics, writers, commentators or investigators. The key point is that your intervention in your field and your approach to your topic should be original. The word 'original' can be subject to catachresis: every time you try to define it the concept falls apart. However, do not be afraid of the idea of originality; what it means is some or all of the following. It could mean you yoke together traditionally dissimilar ideas; in other words, your approach combines elements, arguments, tests or texts that have not been used in the same context before. It may be that the methodology you choose to apply has not been previously adapted to your context. It may be that you have alighted on a principle or problem or archive, a writer, artist or theorist, or a zone of intellectual engagement that is yet to receive sustained critical attention.

Your current or former tutors and your potential supervisors will often act as guides to signal whether the topic you propose is tired or too well-trodden, unrealistic or impossibly ambitious. It may be none of these things and your first attempt may provoke interest and a willingness to support the project. However, it is not unusual for it to take as many as six or more attempts to refine your thesis proposal in consultation with your potential supervisors. If they feel that you have an idea that could work, they may help you to test its validity by asking tough intellectual questions about your conceptualisation. You should accept constructive advice. Although the project is yours and it is your responsibility to produce the proposal, you should welcome questions and suggestions from experienced academics practised in reading successful proposals and who are experts in the area you wish to enter as a researcher. You should keep in good and regular contact with potential supervisors who will also help you prepare your proposal for a funding body. Your contact with them should be targeted and professional.

Step-by-step Guide on Putting a Research Proposal Together

In summary, the following is a suggested set of stages you may wish to follow when writing your research proposal. It is not a definitive list but it will be helpful in getting organised:

1   Assuming you have been inspired by a field of enquiry, discuss it with your tutors at your university or anyone who will talk to you about it. Verbalising your ideas is important and you will learn more about your subject.
2   Talk to your potential supervisors and other key contacts at your potential university. (The next section will look at how to choose a university.)
3   If you have several ideas for a proposal, write summary documents for each outlining, as clearly as you can, what your thesis would be about.
4   Divide your proposal into clearly defined sections. Start with a short introduction and then consider the following questions which may be presented in separate sections.

    a   Why is the research important?
    b   What is the research about?
    c   How will the research be done?
    d   What intellectual field is the research located in?
    e   Will there be cost implications to the research?
    f   Will you need to travel to consult an archive or to interview subjects? Is the research manageable in the time allocated (most doctorates are completed over a three-year period)?
    g   Am I interested enough in the subject?
    h   Will the research keep me interested?

5 Test these ideas to establish, as far as you can, whether the research will be groundbreaking or original.
6 Share your proposal with others. Ask for their comments and advice.

Choosing a University

You should select a university on the basis of the academic 'fit' between your chosen field of enquiry and the supervisors whose expertise will underpin your studies and support you in your professionalisation as a postgraduate researcher (this is explored more in Chapter 6). This is especially important if you are planning an academic career. In other words, who are the experts in your field? Who would be the best academics to oversee your research?

In the first instance, the contact will probably be via email. If you are an international student applying to the UK but living abroad, email may be the primary or even the only means by which you introduce yourself and your project to those who will help you to realise it. Whether writing from home or abroad, it is especially important that you are aware that a poorly written email creates a poor first impression. Colleagues in different institutions confide that it is irritating to be addressed by the wrong title, to have their names spelled incorrectly or to be approached to supervise a topic that bears no relation to their research or publications as publicised on the department website or as available for applicants to search for in a large online bookstore. It may seem very surprising that carelessness of this type is in evidence in initial communications with universities and academics who might be expected to support your work.

However, there are a number of issues to bear in mind. Do not fire off emails to each and every member of an academic department in the hope that any member of staff will reply: either select the two individuals whose expressed research interests, expertise and publications relate to your own (best practice in the UK is always to allocate a research student at least two supervisors) or write to the person designated. In most departments and institutions a member of academic staff is designated the department's Director of Research and/or the person in charge of postgraduate applications and their name is usually flagged on the website as the individual to whom you should address expressions of interest in the first instance. That person will respond and put you in email contact with those researchers whose interests map on to your own. Bombarding an entire department with emails is a mistake; rather than presenting yourself as a keen and serious applicant with an academic purpose, you risk being read as taking a 'scattergun' approach because you are ill-prepared for your studies or because you wish to study for study's sake rather than follow a directed and focused project in the academic environment that best serves your goals. So, in summary, the email should include (a) who you are, (b) no more than two pages about the research you wish to pursue and why that research is important and original, and (c) a brief Curriculum Vitae that contains the relevant information about you.

Timing

One of the most obvious things that you can do to afford yourself the best chance of securing funding for your studies is not to leave your application until the last moment. If you do, it may be that the academics you send it to will have no time to read and return their comments before a funding body's application deadline – or it may be that a university will not consider you for funding for the following year because all other applications have been assessed. In any case, it is supremely obvious that a rushed proposal will neither define its intellectual challenges nor be situated clearly within the field in a way that will do justice to your ideas.

Funding Advice

It is equally important to read and digest the guidelines as specified by a funding council and/or a university faculty or a school advertising studentships. Although this may seem a very obvious piece of advice, we are very aware that some applicants who are ineligible according to the specified criteria made available on websites sometimes spend considerable time preparing an application that rules them out of a competition. In other words, attention needs to be paid to criteria in addition to those that relate to the intellectual component of your application. Most award-givers accept applications for part-time as well as full-time study, but again, it is important to reassure yourself of the criteria. A contact name is always provided for the person best able to answer administrative and/or intellectual queries and there are often web pages wherein answers to 'Frequently Asked Questions' (FAQs) will be spelled out. Similarly, failure to read and apply the criteria that relate specifically to conveying the significance of your project may result in a weak and unfocused application. For example, word counts are specified for each application and these can be very differently loaded. As we write, for instance, the Economic and Social Research Council (ESRC) currently requires student applicants to prepare a lengthy outline of a research project, whereas the Arts and Humanities Research Council (AHRC) expects that students will summarise the project in its entirety, as well as speak about the project's match to supervisors and institution, in no more than 500 words. Types of funding application vary and institutions will choose formats and processes that they believe are both informative and revealing of a candidate's commitment to follow set guidelines; such guidelines also work as a preliminary means of selecting between an organised applicant and a focused proposal and a loose and baggy general exploration that is poorly presented by an ill-prepared applicant.

It is always useful to see successful proposals that have secured funding from external bodies and that constituted the first stage of successfully completed studies. *Therefore the appendix to this chapter contains a selection of indicative examples.* These may not fall within your own field of research but you should note the ways in which, whatever their topic, they present their research concerns in a phased and focused way. It is important for your research proposal to stake a claim in a subject area and/or make clear its interdisciplinary qualities so that it may be judged by the most appropriate of assessors. Funding bodies often have very broad subject domains.

They also have different funding mechanisms. You may decide to apply for a funding council's open competition, whereby the individual proposal is judged according to its individual merits alongside and including the expertise of, and relevance to, the university department to which it will be attached. Or, you may decide to apply to a university faculty or department which has either a specified number of funded studentships or has been allocated a quota of studentships by a funding body with emphases placed on quite broad, or alternatively very specific, subject areas. Ensure that you always direct applications appropriately.

The Formal Application Process

The process for applying to UK universities for postgraduate study is broadly similar. It will always involve completing an application form. You will be asked to supply the names of academic referees who will, in turn, be asked to comment separately and confidentially on your scholarly abilities. You will also be required to attach relevant supporting information and documents to supplement your application and to provide clarification of your educational background.

For many potential research applicants this official process will follow initial contact with your potential supervisors; you may even have had an interview and/or have met with potential supervisors. Further, you may have already been given an indication about the likelihood of your success in gaining a place at a university of your choice following a discussion or formal interview. Whether you complete an application form at the beginning of the process or towards the end, it is important to stress that this paperwork should not be overlooked or treated as merely a formality. Omitting vital information or not completing a form properly could at worst, lead to your not being offered a place, and at best, delay the process of being admitted to a university.

Although developing and writing a research proposal is often a fairly intimate affair, largely undertaken by you and perhaps with support and guidance from prospective supervisors, or academics in your current or former institution, the formal process of application is also important for a number of reasons. First, universities usually have central registry and student support systems, and these are responsible for communicating directly with applicants about all sorts of relevant issues, from registration details to graduation ceremony organisation at the end of your degree. Often, important information is sent directly to applicants from central departments (rather than academic departments) and so it is important you are 'in the system'. Second, central admissions departments process and check applications to ensure that rigorous university entry standards are met. Departments have different minimum entry requirements and it is usually the task of the admissions departments to check them. Finally, many universities need to assure themselves that you are a serious applicant by signing an application form so that they may make provision for your registration. In fact, some universities charge an application fee to postgraduates in order to test that you are indeed serious in making your application.

Different universities employ different methods of application. Virtually all institutions provide either downloadable forms from the internet and several provide an online application service. It may seem an obvious point to make but ensuring you read the guidance notes and making sure you treat the application process seriously is of primary importance. It is also important to note what documentary evidence you need to provide which will probably include the following:

- Original certificates of undergraduate/postgraduate degrees
- Original transcripts of your degrees
- Original certificates of English Language tests if you are an overseas applicant
- Signed referee reports (these may be sent under separate cover)
- Portfolios – sometimes required for specific subjects
- Research proposal
- Curriculum Vitae (CV)
- Personal statement (this may be included on the application form).

Usually, if the application process is online, you will need to submit your supporting documents by mail. Some systems allow you to upload scanned documents through their online form. However, at some point, a university will always ask you to provide the original documents, usually before you register. To ensure that your documents are checked, the institution will normally extend an offer that is conditional upon the need to verify your documentation.

Application review can sometimes be a slow process and it may take up to 4–6 weeks for the processing to be complete. It is wise to find out how long the process usually takes so you may plan accordingly and it is useful to make sure you have the contact name and number so that you may get in touch with the university to check the status of your application.

Advice on Completing Your Application Process

References

All universities will need to see at least two references to support your application. The same referees may also be required if you submit a funding application too. You should think very carefully about who you choose as your referees. The ideal referees will be academics who know you and who have read your work recently. It does seem obvious, but it is amazing how many times applicants do not request permission from academics to use them as referees. You should do this, not merely out of politeness and basic courtesy, but also because if they are away on study leave, or researching in another country, or have left the university, it will cause delays for you. Similarly, if they feel that they do not know you well enough to comment positively on your application or have any queries about your research, they can enter into a dialogue with you before they write a reference. Try to give potential referees as much information as possible – a copy of your application which will include the reasons why you want to embark on the research. If there is a deadline for the reference to be sent to the institution, tell your referees when you want to start and also tell them details of where to send their reference. Most importantly, but again, it is surprising how many applicants fail to do this: you should send your referees a copy of your research proposal. In this way, they can be specific in their reference about the ways in which your current ideas build on your previous work and/or interests and they can situate your broader qualities within the framework of the proposal according to which you will be judged. Always allow them sufficient time to complete their references.

If you have been away from full-time education for a while and you feel that references from members of academic staff who knew you while you were studying for your undergraduate or masters degree will not be able to give you an informative reference, check with the admissions department at the university to which you are applying and ask them for advice. It will probably be possible for you to ask a line manager at your place of work for one of the references.

The Form

1   University structures can be complex. When you apply, the form will ask for the school or department to which you are applying. Do make sure you have the correct information so that your application does not go to the wrong place and delay the process. For example, literary studies take place across different departments. If you are applying for French literature or American literature you may need to specify a department of

Modern Languages or of American Studies. In an institution where such departments are not in place, comparative or American literature may be taught in the English Department. It is important that you are clear about the department to which you intend to apply. An application may not only be turned down by a department that does not have expertise in your topic but may also not always be passed on to another, more appropriate, department. It is your responsibility to follow up closely and get this right.

2   In recording your academic history, institutions will generally only be interested in your higher education record not your schooling, so you need to make sure that you place emphasis where it is required.

3   Make sure that you complete the application form as fully as possible. Do not be sparing with the information you provide. The central admissions office will require you to provide any information that is missing, and this can cause delays.

4   Be as specific as possible about the development of your research proposal, as described above, and always ensure that you mention the name of your prospective supervisors in the application.

5   The application form will ask you about your career experience. If this is minimal and the work is not relevant because you have just finished your masters course or your undergraduate degree course, you may make very brief notes about this. Make more of the information about previous posts if you are a mature student, or if you are returning to study for a research degree after a period in work. If your previous employment is relevant, it may sometimes compensate for not having the exact or standard entry requirements. Separate permission usually has to be accorded for entry to a research degree when you have non-traditional or non-standard qualifications or are claiming work experience as an entry qualification. Allow extra time for this process and make sure you are clear and detailed in making a case for special consideration.

Attitude and Approach

1   Make a photocopy of all your documents and your application form and note the dates when the forms were submitted.

2   Inform your potential supervisors that you have made a formal application and keep in touch with them.

3   Be proactive after you have submitted your application. Keep in touch with the central admissions office and with prospective supervisors to make sure your application is being processed and keep reading and researching in your area while you are waiting for an offer letter and registration documents.

4   Treat the application as you would an application for a job. For admission to a very good UK university there is competition for places and you will need to present yourself as well and as fully as possible.

5 You must make sure you have checked your application and proofread it carefully. Give it to other readers who may not be in your discipline but who will tell you whether your proposal makes good general sense and is expressed clearly. At each stage of the application, make sure that you have been professional in all aspects of the process in order to secure an offer from a university to pursue your research.

Interviews

1 You may be requested to attend an interview at some point during the formal application procedure, or you may have had an interview with your potential supervisors prior to the application procedure. Some universities may not invite you for an interview.
2 Ensure that you treat the interview process as you would an important job interview. It is not unusual, in the experience of the authors, for some interviews to seem informal. However, even if this is the case, the interviewers will be assessing very seriously your ability to undertake a doctoral degree.
3 The interviewers will be looking for a demonstration of your intellectual abilities. They will be looking at your ability to communication generally, your expertise or knowledge about your research area and for signs that will indicate that you will be able to organise and complete your degree.

Registration

Although most research students begin their course at the beginning of an academic year – in September or early October it is usually possible for you to begin at any time of the year. If you do consider registering at a different point, you may miss informative and useful welcome sessions that take place at the beginning of the year, unless your university offers them more often. Make sure you take extra care to find out everything you need to know when you arrive and that you know who to contact when you do.

Conclusion

You should note that the applicants who are hardest to help are those who do not develop their ideas or stance as a result of constructive feedback. Those who write the most successful research proposals have usually taken advice and worked through their application with the academics who will best support it. A research proposal should be a considered and coherent representation of the research which will sustain your studies over three years. It should be presented clearly and coherently so that a variety of audiences may use it as a guide when assessing your application for a research studentship. It therefore has to speak to referees who will see it as a culmination of your earlier work and interests; to prospective supervisors who will detect within it the germination of ideas that are sufficiently profound and analytical to locate your study within wider research culture. It should speak to potential funders—whether the university or an external funding body— who will judge your proposal competitively against applications on similar topics, by similarly qualified applicants, for its intellectual promise and rigour; and it should speak to central admissions who will see your proposal in the wider context of your complete application. Most importantly for you, your research proposal is the template for your future successful studies.

Appendix

Examples of Research Proposals That Have Formed Part of Successful Application for University Places and for External Funding

These are presented with the permission of the ESRC and AHRC research students who authored them and are indicative examples from across the disciplines. Full bibliographic details have been removed for space reasons; this should not prevent you from gaining an insight into how proposals are structured while reading them.

Application for PhD to the AHRC

Project Title: The Aesthetics of Suffering: Arthur Schopenhauer and the Literature of the American South

Reasons and Purposes for Undertaking This Project. My PhD thesis traces the origins and development of a particularly Schopenhauerian aesthetic in the literature of the American South, a region which, although it has often been seen to exemplify the moral and cultural pessimism so often associated with the philosopher, has not yet been discussed in this context.

The Research Project. In his recent book on Arthur Schopenhauer's philosophy, Dale Jacquette notes that if one were to compile a list of figures who 'owe an intellectual or inspirational debt' to the German thinker, it would have to include not only those who came into direct contact with his work, but also everyone influenced by those figures in turn. Rather than seeking to prove direct Schopenhauerian influence, my thesis explores the complex filtration of the basic tenets of Schopenhauer's world-view through the work of key individuals. Schopenhauer saw the nature of existence as grounded in want and suffering, the ubiquity and inevitability of which have their fruits in the very vices which W. J. Cash, in *The Mind of the South* (1941), saw as characteristic of the region. Given Cash's indebtedness to H. L. Mencken, who as well as being an outspoken critic of the South was also a translator and scholar of the works of Schopenhauer's one-time disciple Friedrich Nietzsche, the first section of the thesis discusses the philosophical context of Cash's cultural pessimism in the light of recent re-examinations of the complex relationship between the writings of the two German thinkers. The section also explores the literary ramifications of this development in works by William Faulkner, Lillian Smith, and Ellen Glasgow, the last a self-acknowledged Schopenhauerian.

Drawing upon Flannery O'Connor's assertion that the presence of the grotesque in Southern literature is emblematic of human isolation and difference—in Schopenhauerian terms, individuation—the second section will explore the persistence of this trope in more recent Southern fiction. Focusing on Lewis Nordan, Barry Hannah, Larry Brown, and Harry Crews, it will consider key texts in the tradition of grotesque southern literature, deploying Schopenhauer's transcendental idealism as an interpretative tool. Focusing specifically on Schopenhauer's insistence regarding the inseparability of metaphysics and ethics, particular attention will be paid to the way in which literary works posit either a renunciatory or a compassionate response to suffering. The thesis will conclude with a detailed case-study and Schopenhauerian analysis of the work of novelist Cormac McCarthy.

Preparation and Previous Experience. This project draws upon previous study of Schopenhauer and McCarthy, undertaken as an undergraduate and, latterly, during the MA American Studies at Nottingham during which I studied the MA module 'Representing the US South'. My studies benefit greatly from the expertise of supervisors who have a wealth of experience researching and writing on contemporary American fiction and the literature and culture of the South.

Thanks to Euan Gallivan studying for a PhD in the School of American and Canadian Studies, University of Nottingham.

Application for PhD to the AHRC

Project Title: Performing Commonwealth and Colonial: A Cultural and Historical Geography of the Royal Commonwealth Society from 1868

Reasons and Purposes for Undertaking This Project. The project will investigate the Royal Commonwealth Society (RCS) from 1868 to the present. The RCS began as the Colonial Society, becoming the Royal Empire Society in 1928, and taking its present name in 1958. Apart from Mackenzie's 1998 essay on the

RCS library, researchers have neglected the society. My undergraduate and MA dissertations, focusing on the architecture of the RCS and the organisation of the library collection respectively, indicate a wealth of unexamined material. The RCS provides a way into the performance of imperial and commonwealth identities in a changing Britain. I wish in due course to pursue an academic career centred on a culturally and historically informed perspective on the geographies of British identity.

The Research Project. The project will explore the performance of imperial and commonwealth identities through the material and metaphorical spaces of the RCS London headquarters. Historians of Geography (Driver 2001) and the Social Sciences (Osborne 1999) have shown how institutions became centres of calculation and interpretation shaping imperial and post-imperial policies, identities and geographical knowledges. The RCS, as a metropolitan institution reinventing its own identity through changing historical contexts, allows a detailed study of the institutional performance of empire and commonwealth, from a site at the centre of a global empire to a position as the focus of a commonwealth 'club' of nations within a world city. The project will have five key empirical foci:

1   The changing architecture of the RCS building, subject to major redesigns in 1936 and 1997 which sought to produce a style of headquarters to suit changing historical and cultural circumstances.
2   The performance of British, colonial and commonwealth identities through lectures and cultural events, the related place of the RCS within London society, and political controversies surrounding events concerning, for example, South Africa and Bangladesh.
3   The imaginative geographies of RCS journals and newsletters, producing particular visions of the world and its cultural and natural environments.
4   The organisational structures of the RCS as a means of shaping power and influence within and beyond the institution, and controversies over society name changes and membership rules concerning gender and ethnicity.
5   The active role of the RCS library in producing and circulating information through which institutional identity was produced.

The primary source will be the RCS library and archive, which moved from its London headquarters to Cambridge University Library in 1994. I have permission from the RCS librarian to access all relevant material, including books, plans, membership records and photos. Oral history interviews with employees, members and visitors, and visits to the current building and events, will supplement archival research. The first year of the research will consist of initial archival research alongside secondary historical and theoretical reading, with the remaining archival work and oral history interviews to be completed by December of Year 3, allowing writing up within three years.

Preparation and Previous Experience. The MA in Landscape and Culture has given excellent preparation in terms of the theoretical and empirical basis for my proposed research, with the Research Design module providing training in research methods such as archival research and interviewing.

Thanks to Ruth Craggs studying for a PhD in the School of Geography at the University of Nottingham.

Application for PhD to the ESRC

Project Title: Network Effects in Mobile Telecommunications: An Empirical Analysis

The aim of my research is to estimate the importance of network effects in the use of mobile telephones. The nature of network effects will be analysed both in the traditional framework of microeconomics, and in a framework focusing on the direct interaction between consumers.

Background. It is recognised that network effects can be a powerful source of economic growth (McGee and Bonnici, 2002). Due to the self-propelling nature of growth in network markets, market expansion tends to be much faster in network industries than in non-network industries. Network industries, like telecommunications, have been among the fastest growing industries in recent years.

After the seminal article of Rohlfs (1974), and the influential papers of Katz and Shapiro (1985) and Farrell and Saloner (1985), there has been a plethora of theoretical studies into the nature of network effects and network effects theory has reached a rather mature state. However, empirical work in this area has been slow to keep track with the advances in theory, and it is only comparatively recently that such studies have appeared in any numbers.

The literature on network effects usually distinguishes between two types of network effects: direct and indirect effects. Direct network effects refer to the case where users benefit directly from the fact that there are large numbers of other users of the same network. In mobile communications, a direct network effect arises when the user can call a larger set of persons. Indirect network effects, on the other hand, arise, because bigger networks support a larger range of complementary products and services. In second generation mobile networks, indirect network effects are only of second-order significance, but they will play an increasing role after the introduction of 3G networks, where usage will be heavily influenced by the availability of data services. While it is widely acknowledged that network effects are a key feature of telecommunications industries and, indeed, that telecommunications networks provide perhaps the leading example of network effects, relatively few studies have analysed the empirical importance and extent of network effects in the telecommunications market (see Kim and Kwon, 2003 for an exception).

The overall aim of my research is to estimate the importance of network effects in the use of mobile telephones. My thesis will contain three major parts: an empirical section using aggregated market level data and available survey data on mobile telecommunications; a theoretical section which will aim at enriching the current network concept used in microeconomics with a focus on local interaction effects and, thirdly, I plan to conduct a survey research which it is hoped will validate the findings.

Part 1: Empirical Work Based on the Traditional Understanding of Network Effects. For the first step, I plan to use a model of discrete choice between differentiated products (following Berry, 1994). I will adapt this model to allow for choice to be a function of different network effects. The technique allows estimating implied mean levels of utility for each network by 'inverting' the market share equation and accounts for correlations between prices and unobserved demand factors. It is, therefore, not necessary to directly observe product characteristics (which might be largely determined by the brand strength in mobile communications); it is sufficient to observe the market outcomes of price and quantities sold by each operator.

The research will use market data from the UK telecommunications regulator (OFCOM) and a survey entitled Home Online with data on individual mobile usage. The OFCOM data consists of quarterly market data on number of subscribers, call volumes and revenues. The data is reported on a voluntary basis by the four UK GSM-network operators: Vodafone, 02, Orange and T-Mobile (data for 3 is not available yet). Furthermore, OFCOM publishes price data for a variety of user types. The Home Online survey was conducted in three waves between late 1998 and early 2001 by the Institute for Social and Economic Research, University of Essex. It consists of data on information and communications technology (ICT) access and behaviour from 1000 households and around 2500 individuals from these households. A subsection of the survey focuses on mobile usage and attitudes towards mobile telephony. One issue discussed in detail is how exactly we should measure the relevant network size for mobile communications. We could in, principle, measure the size of the total mobile network, the size of a particular operator's network, or indeed the total telephone network. Or, noting how Orange and T-Mobile have achieved market success in the UK by targeting different customer groups, we could define relevant network size as the network of friends. To resolve this question, I will follow the approach in Swann (2002). There, it is argued that many (or perhaps even all) other users are a potential source of network effects, but some users matter more than others. Network value is defined as a weighted sum of all other users, where the weights depend on the probability that one type of user would call another. In this way, the resolution of the issue of measuring network size is to attach high weights to friends using the same network, a slightly lower weight to friends using different networks, and much lower weights to other mobile and landline users.

Part 2: Theoretical Work on Network Concept Based on Local Interaction Effects. The first part of my thesis is based on the use of aggregated data and a survey on technology use. However, the survey does not allow for a full identification of the relevant network that influences the choice behaviour of consumers. To estimate the network that is relevant for the consumer when purchasing a network product, i.e. subscribe to a certain mobile network, it is necessary to get data on the social network of people.

There are a number of contributions looking at local interactions in economics (see Kirman (1997) for an overview). Typically, agents are assumed to be located in a highly structured network (a lattice or a torus). These studies have demonstrated that multiple equilibria can occur in a wide range of settings, especially if local externalities are strong. However, many real world networks have small-world properties, i.e. besides a strong local clustering there is often a short path length between distant agents, as there are direct connections between some agents located far away. Watts and Strogatz (1998) show that these networks have very different properties from traditional networks. I plan to apply such network concepts in the mobile telecommunications context.

I hypothesise that the relevant network for the user basically consists of two layers. The first is the overall number of subscribers to a particular network, of which there is data publicly available and where I assume that the consumer at least has some basic knowledge, e.g. provider A is much bigger than provider B. The second layer, and the focus of my research, is the network of 'friends', where I assume that there typically exists a small number of people with whom there is intensive social contact. There is circumstantial evidence that the latter layer is important and that this is recognised by network operators. For example, there are tariffs where you can choose a number of people for which there is a price discount.

Similarly, the strategy of co-branding can be seen in the light of increasing the awareness of the consumer of what operator the peers are using.

Part 3: Empirical Work on Social Networks in Mobile Telecommunications. To analyse this second, personal layer, I intend to develop a questionnaire to identify social networks. The most useful sampling technique for such an endeavour is snowball sampling (Goodman, 1961) which means that a relatively small group of prime respondents are chosen who then identify the persons with whom they have a close relationship. In a subsequent step, these secondary respondents will be targeted.

Besides the information gained about the personal network, further network questions will be used to further substantiate the exact constitution of the network (e.g. type of relationship). The second part of the questionnaire will enquire about the use of mobile technology by the user. It contains questions about network operator choice, reasons for network choice, use of services etc. and questions targeted at getting information on how the personal relationships identified in the first part reflect on mobile telecommunications usage. Furthermore, there will be questions to elicit whether the respondent is aware of the network choice of his/her network 'neighbours'.

Contribution of the Research. By exploring the network constitution that is relevant for the choice of a mobile network operator, the research will be able to shed further light on how the abstract concept of network effects of economics operates in reality. It thus helps to bridge the gap between the parsimony of economic models and the practical strategic management and marketing requirements of the companies competing in the mobile telecommunications market.

The thesis will close by discussing implications of the findings for our understanding of the mobile market, and the implications for company strategy and regulatory policy. As discussed in Swann (2002), the functional form of network effects has several important implications for business strategy. The extent of network effects especially influences operator's pricing strategies and is related to regulatory questions such as pricing of on-net and off-net calls. The results will be directly relevant with regard to the current introduction of 3G networks in Europe. As mobile telephony is an important part of information technologies in general, the results from my thesis will be highly relevant for the theme 'Knowledge, Communication and Learning'. It can be expected that effects found in mobile telecommunications are present in similar forms in other information technologies too. Furthermore, the study of social networks is related not only to the adoption of new technologies, but might also help to better understand the diffusion of knowledge.

Thanks to Dr Daniel Birke who completed his PhD at Nottingham University Business School and who is currently Head of Research at Idiro Technologies, Dublin.

Application for PhD to ESRC

Project Title: The Interaction between Social Stereotyping and the Maintenance of Cognitive Abilities in Older Workers and Their Impact on Health and Performance

Demographic transition has reshaped the age structure of the global population, particularly in more developed regions, by shifting relative weight from younger to older groups (United Nations, 2002). The 'greying' of the population (Buchan, 1999) is reflected in changes to the structure of the British work force, and by 2006 older workers (i.e. over 50 years of age, as defined by the National Audit Office, 2004) are predicted to comprise its largest age group (Overell, 2004). The economic implications of ageing populations are considerable (Coleman, 1993), and reduction of potential economic deficits in future will be difficult without increasing the size of the labour force, partly by the further retention of older workers (Griffiths, 1997). It will soon become necessary for people to work to a greater age than previous generations, meaning later retirement will become a reality for many people (Miles, 1997).

With an increase in the number of older workers, it is increasingly important to understand the implications of later retirement on employee health and productivity. Work environments will soon be bound by law to be designed and managed to accommodate older workers, and to facilitate tasks that may be affected by age-related changes at physiological, psychological and social levels. Previously, some employers have failed to recognise the importance of older workers' contributions. Indeed, considerable evidence exists to suggest that older workers have often been misunderstood or ignored, and may be targets for age-related stereotyping and discrimination (Chiu, Chan, Snape & Redman, 2001). The British government, along with other member states of the European Union, has recognised the need for legislation to distinguish between the types of age-specific treatment at work that are acceptable and those that are not (Department of Trade and Industry, 2003). Age-related changes in cognitive abilities associated with job performance, and discrimination against workers on the basis of increased age are central considerations of the present research.

Age-discrimination legislation aims to alter the psychological and behavioural basis of age-related stereotypes of older workers, and increase understanding of work demands peculiar to the older worker. As such, many organisations will be required to adopt new styles of management, while implementing new/revised policies and practices relating to the job demands faced by employees. While legislation will affect organisational practices, additional factors affect employment of older workers and their retention. Two of these factors, age-related change in cognitive abilities (e.g. language, attention, memory, and fluid and crystallised intelligence) and social constructions (specifically, age-related stereotypes of older workers) are central to the proposed research. My research brings these two areas together and explores the interaction between the key factors in relation to health and performance at work. The context is the way in which older workers are seen and managed and the organisation's policies for handling this increasingly important resource.

Summary of Research Literature. Older workers may be subject to a number of age-related declines in physical and cognitive ability. At a physiological level, progressive deterioration occurs over time in skeletal, neuromuscular and energy delivery systems (Kemper, 1994). More than one third of older workers suffer from at least one chronic disease, while workers over the age of 40 are less tolerant of shift work (especially night work) than are younger workers (Ilmarinen, 1994). Moreover, joint movement and muscular strength have been reported to decrease by up to 25 per cent from maturity to old age (Hitchcock, Lockyer, Cook & Quigley, 2001) while the ability to maintain a constant body temperature is also reduced (Blackwell & Blackwell, 1980). Declines in ability have also been reported in a number of cognitive faculties. Horn and Cattell (1967) proposed two types of intelligence which they labelled *fluid* (a measure of speed of reasoning) and *crystallised* (a construct similar to a lay definition of knowledge) intelligences. Evidence suggests that fluid abilities decrease from maturity to old age (Salthouse & Maurer, 1996). Age-related declines have also been reported in selective, sustained and divided measures of attention (Babbitt, 1965; Giambra & Quilter, 1988; Salthouse, Fristoe, Lineweaver & Coon, 1995), various measures of memory (Verhaeghen, Marcoen & Goossens, 1993), and language comprehension (Sommers, 1996).

The fact that ageing decreases ability in some respects may dominate social perceptions and be at the root of the negative stereotypes attached to older workers' abilities. Job performance may be assumed to decrease into old age as a result of the availability (Tversky & Kahneman, 1974) of multiple decrements in physical and cognitive abilities. However, most reviews fail to demonstrate a consistent relationship between job performance and ageing, suggesting that the two may not be directly related and may operate through complex interactions of organisation-level factors (e.g. Warr, 1994; Salthouse & Maurer, 1996; Griffiths, 1997). Furthermore, evidence from psychological gerontology suggests that focused attention remains relatively unaffected by processes associated with ageing (Wright & Elias, 1979), while discourse quality (a measure of language production) and crystallised intelligence may actually increase from maturity to old age (Kemper & Kemtes, 2000; Horn & Cattell, 1967). Moreover, evidence exists to suggest that variations in job performance within age-groups may exceed variations between age-groups, thus highlighting the importance of individual differences in the way people age (Warr, 1994).

Compensation theories. Of ageing suggest that as chronological age increases, physical and cognitive deterioration in some domains may be counteracted by strategies derived from experience, such as job knowledge or physical/mental load-reducing strategies (Griffiths, 1997). For example, one study demonstrated that older typists compensate for decreased perceptual-motor speed by looking further ahead and processing larger chunks of information than younger typists (Warr, 1994). Compensatory techniques have also been reported in older chess and bridge players (Charness, 1989) and in older bus drivers (Shephard, 1997). Additionally, older workers demonstrate more consistent work performance than younger workers (Walker, 1964), receive more positive appraisals of conscientiousness and good attendance than younger workers (Warr, 1994), and are involved in fewer work-related accidents than their younger counterparts (Dillingham, 1981).

Reduction of excessive physical demands and maintenance of optimal physical working conditions with respect to temperature and environmental noise are known to be beneficial to older workers' job performance (Ilmarinen, 1997). The importance of adapting modern technology to the needs of older workers has also been recognised (e.g. Rudinger, Espey, Neuf & Paus, 1994). However, less attention has been paid to psychosocial work environments (subjective perceptions of work, the work environment, interpersonal relationships at work, and work organisation: Griffiths, 1997), which are likely to play a large part in workers' stress reactions. Negative psychosocial work environments can exacerbate ageing processes and can contribute to the development of additional diseases (Goedhart, 1992). Work-related psychological ill-health, associated with poor psychosocial work environments, is twice as prevalent in older workers as younger workers' (Crones, Hodgson, Clegg & Elliott, 1998). Moreover, Ilmarinen (1995) suggests that psychosocial factors such as poor supervision and lack of recognition or feedback can be as important a factor of poor job performance, as can excessive biomechanical demands.

Discrimination against Older Workers. Older workers are often viewed as less effective than younger workers, despite a large amount of empirical evidence suggesting the contrary, and in some instances organisational practice is regarded as disadvantageous towards older employees (Taylor & Walker, 1998). Traditionally, younger workers have been viewed as a better financial investment (Crew, 1984) and offering early retirement to older workers has become an easy option for employers (Taylor & Walker, 1998). Although perceived as loyal, older workers are also viewed as less flexible and motivated, as having out-dated skills, and poor fitness compared against younger workers (Tillsley, 1990). Older workers may therefore be disadvantaged in relation to aspects of work such as recruitment, selection and redundancy (Griffiths, 1997) as well as learning/development opportunities and, in turn, promotion and career development (Salthouse & Maurer, 1996). Social stereotyping can lead to discrimination. Evidence exists to suggest that non-discriminatory work environments may allow older workers to escape social stereotyping and the self-fulfilling prophecy of age-related declines in job performance (Warr, 1994).

The Gap in Academic Research. The proposed research will explore new evidence that relates to the nature and effects of social stereotyping against what is known and can be discovered about the reality of cognitive ability with respect to work. The impact of these factors on health will be explored. It should make clear the strengths (and weaknesses) of older workers compared to younger ones. Such data should inform managers' attitudes to older workers and, hopefully, organisational policies and practice.

The study of older workers' abilities within occupational psychology and occupational health psychology is a popular area of study. Similarly, the extent to which various cognitive abilities are maintained over the lifespan has been studied extensively within mainstream psychological gerontology. However, a research gap exists in linking these two parallel streams of research. Establishing the nature of age-related differences in cognitive abilities and strategies in relation to work tasks, should allow the validity as well as the nature of social stereotyping to be established. This will allow something of a theoretical fusion of these two streams of research, as well as eventually feeding policy formation in this area (see above).

Relevance to the ESRC's Thematic Priorities. This proposal examines issues relevant to occupational psychology and occupational health psychology. The aim will be to answer the following *research questions*. [1] what is the nature of social stereotypes of age, cognitive ability, work performance and health in samples of skilled workers in engineering (and manufacturing)? [2] what cognitive strategies, developed through experience or training, do older workers use to maintain their performance on work tasks in these sectors? Do these strategies differ from those used by younger workers and to what effect? [3] what is the relationship between social stereotyping and 'reality'? and [4] what effects do social stereotyping and cognitive ability have in relation to work and health? These are the core research questions. There is also a set of subsidiary questions relating to the organisations' (managers') understanding of these data and of the literature and how this understanding shapes and drives management decisions and behaviour.

Data from the proposed study will provide an empirical basis for the development of a theoretical model regarding the work ability and management of older workers and of their occupational health. At the same time, it may help to articulate the arguments that older workers may be encouraged to remain in employment. The research will contribute to the literature on reduction of age discrimination in the workplace. Although there are clear parallels between this research and *Theme 7: Work and Organisations*, the main focus of the research is inclusion of older workers and the importance of helping society and work organisations adapt to future demographic challenges: *Theme 6: Social Stability and Exclusion*. The research clearly relates to the ESRC's investment in *age research*.

Research Design. The proposed research will combine field studies with laboratory testing to explore the maintenance of cognitive abilities in older workers, their relation to social stereotyping, and the impact of both on health and productivity.

Essentially, younger and older workers from a sample of skilled workers engineering (and manufacturing) companies will be surveyed and compared with respect to social perceptions of ageing, cognitive ability, work performance and health. The cognitive and other strategies that both groups of workers use to maintain cognitive and task performance at work will also be explored. The relationship between social perception and individual 'reality' will be examined. The initial study will be cross-sectional in design but, it is intended, if continued access is possible, that this study transform with further testing into a limited prospective study. The design of the survey will be informed by a series of semi-structured interviews, and focus groups, held with sub samples of the study group. In the survey-based research, an appropriate combination of quantitative and qualitative methods will be used. The qualitative methods will be used in two ways. First, such methods in the pre-survey work establish a working model of the nature and impact of social stereotyping at work and of differences in cognitive ability with age. This model will inform the design of the main survey (and prospective study if possible). Second, qualitative methods will be used to illustrate the findings of the main survey. If necessary, further interviews and focus groups will be employed to clarify and study in greater depth any areas of uncertainty in the main survey.

To allow particular micro theories relating to cognitive ability and strategy to be tested with respect to [1] age-related differences and [2] work (task) performance, a sub sample of the survey group will be invited to attend for laboratory-based testing. Laboratory-based challenges to participants will be informed by the survey-based studies and by the literature. Essentially, they will be used to bridge *the gap* between knowledge derived from the survey studies, and related literature, and that derived from the more experimental literature. Testing the nature and role of the compensation hypothesis through a comparison of younger and older workers on 'extracted' skilled tasks of relevance would be one example.

The two lines of investigation are interconnected: each informs the other over time. During the course of these studies, and built into the work with participating organisations, managers will be interviewed on their understanding of the literature on older workers and their abilities and how they use such information, and will use the present information, in terms of person and work management and policy development.

A range of multivariate statistical techniques (e.g. regression, analyses of variance and structural equation modelling where appropriate) will be used to analyse the quantitative survey data. The qualitative data will be analysed using a software package (e.g. QSR's NUD*IST qualitative data analysis system). The laboratory-based studies will be analysed using MANCOVA (as appropriate).

Key Variables. Age is not an independent variable in the strict sense of the word, as participants cannot be randomly assigned into groups with respect to this variable. Nevertheless, the age group to which participants belong will be a variable of fundamental importance in the study which is based, in part, on the comparison of younger and older workers. *Attitude toward work, attitude toward ageing* and *attitude toward older workers* will be the important social variables. Measures of cognitive ability and strategy in relation to work will be the important cognitive variables. Task performance (to be more exactly defined as the study progresses) and general health will also be measured. General health will be measured using the *General Wellbeing Questionnaire* developed at Nottingham and employed in its other related studies.

Participants. Organisations will be sought, which have a homogenous or near-homogenous spread of employees at various age-ranges including younger ($<$ 45 years of age) and older ($>$ 45 years of age) workers. Large companies with existing links to the Institute's research programme with the Engineering Employers Federation will be approached and invited to participate in the proposed research. Participants will be the skilled workers in these organisations.

Ethical Issues. Age discrimination may prove a sensitive issue for organisations and for older individuals alike. As such, it is possible that in the course of the project some aspects of the research may challenge participants, and/or may worry their managers as to how the data will reflect upon their organisation. In order to address these concerns, participants' anonymity will be ensured, as will the confidentiality of the data they provide. Participants will be made aware that they have the right to withdraw from the surveys or laboratory testing at any time, and informed consent will be sought in all cases as a prerequisite to any data collection. Information relating to the purpose of the research, the methods employed, and the intended use of data collected will be made available to all participants so as to engender an honest and open relationship between researcher and participants. Each aspect of the proposed research will be submitted to the Institute's Ethics Committee and will only proceed when approval is formally granted.

Usefulness of Research. The proposed research will advance our understanding (and theories of) age, work and health combining two different lines of existing research. It will inform the management of older workers in the coming scenario where they need to be persuaded to remain at work and need to do so productively and without challenge to their health. The research should (eventually) inform policy development in this area at the organisational level. By identifying and accommodating the needs of older workers, and developing inclusive (rather than discriminatory) policies (so-called transgenerational design; Woudhuysen, 1993), the research will be of potential benefit to all employees, not simply those over the age of 50. The inevitability of ageing means that taking into account the needs of older workers will benefit the whole of society, and indeed our future selves (Coleman & Pullinger, 1993). Organisations will benefit from a diverse workforce, and an increased potential customer base (Hitchcock et al., 2001). Hopefully, the proposed research will make some contribution to bringing about necessary organisational and societal change.

Thanks to Alec Knight who is completing his PhD in the Institute of Work, Health and Organisations at the University of Nottingham.

SOURCES OF SUPPORT

www.findaphd.com/students/explain.asp – contains some helpful advice regarding the research degree process.

www.le.ac.uk/ssds/careers/interviewspgstudy.html – guidance, hints and tips direct from a research-intensive university careers service.

Bentley, P.J. (2006) *The PhD Application Handbook.* Maidenhead: Open University Press – useful guide focused on the issue of applying to do a PhD in the UK.

Section II

Getting Your Research Degree

8 The Supervision Process and the Nature of the Research Degree

Professor Pam Denicolo and
Dr Lucinda Becker

Introduction

Whatever your mode of study, whether you are registered full or part time, whether you spend most of your time in the university or whether you are studying at a distance, whether you are engaged in a traditional research degree or a 'professional' or 'taught' doctorate, the key difference between your life as an undergraduate (or taught postgraduate) and your new role as a research postgraduate student is an increased sense of control. You are expected to be in control of your time, your intellectual development and, to a large extent, your area of research, in a professional way. This is not to suggest that you have no support in these areas, but it is worth considering for a moment how profound this difference can be.

So, although you will be given guidance and support (see later section), you will be expected to be independent in seeking and responding to advice, to find out about the norms of professional behaviour in your discipline's culture and to make your own niche within it. This has obvious huge advantages and disadvantages (the main one being the burden of responsibility). For instance, you are relatively free to pursue your area of research in your own way and to some extent in your own time, within the boundaries of some general stages (about which more appears later in this chapter and the next one). If you are registered full time your activities beyond your research (any teaching/ tutoring commitments, attending conferences, earning money etc.) should generally be scheduled around this core activity. If you are registered on a part-time basis, whether accessing resources directly or by e-learning, then the activities that constitute 'the rest of your life' also need to be organised to provide dedicated time for engaging with your research. We will address some further implications for students in this large group later, but by and large the rest of what follows still applies, albeit in an adjusted form.

If you are used to the support of fellow students within a structured timetable or enjoy the sense that every moment of your day is filled with planned activities or find security in knowing that you will be directed each step of the way, you might begin to find this new-found freedom disconcerting within a relatively short time. For some students this is the greatest hurdle within their life as a research postgraduate, so, if this describes you, we provide in this chapter some guidance on how to draw on resources within your institution to help you cope with this new situation. For other students, the freedom to arrange their own time and research pattern seems nothing but a blessing – that is, until deadlines loom or the pace escalates, so the guidance provided can be useful for those of you who want to avoid such problems. Learning to recognise and deal to best effect with your own personal working styles and inclinations is part of the process of becoming a good researcher – the role to which you aspire or you would not have read this far.

By the time you have read this chapter you should have a good idea about the following:

- Your role and some of the responsibilities of being a postgraduate research student.
- How you can help yourself by structuring your life appropriately to fit the practicalities of research student obligations?
- What some of those obligations are in relation to key stakeholders?
- What sources of help there are available and how you can access them?
- What variations from the norm can be expected if you are a part-time or distance-learning student?
- The variation that can come about because of disciplinary differences.

We will start first with the place of research students in the academic structure and the professional responsibilities that you will be expected to shoulder.

The Role of the Research Student

In the UK, the role of the research student is different to his/her counterpart in many of the countries of continental Europe and North America (refer back to Chapter 2 for differences in national models). In those locations research students are generally also members of academic staff in some form or other, albeit often in a junior capacity, which means that certain legal rights and obligations apply. In the UK, unless they are members of staff entering academia from a professional background (education or law or from the health and social service professions, for example), research students are in a middle position, sandwiched between the student groups (undergraduates and taught masters-level students) and the 'employed' group of academics and research staff.

This difference may reduce in the years to come, since the Commission of European Communities (2005) is encouraging all EU countries to move towards increased homogeneity in this and other respects related to research, through the European Charter for Researchers. The explicit motive is to 'ensure that the nature of the relationship between researchers and employers or funders is conducive to successful performance in generating, transferring, sharing and disseminating knowledge and technological development, and to the career development of researchers'. In so doing, it emphasises that research students should be afforded respect as important contributors to the intellectual capital of their institutions and countries.

A very condensed version of the *general principles and requirements* applicable to researchers follows, which gives an overview of core aspects of the role. The first principle is presented in full since it incorporates key aspects of the role:

> Researchers should focus their research for the good of mankind [sic] and for expanding the frontiers of scientific knowledge, while enjoying the freedom of thought and expression, and the freedom to identify methods by which problems are solved, according to recognised ethical principles and practices. Researchers should, however, recognise the limitations to this freedom that could arise as a result of particular research circumstances (including supervision/guidance/management) or operational constraints, e.g. for budgetary or infrastructure reasons or, especially in the industrial sector, for reasons of intellectual property protection. Such limitations should not, however, contravene recognised ethical principles and practices, to which researchers have to adhere.

The document goes on to provide suggestions that researchers (including those early in their careers, for example, research students) should:

- avoid plagiarism
- seek necessary approvals before starting their research
- adhere to contractual obligations and regulations
- be accountable to their employers, funders, professional bodies and society at large
- make details of methods of data collection and analysis and the data themselves available for public scrutiny, as requested by appropriate authorities
- adopt safe working practices
- be familiar with legal requirements regarding data protection and confidentiality
- disseminate their results, both to specialists and the lay public, in an appropriate form
- establish a structured and regular relationship with their supervisor/s and keep records of work progress
- seek feedback and apply it according to agreed schedules and milestones
- improve their skills and competencies through regular updating opportunities such as formal training, seminars and e-learning.

There is clearly a lot to do as a 'research student', and your institution will provide training and support resources to help you develop all the skills needed while you are engaged with your research. Your responsibility is to use these resources well.

Taking Responsibility for Structuring Your Life

Whether or not you expect to enjoy or loathe this level of control over your life, it is a good idea to put in place some structured elements within your personal timetable in order to ensure that you have regular access to sources of support. This is also important in relation to that well-publicised challenge for research students – isolation. Doing research means working on something relatively novel and unique, while a PhD is awarded for an independent piece of research so it is inevitable that much of your study will be conducted on your own. Thus, it is important to build in interaction with those who can support you, or at least understand your new obsession, to prevent the possibility that you might become first isolated, then unfocused and finally demotivated. Instead, they will help you to remain enthusiastic about your research and confront inevitable setbacks and hurdles with confidence.

The ways in which you can expect to structure your life as a research postgraduate will depend upon your personal circumstances and the organisation of your university, but some of the features, which can help you retain a sense of community and structure and/or prevent you being overwhelmed by the task, might include the following:

- Developing your own, personalised timetable, in which you will include your teaching/work commitments, research tasks, deadlines for conference papers, supervisions and research seminars, domestic obligations and so on. If you can produce a weekly 'task list', differentiating between the differing areas of your life and giving some sense of the urgency of each task, you will feel in control of your research and your wider academic and social life.
- Ensuring that your teaching or other work/domestic commitments suit this timetable, wherever possible, and give you enough opportunity to interact with other colleagues. For example, for full-time students taking on more teaching than is strictly required need not be a bad thing; for some periods it can be productive to move away from pure research and to look outwards to other developments in your field. For part-time students, keeping other work and domestic chores to a minimum can provide time for interacting with fellow researchers.
- Subscribing to department or school email lists so that you know what is going on, from research seminars directly or indirectly related to your areas of research, to activities in other departments which might be tangentially related to your work but nevertheless intellectually stimulating.

- Registering with conference-alert websites so that you remain aware of all of the possibilities for wider interaction within your field.
- Gaining peer support for your activities; we consider this in greater detail later in this chapter.

You will find more useful guidance on planning your schedule in 'Planning a Doctorate' from the UK GRAD website www.grad.ac.uk/planner/

You will find that the contributors of that section also emphasise the importance of early planning. In the next section, we will introduce some notions that will form the foundation for your future planning.

Practicalities and What to Expect: Working Hours, Holidays, Environment etc.

For most of us, the academic year is engrained in the rhythm of our lives from an early age. Despite recent changes to some academic calendars, most students will be used to the traditional annual cycle beginning with the start of the academic year, usually in October, when new ideas are explored, new courses begun and new pursuits encouraged. This is followed by a period during which these ideas are consolidated and data is reinforced; then the – sometimes seemingly never ending – stage that requires students to finalise their knowledge acquisition through examinations or coursework. The reward for all of this hard work is the long 'summer vacation', a time in which to rest, regain your energy and your enthusiasm for your subject. But that was undergraduate study … it is now time to dispel the myth of the long academic vacation!

For research postgraduates, this engrained timetable can be challenged by a new regime. The academic year 'proper', which might begin at different registration points than October, can be a frantic rush to cope with all of the competing demands upon your time: research and generic, transferable skills training, the research process itself, research seminars and meeting with your supervisor, plus teaching or your other work. In addition, the 'winter' and 'spring' vacations can be taken up with attending conferences or preparing or giving conference papers. You are left, at the beginning of what used to be the 'summer vacation', with a mountain of work still to complete and a sense that you have been running just to keep up with yourself all year, never really getting ahead as you had hoped. The long days of summer for research students and their academic tutors and supervisors alike are times to catch up on a backlog of reading, writing and organisation for the next period of research. It is wise to allow some time for rest and recuperation, but this should conform to normal work practices rather than the popular idea of what constitutes an academic long vacation.

The experiments of science students that may tie them to the laboratory; the availability of participants for social science research and the accessibility of materials for arts and humanities students are examples of some factors that also impact on when a vacation can take place and for how long. Other influences on your timetable may be the availability of technical support, safety issues and the working patterns of others working in the same laboratory (generally in science subjects) or the seasons of the year (in biological or agricultural sciences in particular).

There are, of course, advantages to undertaking major elements of your research in the summer. University libraries and research facilities should be a little quieter and your supervisor will still be available to support you. If you are working at some distance from your research institute, making time to be on campus during vacation, without the distractions of teaching, meetings or seminars, can offer you uninterrupted access to the facilities with the chance to develop your thoughts without distractions.

The secret to harnessing the opportunities offered by this new way of managing your time is to be rigorous in planning through your personalised timetable, in which you will be able to prioritise a variety of tasks, including the following:

- Tasks which simply have to be undertaken (regular meetings with a research panel, the submission of paperwork in connection with your degree, teaching or other work commitments) at a certain time
- Activities which you might be able to complete at a time of the academic year which suits you best (giving a conference paper, beginning a new area of research, working on your bibliography).

You can then include the compulsory elements in one section of your personalised timetable, safe in the knowledge that these will be completed on time, giving you a firm sense of achievement.

Those tasks which are not compulsory at any particular time will also, for the most part, be completed, but if they slip by a few weeks (perhaps from the term time to a vacation), this will not be a disaster, and the fact that you have them scheduled in your timetable means that you will not begin to panic; they are still under your control.

Many of your activities are, as you can see, under your control, but be prepared for some surprises if you were assuming that the postgraduate schedule mirrors that of undergraduates. Certainly a 9 am to 5 pm working day, with weekends sacrosanct, is another myth to dispel. Evening teaching sessions might be part of your weekly routine, as might evening or weekend research seminars or conferences. Lest this sounds like a recipe for all work and no play, rest assured that what we are advocating is carefully incorporating flexibility and deliberate space into your timetable, so that you can ensure that you have time for some very important rest and relaxation that will stimulate your creativity. There are several things to bear in mind when tackling a routine such as the following scenarios:

- If you are working to earn money outside your institute, it is a good idea to remain flexible, if you can, about the hours you can offer an employer, until you know each term what your university commitments will be, whether those are research related or part of a teaching/tutoring brief.

- Your supervisor is unlikely to be too rigid about the time when your supervision meetings can take place, so arranging them on those days when you are already in your department, for teaching/tutoring or attending methods or skills courses, makes sense.

- If you have regular family or work commitments that prevent you from being available all of the time, make sure that your supervisor and, crucially, your departmental administrators know about these before the teaching/tutorial timetables are finalised.

- Work towards using your time as efficiently as you can. It is not always a good idea to aim to be on campus just one day a week, as this can leave you feeling isolated on the other days, but it is a good idea to plan to undertake some library work on those evenings when you are attending a course or teaching during the day, or to arrange a research seminar when you have to be on campus for a supervision session.

- Be sensible in your planning – don't expect to engage in a demanding intellectual task (writing the first draft of your literature review for instance) on the day after your birthday party; try to balance during any one day tasks that require concentration (that chapter again!) with some that are relatively undemanding but give you a sense of making progress (checking that all your references are noted appropriately for instance).

In these ways you will reduce your stress level and remain confident that you are making the most of your time and fulfilling the expectations of those who have a stake in your project.

Expectations of the Research Project: What Do the Various Stakeholders Want?

The various stakeholders in your project are, in addition to yourself, those who are funding the project (which, of course, may again be you), the institution as a whole and those who are involved with supporting you directly through giving time and making effort. The latter includes, within the institution, your supervisory team and, externally, your family members and friends who help make your study possible. The main expectation of all of these people is that you complete your project and write up and submit your thesis successfully and in a timely manner – and survive the process!

A successful thesis is one which meets the criteria set out in institutional regulations (see Chapters 20 and 21) while 'timeliness' relates to the deadlines generally determined by the Research Councils for your discipline. A general estimate is the equivalent of 3.5 years of full-time study.

In addition to a title and qualification, your project should provide you with the interest and impetus for further work in an area in which you can be proud to have become an expert. This will be important for your future (you may live with this area of research for many years of your professional life) and also to help you maintain your enthusiasm and stamina – the key ingredient for gaining a research degree! When you are considering how you might develop your research ideas, how you might expand into new areas, your level of interest in, and passion for, your area of research should always be a motivating factor. Equally, you should ensure, as much as you humanly can, that potential major distractions from your research that lie within your control, such as family relocations or religious pilgrimages, have been identified and can be organised appropriately to allow you to retain stamina to cope with unexpected events, joyful or sorrowful.

The funding bodies and employers, who have invested in your success financially and otherwise, will want a project that contributes knowledge and understanding to the field of study – so your responsibility that we mentioned earlier, to manage your research well, is particularly important to them.

The institution and your supervisory team too have a vested interest in your timely success: their reputations will be enhanced by it while resources will have demonstrably been well invested. Your project may also contribute to a wider study going on in your university, so on many counts you can be reassured that you are an important person to your institution and your supervisors.

What Support Can You Expect from Your Institution?

Supervision

The most important support provided by your institution is your supervisory team. Although some institutions still follow the traditional pattern of each research student having only one supervisor, most have now taken up the recommendations in the Quality Assurance Agency (QAA) Code of Practice for Research Students and the European Researchers' Charter that research students should benefit from a wider range of academic support. However, how these recommendations are implemented varies between institutions, or between disciplines within an institution; although they all have a common theme, that is, the provision of different kinds of personal and academic support, and serve similar purposes, such as ensuring that some continuity of support is available and that the student has recourse to more than one academic contact.

One variation of this is that you could be allocated two supervisors, perhaps each focusing on one particular aspect of research, such as topic or methods, or one particular aspect of the supervisory role, for instance, the academic or pastoral dimensions. Another variant is the supervisory team of several people, each of whom you meet individually for particular purposes though you should meet the whole team together on a regular basis. A third version involves a single supervisor with whom you work fairly continuously, with both of you benefiting from review, feedback and advice from a small panel of advisors with whom you meet, say, once a term. These patterns of support are particularly useful in the very rare event of disharmony between the main supervisor and the student. In the next chapter we will provide some guidance on how you manage your research and the supervisory relationship to diminish the possibility of clashes even further – so that you effectively interact with the many activities which supervisors engage in on your behalf.

The core duties of a supervisor are as follows:

- Ensure that an appropriate topic is selected and developed to the required depth, from their expert knowledge of the field
- Agree on and regularly review a training programme, and advise on any additional training requirements
- Provide feedback on skills development, research and thesis-writing progress
- Give advice on appropriate completion dates for successive stages of the research
- Provide detailed guidance and advice about the following:

  a   Literature sources
  b   Literature evaluation and review
  c   Planning the research
  d   Choice of research and data analysis methods and techniques
  e   Ethical issues and review procedures
  f   Codes of conduct and safety procedures

- Regularly monitor progress and ensure that formal procedures (see next chapter) are followed
- Support dissemination activities (conference presentations and article writing)
- Prepare the student for the examination process.

Of course, supervisors will expect you to reciprocate by fulfilling the matching half of these duties, such as attending recommended courses, engaging well with the research process etc. Since they are also busy people, with equally demanding research commitments, they will probably expect you to be professional in relation to scheduled meetings, so do turn up both on time and prepared for the topic to be discussed.

Other Staff Support

Academic staff, in addition to your nominated supervisors, will also be able and will usually be willing to contribute their expertise and encouragement to your studies, either as teachers and leaders of workshops in your training programme or in response to a direct request from you. Most institutions now provide training in research approaches and methods, in the laboratory and/or through workshops, seminars and/or through e-learning and they are now building up programmes, either individually or in groups, to develop generic research and transferable skills (see Chapter 14). Some institutions combine the provision of such training with other postgraduate research support in some form of Graduate School, while yet others provide the means for students to engage in such courses and training at other venues outside the institution.

It is from such programmes or through the Graduate School that you can identify and locate academic colleagues who may be interested in helping you, at least by talking about how your research interests (either topic or methods or common participant groups) overlap with theirs. Do not be too shy to seek such discussions – most academics love talking about their research interests and will feel flattered by your recognition of their expertise – but do ensure that such interactions have the approval of your supervisor.

Institutions also provide more tangible resources, though this will vary between institutions, disciplines and may be dependent on your mode of study. You should make it your business, as appropriate, to find out the following before you register:

- What study facilities you will be provided with (such as desk space, computer and other IT equipment and support)?
- What research facilities you will be provided with (such as a well-equipped laboratory or access to fieldwork locations)?
- How vibrant the research life of the institution is (such as whether there exist active research centres in your area, regular seminars for postgraduates, social and academic support networks, etc)?
- What is the policy on charging for photocopying?
- How well your topic area is supported by the library (or how reasonably priced are the inter-library loan facilities that may be available to you)?

The variation, and the parlous state of funding support for universities, may mean that you have to balance some advantages and deficits but it is wise to prepare yourself in advance.

Other Services

Other sources of support are available in Higher Education Institutions, such as careers, IT and counselling services, which you may be familiar with from your previous study opportunities but if it is some time since you graduated or if you are changing institution then you will probably find a Welcome Week, or an Induction Programme that will identify and introduce the range of services available, absolutely invaluable. Thus it is very important to try to attend these events, even if you have not completed your registration fully, or have already completed a course in the same institution, or have to make a large effort to attend. (Institutions are often willing to let students attend induction meetings on a 'visiting-student' basis, even if they are not yet completely registered, because of the helpful orientation to studies and resources provided.) Even if you have already been at the university for several months before these sessions are scheduled, it is not safe to assume that there is no need for you to attend. There is little worse than struggling for many weeks with a problem only to find that resolution was on your doorstep all the time, if only you had known. One important resource right on your doorstep is the current group of research students in the department and in the wider institution. We will consider this resource further after looking in more detail at what you might expect to be included in the induction programme.

The Induction Process

Most institutions schedule some form of welcome and orientation programme at the beginning of the academic year and some reduced form of it at entrance times throughout the year (at the beginning of semesters or terms). The traditions of academic life ensure that the programme presented at the beginning of the academic year is longer and richer because of the larger number of students enrolling then. It would be ideal if we could guarantee that each induction programme would be equivalent, but universities have practical constraints to consider too. If you should happen to register later in the year then it would be worth making contact with at least one fellow student who began at the traditional time so that you can borrow from them a copy of the scheduled programme to ensure that you can spot what you might have missed and make an effort to contact the original presenter for more information. If you are intending to study at a distance, it would be worth considering making an effort to attend in person any induction programme provided by your institution so that you can get to know the people you will correspond with and the level of resource available.

The kind of things that you might find on such programmes can be divided into three groups: absolutely essential information that you are sure to need, and probably soon; information that may be extremely useful at some point in your registration period; and opportunities to get to know people and services that, while not necessarily essential, will at least ease your progress and at best make it thoroughly enjoyable. We will address each of these but first it is fair to alert you to the range of reactions that research students have when first embarking on their studies.

A very small minority of students begin their journey confident about the process and procedures involved in higher degree by research study, about what they intend to research and how and about their own capacity to complete their research degree successfully. A majority of them will be very nervous about all of these aspects; some only having a tentative idea about what the exact focus of their study will be, with only a rudimentary knowledge about research methods and the skills they will need, while many will harbour a secret concern that 'every other new recruit is really clever and some-day someone will find out that I am not as clever as my paper credentials promise – my being accepted was a fluke!' It is worth holding on to the following ideas at this point:

- Most initial research proposals have to be amended during the course of the first year as the literature is searched more thoroughly and the practicalities of the project are explored in depth.
- Studying for a research degree is a form of apprenticeship during which it is expected that knowledge and skills will be developed – you will not be expected to know everything at the start.
- The main ingredients for success include a modicum of creativity and versatility and a bucketful of stamina and perseverance – there are very few actual geniuses amongst the group of successful doctoral candidates.
- Reading this book will stand you in good stead by dispelling myths and rendering the unknown less daunting by making it familiar.

The topics that fall into the 'absolutely essential' category, as noted above, are likely to be included in your induction programme which will provide information on the research methods courses available, details about generic research and transferable skills training provided and how these are organised, presented and assessed. You will be introduced to the institutional code of practice for research students, which usually includes guidelines and procedures for health and safety, accident and incident reporting, safety training and the legal obligations related to your particular field of work. This could include your responsibilities under the COSHH (Control of Substances Hazardous to Health) regulations. While health and safety procedures are particularly important for students working in laboratories to become very familiar with very quickly, they should not be neglected by anyone embarking on fieldwork/practical work of any kind. We emphasised earlier that you will be considered an independent researcher with responsibilities in this student role and one of these responsibilities is to work with due care and attention in whatever environment your research is conducted. The staff of the institution also have a duty of care to you so they will want you to understand and respect the precautions that they advise.

The 'extremely useful' information often may be in the form of introductions to the staff of the services provided by the university, like the library, IT and counselling services mentioned above, who will explain how to access them, or in the form of information sheets that clarify policy and procedures in relation to, for example, 'ethics approval' and 'reporting' stages.

Perhaps not essential, but certainly adding some spice to the pot, will be the advertisement of opportunities to engage in sporting or artistic pursuits or other activities that refresh the brain, body and soul. Induction programmes are also the place in which lasting academic friendships and networks are first forged that will serve you well for years to come. Some institutions or schools operate a 'buddy' system in which a second- or third-year student undertakes to show a new recruit around and alert them to useful resources. If this is not offered in your institution, you could ask your supervisor to arrange a similar support for a few weeks, perhaps with one of their own students who is a little further on in their research degree. The next section explores other ways of making the most of time with your colleague students.

Peer Support within the Postgraduate Community; Benefits and How to Set Up Such Groups

The level of peer support available to research postgraduate varies from place to place, but there is no doubt that such support is needed by every postgraduate, whether your university makes this obvious or not. Some research postgraduates will choose a university specifically because it offers a plethora of support groups, research seminars and online learning opportunities; most postgraduates overlook this element until they have begun their course of research. In fact, this need not be a problem at all, as long as you are prepared to take the first steps towards creating your own support network.

Your need for support will vary during your time as a postgraduate. At some stages of your research, you will want nothing more than to be left alone to progress with your research, or write up a chapter of your thesis, or prepare a conference paper. At other times, you will feel in desperate need of some support, some input into your work and, at its most basic, just the company of like-minded people who are sharing similar experiences.

The ways in which you might develop, or take advantage of, support networks will depend upon your personality. One postgraduate will find it easy to stroll along a corridor and make friends and enlist support. Another would find it difficult even to attend a research-support group meeting. For the latter, support groups can seem more of a trial than a help, particularly if you are hampered by a feeling that you are behind with your work and/or too busy to attend, or are naturally shy/an independent worker by nature. Whichever type of person you are (some or all of these descriptors will probably apply to you at some point during the course of your studies), it is always a good idea to have some support from your peers, even if you have to dip in and out of it, as your work progresses. Support groups can throw up new research ideas, helping to move your research forward when your work stagnates; they can be a useful practice ground for conference and research papers and, most importantly, they can reassure you that you are not alone in facing particular challenges in research. They are also the only ones who can really appreciate the little successes along the road of research (who else can recognise the elation of finding just the right reference at just the right time?) and help you celebrate.

You will want your support groups to be as productive as possible, and you will approach them in your own way, but trying out some of these suggestions will help you to gauge what help and encouragement you need, and how to get it:

- If your department or school already has a system of postgraduate-support seminars set up, attend at least two or three meetings. These can be distinguished from the more formal research seminars in that they are often led by postgraduates (sometimes with a supervisor there just to answer any queries and offer support) and the topics that are covered at the meetings will be wide ranging. These groups often allow postgraduates to try out conference papers, or to raise an issue that is relevant to everyone, such as how to prepare work for publication. They often vary greatly from one meeting to the next in their subject matter and attendance, so going two or three times will give you the best idea of whether they suit your needs or not.
- Your department or school will likely have a Postgraduate Student's Association, and this may be linked to a Staff Student Committee. These groups are open to all postgraduates, and joining such a group would allow you to keep in touch with what is going on: if you act as a student representative, you will be in a position to have a say in the development of activities and policy within your school or department.
- Remember that research postgraduates will be working together all over your university, so make sure that you check the notice boards and websites of other departments, or other specialist areas of your department. A research group which is only tangentially linked to your field of interest might still throw up interesting possibilities and might help to support you in general aspects of your work such as writing up or research methodologies.
- Teaching at the undergraduate level can be stressful for research postgraduates, particularly if this is your first experience of teaching. Your department might hold regular meetings for postgraduate or part-time teachers, and these can offer substantial support in this aspect of your postgraduate life. You can find out more about the expectations of postgraduate researchers as teachers in Chapter 17.
- If you are struggling to find a support group in your department, then simply set one up yourself. These groups need no official sanction beyond offering you a room in which to meet, and it is probable that your supervisor would be happy to attend at least some of the meetings. These groups tend to appear and disappear within departments over the years, so there is no reason why you should not set one up with little effort: just one notice on the notice board should produce a result.
- If you find the idea of setting up a support group daunting, or feel that it might be too time consuming, you could try an online support group. These are also especially useful if you are geographically isolated from

your institute. Your supervisor can let you know if one exists already, but if not, the e-learning website of your department is the place to start. It is relatively straightforward to set up a 'chat room' for all of those interested in joining such a group and your department administrators should be able to help you in this.

- Whilst an open invitation asking postgraduates to join an online group is a good way to set up your own support structure, it is also effective to develop a wider online network of your own. Every conference you attend will offer you the chance to take the email address of fellow academics; research seminars with guest speakers offer the same opportunity. Store every email address that you can get hold of, making sure that you have noted down each person's area of expertise and perhaps add a note about why you might need to contact someone in the future. In this way, you have an online support network that simultaneously develops, as your research progresses.

- You might like to check whether your institution has an active Postgraduate Committee as part of the Student Union. There is also a national network that you might like to become involved with: the National Postgraduate Committee, the representative body for postgraduates in the UK; you can find details about the Committee on the web at: www.npc.org.uk

Special Implications for Part-timers and Distance/E-learners

Part-time research postgraduates and those working online tend to fall into one of two categories. For some, their research life reflects most aspects of the life of a full-time research postgraduate but at a reduced number of hours per week. For these students, all of the advice offered here will be as relevant as it is for full-time postgraduates. You will work in a similar way, with as much need for support groups, a personalised timetable and a coherent working structure. For other postgraduates (perhaps the majority), working through your degree on a part-time basis or as an e-learner means progressing at a rapid pace for some periods, but working very little on your research at others. If you fall into this latter category, there is no need to feel unsure about your effectiveness as a researcher, but there are some aspects of managing your research that you will need to control:

Managing your time. Although it is quite common now for research aspirants to study as part-time students or e-learners, which is as effective as any other way to work towards a research degree, you are likely to find that, whilst you can vary your workload on research, external factors will dictate that you have to keep up a regular work schedule for other aspects of your life (earning money, teaching, completing updates for your supervisor). This is not a disadvantage, but it will make your personalised timetable even more important. If you must spend several weeks devoting much of your time to your teaching commitments, or you find that other paid employment has taken you away from your research for a month, it is easy to feel that you are behind schedule in getting your degree, and that you are neglecting this important area of your life. In fact, this is unlikely to be the case if you have planned well in advance: you will simply have been prioritising other tasks over your research for a time, and you will return with renewed vigour to your research as soon as you can. Accepting that this could be the case for you at times during your degree is the key to reducing your stress levels. If you have incorporated all of your commitments in your timetable, you will be able to see at a glance that you are on track, even if you feel that you are neglecting your research for a while. You will need to include some space in your timetable to reacquaint yourself with your research when you return to it, but it is often the case that taking a break in this way allows you to assimilate your research without conscious thought, and you may find yourself overflowing with ideas when you return.

Working with your supervisor. Supervisors are, of course, used to dealing with part-time research students under many different circumstances, and yours will be looking for clues as to your work pattern, your commitments beyond your research degree and the ways in which you tend to work best. Rather than simply assuming that your supervisor is not interested in your plans, take the time at the outset to discuss your other commitments and to work together to ensure that your personalised timetable and your research plans are realistic. Your plans will change – they always do – but a detailed plan or timetable which reflects your life as it is (rather than how you might like it to be!) is the most constructive way to begin work on this important relationship. It will be reassuring for your supervisor too that you are so well organised!

Maintaining your support structures. It is obviously going to be important for you to maintain your support structures during your research, and the most productive way to achieve this, when you do have to shift your focus from your research, is to adopt a similar approach to that of maintaining your relationship with your supervisor. Make sure that your fellow research postgraduates are aware, in general terms, of the working pattern that you expect to develop, including the fact that you might be less involved in research seminars or joint projects at some times. In this way, you can reassure your fellow academics that you are still a reliable and keen member of your support groups, even when you might be occupied elsewhere. If you know that you will find this pattern of work stressful, make sure that you include some minor research tasks within your personalised timetable, such as working on your bibliography or undertaking some background reading which is not too taxing but which you need to complete nevertheless. These tasks will not be time consuming, but they will reassure you that you are still undertaking a research degree, even though you have not had much time to devote to it for a few weeks.

As with so much else in your research degree, working effectively as a part-time research postgraduate is all about control: controlling both your time and your research development. If everyone around you is not only aware of the competing demands on your time, but can also recognise your commitment to your research and determination to do it justice, you will find your course or research more rewarding and far less stressful.

You can find more information about how to make the most of your time as a part-time research student in Bourner and Race (1995).

Variations across the Disciplines

Working on preparing this chapter with colleagues from a wide range of subject areas within higher education, we have, as discussed in the foregoing, noted that some differences do exist between disciplines, though these tend to be related to 'the scale rather than the nature' of the research process. Scientists and engineers are more likely to join a team of research students led by a senior academic with the help of more junior colleagues who are involved in a common research project – because of both traditional ways of working and the practical demands for resources such as equipment (kit) and laboratory space. Thus loneliness may be reduced, and so will the range of choice of topic area for study.

Arts and humanities, and social science students tend to be able to follow a more personally developed study area, even if it is located in a general area defined by a funding organisation. In that case, they will develop a proposal with an interested supervisor with relevant expertise. If they are self-funding or supported by their employer, then they must identify a suitably qualified supervisor willing to work with them on a topic of their own devising. Whatever the source of funding and topic idea, they are less likely to find themselves working in a team.

Similarly, because of the constraints of experimental work, most science or engineering researchers study on a full-time basis with few places and topics available for part-time study. The reverse is true for arts and humanities, and social science researchers. This is one of the reasons why there are more mature students in those latter discipline areas, another being that professional people (social workers, teachers, lawyers, health service personnel etc.) sometimes find 'burning issues' that require investigation in the course of their working lives.

Conclusion

We hope we have conveyed in this chapter that being a research student is not just a demanding but a potentially liberating role which, managed with care, can provide a myriad of opportunities for self as well as career development.

The key points for you to remember from this chapter are listed below:

**KEY POINTS ABOUT THE RESEARCH STUDENT'S ROLE AND
RESPONSIBILITIES AND SOURCES OF SUPPORT**

- You are now in firmer control of much of your academic life: self-organisation and heeding safety-critical advice (about both lab practice and the requirements of research degrees) from supervisors will be the key to success
- Research students take on several roles as they develop and each role needs to be understood and developed
- The use of a personalised timetable will help to ensure that you keep on track
- Your working pattern may vary widely over the year and throughout your registration period: this is to your advantage as long as your timetable reflects these changes
- All the stakeholders within a research programme will have different responsibilities and duties: making the most of this range of support will be your responsibility
- You may have more than one supervisor: communication with everyone involved will help you to achieve your goal
- Planning ahead of supervision meetings will enhance the supervision process
- The induction programme to your course will give you the core information and support you need to get started
- Postgraduate support groups can be an invaluable source of help and encouragement
- Part-time and e-learning postgraduates are in a strong position in managing their time and resources.

In the next chapter, we will look at other aspects of the research process and will provide further suggestions to help with organising your activities effectively.

References

Bourner, T. and Race, P. (1995) *How to Win as a Part-time Student*, London: Kogan Page.
Commission of European Communities (2005) *Commission Recommendation on the European Charter for Researchers and on a Code of Conduct for the Recruitment of Researchers*, Brussels, 11.3.2.

9 Managing the Research Process and the Supervisory Relationship
Dr Lucinda Becker and Professor Pam Denicolo

Introduction

In the preceding chapter, we presented perspectives on some of the challenges faced by research students in terms of their role and, in broad-brush terms, some of the activities in which they are engaged, particularly focusing on how their efforts might be supported within institutions. In doing so, we provided some suggestions and ideas about ways of interacting within the system for you to consider as you take on that role. In this chapter, we will focus at a more detailed level on what to expect at different stages in the research-degree process and how to manage these stages to achieve a positive outcome. We will also explore in more depth the student–supervisor relationship and how to manage it effectively. In this chapter we will assume that you have taken to heart the notion, conveyed in the previous chapter, of being responsible for your own learning and for decisions about the progress of your research, albeit in consultation with your supervisors. By the time you have read this chapter you should:

- know what to expect during different phases of the research process
- be aware of the different forms of institutional monitoring and how this supports your progress
- have gained some ideas about how to manage your time effectively
- be in a position to work positively on developing your relationships with your supervisors.

Major Stages, and What to Expect at Each Stage

It is not possible to divide up the registration time for a research degree into distinct, separate, consecutive stages because the process usually involves engagement with several tasks at once, though one may predominate at any one time. Thus, although the main focus of the first few weeks of your first year will be on learning the ropes, and finding your way about, you may also be attending a research-training course, beginning to read the literature and to write down ideas. Concentration on research training and reviewing the literature will come next, and as this begins to subside, your attention will turn to designing and then implementing your research and so on. Thus, although in what follows we have discussed the main stages as if they were discrete, remember that there will be overlaps.

In the previous chapter we noted that the *Induction Process* was an important stage, one that you should make every effort to engage in because it provides important orientation to resources and services/people within the institution that can make the research process manageable. The activities and sessions provided will also help you to begin to feel like a research student, part of a group of people with common interests and challenges to face, as well as providing clues about the particular style of your institution in relation to its support of research students. Whether or not you choose to attend sessions in person, you should ensure that you check out what documents are provided over this period because they will contain information about facilities and training available to you. In particular, make yourself familiar with your institutional Code of Practice for Research Students since it will provide contextual detail, relevant within your own institution, about the points that we will make at a generic level in what follows. You will also find the UK GRAD material 'Planning a Doctorate' useful at this stage.

New students begin their research degrees with different views and expectations about the *training* on offer. Some are anxious to get started on what they see as the main element of their degree, the actual research itself, and see the training programmes as distractions from that main task. Others, in contrast, focus on the training programmes as a means of avoiding the plunge into the unknown chasms of research, feeling confident that they know how to learn through being taught. Both of these extremes are unhelpful attitudes to adopt. Your institution, like others in the UK and Europe, will provide 'research methods', relevant to your discipline, and 'generic and transferable skills training programmes' that will not only contribute to the knowledge and skills you will require to complete your project but will also provide a firm and broad basis for future research work. It is important to recognise that future employers will consider not only the expertise that you have developed in the course of your research project but also will want to know that you have become a good researcher in a more general sense. It is often worthwhile attending methods sessions, for example, even if you think that you have 'covered them' in a previous degree.

First, research at doctoral level has more and more complex demands than at masters- or first-degree level, so there may well be more to learn while, second, you may have the opportunity to discuss with other academics and peers how particular approaches and methods might be relevant in your new project. In some institutions you may find that either attendance and/or assignments related to the training programme are compulsory, and certainly you are likely to be expected to engage in the generic and transferable skills programme sufficiently to be able to identify your current level of skills across a range and then focus on a relevant few to develop further. See Chapter 14 for more information on this aspect. Remember that the training provided is likely to overlap in time with the development of your literature review and the design of your project, testing your planning and organisation skills.

The next chapter provides considerable guidance on how to conduct your *literature review* – a process that begins while you are developing your research proposal and continues until at least the day before your viva, although there is a stage when it is the most predominant activity. One thing that you may not have thought of is that you will need to review literature about the substance or focus of your research and also literature on research approaches and methods. You will be seeking both 'gaps in the literature' about your topic area and 'evidence' to inform appropriate ways of researching it.

This latter literature will inform your work during the period when you will be addressing your *research design*. Although some research projects evolve over time, exploratory studies in particular, it is important to devote sufficient time and thought to planning what you will do, who or what with and when, before embarking on your field or labwork. One important consideration, for instance, is the economical and appropriate use of resources. These resources may be tangible things like chemicals or plant material, or less tangible, such as opportunities to use expensive equipment in engineering or physics or access precious documents or artefacts in history or archaeology, or to attend conferences and seminars that include important guest speakers. They may be ephemeral or subject to being 'contaminated', like people who may only be available for a short period or who cannot be asked the same questions, or take part in an experiment, on a social science topic more than once. To be more colourful, it is important not to 'muddy the field' by trudging about hap-hazardly before you have examined it for what might be there in its natural, untrammelled state. In short, time spent on the design stage will pay dividends even if, or especially when, you intend to produce a flexible structure that can be adapted to meet changing circumstances and developing knowledge. This is likely to be followed, particularly in arts and humanities and indeed in other disciplines, by a formal testing of your working hypothesis, usually by a research panel interrogating your ideas.

For many of you, *fieldwork/labwork* will start with a pilot study, designed to explore possibilities or refine research tools or research skills or combinations of these. Once these have been successfully completed, then you will begin the research proper – an exciting time that you have been preparing for up until this point. As you gather your data you will have much to fascinate and interest you and it is important not to get too distracted by the 'collection' process to the detriment of recording exactly what you did, why and how, including any changes you make as you go along to your research design – and why! In the sciences, there is a tradition of compiling a lab book to ensure that such details are recorded while in the social sciences some supervisors set store by the completion of a research diary. We would recommend that students in any discipline should keep some kind of log, no matter how informal, about how their ideas develop during this phase in particular. This then forms a useful record and reminder for when you are writing up the 'results' and 'discussion' chapters and polishing up your field/labwork and methods chapter(s).

You will find detailed advice in Chapter 12 to help you get started on the *writing* process, and we will pre-empt that a little by emphasising that it is never too soon to start writing – registration day is a good choice! This is because the writing style for a thesis is probably different to that you will have become used to – it is a very special piece of academic writing for which you will find guidance, particularly on style and conventions, in Chapter 19 as well as on what issues to cover and in what way during the construction of your thesis. Starting writing early not only ensures that the creative thoughts that you have early on in the process can be revisited for inclusion, revision or deliberate excision later on, but the process provides opportunities for feedback from supervisors to help you hone your writing skill.

As you complete the writing-up phase you will also be mentally *preparing for your viva voce*. In your final review of the thesis, you should be considering what questions your work might stimulate in the mind of the reader, what they might want to know more about and what information, not included in the written version, will convince an examiner that this is your own unique work.

This process will continue beyond *submission*, an important final stage. You should find information about the submission process in your student handbook or on an appropriate section of your university's website. Although there will be specific instructions therein about how and when to inform the authorities about your intention to submit, the general procedure will be the same for all students. You will be expected to let Registry or the Exams Office know in good time about your intention to submit so that procedures can be set in motion to select and appoint your examiners. Importantly, it is the student's responsibility to start this procedure by declaring that she/he intends to submit, although she/he would be well advised to have his/her supervisors' support in doing so, although it is seldom officially strictly necessary. This really is the culmination of the process of your development as an independent researcher, able to shoulder responsibility – as we discussed in the previous chapter.

Chapter 21 provides a good overview of what to expect from the *viva voce* and how to prepare for it, while subsequent chapters address life beyond the viva. One thing we will alert you to here though is that it is becoming increasingly common for candidates to have to make some form of amendments, usually minor, to their theses immediately after the formal viva and before the final award. Although you should arrange some festivity (for celebration or commiseration) on the evening of your viva day, you would be wise to allow at least a few weeks for this 'tidying-up' process beyond the viva. If you are one of the lucky few with no corrections or amendments then you could use this time to start drafting a paper at a gentle pace to help you wind down from the pressured time leading up to this stage. Certainly do not rely on there being something interesting on the television (that you have not seen for several months) – you are likely to be disappointed! Hopefully you will not be disappointed in this final assessment of your work because you will have gained both feedback and confidence from the preceding institutional progress-monitoring process.

Institutional Progress Monitoring

When you first contemplate undertaking a higher degree by research, the three to four years full-time equivalent registration period may seem like a very long time, but by now you may be realising that a lot of diverse and intense activities have to be crammed into that period. Since it would be very unfortunate if people expended that time only to fail at the end, institutions have established what amount to check points spread over the period. These are called progress-monitoring activities because they are intended to be formative (providing developmental feedback) and thus supportive. For your part, you will be expected to provide up-to-date summaries of your work which will be useful as a contribution towards your thesis, helping you to demonstrate in writing how your thinking has developed in the interim period and to articulate your plans for the future.

It is usual for these reports to be required on an annual basis, though often the 'first year annual report' is often required nine months after registration. This first formal report is used by your supervisor(s) and yourself to judge whether there is a possibility that the topic of your research, and the way you are addressing the task of learning about research, will meet the requirements of a higher degree by research. Having to prepare and submit this report after nine months does give you and your supervisor(s) time to address and remedy any obvious problems before another year of registration needs to be paid for. This protects all the stakeholders, including yourself, from investing further in what appears to be an unproductive activity.

Generally all annual reports require you to describe your research activities to that point, including literature read, classes attended, data collected and how, and plans for the future. At the same time, your supervisor will be required to provide a report indicating how well they think you are doing in these respects. These reports are generally reviewed alongside each other by a school or departmental committee who will recommend to the institution whether it will be sensible for you to continue. This may sound a little frightening but remember that there is a vested interest in your success. Everyone will consider whether it will be in your interest to continue as you are doing, or whether you need to be encouraged to do more or differently or whether, in the last analysis, you would be well advised to withdraw gracefully.

Usually at about the same time as your annual progress report, many universities ask you to provide feedback on a form about your supervision – basically asking you to describe its adequacy and how it can be improved, if at all. This gives you an opportunity to air any concerns that you have and is useful for future planning of research students loads for staff. These forms are not automatically shared with your supervisor but are reviewed by a senior academic with responsibility for postgraduate research-student support. Should you report a problem, this person will talk to you about a productive way of resolving it. However, this is really only a 'fail-safe mechanism' because your Code of Practice should encourage you first to raise any problems directly with your supervisor so that they can be resolved in a mature and professional fashion. If you cannot resolve the issue together then the Code will indicate who can neutrally help you both come to a resolution. Thus the annual 'Report on Supervision' should be a last resort for airing problems and hopefully will rather reflect the working together of a successful team.

A particularly critical process that can be regarded as part of the institutional monitoring process is what is called in some universities the *transfer process* or in others the *upgrade process*. These refer to what is essentially the same thing. In only very few universities, or only for very particularly qualified candidates, is a research student registered directly and immediately for the award of a PhD. You may initially register as an MPhil or an MPhil/PhD student, or even as a higher degree by research student. This is because it is difficult to tell at the outset whether a research topic is one which can be researched to the level that meets doctoral requirements or whether it is more suitable for the award of an MPhil. Equally, you may not have the time, energy or inclination (or stamina – see earlier comment on aptitudes required for PhD study) to complete a project to PhD level and may only wish to conduct research to the MPhil level.

Usually early in the second year of study, if you are registered full time, or a little later, if you are registered part time (your supervisor(s) will advise on the most appropriate time), you will prepare and submit a 'transfer' or 'upgrade' document that is an extension of your annual report and contains an argument about the potential of the project to meet either MPhil or PhD standards. Sometimes a sample chapter of the thesis is also required to provide an indication that you are on your way to writing in the required academic manner. This document will be reviewed by your supervisory team or committee and at least one academic in your discipline area (usually from within your institution) who has not been involved in supervising your research and, in most cases, a small-scale viva voce will also be held. The objective is to determine which level, MPhil or PhD, you should be aiming for although most students also find it very useful indeed to hear the views and suggestions of the 'independent internal examiner'. This process is, of course, also good practice for the final assessment process.

You should by this time feel reassured that although your research study is intended to be independent, and is oftentimes lonely, there are systems in place to help you keep on track towards the degree to which you aspire. In the previous chapter we urged you to contribute towards this process by organising your time, perhaps by drawing up a personal timetable. Obviously, the annual reports and transfer/upgrade process need to be included as important milestones in your planning and adequate time should be set aside to accomplish them well. Now that you know more about the structure and content of your course, we have some more suggestions to help you stay in control of the myriad tasks that await you.

Planning and Time Management

Effective planning and time management are obviously of paramount importance to a postgraduate, and there are several issues to consider as you begin to develop these skills:

- *Know how you work.* You are likely to be one of two types of academic – either you work at a steady pace to complete tasks, or you tend to allow a lull in your work pattern to develop until you work at speed, under pressure, as a deadline looms. There is no point in supposing that you will radically change your preferred approach now, although it might be helpful for the future to at least try to cope with your non-preferred style. Nevertheless, both can work equally well for postgraduates, but you do need to recognise your natural work pattern. If you are a steady worker, you can be fairly sure that you will stick to even a fairly loose personalised timetable, although you will have to accept that you might find it stressful if your work pattern is disrupted; altering your timetable to accommodate such changes will help to reduce the stress. If you work best under pressure, it is easy enough to insert a series of self-imposed deadlines into your timetable so that you maintain your work rate. Recognition of your preferred working method is the route to success.
- *Analyse your time.* Time management is often perceived to be no more than a way of cramming more and more work into the time available, but this is not necessarily the most productive way to proceed. Of course, you will have times when you are working frantically to meet a deadline, or because your research has reached a crucial and fascinating stage, but at other times it is important that you rest or work at a reduced pace. Some of your personal tasks will be timetabled for you (teaching, conferences, seminars and so on) but your other academic tasks need to be analysed to categorise them into intensive (e.g. writing up a chapter), ongoing (such as

working on your bibliography) and light (background reading and so on). If you can categorise your tasks in this way, you can find pockets of time in which to place the latter categories (after teaching, in the hour before the library shuts, on a train or last thing at night) whilst recognising that more intensive tasks will have to have dedicated blocks of time allocated to them.

- *Accept the pattern of your degree.* A research degree is not intended to be planned to perfection within the first few weeks of your course: indeed, your supervisor would be concerned if you had a finalised plan in the early stages of your work. You might find it comforting to produce a plan early on of how you think your dissertation or thesis might look, but it is essential that you are prepared to change. A rigid plan suggests rigid thinking, a refusal to allow the research to lead your work and a reluctance to accept new avenues of thought as they develop. Expect to produce many plans, both broad and detailed, as your research evolves: producing a dissertation or thesis is an organic process; change is a good thing and plans are put in place in the early stages merely so that you can chart your progress, accepting that they will change over time.

- *Recognise the shape of your development.* Your own intellectual and academic development is also an organic process: you will change over time too, and what is a huge hurdle in the first term of your course will become second nature within a relatively short time. Allow this to happen; assume that you will have to give more time to certain tasks in the early stages, recognising that these will become easier as your skills and understanding develop.

With these points in mind, it is worth considering the best way to plan your time and your research. You will know how you work best, and you will be aware that the nature of the task before you will change over time. What you need is some way to harness your skills and your available time, and to anchor your research in the reality of your everyday life. The most effective way to achieve this for most students, as we have already mentioned, is to produce a personalised timetable. At some points in your degree this might be a detailed, weekly chart of tasks to be completed and events to attend. At other points it might be no more than a monthly plan with a list of tasks. The secret to success with a personalised timetable is to categorise the tasks before you. You will have your own priorities, but a useful set of tasks might include the following:

- *Scheduled tasks.* These are the tasks which you cannot avoid without some trouble, such as your teaching commitments, meetings with your supervisor and such like. By including them in your personalised time-table you will ensure that you never forget a scheduled task, even when you are working under pressure. This will reduce your potential stress levels.

- *Research tasks.* These tasks will often be solitary, as you carry out the research necessary and write up synopses of your findings or sections of your dissertation or thesis. Including these tasks in your timetable, with deadlines for completion, will be particularly useful to you if you know that you tend to work best under pressure, even if the deadlines are self-imposed.

- *Long-term plans.* Activities such as specific areas of background reading, working on your bibliography, beginning to prepare some material for a possible publication will fall into this category. It is useful to include these in your timetable because you will feel a surge of satisfaction as you tick them off as completed for that period, but you will not have to worry too much if they are not completed in that particular week: you can simply transfer them to the following week, aware that they are becoming a little more pressing and some of them might be moved to your 'research-tasks' section to guarantee that they will be done in time.

- *Personal goals.* However busy you are with your research, including personal goals in your timetable will remind you that you do have a life beyond your degree. They also give you something beyond your work to aim for as things progress, for example, taking a holiday, redecorating, attending a family gathering; all of these can be included in this section. You might not achieve them all in the time you planned, but they will at least be there to remind you how important it is to rest and enjoy yourself as well as to work.

If you are the type of person who loves to plan you will by now be eager to create a spreadsheet, with a row for each week and a column for each category of task, complete with tick boxes ready for that satisfying moment when you can tick off a completed task. Even if the idea of a spreadsheet leaves you cold, it is still a good idea to put some type of timetable in place, however broad it is in outline. Your timetable will run alongside your developing plan of your final research outcome, and you will alter your timetable as your research progresses to take into account developments and variations in your dissertation or a thesis plan that might dictate an altered work pattern. Most importantly, perhaps, you will now be able to share your plan with your supervisor. Rather than vaguely discussing how you might proceed over the next few weeks, you will be able to email a copy of your personalised timetable in advance of your next supervision, so you can discuss how realistic your plan is, what tasks you might have overlooked and how the shape of your research can relate to your future planning.

If you produce a personalised timetable from the very outset of your course of research, you will be reducing your stress levels, and most importantly, you will feel in control of the process of successfully completing a research postgraduate course. Control is the foundation of success for postgraduates, and your timetable will be one of the cornerstones of that success. Another critical cornerstone is your relationship with your supervisor. We mentioned this in the previous chapter but we will now provide more practical and detailed suggestions to help you manage that relationship well.

Patterns of Student–supervisor Relationships: How to Achieve the Right One for You?

There are as many differing supervisory relationships as there are supervisors and students, but as a research student one thing will rapidly become clear to you: this is the most important academic relationship you are likely to form, and as such it is worth taking the time to make sure that it is a positive one.

Communication

Communicating with your supervisor(s) is clearly going to be an important part of this relationship, and will be a fundamental aspect of your research. Your supervisors are there to help with the logistics of your degree (the paperwork, dealing with research panels, helping with conference papers and funding bids) and also with your intellectual and research development, so communicating effectively is of paramount importance. There are several communication questions that need to be asked at the outset:

How to Communicate?

This may seem an odd question to ask, but supervisors, like all human beings, have their preferred methods (media) of communication, so working with these is clearly to your advantage. You have three potential ways to communicate: face to face, on the phone and via email, and there are advantages and disadvantages to each. (Of course, not all of these options is open to all students all of the time. If you are working at a distance, or your part-time registration limits your visits to your institution, then you will need to hone your telephone/email skills – and perhaps even your hardcopy letter- writing skills! You should make doubly sure, in such instances, that you have discussed best ways to communicate with your supervisor. You might both explore the possibility of using resources such as Skype with a webcam so that you can talk cheaply to each other while seeing your images on the computer screen.)

Face-to-face communication. It has the advantage of being spontaneous and allowing a conversation to develop, which can result in a more wide-ranging and productive discussion than if you simply rely on email. However, in face-to-face discussions it is easier to forget what you wanted to say, or to overlook a point to follow up, or simply to become flustered and miss an opportunity. Although you might not expect to find this difficult, face-to-face communication can suffer from pressure of time (supervision meetings are rarely long enough, however hard you both try to set aside enough time) and from a sense that there is so much to cover that you have to prioritise your points. Sticking to an agenda has some benefits but it can sometimes be to the detriment of your emerging research ideas and the potential creative process of exploring ideas together. You might also have the potential problem, at the outset of the supervisory relationship, of finding yourself feeling awkward. You are dealing with a supervisor who may be a relative stranger, whose ideas for your research may vary radically from your own, and who is unused to your working methods. The answer to this potential problem is to plan for every conversation in advance. You will have face-to-face supervision meetings, even if much of your communication is carried out by email in between, so working through the planning section of this chapter will help you to capitalise on this opportunity.

Telephone communication. It is fraught with dangers. You cannot see your supervisor, so cannot pick up on any facial expressions such as a puzzled frown or a delighted smile, and you cannot be sure that you are talking to someone who is able to offer you undivided attention. If you do have to work together on the phone, there are two ways to ensure that this method of communication works. First, keep your queries as succinct and clear as possible. A vague question will result in a vague answer, which might be of little help. It is easy for your supervisor to miss your point altogether if you are unclear, perhaps misreading your emotional state or misunderstanding the real thrust of your questions. If you write down your questions in advance, and have a pen and paper to hand for noting any answers, the problems of miscommunication are diminished. Second, make sure that your supervisor has time to talk at the outset of the call. Offer to call back at a more convenient time, give some indication of how long you think the call might last, and be clear about the number of questions that you want to ask. If you are asked about something to which you have no ready answer, be prepared to ask for time to think through the issue before calling back later with an answer: that way you will not find that you have mistakenly committed yourself to anything.

Email. It is, for many research students, the most important method of communication in the supervisory relationship. It can be used in three main ways: to offer regular updates to your supervisor, to prepare for supervisions and to recap on discussions. If you have a personalised timetable, you can update it regularly and email it to your supervisor(s) so that your intentions and progress remain clear. This will reassure your supervisor(s) that you are working according to schedule; it also makes it easier if you intend to take a break from your research at points during the academic year. When you have a supervision meeting due, emailing your main questions ahead of the date will ensure that you are both making the most productive use of the face-to-face time that you have; your supervisor(s) may well choose to email you in advance as well. One of the most positive ways to use email in this relationship, and one that is overlooked by many research students, is to email your supervisor(s) after every supervision meeting or telephone call, to reiterate what was said and to confirm your understanding of what was agreed. By doing this, you are offering your supervisor(s) the chance to look up the titles of books that were mentioned only in passing at the time, or to confirm the dates of conferences, or to embellish advice that was offered only sketchily during the supervision meeting. If you have, as is likely, more than one supervisor then making sure that all of them are copied into such reviews ensures that everyone is kept up to date with your thinking and progress. One simple but effective device for this is to draw up a form that you can use repeatedly. It could sensibly include: the persons present at the meeting, and the date and duration of the meeting; what the main topic of discussion was; what main decisions were made and what advice given; what commitments before the next meeting were agreed; what was expected to be the topic of that next meeting and when it was planned to take place. Such a 'report form' can act as a log of your progress, useful for all concerned. A great advantage of email is that it allows both you and your supervisor to monitor research progress at times which suit you both, yet still keeps the lines of communication open in what will be a continued and developing dialogue. There is, though, a need to consider with your supervisor(s) the 'etiquette' of such correspondence, for it can be a burden as well as a boon! Some supervisors will prefer to answer emails from students only on certain days, rather than as soon as they come in, while others like to be warned slightly in advance that the next mail will have a very large file attached (we can't be the only ones who seethe with frustration when we inadvertently open such a mail and have to wait for it to download!). Each supervisor will have their own preferences and peccadilloes, so be sure to check these out early in your relationship.

When to Communicate?

You will have regular sessions with your supervisor(s), but the frequency and nature of these will vary between different supervisors. When we refer to 'supervision meetings' we mean semi-formal meetings that focus on supporting you through your research degree, rather than the 'passing in the corridor' or 'working side by side in the laboratory' or informal encounters over coffee or lunch that might occur, or indeed, more formal official progress meetings such as the 'transfer' stage mentioned earlier. For some students at certain stages in their work, a supervision meeting each week or fortnight will be a regular part of their programme, and for others a once-a-term supervision meeting is all that is expected.

There is no 'right' number of supervision meetings in general terms, but there will be a right number of supervision meetings for you. Over the period of your research you will need, at times, to have fewer supervision meetings, whilst at other points you might need to see your supervisor more frequently. The best way to approach this is to let your supervisor guide the frequency of supervisions in the first term, whilst you get your bearings, and then use your personalised timetable to forecast when you might need more-, or less-frequent, supervision meetings. This will allow you to forewarn your supervisor of your needs.

A good supervisory relationship is one in which neither side dictates what will happen: it is a developing dialogue between two academics and as such there is no reason to hesitate in setting the pace of your supervision meetings, always bearing in mind that other commitments might force your supervisor(s) to restrict supervision time at some points, just as you might have to do on occasion.

What to Communicate?

There are three prime causes for contacting your supervisor(s), and each of these will be handled differently:

1   *Regular supervision meetings.* The frequency of these, as has already been mentioned, will vary over time, but your preparation for them will be similar throughout your research degree. You will need to review your last supervision, make notes on developments within your main project, decide on the next set of research questions that you are formulating, and ponder any other queries that you should raise about the logistics of your course. Crucially, unless you have used the report form noted in the previous section or if the proposed topic has changed, you need to email these to your supervisor in advance of the supervisions, so that you are both clear about the topics to be discussed, and to allow your supervisor to respond in advance of the meeting with any other points that need to be covered. Early in your registration you will have one or more sessions focusing on reviewing your current skills and what training/learning needs you have in order to develop them. Thereafter, there will be review sessions to check on those developments. As you progress, you will certainly have meetings focusing on drafts of chapters that you have been working on. Bear in mind the pressures on supervisors and ensure that such drafts are sent, either by email attachment (note the large file caveat above!) or as hardcopy, if that is their preference, in plenty of time for them to read and comment on the material in advance. As a rule of thumb, three working days would be reasonable, but agree these general timings in advance.

2   *Unexpected developments.* Academics choose to supervise research students because they have a genuine interest in the research and enjoy the challenge of developing young academics. With this in mind, it becomes easy to see that your supervisors are not there simply to help you with form filling, or to run through a series of predetermined points with you. If something unexpected happens (you are asked to give a paper at a conference, you have just discovered an exciting new avenue for your research, you are thinking of submitting an article to a journal), your supervisor(s) will want to know. You are not asking for help, the response need be no more than simply congratulating you on this unexpected development, but this type of communication will help to make your relationship stronger, to ensure

that it develops beyond simply the formal, regular supervision sessions that you undertake together.

3   *When things go wrong.* It is highly unlikely that you will go through your postgraduate career without anything going wrong. Indeed, if this were to happen your supervisor(s) might be concerned about whether you were truly interrogating your research questions. Problematic research results, unexpected new demands on your time, deadlines for articles or conference papers and lack of time and money are just a few of the hurdles that you might have to face, and your supervisor(s) will hope to be involved in helping you to succeed. Your relationship with your supervisor(s) is one of trust, not one of constant testing. You are not communicating with your supervisor(s) in order to see if you have reached a 'correct' stage in your research, or to test your knowledge base. Your supervisor(s) will be ready to help you, because, as we pointed out in the previous chapter, it is important to them that you succeed. If you are experiencing a problem, try to be as clear as you can about why you are finding an aspect of your postgraduate life difficult, and then take the problem to your supervisor, the most appropriate one in the team if you have more than one, as early as you can. The clearer you can be about the root cause of the problem the easier it will be for someone to help you. What might seem like a huge, unique problem to you is unlikely to be surprising to your supervisor(s), who probably will have helped other students overcome similar difficulties in the past. If they cannot work with you to identify a range of solutions, they will know of other people in appropriate services (financial, counselling, accommodation, etc) who can.

Feedback

You will expect to receive feedback on your ideas and research developments from your supervisor(s) and the quality of this feedback will depend, to some extent, on mastering the communication within the relationship. A research student who is well organised, whose supervisor(s) have seen a personalised timetable that makes sense and who have been kept in touch regularly with updates, is more likely to receive relevant and inspiring feedback.

However, there is a potential problem here. You may not always appreciate the feedback (it can be frustrating to spend weeks on an area of research which your supervisor feels could be abandoned) or you may not agree with the direction which your supervisor is suggesting that you take. You have to face up to this problem head on, rather than being polite during your supervision meeting and then seething with resentment after the event. Your research degree is about your work, your ideas and, ultimately, your dissertation or thesis. Naturally, you will not lightly dismiss any advice or suggestions from your supervisor, but these are what they are, not instructions as you might expect to receive as an undergraduate. As such, you might choose to modify your work in the light of these suggestions, but you are under no obligation to follow such advice slavishly: your supervisor(s) would be disappointed if you did because they are expecting you to be able and happy to defend your research in public at conferences and in seminars before and after you have achieved your degree.

In some cases, a supervision meeting will be simply a highly structured conversation, in which it will be easy for you to argue your case for pursuing a particular avenue of enquiry, or to give good reasons for not following an avenue of research which is being suggested. In other cases, particularly if you are pushed for time, or a comment is made at the close of the supervision, you might feel less able to voice your opinion. If this happens to you, avoid becoming flustered by allowing yourself time, after the meeting, to consider what has been suggested. The chances are that your discomfort is no more than a misunderstanding between yourselves; perhaps there was not enough time to explain yourselves properly, or one of you misunderstood a point. If, on reflection, you feel that this is the case, it is an easy matter to email your supervisor and ask for clarification, or to re-state your case more cogently. If, on the other hand, you feel that you have both understood correctly and yet you still do not feel that a course of action would be productive, email your supervisor to explain this, putting forward your reasons for making this decision and asking for an additional meeting to discuss the issue further. If you do nothing, hoping that the problem will disappear in time, you will be distracted from your research and you could hinder your working relationship with your supervisor, so it is always best to tackle the issue in as straightforward a way as it can be.

A similar sense of awkwardness can arise if you feel that you would like a wider supervisory input for one aspect of your research. You might, perhaps, meet an academic at a conference who is currently working directly on an area that is of interest to you, but which is of less interest to your supervisor, or you may realise that another academic within your school or department can help to support you in one area of your work. Changing your supervisor entirely as a result of this would be counter-productive and unnecessary, but there is no reason why you should not, while working with your supervisor, approach another academic for some specific support in one particular area. This need not be a problem at all: both academics will want to get the best out of your abilities and research ideas, and will be happy to allow for this joint approach to be an aspect of your work.

The Wider Relationship

As a research student you are rather like an amphibious academic. You are a student in some ways, a scholar in others and a teacher in yet others. Sometimes you will be working under the supervision of an academic, and yet you might on some occasions be working alongside that same academic within a teaching situation, or on a conference platform. This is an exciting prospect, but it is one that must be recognised by you and your supervisor(s) if you are to forge the most productive relationship. Rather than seeing your supervisor(s) as your instructors, you need to try to reconcile these potentially conflicting roles, being happy to take advice on the direction your research might take, whilst recognising that at times (such as before a group of undergraduates) you will be fellow academics, working on an equal footing. Your supervisor(s) will be a rich reservoir of ideas, experience and common sense, and you can take advantage of all of these as the relationship develops. It is not necessary (or necessarily desirable) for you to develop a friendship with your supervisor(s), but an open approach to the relationship, from which you can talk comfortably about the skills and experience which you bring to the situation as well as a recognition of the experience of your supervisor(s), will ensure that you make the most of this opportunity.

Further Help

Although the focus here has been upon the academic and intellectual support offered by a supervisor, there is still more to be gleaned from this relationship. The mechanics of your course, such as facing a research panel, applying for additional funding, taking a break in your research, undertaking more teaching and so on, can all usefully be brought to your supervisor(s)' attention. If you find paperwork stressful, remember that your supervisor(s) may hate form filling as much as you do, but will be in a position to send you to the school administrator, for example, for further help, and will be able to give you details of the funding or research office if you are having financial difficulties. The default position here is that you will approach your supervisor(s) with any queries that you have, regardless of what they are, but that you will be ready to be guided towards another expert if this seems to your supervisor to be the best way forward. This approach also has the advantage of guaranteeing that your supervisor(s) is fully aware of all aspects of your postgraduate experience.

Your relationship with your supervisor(s) will not end just because you have successfully completed your research degree. It will be to your supervisor(s) that you return in the coming months and years for references, both professional and academic, and perhaps for guidance as to the direction that your career path is taking. You might also, of course, find that one of your supervisors is on the interview panel for your first academic post, and all of this is worth bearing in mind. You cannot guarantee that you will get a job just because you have a good relationship with your ex-supervisor, nor would you want to work under such an unfair system, but if your supervisor's only memories of you are missed supervisions, desultory emails and forms submitted late, you are asking for problems. The key issue here is, again, communication. It is impossible to suppose that you will never miss a supervision meeting, or a deadline, or that your research will run so smoothly that you never hit a crisis, but as long as your supervisor(s) are made aware, in advance, of any of these problems, they need not jeopardise your good working relationship.

Once you have avoided any negative impact upon your relationship, you can work towards using it in the most positive way possible for your future career. From what we have said so far, you will recognise that student–supervisor relationship, like any other important relationship, requires some tending and, unlike some relationships, it cannot be left to chance or the vagaries of fortune. If your supervisor(s) don't suggest it, you might like to start the ball rolling by discussing a form of learning contract, one in which at least your mutual expectations of each other are explored and ways of operationalising them are debated and agreed. This gives you both a structure to work on albeit one that may be amended as your needs develop and change. Being clear with each other about expectations is a particularly helpful way of avoiding conflicts but even with the best will from both sides, sometimes relationships can founder. This is exceptional in terms of the student–supervisor relationship but it can be devastating if it happens. That is one of the reasons why the Quality Assurance Agency recommends the use of Supervisory Teams so that there is always someone you can turn to in problem situations. Each institution will also have procedures written into its Code of Practice for Research Students to deal with such eventualities. However, don't resort to official procedures too precipitately – decisions made in the heat of the moment are seldom the best ones, so give each other time to think clearly and review alternative strategies, and do not be too proud or too stubborn to consider some form of arbitration by another member of staff or member of the research team.

Further, on a more positive note, as this is not intended to be a situation in which you are constantly being tested, there need be no shame in sharing your fears and frustration, nor any embarrassment in being bold about your ambitions and hopes for the future. There are five important areas in which you might expect to receive this type of support:

1 *Publication.* You will need to think about publication early in your research programme, particularly if you are hoping to develop an academic career. Articles take a surprisingly long time to transfer from your computer to a journal, and there is a plethora of options, all with advantages and disadvantages. Traditional academic journals exist, of course, but so too do online versions of journals, some peer reviewed and others not, and academic papers can sometimes become publications merely as a result of you having given the paper at a conference. Working with other academics to contribute to an edition of a journal, or to write individually authored chapters in a more lengthy publication, are all possibilities that your supervisor(s) can help you to pursue by guiding you through the minefield of publication and advising you as to the best way forward.

2 *Conferences.* Although you are able to subscribe to conference-alert websites and will have a growing list of conference contacts as your work progresses, it is still worth making it clear to your supervisor(s) if you are keen to attend conferences, perhaps to give a paper at some. As some students are less interested in conferences, finding the cost of travel prohibitive or

feeling they have too little time to attend them, you cannot assume that your supervisor(s) will keep you updated on conferences unless you speak up. Your supervisor(s) will also be able to alert you to group-mailing lists of series of conferences that can sometimes run over several years, offering you the chance to increase your list of contacts. The proceedings of conferences are often lodged on the internet, and again your supervisor(s) can help you to access the proceedings of any past conferences which might be of interest to you.

3   *Networking.* It is difficult to overestimate the importance of academic networking for research postgraduates. Not only is it useful in terms of your academic development, as you draw on the widest possible pool of the expertise around you, it could be vital to your career development, as you hear about opportunities in your field. You will naturally develop your own network as you attend conferences and seminars and talk to visiting academics within your institution, and this will be reflected in an ever-increasing email address book. Beyond this, it makes sense to check with your supervisor if you feel that you need additional input in an area, if you have read the work of an academic, for example, and would like to make contact, or if you have heard only vaguely of another researcher in your field and would like to discuss ideas. Your supervisor(s) may well know the academics in question or at least might know something more about them.

4   *Teaching.* You may be allocated some teaching of undergraduates as part of your commitment to your university, but this might need some adjustment during your course of research. You might, for example, need to reduce your teaching hours at critical points in your research, making up those hours, if they are part of an agreement with your institution, at a later time. You might, alternatively, wish to increase your teaching hours in order to earn some much-needed cash. If you hope to develop your teaching within a particular area, perhaps to enhance your CV or to play to your strengths, you might be looking to alter your teaching load. Whilst teaching allocation is likely to be undertaken by the administrators and senior staff within your department, discussing the situation with your supervisor(s) is the best way to begin the process of trying either to increase or decrease the amount and type of teaching which you undertake.

5   *Career development.* As well as helping you to network, your supervisor will be able to advise you on your academic CV and your references, as well as encouraging you in any publications you produce. You will be pursuing any career possibilities that you find as your research nears its end and if your supervisor(s) are made aware of your plans you will be sure to hear of opportunities in your field as they arise.

Conclusion

We hope that in this chapter we have provided you with a framework for understanding the way your research is likely to progress through the different stages of the research process and how these articulate with institutional progress monitoring. The chapter that follows will address the foundation of all research, the literature review. We have also provided some more guidance on how to manage your time and your relationship with your supervisor. Again, key points included in the chapter are summarised below.

Key Points for Managing the Research Process and the Student–supervisor Relationship

- There are distinctive stages to your degree; all are important and there will be some overlap. If you miss any part of a stage, it will be possible to catch up but this will be your responsibility
- Training as a postgraduate researcher goes beyond your subject area to include generic training. This is attractive to future employers and vital for your academic development
- Progress monitoring takes various forms and is designed to ensure that you get maximum reward for your efforts
- Planning your time around different categories of task will allow you to maximise both your efficiency and your enjoyment of the research degree process
- It is helpful to decide on the best principal form of communication with your supervisor(s) and use this to make the most of your time together
- You can expect to communicate with your supervisor(s) in a variety of ways and for a range of reasons: recognising this will help you to get the best form of supervision
- In the rare event of experiencing problems with your supervision, you should first raise the issue with your supervisor(s): the formal reporting procedure should only be used as a last resort
- There are many opportunities to progress beyond your immediate research: your supervisor(s) can support you in all of these endeavours. They may become your key point of academic contact for many years.

SOURCES OF SUPPORT

The Society for Research into Higher Education (SRHE) Postgraduate Issues Network welcomes research students and produces a series of Guides for Supervisors and PGR Programme managers that would also be informative for students. You may find the Guides in your institution's Staff Development Unit or find out more about them at: www.SRHE.ac.uk

The National Postgraduate Committee (NPC) is the independent representative body for postgraduates and also produces its own guides; to find out more visit www.npc.org.uk

UK GRAD provides a range of support for research students; to know more visit: www.grad.ac.uk

10 Searching and Reviewing the Literature and Information Skills

Dr Chris Hart

Introduction

After reading this chapter, you should be able to do the following:

- Explain the reasons for the literature review for your research degree
- Plan and conduct a literature search using paper and electronic sources and resources
- Construct competent bibliographies and do correct citations
- Identity the basic argumentative structure of different literature reviews in terms of the purpose of their research
- Say what a literature review is and is not
- Select an appropriate structure for writing a literature review.

There Is No Magic Formula

I wish I could tell you just what a literature review is, what one would look like for your thesis and show you an easy way to searching, gathering, organising, reading and understanding 'the literature'. All literature reviews are unique. No one researcher will search the literature, chose texts, read and understand them in the same way. Scholarly life is largely about participating in discussions (sometimes arguments) about the meaning, intent and usefulness of what another scholar or group of scholars have written on a topic (their interpretation) or gone about doing the research they have (their methodological assumptions and methods).

I can, however, show you some of the tools and techniques you can use to search for literature relevant to your topic and methods. This is largely technical knowledge. You will have to provide a degree of common sense to make the techniques effective, in terms of finding what you need, and efficient, in terms of the use of your time. What is more difficult is showing you how to make sense of the literature. The interpretation you make of what you read will be shaped by many factors including your discipline, political and moral standpoint, prior learning and academic interests. What I can show are some techniques which may be useful to structure your review of your chosen literature.

What Literature Search and Review Are Not

Let us begin by saying what a literature search and literature review are not. A search of the literature is not a search of the internet, browsing (though I would argue library browsing is important) of what's in the library, local bookshop or on Amazon. A literature review is not a list of items you have come across, or a bibliography or summary of one text after another. These are things developed in the early stages of searching, organising (classifying) and evaluating the literature.

This is not a literature review.

BIBLIOGRAPHY: AN EXAMPLE

Beck, U. 1999 'Introduction. The Cosmopolitan Manifesto', in U. Beck *World Risk Society*, Cambridge: Polity Press.

Beck, U. 2000 *What is Globalization?* Cambridge: Polity Press.

Beck, U. 2000 'The Cosmopolitan Perspective. Sociology in the Second Age of Modernity', *British Journal of* Sociology, 151: 79–106.

Beck, U. 2002 'The Cosmopolitan Society and its Enemies', *Theory, Culture and Society*, 19(1–2): 17–44.

Beck, U. 2004 'The Truth of Others: A Cosmopolitan Approach', *Common Knowledge*, 10: 430–49.

Boehm, M.H. 1931 'Cosmopolitanism', *Encyclopedia of the Social Sciences Vol. 4*, New York: MacMillan.

Cohen, R. and Fine, R. 2002 'Four Cosmopolitan Moments', in S. Vertovec and R.Cohen (eds) *Conceiving Cosmopolitanism. Theory, Context, and Practice*, Oxford: Oxford University Press.

Featherstone, M. 2002 'Cosmopolis. An Introduction', *Theory, Culture, and Society*, 19(1–2): 1–16.

The following is from a review of the literature.

LITERATURE REVIEW: A SAMPLE EXCERPT

In the Western world there is growing concern at declining levels of participation. Of particular concern is the increasing non-engagement amongst young people (UK Electoral Commission, 2004, 2002) and the worrying signs of alienation and cynicism among young people about public life and participation, leading to their possible disconnection and disengagement with it (Kerr, 2003). We might argue that as each generation reaches middle-age and positions of influence it despairs of the attitude of the young. However statistics do suggest that the non-participation of the young is both higher and lasting for longer. Participation, when it occurs, is of a different nature being more apolitical, such as helping in a soup kitchen (Horwitt, 1999) and individual rather than collective action (Pattie, Seyd & Whiteley, 2003). A UK study found that young people increasingly feel disconnected from the wider society, are proud of being outside and against the mainstream, and have opted out of party politics (Wilkinson & Mulgan, 1995).

A paper delivered in the symposium *Citizenship: Learning by Doing*. Children and young people as citizens: Participation, provision and protection 6th child and family policy conference, University of Otago Dunedin, July 2005 Dr Helena Catt.

What Literature Search and Review Involve

A literature search is: a systematic search of the accredited sources and resources used to record written works. It involves identifying paper and electronic sources relevant to your topic and method(s) and preparing a clear plan for the search that includes a justifiable vocabulary. The search will include establishing a robust scheme for the management of what will be a massive amount of information and paper. A review of the literature selected and obtained is, the analysis, critical evaluation and synthesis of existing knowledge relevant to your research problem, and thesis or issue you are aiming to say something original about. In your analysis you are selecting from different texts concepts, theory, argument and interpretation relevant to the development of your particular theoretical frame of reference. It involves classifying these parts into schemes which enable you to critically evaluate those concepts, argument and interpretation. When critically evaluating you interrogate the work of others (regardless of their standing in the academic community). You are scrutinising the chain of reasoning another has used and the evidence they have offered to support their argument. You are aiming to follow the use of a seminal work by successive authors; to evaluate their assessments and use of that work; to evaluate the synthesis which have been developed with other land-mark publications. Your reason for doing this is to identify fallacies in arguments, methodological assumptions or theory or to show how an issue and problem could benefit from the application of an existing theory and/or methodology. This is 'finding the gap' for your research: the basis for making an argument that your research will make an original contribution to knowledge (doctorate level) or demonstrate the application of theory and method (masters level).

Initial Search and Review Precedes the Full Search and Review

If all of this sounds like a lot of work, well it is. But it is also, say many researchers, one of the most enjoyable parts of doing research. The main thing is to see the search and review as a series of stages. Each stage successively builds on the previous ones to construct the review for the thesis or dissertation. There are two main kinds of search and review for most research: the initial (or indicative) search and review and the comprehensive search and review. The initial search is like a reconnaissance of the landscape: what literature is 'out there' and readily obtainable; what databases exist and where and how they can be accessed. Your academic librarian can be an indispensable source of information and guidance at this stage. It is worth making an appointment to discuss your research with them. From what is readily available a short review can be constructed that 'indicates' the key ideas, concepts, authors, works and arguments of the broader literature. At this stage the internet, library catalogue and online book stores such as Amazon can be helpful – but only as indications of the themes. The indicative review is often used for research proposals. If the indicative review has been done competently then the skills and knowledge acquired can be rapidly developed. A more comprehensive search can be planned on the basis of the databases identified, articles and books ordered which are not in the library, and more time given to 'mining' the literature.

Why Search and Review the Literature?

If so much effort is required what are the main reasons for searching and reviewing the literature? To be counted by your academic peers as a competent professional (to be awarded your degree and/or have a career in research) you will need to be able to demonstrate a knowledge and experience of the main tools and techniques of research. These include the essential and generic tools and techniques of searching for information, managing, categorising and applying information. By information we mean data, statistics, formulae, ideas, arguments, concepts and theories. By managing information we mean using paper, mechanical and electronic methods to store, organise, relate and retrieve what you have found. By applying information we mean developing the cognitive capacity to make connections between different kinds and sources of information, find problems with existing connections and arguments and, importantly, be able to apply imagination.

A search and review will provide you with two essential parts for your research; these are shown in Figure 10.1. One is information on your topic: how it has been defined, its historical development, key studies and authors/researchers, the main concepts, theories and themes. An essential part of this is that you will come to know the kinds of questions which have been (and may still be) deemed important by your discipline and how these have been addressed, argued over and developed. The second thing you will get out of doing a search and review is methodological knowledge. This will include knowledge of the methods and procedures which have been used by other researchers, what assumptions they made, the issues that exist with the

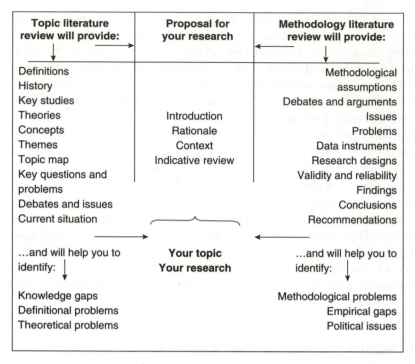

FIGURE 10.1   What the search and review of the literature will contribute to your research and thesis? (Source: Hart *Doing Your Masters Dissertation.* London: Dr Chris Hart, Sage, 2004: 157)

methods and assumptions used, access to the data collected, the research designs employed and information on the degrees of validity and reliability achieved. Put these two together and you will have achieved a state-of-the-art understanding of your topic. You will have achieved this level of understanding, something which is much greater than its parts, and have knowledge on how to apply critical evaluation, analysis and synthesis of information.

The main elements of Figure 10.1 can be turned into a series of questions (Figure 10.2). These are questions which will guide what you search for and how you develop your definition of your research problem. The questions are in sets and start with the most basic, which will help you become familiar with the terrain of your 'literature'. As you work through the questions you will soon develop the necessary technical skills and knowledge of the ways in which information is organised. This pedagogical knowledge will soon become second nature for you. As you move through the other sets of questions you will be developing your *andragogical* knowledge; the ability to apply what you have found.

More advanced questions:

1 What inconsistencies, shortcomings or contradictions are there in our knowledge of the topic?
2 What evidence is lacking, inconclusive or too limited?
3 What alternate approaches are there for understanding the topic which have not been used?

Intermediate questions:

1 How has the topic or problem been defined?
2 What are the different frames of reference for researching and discussing the topic?
3 How has theory been related to practice or to empirical research?
4 What methodological assumptions and approaches have been used?
5 What key concepts, variables or factors have been identified?
6 What are the main debates on my topic?
7 What gaps in knowledge, theory or application of a methodology are there in my topic area?

Basic questions:

1 What are the databases I can use to search for relevant information?
2 What is the language (vocabulary) of my topic and how is it used?
3 What are the key sources (books, articles, reports) on my topic?
4 What research, methods and theory are there on my topic?
5 Who are the main researchers in this area?
6 What is the history, chronological development, of the topic or problem?

FIGURE 10.2 The hierarchy of questions

What Is Literature and a Literature Search?

All of this begins with understanding what the literature is and how it is organised. By the word 'literature' we refer to all kinds of published information relevant to your research. Information is published in a wide range of formats including the following:

Monographs	Anthologies	Reports	Conference proceedings
Theses	Internet	Textbooks	Official publications
Statistics	Articles	Trade literature	Patents and Trademarks

There are many different ways in which research and ideas are published. Electronic or digital publications have become established but are not a substitute for other, printed documents. Your search must therefore use the tools which make available records on as many kinds of literature as possible. The good news is that the library profession have spent a lot of effort into organising knowledge, have collected unbelievable amounts of it and have the tools to help us find and retrieve a lot of it (often too much of it).

Always Do a Plan

Doing a literature search needs planning, preparation and a little thought. The aim is to be systematic and precise. You can, of course, begin without a plan with little idea of the ways knowledge is organised; if, that is, chaos and the high probability of failure are risks worth taking.

There are a number typical sequences to a search of the literature. Table 10.1 shows the main elements of a search and what kinds of information you can expect to be looking for, from which type of resource.

TABLE 10.1   Initial preparation for the generic literature search

Things to do	Sources to consult
1 Define your topic	Consult the dictionaries and encyclopaedias in the *quick reference section* of the library to develop a list of key words that can be used to search the library catalogue, abstracts and indexes Write down the main topic and what disciplines you think will have had something to say about it
2 Think about the limits of your topic	Use materials from the encyclopaedias and dictionaries to define the scope of your topic and to write a working title. Write down the criteria for your search – what to include and what to exclude Limit your search by placing parameters around the time frame (dates), language(s), place, population or variables
3 Identify the main reference which lead to information on your topic	Use *guides to the literature* from the *quick reference section* of the library to identify relevant indexes and abstracts and reference sources including internet gateways. Check which reference tools the library holds that you can use and which you need to order through the library. Identify the main indexes and abstracts and any other reference materials that cover the disciplines for your topic
4 Think about the housekeeping	Use ring binders to store notes and index cards to record citations Design a means of recording what you find and how you will cross-reference materials
5 Plan the sources to be searched and start your search	Use your notes to construct a list of abstracts, indexes and other reference sources to be searched List the sources you intend to search in the order in which you intend to search them

Source: Adapted from Hart *Doing a literature search*. London: Sage, 2001: 25.

Use Guides to the Literature

Your main resources are the guides to the literature. All subject disciplines have a range of sources which have been developed over the decades to record, in indexes, published outputs (print and electronic). There is a large range of these indexes and bespoke sources. Guides to the literature will tell you which indexes and abstracts (paper, online or CD ROM) are relevant to your topic and methodology. Many, such as the ones listed below, will show how to do a search of the main indexes and also list 'special collections' in libraries and on the internet. Useful guides include the following:

- *Guide to Reference Books.* Balay, Robert (ed.) (1996), 11th edn, Chicago, IL: American Library Association. This guide lists and describes the most important reference sources for all disciplines.
- *Information Sources of Political Science.* Green, Stephen W. and Douglas J. Ernest (eds) (2005), 5th edn, Santa Barbara, CA: A guide to print and electronic reference sources for the field of Political Science.
- *Manual of Online Search Strategies.* Armstrong, C.J. and Andrew Large. (2001), 3rd edn, Aldershot, Hampshire, UK: Gower Publishing Ltd., 3 volume set. A comprehensive work, this three-volume covers the whole range of Internet, CD-ROM and dial-up online services. International experts on each subject area describe in detail how to identify and exploit specialist bibliographic and non-bibliographic databases, the best search methods and delivery modes, and the relative merits of different services and online hosts in their different disciplines. Numerous examples of search results are used to illustrate different strategies and commands. The Manual can be used as a subject hand-book, a directory of recommended resources and as a textbook. This new edition provides extensive guidance for searchers of electronic information and is particularly useful for those working in a subject area other than their own.

  a   Volume I: Sciences: agriculture, earth sciences, chemistry, biosciences, engineering and energy
  b   Volume II: Business, Law and Patents: patents, business and economics, news and current affairs, law
  c   Volume III: Humanities and Social Sciences: citations, social and behavioural sciences, humanities and education resources

- *Political Science: The State of the Discipline.* Katznelson, Ira and Helen V. Milner (eds) (2002), Washington, DC: American Political Science Association. New essays on all fields in the discipline.
- *Reader's Guide to the Social Sciences.* Michie, Jonathan (ed.) (2001), 2 vols, Chicago, IL: Fitzroy Dearborn. Provides brief overviews and recommended reading lists on topics in the social sciences.

Also see,

- *A Guide to Finding Quality Information on the Internet: Selection and Evaluation.* Cooke, A. (2001), 2nd edn, London: Library Association
- Your supervisor – she or he will know the literature and should be able to guide your efforts.

These and other guides will help you to find indexes and abstracts for planning a literature search. The key words used to index articles can be a useful source for your own search. Subject encyclopaedia and dictionaries can be useful for identifying the key ideas, concepts and references on a topic.

There are many good and reliable internet sources, such as the following. These represent a small selection of those available and show the spacialisation of many. Have a play with them and follow some of the links to build up your own library of links and sources.

- A resource guide from John Hopkins University (USA)
  www.library.jhu.edu/researchhelp/polisci/index.html
- A Collection of links on politics and political corruption in relation to financial scandals
  www.exeter.ac.uk/~RDavies/arian/scandals/political.html
- Alternative news sources
  www.world-newspapers.com/alternative-news.html
- Conflict and politics in Northern Ireland (1968 to the Present)
  www.cain.ulst.ac.uk/
- Political sources in the internet
  www.socsciresearch.com/r12.html
- Sources on politics
  www.livjm.ac.uk/SOC/70268.htm
- My personal site dedicated to literature reviewing:
  web.mac.com/theorists/literaturereviewing

Citing Your Sources

As you find items of information (publications) you deem may be useful cite their bibliographic details; it is an absolute necessity not to leave this task unattended. If you skip this part the outcome is usually frustration; you will not be able to remember all the details (Chapter 20 reminds you of this). You cannot, normally, cite an item if you cannot provide all the bibliographic details. Key things to do are the following:

- Make notes on where you found the main ideas, words, phrases and other materials you intend to use so that you can include in your dissertation citations which attribute the origins of those ideas, words, phrases. This shows you have a clear understanding of ethical standards, that you have done your literature search and have been able to incorporate materials. It will also protect you from claims that your ideas cannot be traced and therefore from doubts about the quality of your work.

- Use a consistent style to cite the sources of your ideas, words and phrases. The two main styles or methods are the Harvard system and the Vancouver method. Check to see if your institution has a preferred style.

THE HARVARD SYSTEM: AN EXAMPLE

Research on fathering has expanded in scope and breadth over the last several decades (e.g. Berman and Pedersen, 1987a; Pedersen, 1987). Nonetheless, investigations of and conceptualizations about men's behaviors in and attitudes toward families are still sparse compared to studies of mothering and family processes, more generally. Indeed, relatively little is known about what residential fathers actually do, how their activities vary, and what the variability means (Harris and Morgan, 1991:541; Lamb and Oppenheim, 1989; Radin, 1994, 1988). (Gable et al., 1992:285). (Source: National Center on Fathers and Families, *Co-Parenting: A Review of the Literature*, by Terry Arendell www.ncoff.gse.upenn.edu/litrev/cplr.htm. Accessed: 1 December 2003)

Each of the references cited in the text would normally be listed as full citations at the end of the chapter or end of the thesis in alpha order (A–Z). For more information on using the Harvard System see the following work:

Holland, M. (1996) *Harvard system* [online]. Poole: Bournemouth University. Available from: www.bournemouth.ac.uk/service-depts/lis/LIS_Pub/ harvardsyst.html[Accessed 1 December 2003].

Chapter 13 discusses how to cite information to avoid the possibility of plagiarism.

Citation Style

There are numerous guides on how to do citations. Before you start any work find out what style is recommended by your university. Commonly used sources on how to do citations include the following:

- Modern Language Association (MLA).
  www.cctc.commnet.edu/mla/practical_guide.html
- International Standards Organization ISO 690-2 – information and bibliographic references.
  www.nlc-bnc.ca/iso/tc46sc9/standard/690-2ehtm

TABLE 10.2   Citation styles

Type	Example and notes
Books	Hart, C. (1998) *Doing a literature review: releasing the social science research imagination*. London: Sage. Some use capitals for the title, e.g. *Doing a Literature Review*. I believe the fewer key strokes needed the better. Include sub-titles.
Articles	Hart, C., Shoolbred, M., Butcher, D. and Kane, D. (1999) 'The bibliographic structure of fan information', *Collection Building*, 18 (2): 81–90. Do not use et al but include all the authors. Some do not have ' at the beginning and at end of the article title.
Chapters in books	Francis, D. and Hart, C. (1997) 'Narrative intelligibility and membership categorization in a television commercial'. In Hester, S. and Eglin, P. (eds). *Culture in action: studies in membership categorization and analysis*. Washington, DC: University Press of America. Some place the ed. or eds in brackets, e.g. (eds). Include as much information as possible, e.g. DC as there are a number of Washington(s).
Thesis	Hart, C. (1993) 'The social production of an advertisement'. PhD thesis, Manchester Metropolitan University/J. Walter Thompson Ltd. DoRs: Dr D.W. Francis (Manchester Metropolitan University) and Dr W.W. Sharrock (Victoria University of Manchester). Give as many details as possible, as theses are difficult to locate and obtain. I always try to include the Directors of the Research (DoRs) and their institutions.
Internet articles based on a print source	VandenBos, G., Knapp, S., and Doe, J. (2001) 'Role of reference elements in the selection of resources by psychology undergraduates'. (Electronic version). *Journal of Bibliographic Research*, 5: 117–123. I use the full 'and' rather than the '&'. While not capitalising the article title I capitalise the title of the journal. No need to use pp. for pages.
Article in an electronic journal	Fredrickson, B.L. (2002) 'Cultivating positive emotions to optimise health and well-being'. *Prevention & Treatment*, 3, article 0001a, from: www.journals.apa.org/prevention/volume3/pre0030001a.html (accessed 7 March, 2000) The '&' is in the title of the journal. Give the full Internet address and the date you accessed it.
Document from a private Internet site	Dingwall, R. 'Oration for Harold Garfinkel', from: www.pscw.uva.nl /emca/oration.html (accessed 5 September, 2002) Some of these sites do not have an obvious author so give all details possible.

Source: Adapted from *Sage Publications authors style guide* and APA Online www.apastyle.org/

Table 10.2 shows how the citations have been done in this book. The style is recommended by Sage Publications.

Bibliographical Software

There are a number of software packages available that can help you manage your citations. The common name for these is bibliographical software. The idea of most is that when you locate documents during a search you use the software to download the bibliographical details to your own computer. In general, they are designed to assist in the following tasks:

- Automated collection and organisation of references from bibliographic databases, library catalogues and online journals
- Integration with word-processing software to automatically insert and format citations and bibliographies
- Formatting of references according to particular bibliographic styles (e.g. MLA, Chicago, individual journals) format records for exporting to other packages and for data sharing.

Some of most well-known ones include: Biblioscape 3.3, Bookends Plus 5, Bookwhere2000 v.3.0, Citation 7, EndNote 3.0.1, Papyrus 7.0, Procite 4 and Reference Web Poster. Details on these can be found from the Internet.

Using Citation Indexes

Once you have identified some sources you can begin to dig deeper and mine for the details. This may involve the use of citation indexes. The culture of justifying your existence in academia has created a range of sophisticated tools which record and organise published output. These are the citation indexes. Citation indexes record not only what has been published but what publications/authors are cited in publications. If you have a key publication you can then consult the relevant citation index and find out who the authors cited in your key publication cited. The basic idea of citation maps is most research is built on previous research efforts and assumptions that we make are based upon existing accepted knowledge. The flow of research can be mapped through connecting the cited references both forward and backward over time. In this way we can see how research is interrelated.

The key site of the ISI web of science (www.isinet.com/) is where you will find the citation indexes for most subjects. These indexes are the basis for index mapping.

Key Questions

An extensive vocabulary has developed around citation and literature searching. Much of it now includes the phrase 'knowledge mapping'. What this amounts to is finding answers to a basic set of questions.

- Who are the most cited authors?
- What are the details of their publications?
- Who have the most-cited authors cited?
- How much has been written on my topic?
- What institutions are key authors affiliated with?
- What are their most influential publications?
- What are their collaboration patterns?
- What are the dominant topics?
- What are the new areas of research?
- What groups of authors have papers related to the dominant topics?
- What groups of authors have papers related to the new areas of research?
- What are the communities of researchers?

Exciting Software

There is a range of software products and websites offering methods to construct maps which map the relationships between publications based on citations. Many now use visualisation techniques. These are web-based diagrams which are interactive. Some of the key websites among these include the following:

- *AuthorMap* (www.project.cis.drexel.edu/authorlink/) The assumption is that if two authors are often cited together by many other authors, these two authors likely have common intellectual interest (in their research and writing). From this a subject domain map is constructed. The map allows the user to drag the names on the maps and drop them to a search box to activate an automatic search, by the underlying search engine.
- *Citation Link* (www.delphion.com/help/citelink/) is an analytical tool that reveals a patent's citations in a graphical map, using multiple visualisation techniques. From a target patent, you can review either forward or backward references, or both at once. You can display your analysis in a citation tree or timeline.
- *CiteULike* (www.citeulike.org/) This is a free service to help academics to share, store and organise academic papers. When you see a paper on the web that interests you, you can click one button and have it added to your personal library. *CiteULike* automatically extracts the citation details, so there's no need to type them in yourself.

A simple word of warning: do not get caught up playing with this impressive technology. It may be visually exciting but it is not a quick answer to doing a search or analysis of the literature.

What To Do with the Information?

Once you begin to find information relevant to your topic you will also begin to write making notes using categories is the foundation of all literature reviews. This is not a linear process but iterative. Initially your indicative search and review of the literature will have suggested the key themes. From these you develop some rudimentary categories to guide your reading and note taking. The literature review in your thesis is the public product of your analysis; the use of categories to extract information from your sources. This often means the review you write for your thesis is a selective and edited, and much shorter, piece(s) of writing. Analysing your sources will result in a substantial amount of paper. Be prepared with a system to manage it all.

There are a number of things you will want from the literature. Among these some of the important things to consider are as follows:

- Concepts which will be useful to guide your observations
- Theories to compare and maybe use in your explanation or description
- Definitions of the topic, issue or problem to compare and from which to construct your own working definition
- Arguments over what something means, how it should be defined and studied
- Data and evidence which can be evaluated.

Evidence Is What It Is All about

Evidence is a core requirement for argument, interpretation and recommendations. Evidence is what your discipline and common sense says it is – subject to the rules of proof, authentification and production. That is, statements made about some phenomenon must (now or hypothetically in the future) have a corresponding proof. That proof must be authentic; not false, not incomplete or be a surrogate. The proof must be able to be produced, in full, and if possible in it's original state. In research the proof must, if produced from a research method be replicable; other researchers must, in principle, be able to produce the same results using the same methods. Figure 10.3 summarises the relationship research has to professional practice, argumentation and critical thinking – placing evidence at the centre of these activities.

What evidence actually is, is not always clear. Nor are the methods or procedures used to produce evidence commonly agreed on. Both are subject to critique and evaluation. How evidence was produced is subject to questions about the reliability and validity of the method(s), process and application of the method(s). Once produced evidence is subject to evaluation in terms of its merit, completeness and utility for recommendations and making changes. Critical evaluation of evidence is essential for reviewing literature claiming

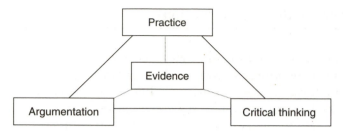

FIGURE 10.3   Evidence, Argumentation, Practice and critical thinking

changes should be made to a practice or procedure (as in medical treatment) or offering an explanation for the occurrence of a phenomenon.

Evidence is published in documents. If your interest is in claims for intervention or explanation then the literature with the evidence should be your focus.

Methodological Argument

Claims about the cause of a phenomenon are not always as 'objective' as they may be presented. In many instances much depends on the level of explanation required for all practical purposes and the context in which the explanation is offered. In philosophy and methodology, argument is sometimes used without recourse to empirical evidence. Argumentation about all kinds of moral, ethical, epistemological and ontological issues are often offered without definitive proof. Argumentation over such matters as deductivism versus inductivism, individualism versus collectivism, nomotheticism versus ideographicism and the like may have empirical examples offered by opponents as proofs but nevertheless are based on conviction and can be overturned by recourse to counter evidence.

Evaluating Arguments

There are three standpoints to an argument: first, the one you take when critically evaluating the arguments made by others; second, the standpoint taken by those authors you are evaluating; third, the standpoint taken when you develop your own argument.

The proposer of an argument needs to marshal sufficient and relevant evidence to support the argument. The method by which this is accomplished is producing valid, sound and coherent arguments devoid of fallacies and not easily undone. The evaluator of an argument needs to identity the structure of the reasoning used; look carefully at the premises and conclusions; seek to show why the proposed conclusion is not the only one to be derived from the reasons provided. Alec Fisher gives some sound advice:

> Starting with the main conclusion C, ask, 'What immediate reasons are presented in the text for accepting C?' or 'Why (in the text) am I asked to believe C?' (Fisher, 1988: 129)

Using methods to evaluate argument, evidence and practices involves thinking critically. There is a lot of advice given on what it means and how to do critical thinking. Some of this is overtly complicated. For practical purposes critical thinking can be characterised as follows. Critical thinking involves developing the ability and capacity to be sceptical – to a degree appropriate to the needs of the project. Fisher's (1988: 128–139) method is a sceptical one. It is about asking questions about an argument in a systematic way, based on consistent application of the *assertibility question*. A common problem is that many authors have a poor understanding of informal let alone formal logic and hence know little about how to structure a clear, accurate, precise, thorough and fair argument.

Critical evaluation involves the following basic steps. Once you have identified the main publications group them roughly into sets based on similarity of argument.

- For each set itemise the reasons given for the conclusions made. Pay particular attention to inference indicators. Group reasons together along with any evidence offered. Group conclusions together. Pick out quotes for each author that illustrate clearly and fairly their argument
- Think about the reasons and conclusions. Ask what assumptions have been made, what are the origins (heritage) of these assumptions, were these assumptions necessary, what other assumptions could have been used? At this level of study you should be familiar with methodological assumptions and traditions
- Think about the logical consequences of the conclusions made based on the assumptions underpinning them. Ask what would the likely outcomes be if the assumptions were taken to their logical conclusions? Look for distinctive chains of reasoning and new ideas
- Assign weights – high weight to strong chains of reasons with throughout conclusions and low weight to weaker chains of reasoning
- Use mind maps (Buzan, 1995) and relevance trees (Hart, 1998: 152) as tools to organise and evaluate the relative usefulness (strengths) of the different camps and individual studies.

Methods to Avoid Bias

Reflect and consider on your evaluation. Look to see if you have introduced explicit or implicit bias into your evaluations. There are various methods you could use here. The Socratic Method and De Bono's *Six Thinking Hats* (www.debonogroup.com/6hats.htm) can be useful. The Socratic Method is based on systematic questioning of others and your own opinions and beliefs. For example, ask of your evaluations, what do I mean by? How did I come to that conclusion? Why do I believe that I am right? What is the source of my information? What assumption led to this conclusion? What happens if I am wrong? What sources disagree with me, why? Why is this significant? What is an alternate explanation for this phenomenon?

Edward De Bono claims that there are several types, orientations and approaches to thinking and that most people only use one or two. People, he claims, use what they have become used to (habitual). He advocates that we learn to use several approaches; in this way we could become much more effective thinkers. He asks us to think about problems using a range of 'hats' (different approaches). These hats are listed below:

- White hat (Blank sheet): Information and reports (*objective*)
- Red hat (Fire): Intuition, opinion and emotion (*subjective*)
- Yellow hat (Sun): Praise, positive aspects, (*objective*)
- Black hat (Judge's robe): Criticism, negative aspects, (*objective*)
- Green hat (Plant): Alternatives, new approaches and 'everything goes' (*speculative*)
- Blue hat (Sky): 'Big Picture,' 'Conductor hat,' 'Meta hat,' 'thinking about thinking' and overall process (*overview*).

Go beyond Factual Questions

The specific questions you will need answering by the literature will depend on your topic. But as a general guide Table 10.3 *A scheme for the systematic assessment of a literature* will give you an idea of what to look for. Adapt the contents of Table 10.3 to your own needs. The basic idea of having a list of questions is that you address the same questions to each study you select to look at. In this way you are building a degree of reliability to your evaluation. Questions like these can help you to refine your 'interrogation' technique; they will take you beyond the level of who said what and when to why they said what they did, in the way they did and what the implications are of what they said.

Managing Information

You will generate much more information that I can possibly warn you about. Research is an information-intensive activity. You will need, from the beginning, a system robust enough to cope with a range of documents, data and information. This includes a way not only of indexing (or categorising your documents) but retrieving what you need quickly. When you can't find

TABLE 10.3   A scheme for the systematic assessment of a literature

Areas for assessment	Amplification
Assessing the questions or hypotheses	What are the hypotheses or questions of the research? How well have these been expressed? Do they show any biases in the way they are expressed and have been tested? What variables or factors has the research identified for comparison or framing the problem? Are these adequate? What others could have been used and why?
Assessing the context of justification	How has context been defined or implied? What influence has this had on framing the hypothesis or problem? Have alternative ways of framing context been given or rejected? If not, what alternatives could you envision? Is the nature of the literature fully understood? Is this selective? How has it been used to formulate the context? Is the context based on a closed- or open-research design? What difference would an alternative make to the aims of the research and findings?
Assessing the methodology	Have the main methodological assumptions of the research tradition and approach been critically discussed? If not, what kinds of assumptions have been made about knowledge? In the design of the research, what is seen as valid data and why and how has this been obtained? Is the design coherent and a systematic application of the methodology?
Assessing awareness of alternatives	Are alternative methodological traditions and approaches acknowledged? What limitations are recognised to the methodology used? Has alternative data been identified? If not, what kinds of data can you find and what does this mean for the research? Is the data presented, whether statistical or textual, coherent and adequately presented? Are there alternative ways it could have been presented? If so, how might these have influenced what significance could be made of it?
Assessing the findings or results	Are the reported findings or results consistent in terms of collection methods and any statistical methods used? What inconsistencies are identified and how are these explained? If a hypothesis was used how has any significance been achieved? How are findings related to other studies? Are there any indications of selective presentation?
Assessing the conclusions and recommendations	What magnitude is given for the findings/results? What level of generalisation is being used? Is this justified by the data and research design? Is the conclusion based only on the results, as it should be? Or are other factors, including values, not introduced in the data? Is there a sense of critical evaluation of the findings or is the conclusion presented as self-evident? Are recommendations (where given) clear, consistent and properly formulated? Do they cite what findings they are based on? What other conclusions can you draw from the data?

Source: Dr Chris Hart, *Doing Your Masters Dissertation*, London: Sage, 2004: 175–176.

something you need, for example, an article that you are sure you have causes (as I'm sure you already know) unnecessary frustration and delay. You will need a lot of physical space, boxes and files and labels. I always recommend the use of a card index and hard-back note book (A4 size). On the cards keep information on your books, chapters and articles. Sub-divide the cards into sources based on the different aspects of the topic. Have a section for contacts. In the US the card index is often seen as an indispensable tool (they call them rolodex). In your book keep notes on where things have been put, what has been ordered from the library, ideas and notions, outline diagrams and the like. In terms of the 'blue hat' (see above for a definition) the whole thing involves the elements shown in Figure 10.4 (*The stuff research generates*).

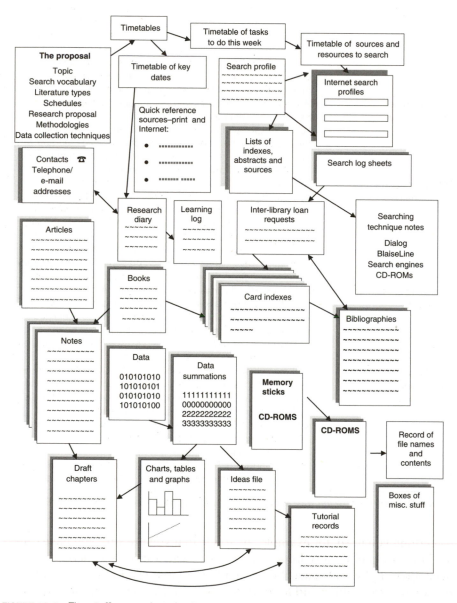

FIGURE 10.4   The stuff research generates

Ideas for Writing

An effective information management system will help you to put your hands on what you need when you need it. This can be useful if you are using your sources on a regular basis to write-up different aspects of the literature. With all types of research, at this stage, there are a number of ways you can begin to make sense of the literature. Mind maps have already been mentioned and no doubt you are familiar with these. From mind maps think about preparing documents on the following:

- *A chronological summary of the literature on your problem.* Using the results from your search of the citation indexes try constructing a history of the topic; ensuring you show the main landmarks (key studies)
- If there is a substantial amount of statistics try constructing meta-analysis
- *Develop your evaluation with similarity and differences tables.* List (possibly in chronological order) studies which show similar findings, have used similar concepts or been done using a common standpoint. Compare these with others, which are different
- *Using the key landmark studies on your topic identify the key critiques.* Produce matrixes of the critiques, identifying points of agreement and difference
- *Develop some diagrams on your topic.* Look at textbooks and at this book. See how diagrams have been employed in this book and others to clarify matters (or not as the case may be; you judge). They can also be an aid to structuring writing. Once you have a diagram, some matrixes and tables you can write about the content of these. Remember to use side headings to break up the text.

Developing Your Argument

Once you have analysed and evaluated the literature you will be at the stage where you need to think about constructing an outline structure for your own argument. This may be the structure that has reasons aligned to a particular hypothesis, proposition or debate over a theory. Achieving a coherent argument can be done by developing a clear chain of reasoning. This usually involves using an argumentative structure. Table 10.4 shows some of the basic templates for argumentative structure. For further examples and explanations see Hart 1998: 79–109 and www.mac.com/theorists/iWeb. Each can be adapted to a particular situation and elements from each combined. Your main need is to explain (rationalise) the need for your research; showing not only why it is needed but what gap in our existing knowledge your research will (hopefully) fill.

Think of each structure as a map to guide the arrangement you will use for writing different parts of your thesis (this is discussed further in Chapter 19). In the introductory chapter you may need to give an overview of your topic

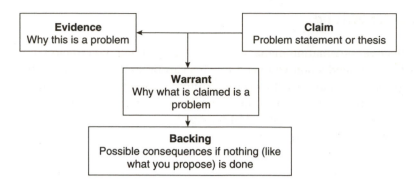

FIGURE 10.5   Structure for developing an argument

and why it should be considered important; a viable one for research at this level. You will be making a claim (statement) that this phenomenon needs to be researched. The reasons you give are the support for the claim. Whatever your claim is, you need to give reasons to support it. Think of reasons as evidence and data. Figure 10.5 adapted from Toulmin (1958) shows this suggestion.

Information from your evaluation of the literature is the main source of your evidence. Remember you can break down a claim (thesis statement) into a number of parts. For each part call upon different kinds of information from your literature including, statistics, data, methods used, definitions, concepts and so on. In an introductory chapter remember to be brief; you will expand on this chapter in subsequent ones, especially in chapters such as 'background' and the 'literature review'.

Uses of the Structures

The *problem awareness* structure is best suited to research that aims to explore a topic. This may be looking at the ways a phenomenon has been defined, how concepts have been applied – the aim being to show that there are alternative approaches. This kind of thesis would be 'methodological'. Your claim would be one of either 'concept' or 'interpretation'. The bulk of the thesis would be a review of existing publications on the phenomenon. The 'cause–effect' structure is best suited to research aiming to test relationships between independent and dependent variables, particularly hypothesis testing. This structure can also be used when looking at best practice and meta-data analysis. Your claim would be one of 'fact'. The possible solution structure is best used in policy and practice research. To propose an alternative method of intervention with a social problem (or other issues) existing approaches and policies need to be shown to have failed or not to have addressed all aspects. Once this has been done your own preferred option can be proposed, backed up by all necessary evidence. Your claim would be one of 'value' or of 'policy'.

You can in your problem statement (thesis statement) employ different kinds of claim (Hart, 1998: 90). If you were looking at the ways in which a phenomenon has been defined you may challenge the language used in the definition, the consequences of that language, the policies developed from the definition, the value of the policies and the facts invoked as evidence for the policies. You should have gathered by now that the structures in Table 10.4 are templates for you to develop. These structures are initial starting points from which you should develop multi-level argument(s).

This chapter has provided an introduction to the skills involved in searching and reviewing a literature. The skills you have been introduced to in searching and reviewing do not in themselves constitute a review of the literature; they are only tools. What you need, in order to apply these tools, is practice, creativity and tolerance. The latter refers to the scholastic practice of giving 'fair play' to the ideas of others – even when you have profound disagreements with the ideas of another.

We will leave you with a checklist to look for things that mark an effective search and review:

1   Shows a clear understanding of your topic
2   Includes all the key landmark studies
3   States honestly the arguments presented in the literature
4   Reaches conclusions which are justifiable
5   Shows the gap in knowledge your research intends to address.

If you can achieve all of these then you have produced a sound review of the literature for your research. Above all, you need to look at your review and be able to say with confidence and pride you have done a good job.

TABLE 10.4   Structures for constructing a rationalisation for your research

Problem awareness rationalisation	Cause and effect rationalisation	Possible solution rationalisation
Describe the character of a problem (or behaviour)	Establish the existence of behaviour (or problem)	Evaluate approaches to a situation (behaviour, problem)
• Give examples of its properties (prevalence, variables, locations, structure) • Develop a definition • Show the relevance of the problem for a situation, understanding or methodology • Explain the consequences if nothing is done • Recommend a course of action to examine the problem.	• Give examples of the behaviour • Define the behaviour, identifying key concepts • Propose potential independent variables as related to or as the cause • Provide evidence for preferred potential relationship between variables • Suggest an hypothesis for investigation.	• Outline the situation • Give examples of approaches already applied • Identify an aspect not addressed by existing approaches • Show why they have failed in this aspect • Identify relevant factors requiring action • Recommend an alternative approach to those already tried.

Conclusion: What to Do Next?

What to do next? The next task now that you have finished reading through this chapter is to get hold of some dissertations or theses in your general field of study. Your university librarian will show you how to do this. Look at how the literature reviews have been done in these dissertations. Look to identify the different kinds of structures employed to 'tell the story' of research on the topic. Use these dissertations as learning tools to help you produce your own dissertation.

References

Buzan, T. (1995) *The Mind Map Book* (2nd edn), London: BBC Books.

Fisher, A. (1988) *The Logic of Real Arguments*, Cambridge: Cambridge University Press.

Hart, C. (1998) *Doing a Literature Review: Releasing the Social Science Research Imagination*, London: Sage.

Hart, C. (2001) *Doing a Literature Search: A Comprehensive Guide for the Social Sciences*, London: Sage.

Hart, C. (2004) *Doing Your Masters Dissertation: Realizing Your Potential as a Social* Scientist, London: Sage.

Toulmin, S. (1958) *The Uses of Argument*, Cambridge: Cambridge University Press.

11 Research Ethics
Dr John R. Gibbins

Introduction

My approach to ethics derives from my experiences as a teacher, a researcher and a research manager in British universities. Teaching researchers how to manage research ethics became the crossroads of the many routes in my personal and intellectual development.

The first call for support came from a social service unit who wished to train social workers on good practice in investigatory procedures after the infamous Teesside child sex-abuse controversy, but which soon led into requests for support from a variety of professions from nursing, radiography, child support, public administration, business and the police.

This grounding in professional ethics has informed my whole approach, which, while being generic, is situational, reflexive and pragmatic. These engagements led me back to the academy from whence I came, how do ethics impinge on the university, how do we prepare academics as professionals to manage their own conduct? I have adopted the term 'ownership theory' to capture my approach, namely the idea that unless academics own the problems of their profession they will neither seek their solution nor own the procedures and processes that will lead to good practice.

Any historian of research in the future looking at the question of, 'how professional research was structured and organised in the twenty-first century?' could do no better than explore the Roberts agenda for generic skills development and the ideals it embeds (Roberts; RCUK). Along with the *Joint Skills Statement* of the Research Councils UK (Appendix 2) we have a clear understanding of what is best practice, what are the ideals, and the expectations of researchers in their professional practices. Amongst these skills are those concerning values and behaviour, which are considered as essential and necessary for each and every researcher, unit, centre and university.

But why is ethics so central to professional research at this time? Why should professionals be ethical? How can ethics be engendered, managed and implemented in research institutes? This chapter will deal briefly with these and other related questions with a view to guiding researchers in good practice for research ethics.

All professionals need to be informed and open to reviews and challenges from all sources, be open to public scrutiny, transparent in their proceedings and ever willing to adapt to legitimate concerns.

Framing the Problems: Professionalism and Ownership

There are many ways to approach research ethics but the one chosen in this chapter has two elements: the professionalism and ownership. Rather than explaining and justifying research ethics in terms of specific disciplines, theories, and governance of disciplines and fields by governing bodies, here it is better to look at professional life as a whole as the appropriate context and explore what researchers need to achieve if they are to be respected as a profession equivalent to medicine, law, accountancy or public service.

Here we can follow the core definitions of professionalism by such classical authors as Durkheim, Macdonald, Beauchamp and Childress, Koehn and Bayles (Bayles, 1981; Beauchamp and Childress, 2001; Durkheim, 1983; Koehn, 1994; Macdonald, 1995). The core criteria and expectations are having the external permission and respect to be self-managed and autonomous in exchange for diligence in performance, acceptance of the norms of a professional body, accountability and self-imposed exercise of the values and ethics agreed by the profession. From this researchers are to gather that if they desire professional autonomy and respect, they need to be diligent in performance, update themselves on the norms of their respective governing bodies and councils, they must be willing to engage policy, procedures and governance from their institution, and own the ethics of their professional group, institution and colleagues.

Ownership is a necessary corollary of being a professional, it is entailed in what it is to be a contemporary researcher. By ownership I mean the acceptance of all parties to a research project or projects, that it is *their* personal responsibility to develop themselves, so that they can play a full role in the management of their own and colleagues' research. The key tenets of ownership theory are that (1) things that are owned (individually or collectively) are valued more highly and cared for better, (2) where the ethics of a project are owned by all parties they are more likely to be diligent and to self-regulate, and (3) best practice is achieved by professional's own self-regulation.

This approach is gaining increased credence amongst Research Councils such as the *Economic and Social Research Council* (ESRC) whose main intention to ensure governance while reducing, as far as is possible, the burden of bureaucracy, instruction and policing (ESRC, 2005). The main device for such ownership is to download ethical decision making to peers as close to the research practice and project as possible, and to train all stakeholders in ethical decision across complex decision- making frameworks (Gibbins, 2006: 21–22; Larsons, 1977: 66–74). The added value of such a policy for institutions is that as the researchers own their own ethics, they are more willing to exercise that policy in practice. So in brief my guidance to any research body would be to look at the following:

- The Organisation should have a set of Ethics and Values built into its Mission Statement, Policy and Procedures
- Ethical decision making be devolved, so far as is possible, to researchers
- It should be open to external scrutiny
- That institutions should support their researchers through the provision of training and development activities appropriate to role; provision of policies, procedures, committees and management, dovetailed to support (and not hinder) researcher implementation.

Theories of Research Ethics

But professional ethics has always had its critics, and for professional ownership to work researchers need to avoid the pitfalls these critics perceive. Feminist researchers for instance fear that patriarchy means that men will impose their governance over a large cohort of poorly paid and temporarily contracted female researchers and subjects (Witz, 1992); Marxists fear research ethics is just another bourgeois ideology to support the fabric of class-exploitatory research (Macdonald, 1995: 36–65); post-colonialists fear that the new ethics procedures are an aspect of imperialist plots to prevent the colonised from seeking to know what their former masters have gained; while Foucauldians witness the flowering of new governance policies and procedures designed by the powerful to normalise research in the interests of ever-changing power networks (Foucault 1977, 1980). However, the current incoming tide in favour of research governance is promoted by theoretical forces of equal persuasion.

The custodians of professional bodies stress the need for the development of organic discipline cultures and shared norms in research to prevent the worst aspects of nihilism and amoralism, which reflects the alienation and anomie experienced by many researchers; while activists and reformers stress revitalised ethical debate and pluralism as the best antidote to the most pernicious forms of contemporary conservatism and governance. So why and how should we manage research ethics today?

Why Be Ethical?

Essentially the contemporary researchers find themselves having to balance and manage the legitimate interests, concerns and demands of the following parties: the *subjects* of research whether human, animal or natural (leaving the divine to take care of themselves); the *researcher* who wishes to explore and investigate a subject; the *sponsors* who are willing to pay; the *host* institution who provide the local context for the operation; various *professional bodies* who regulate and oversee research in a particular discipline or field; the *public* who are the support for much research and who are often the beneficiaries.

Each of these parties to research has perfectly legitimate interests, rights (entitlements); and responsibilities to reduce risks to the other parties from the conduct of the research. But these interests, right and responsibilities come into conflict and hence either governance procedures or the researcher are left with the difficult diplomacy of negotiating a suitable research protocol of each project. The first reason why we need research ethics is to unpack the various issues, tensions and options to assist the process to completion. Another reason is to make sure that no single party to the research process achieves domination leaving the interests of the others marginalised or excluded.

The largest threats today come from the sponsors and the professional bodies, such as the National Health System; having responded to public anxieties raised by the media, these bodies are managing risk reduction for subjects by adopting top-heavy forms of governance that reduce the rights of researchers and host institutions in their legitimate role as protectors of the public.

But there are other good reasons why professional researchers should be ethical for the researcher must not only be ethical but also have a fear of discipline or recompense through penalties and sanctions. If every party with a legitimate stake in a project's success has its interests protected and promoted the best outcome maximisation seems to be guaranteed.

Next, it is an accepted generalisation that most actors would prefer to work on and with a practice that they feel is ethical, to work on or with a project that risks damage to parties can result in parties feeling disturbed, guilty and half-hearted as a result. Most researchers, like the public, would prefer to know whether what they were doing was right, and more, whether what they were doing was perceived by others to be right.

Finally, many researchers have worked out the politics of the contemporary global market in research, which dictates that unless you regulate yourself by ethics, others may regulate you via some form of national or international governance.

Existing international codes, such as Helsinki, Bologna, take the form of guidance and exhortation and generally lack regulatory force. In other words, the strongest case for research ethics today is that it supports both responsible governance and the model of the researcher as autonomous, self-regulating professional. However, the alternative model of powerful regulatory governance, of a line-managed, de-professionalised researcher subject to external governance, hovers over and around contemporary research communities.

There are many reasons for knowing the boundaries and being ethical in research, which tend to mirror the answers proffered by philosophers in the field. The first group, generally known as utilitarians, stresses consequences and wishes to ensure best outcomes by managing out risks and managing in efficiency, effectiveness, fairness and welfare. The second group, generally known as deontologists, wishes to focus on doing the right thing whatever the harms and costs or beneficial outcomes. A third group, generally known as virtue ethicists, stresses that the best way to ensure best practice is to teach, generate and maintain a culture of good practice and beneficence in researcher and the researched, and institution.

Ethics and Governance

If the choice today is reduced, crudely perhaps, to a binary, it is between a *professional ethical* and a *governance* model for researcher management. But first we should be clear with our terms (Gibbins, 2006: 21).

By ethics in this context we generally mean not a discipline, but a self-regulating practice of shaping one's behaviour and actions, around some preconceived principles, rules or theories of what we ought to do rather than what we have done, do and might prefer to do.

By governance we mean a set of practices, internal but emanating from the external, which oversee and regulate thought and behaviour through complex mechanisms of surveillance, discipline (normalisation) and control. The first is represented most effectively in a wide variety of codes, mission statements and researcher development courses on offer such as the CIHE Ethics Matters programme; UKCGE workshops on Research Ethics for Research Managers and Supervisors and many self-regulating policies and procedures in such diverse institutions as Kings College, London and Teesside University.

The governance model is best exemplified by the numerous policies, procedures and enforcement agencies proliferating around the British NHS; by such documents as 'Good Governance: A Code for the Voluntary Community Sector' at the other extreme (www.governancehub.org.uk). One governing body at least has managed a clever and effective balancing act between the two competing options, through the devices of central agenda setting and guidance, twinned with the requirement that local bodies devise their own protocols for meeting the central requirements.

The policies of the *Economic and Social Research Council* in Britain might be a useful guide to aspiring researchers and research bodies on how to get it right (www.esrcsocietytoday.ac.uk/ESRCInfoCentre/opportunities/research_ethics_framework/). The main reasons for preferring the ethical to the governance model for researchers are legion: it allows more personal and local autonomy; it provides a greater chance for innovative local protocols to develop, it is less bureaucratic; and less burdensome on time and money in operation. However, when human lives are at risk, as they are with medicine and many other public services, it is unsurprising that when local bodies have mismanaged, that government has intervened to manage risk reduction by central enforcement.

It is a necessary warning to all researchers that, unless they gain awareness, training, transparency in their work, and effectively regulate themselves ethically, they run the risk of central bodies regulating them further. During the last ten years there has been a shift in public opinion from paternalism towards autonomy in ethical thinking that has accompanied media coverage of several high-profile lapses within research communities, around organ removal and storage, covert research and treatment trials. These that have led to scandals in Britain have invited more interventionist governance regimes into the academy, and which have to be managed out via ethics, if professionalism is to be protected. How can the professional model be embedded? What do we need to do to allow us researchers to be ethical?

The Ethical Aims of Your Research

The answer to how we can embed good ethical practice into institutions was outlined in my online units for the CIHE and should be consulted there (Gibbins, 2006). Here I will unpack the requirements for the professional researcher and research institution. Using my reasons for research and my theories of research ethics above we might deduce that there are four aims/requirements that you should set:

- Competence and virtue – have I ensured that I am competent to conduct the research in a professional and ethical manner consistent with the values and needs of my own and other stakeholder communities?
- Effect, beneficence and non-maleficence – does the research activity and process produce more good than harm? How can we manage the project to produce the most favourable outcomes with risk and harm reduced to the minimum?
- Right, rights and duty – is the research project conducted rightly in a fair, just and respectful manner for the rights and needs of others and duties to them?
- Support and recompense – are we able and willing to offer an aftercare support and remedial help service to subjects that are damaged and to recompense any damaged party for any harm experienced?
- Has my project been subjected to external review?

Duties of Care

Each of these aims imposes a *duty of care* on you and other stakeholders as follows:

- *Competence and virtue.* Ensure that you have engaged the appropriate development activities to perform effectively in your field of research, including theory and methods, and in the generic wider field (identified in the Roberts and JSS Skills Agendas above and below). Engage with the professional body or bodies in your discipline or fields in your institution, region, national or international community, and acquaint, engage with their ethical codes and procedures. Seek to become a professional who shares the missions, cultures, rules and values of each community. Ensure you have appropriate professional peer review and supervision for your work. Ensure that you are trustworthy, honest, open, respectful and caring.

- *Effect, beneficence and non-maleficence.* Ensure that your choice of field, research design, methods for data collection and analysis, and form and mode of publication are informed by considerations of potential harms and benefits. Conduct a risk-assessment and health and safety audit to ensure risks are reduced to a minimum and beneficial outcomes managed for. Ensure before you engage fieldwork that you have negotiated ownership of the project and its outputs; have agreed shares in any profits or income in every form and that you have an adequate accounting and management scheme for the project.

- *Right, rights and duty.* At the most general level operate with the Kantian principle that you should not consider doing to others what you would not consider right and appropriate conduct if applied to yourself. For example, if you would not wish to be the subject of a medical, psychological, socio-logical or artistic experiment or test without your consent, then do not apply these to others. Try some empathy: have you placed yourself in the position of each other party to the project and considered how you would wish to be treated by them? At a particular level draft an inventory of the right claimable by and duties owed to each party to a project, prioritise these in rank order and compute a protocol that produces the most balanced and morally defensible final agreement. At the legal level have you considered the national and international legal context for your research, including such new legislation as the Mental Capacity Act fully in force in 2007.

- *Support and recompense.* Have you ensured that all stakeholders have given informed consent for the project that you intend to conduct? Is there complete transparency in the methods and intentions and beneficiaries? Have you ensured that you and the project are covered by indemnity insurance? Make sure that you have an aftercare service in place that can offer guidance, support and restorative interventions if unforeseen harms arise in and after the project is completed?

Ethical Agenda for Research

If the above is a check list of guidance on how to achieve best practice, the information below is a set of principles and of areas to which these should be applied, though each project will require a different agenda and resulting protocol contingent upon discipline, field, theory, method and other factors.

AN ETHICAL AGENDA FOR RESEARCH

Rights. Consideration of what each party to a project are entitled to from each other party, but you especially. Stipulations of the various Human Rights Acts (1998) and Data Protection legislations

Duties and responsibilities. Considerations of what you owe to each other party in the project, including the general duties of care and diligence. The ethical management of expectations and fears of all parties

Legality. Considerations of legal obligations under a variety of legal frameworks, plus consideration of protocol where these come into conflict

Justice and fairness. Considerations of who deserves what in the distribution of burdens in the conduct of the research and allocation of the benefits accruing

Discrimination and neutrality. Consideration of appropriate attitude towards each party, issues of whether you are appropriately partial to a group, should be impartial or are entitled to positively discriminate. Issues of whether you should be neutral or participatory in the conduct of the research and with its findings

Freedom and confidentiality. Consideration of the balance between your right and the rights of users to investigate and know, versus considerations of privacy, confidentiality and corporate interest in intellectual property

Openness and transparency. Considerations of prior information provided to all parties, the honest and openness of information provided, the transparency of intention, benefits, risks, benefits and potentialities, informed consent and considerations of the mental capacity of subjects to consent

Ownership and plagiarism. Considerations of who owns the project, the resources including staff, who owns the risks, the data and intellectual property most widely. Who will disseminate the results and how? Who will accrue commercial benefits and how? Considerations of acknowledgements, recognition and permissions to use resources owned by others (e.g. software systems, data sets), plus legal protections and copyrights to protect the projects assets

Resources, finance and payments. Considerations of the ethical propriety of funding sources and sponsorship, the management of the income, expenditure, expenses and profits

Techniques, methods and equipment. Consideration of the appropriateness of the methods and techniques used in the project, in the training to use methods and techniques and the safety and maintenance of equipment

Monitoring, supervision and audit. Considerations of how the project will be overseen, progress monitored, staff and data collection overseen, and how the project will be managed and audited against objectives and the results posted. Considerations of the duty of all parties to attain prior ethical approval, risk assessment, insurance and ethical consent from the appropriate local (Local Research Ethics Committee), regional, national or international approving body

Whistle blowing and discipline where research discovers bad practice. Considerations of the rights of parties to the project to inform others of their concerns, and have their concerns taken seriously, throughout the project. Considerations of the rights of parties to make known their concerns to an appropriate higher authority, if concerns raised by them are not dealt with satisfactorily.

Protocols and Project Proposals

Ethics is always harder to practice than to preach and the operationalisation of my guidance above will throw up a variety of expected and unexpected conflicts and tensions as I argue in my essay 'In the Field' (Gibbins, 2004; Oliver, 2003: 45–61). It is to be expected that you will encounter incommensurable tensions between: the rights and expectations of each party; recognition and ownership of respective duties and burdens; levels of ownership; direction of travel; interpretations of data; levels of financial support and recompense; the trade-off between risks and benefits; acknowledgements and plagiarisms.

In the practice of a project unexpected issues may arise: such as the discovery of adverse effects of the techniques used; withdrawal of subjects or sponsors, or loss of access to data, expertise or equipment. It is for these reasons that we should argue for and expect that the managers of ethics, usually Ethics Committees, should be willing and able to provide on going support and guidance as well as initial Ethical Approval.

Ethics Advisors are as important as Ethics Committees and Ethics Training in the achievement of good practice, and you should locate the best sources of advice locally and nationally before you begin any project and consult with them as and when issues arise. An essay on best practice with Ethics Committees is presently being prepared for the *Issues in Postgraduate Supervision* series published for the SRHE and the readers should consult that, and the CIHE files for assistance and guidance on the best forms of structure and best practice in negotiating Ethical Approval (Oliver, 2003: 26–44).

Best practice suggests that Ethical Approval should be sought and provided as close to the location and subject field as is possible, and that while central Committees are essential for provision and oversight of policy making and guidance, that management should be devolved as far as is possible to local sub-committees. However well- organised locally, tension and overlaps of authority will exist in each area, and it is important for you to establish who does what, and in what order, before engaging the approval process.

Trust and openness between all parties is essential for good practice to flourish and be effective, so sharing doubts and fears with colleagues and experts is to be encouraged. Consulting the advice and guidance of each approving body before embarking on the approval process is essential if you are not to waste every parties time, and the *Association of Research Ethics Committees* and Kings College, London offer useful advice and exemplars on their website (AREC; KCL).

If you are an overseas researcher, it is vital to access and meet the requirements of both your home and host communities and bodies. In all cases you need to follow the rules provided and keep to the timetables diligently.

Questions to you should be answered promptly and all parties consulted where major changes to the proposal and protocol change as a result to the approval process. It is vital to make collectively owned proposals, properly supported with requested support materials so that your proposal has the highest chance of success. You can take comfort from the knowledge that committees are in the business of progressing research as well as promoting good practice and that they wish and will support your success. Working through case studies, whether real or hypothetical, with colleagues is a tried and tested way to improve your awareness, proficiency and practice.

Conclusion

I started with several problems, about which advice and guidance have been given. Ethics is entailed in what it is to be a professional researcher – it is a part of what it is to be professional and to be a professional. Its high profile today is more to do with professionalism than a current response to the media focus on high-profile cases of mismanagement, and large restitutive legal awards against research institutions. We should be ethical because that is a part of what it is to be a professional, as well as the fear of loss of professional status if we fail to be ethical and diligent in our practices.

Ethics can best be engendered, managed and implemented in research institutes where there is a genuine academy and community of knowers, supported and respected for their professionalism. Ethics rarely flowers and flourishes in a heavily regulated governance context, where surveillance, discipline and control counter and extrude professional self-regulation. Flourishing requires a sensible blend of the following: effective committees; promoting authoritative and widely supported and informed policies and procedures; amongst colleagues who are developed and fit for purpose; sharing a common cause to promote high-quality research; a shared duty of care (National Research Ethics Service, 2007).

Acknowledgements

Many of the ideas and prescriptions found above developed in the practices of preparing, operating and reviewing the provision of training and development courses for a number of institutions. These include the Universities of Teesside, Newcastle Northumbria and York; the UK Council for Graduate Education (UKCGE); UK GRAD; Society for Research into Higher Education (SRHE); and the Council for Industry and Higher Education (CIHE). While it is impossible to name all those who have conversed with me on ethics for research I would like to recognise in particularly the influences of Kathy Ludlow, Colin Chandler, Jan Deckers and Tony Fell.

Bibliography

Association of Research Ethics Committees (AREC) www.arec.org.uk (accessed 7 October 2007)

Bayles, Michael D. (1981) *Professional Ethics,* Belmont, CA: Wadsworth

Beauchamp, T.L. and Childress, J.F. (2001) *Principles of Bio-medical Ethics*, Oxford: Oxford University Press

Durkheim, Emile (1983) *Professional Ethics and Civil Morals*, Glencoe: Greenwood

ESRC Research Ethics Framework (REF) (2005) www.esrc.ac.uk/ESRCInfoCentre/Images/ESRC_Re_Ethics_Frame_tcm6–11291.pdf (accessed 5 October 2007)

Foucault, Michel (1977) *Discipline and Punish: The Birth of the Prison*, Harmondsworth: Penguin

Foucault, Michel (1980) *Power/Knowledge*, Brighton: Harvester Press

Gibbins, John (2004) '"In the Field and In There": Some Ethical Dilemmas in Researching Sexualities', in *Sexual Consent*, ed. M. Cowling and P. Reynolds, London: Willans Press

Gibbins, John (2006), 'Ethics for Higher Education – Training and Development, Part Two – A case study: Training stakeholders for research ethics', Council for Industry and Higher Education, London:

Kings College, London www.kcl.ac.uk/schools/law/research/cmle/

Koehn, David (1994) *The Ground of Professional Ethics*, London: Routledge

Larsons, M.S. (1977) *The Rise of Professionalism: A Sociological Analysis*, Berkeley, CA: University of California Press

Macdonald, Keith M. (1995) *The Sociology of the Professions*, London: Sage

National Research Ethics Service (NRES) (2007) www.nres.npsa.nhs.uk/ (accessed 7 October 2007)

Oliver, Paul (2003) *The Student's Guide to Research Ethics*, Maidenhead: Open University Press

Research Councils UK Joint Skills Statement www.grad.ac.uk/jss/ (and in Appendix 2) (accessed 1 October 2007)

Roberts Agenda www.grad.ac.uk/roberts/ (accessed 1 October 2007)

Witz, Anne (1992) *Professions and Patriarchy*, London: Routledge

12 Getting Started with Writing

Dr Rowena Murray

Introduction: Why Write in the Early Stages?

Anyone who is accepted for a research degree programme has demonstrated much more than basic competence in academic writing. However, it is a premise of this chapter that you can develop your academic writing further in the course of writing your thesis. More controversially for some, another aim is to show how you can learn about your research through writing.

Clearly, you will not write your thesis in the same way as you wrote undergraduate assignments. How the differences between undergraduate and postgraduate writing are defined may depend on your discipline of study or may be determined by the type of research you are doing, or your supervisors may define them for you. There is plenty of room for confusion, or, to look at it positively – and proactively – this is a subject for creative, problem-solving discussions with your supervisors about thesis writing. These discussions will help you to start writing at an early stage. Even if you have done no writing about your research so far, and are not sure what to write about, this chapter will help you start.

'Writing in the early stages' will seem an odd concept to those who see writing as something to do *after* research is completed, but there are two main reasons for writing earlier. The first is that, like the conference presentation or the journal article, writing is one way to test your work. At this level, at this stage, only when you get feedback will you be sure that you have made progress. The second is that, like other kinds of experiment, you can try things out in writing. You can experiment with writing using the prompts in boxes and checklists in this chapter. Research involves thinking creatively, and some of that thinking occurs as you write.

Using writing to develop, and not just to document, your work, constitutes a radical switch in the role of writing for students in some disciplines, but your role as researcher requires much more than simply 'documentation'. You have to break new ground, and to do that you need new strategies for writing, as in other aspects of research. This chapter introduces strategies that, while they might seem odd at first glance, have helped research students in the early stages and are therefore worth trying.

The purpose of this chapter is not to tell you how to write a thesis – a subject covered elsewhere (Murray, 2006; Chapter 19 in this book) – but to get you thinking about your writing, right from the start, in a strategic way. This is not to say that you should 'just get on with writing', which some may tell you to do (or may be something you tell yourself). Instead, this chapter will prompt you to think carefully about the writing you do, to ask questions about it, till you understand exactly what is expected of you, and, more importantly, to find out how the writing you do during your first year will be evaluated.

Start thinking about the stages you foresee, not only in your research and writing, but also in your learning, since writing a thesis is, in many ways, a learning process. You can start with two questions – what are the stages in this learning process, and how can each stage be represented in specific writing tasks that you will do?

When the stakes are high, as they generally are for thesis writers, you may feel under pressure. This can mean that even when you do know what is expected of you, you are anxious about writing. It is difficult to see how you can completely resolve this anxiety. What you can do, however, is develop strategies for planning your writing, checking expectations with your supervisors as you go along, so that you become relatively secure that what you deliver is appropriate and that progress in your research, however gradual, is apparent in your writing.

This is not to say that starting a thesis is inherently problematic. Instead, this chapter shows how you can take a problem-solving approach to thesis writing. The key message, and this may be one of the main differences between undergraduate and postgraduate study, is that you should write often and in different forms.

More specifically, this chapter covers three topics designed to help you start. The first section covers forms of writing, including topics you can write about now. The second deals with issues raised by the audiences for your writing, in order to help you define your task further. The third deals with the potential purposes of early-stage writing, including a range of options for specific writing tasks you can start now. The sooner you write, the sooner you can get feedback on your writing and your research.

Forms of Writing

At the start of a research project many students feel least ready to write, and many have quite clear reasons for not writing:

- Not knowing enough to do any writing
- Not being confident about what they do know
- Becoming even more anxious about their knowledge as they read more
- Feeling that it is too early to write with authority

- Worrying that writing without authority is too weak
- Assuming that it's inappropriate for them to define their writing tasks for themselves.

Some of these barriers arguably have their origin in how new research students position themselves – or how others position, or appear to position, them. Or there may be a lack of understanding of the role of writing in a research project of this scale, and, if you are new to this level of study, it is to be expected that you do not yet fully understand the expectations, even when they have been articulated for you.

Whatever their origins, each of these problems requires you to develop a solution, probably in the course of several drafts of, to take the example of 'writing with authority', your literature review (Chapter 10). It is highly unlikely that you will find an immediate solution to this problem, since you are still developing your understanding of the literature. Nor should you put off till later, till you know more, the process of writing about the literature, since it is through writing about it that you will assimilate and test your knowledge. Even if you do not have a 'review of literature' chapter or phase in your thesis, these principles apply: you can learn about your subject through writing.

As you start to think about writing you can do now, you should probably have a general understanding of the whole thesis-writing process. Then you can think ahead, from time to time, to the form, structure and style that your thesis will ultimately take (Murray, 2006; Chapter 19 in this book). This can be quite creative, as you consider different possibilities. Once you have an overview, you can relate the early stages in your writing to other, later stages. The overview helps you to think ahead, in writing, as in other aspects of research. It may be that you will be writing chapters from the start, or in some other form.

FORMS OF EARLY WRITING LEADING TO THE DEVELOPMENT OF A THESIS

A 'Paper' (not for journal publication)
Paper for journal/conference
A specific type of paper, such as literature review
Work-in-progress paper or progress report
A report/record of your work to date
A record of your achievements, measured against your objectives, to date
Paper developing/revising/updating your proposal
Outline of thesis
Outline of chapter
Summary of your argument
Descriptive account of your method/approach/critical framework
Mini-argument providing rationale for your method/methodology
Introduction to your thesis
Thesis chapter – first draft.

Each of the forms of writing listed above can be defined in more detail. For example, if you are asked to 'write a paper', what exactly does that mean? Does it mean a paper for a journal or a paper that is just for your supervisors to read? Writing a journal article is a good way of testing your work, receiving peer review and developing your understanding.

If you are intending to write a journal article, consider the questions of audience and purpose dealt with later in this chapter – they are usually very different for thesis and journal article. Seek advice about how to develop paper. For example, some students think they should write a paper, then try to find a 'home' for it, when, arguably, it is better to analyse potential journals and shape your paper to suit, while still saying what you want to say, as far as possible (Murray, 2005).

These are writing tasks that you can do now. Think about which seem more relevant, appropriate or useful to you at this stage. Discuss these options with your supervisors. Define each form further. Set limits to scale, scope, length, content, etc. Agree an output. Set a deadline. Think about what the stages might be in meeting that deadline: outlining, discussing, drafting and revising?

If you are unsure of how to produce any of the above forms of writing, ask your supervisors for clarification. Find out what is expected of you. The box below provides some straightforward prompts to help you initiate such discussions.

DISCUSSING THE FORM OF WRITING

How long is this paper [for your supervisors] to be?
I could write a 10-page paper on ... including ...
I'd find it useful to write a short 1000-word paper on ...

Which topics would you like me to cover?
I'd like to write about three topics ...
I'd like to use this writing to develop my ideas about ...
I'm not sure about ... yet, and want to write about that to see what you think.

For example, should I cover some of the literature I've been reading lately?
For example, I could cover the literature on ... and the work of ...

I could summarise the reading I've done recently and show how it has sharpened the focus of my study. Would that be appropriate?

How much should I write on what I've done already and what I plan next?
I think five pages on taking stock and five on the next steps – do you agree?

You may also, at this early stage, be getting a feel for your supervisors' styles. For example, do they respond better to questions asking for guidance or instruction or seem more comfortable when you make suggestions and check for agreement?

As you consider your options, note that sometimes a shorter paper can, paradoxically, be more challenging to write. This can be more useful, since it prompts you to find a focus early on: it makes you decide what is really important, and lets you cut what is not. In longer papers, you can include everything, and sometimes focus is lost, both for you and your reader, potentially for your writing and for your research. The most difficult papers I ever wrote were 500-words long, for a graduate-level seminar. That was when I learned most about academic writing.

Whatever form of writing you are asked to do – whether it's 500 words or 5000 words or more – require further definition.

DEFINING WRITING TASKS: A CHECKLIST

 1 What is the purpose of your writing task?
 2 What should you include?
 3 What can you leave out?
 4 How long should it be?
 5 At what point will you start to write chapters/sections?
 6 What form will they take then?
 7 What types of chapters/sections?
 8 What type(s) of thesis are appropriate for your research?
 9 What are your options?
10 What is not optional?

Be ready to make a case for your approach – writing is quite an individual thing. If one approach helps you get started, or if another does not help, it is up to you to find ways of articulating your view and address the problem. It may be that thesis writers and supervisors, who in some instances do not, at the early stage, know each other very well, do not share a common set of understandings or a common language for talking about writing. This may take time to develop; another reason for you to initiate this discussion early.

In spite of all this encouragement to write early and often, you may still feel that it is too early to do any serious writing. Research students often say that they don't know what to write about (Murray, 2006). Some students have found the following framework below, from *How to Write a Thesis*, useful in outlining a paper early in their research.

WHAT CAN I WRITE ABOUT? THE CONTEXT/BACKGROUND

My research question is … (50 words)
Researchers who have looked at this subject are … (50 words)
They argue that … (25 words)
Smith argues that … (25 words)
Brown argues that … (25 words)
Debate centres on the issue of … (25 words)
There is still work to be done on … (25 words)
My research is closest to that of X in that … (50 words)
My contribution will be … (50 words)
Murray, R. (2006) *How to Write a Thesis*, 2nd edition, pp. 104–105.

This is a writing task that you can do now. It may also be one that is worth repeating, as your research progresses. Presenting this type of short paper to your supervisors allows you to get feedback on the 'big picture' of your research at various stages. This is an important aspect of thesis writing, as the 'big picture' will clearly shape how you write sections and chapters. Other useful prompts for writing are provided in Chapter 19.

Audience

This section explores the issue of audience for your writing. Because it influences what you write and how you write, it is important to develop a sense of audience when you write.

Who are you writing for? In the context of undergraduate writing, this question often seems irrelevant to students. The audience you wrote for then was obviously a tutor or lecturer. For postgraduate writing, however, the audience is more complex. Initially, you may see the immediate audience for your writing as your supervisors, but there are others: the Internal Examiner, the External Examiner, and the research community.

In addition, even when you are writing for one or two people – your supervisors – it is not always as straightforward as it seems, since supervisors play several roles during a research project. These roles can be as different as 'enabling' and 'evaluating'. For example, at one point your supervisors may simply prompt you to 'write something', but later they may use your writing to determine whether or not your work is up to standard.

As you prepare to write, you will be influenced by how your immediate audience – your supervisors – position themselves: how do they represent themselves as your audience? How do they describe the kind of reading they will give your writing? These various roles are shown below.

THINKING ABOUT YOUR AUDIENCE – DEFINING YOUR SUPERVISORS' ROLE AS READERS

As an 'interested reader'?
As your mentor in the subject?
As your teacher?
As your writing and/or research 'coach'?
As an expert in the area/specific subject of your research?
As manager of your research project?
As marker/assessor?
As editor?
As two or more of the above?

You can probably see that each of these roles will make specific demands on your writing. This is how your audience influences your writing directly. That is not to say that you should interrogate your supervisors as to their roles, but it does imply that it would be reasonable, and sensible, to discuss their expectations of your writing and the kind of readings they intend to give it, and to do this as you prepare to write. Since their answers to these questions are likely to vary over time, you may have this discussion several times.

In addition, check if there is an 'early warning system' in your university, a process whereby departments weed out new researchers whom they judge, on the basis of performance in the early stages as unlikely to meet the required standard and unable to complete the research project or thesis. Your supervisors will probably base this assessment on your performance in early writing, talking and research tasks. That is why it is so important that you find out whether, for any early writing you do, your supervisors will be reading as assessors, or as 'interested readers' or in other roles.

In practice, you may find – or you may feel, in spite of what you are told – that everything you write for your supervisors 'counts' in some way as a measure of your performance and/or progress, and this may, of course, be true. However, you may meet people who disagree with this interpretation. You may hear it said that free expression of ideas, in writing, is an essential component of research and/or a valuable means of developing your thinking in the early stages.

To complicate matters further, expectations may shift, explicitly or implicitly. Your audience's expectations can shift between the point at which you agreed a definition of a specific writing task and the point at which your supervisors read your writing. This is not because your supervisors are trying to confuse or trick you; it may be because their thinking has moved on since the writing task was agreed. This too merits discussion, if it happens.

This is a powerful reminder of the value – to both writer and audience – of a written record of what you are asked to write and, more importantly, of explicitly stating it at the start of your text, or in a separate note, or on a separate page, before your text. In many contexts this is considered good writing practice, and it seems sensible to adopt it as you get started. It means that your audience's role is not simply assumed, but is built into your text. It can also be a useful reminder for your supervisors.

Purpose

Like the question of audience, the question of purpose – why are you writing, what are you intending to achieve in your writing? – seems irrelevant in the context of undergraduate studies, but it is more relevant, and more complex, for thesis writers.

More specifically, as you start your research, what are the purposes of the different pieces you are asked to write, in order to 'get you started'? Is it likely that they will all have the same purpose? Is it not more likely that different writing tasks will have different purposes? The box below suggests common purposes for your writing.

DEFINING THE PURPOSES OF WRITING TASKS

To document your reading
To demonstrate your developing understanding
To identify gaps in your understanding and/or reading
To develop your ideas
To describe the relationship between your ideas and others'
To describe the distinction between your work and others'
To define the rationale for your work
To propose a course of reading/research/actions
To raise questions for analysis and discussion
To give you something to talk about at supervision meetings.

Many of these are appropriate purposes for early writing. You can do these now. Match your chosen purpose with one of the 'forms of writing' suggested in the previous section.

Once you have established the purpose of a specific piece of writing, reveal it to your reader. For example, thesis writers often find it useful to think about the purpose of their writing in terms of some of the verbs as shown below.

SIGNALLING PURPOSE AT THE START OF YOUR WRITING

The purpose of this paper is to	explore ...
	report on ...
	assess the ...
	comment on ...
	critique ...
	integrate ...
	compare and contrast ...
	show progress since ...
	make a case for ...
The purpose of this chapter is to ...	
The purpose of this section is to ...	

This box shows how you can define the main purpose of your writing, while also defining its form. You can, of course, define the purposes of sections in your writing – also in the form of verbs. This approach helps you to make explicit – for yourself and your audience – what you aim to do in each piece and each section. This makes your writing, and its logic, more overt and potentially easier to follow. It can also make it easier to write, since your thinking may be more focused once you have decided on purpose and form.

You can also state, in verbs, what your writing will *not* do, in order to strengthen the case for what you decided to write about, showing that you were aware of other approaches or topics and dismissed them for sound reasons.

If you feel that this makes your writing too direct, you can modulate these verbs with, for example, a signal that the writing marks an early stage: 'The purpose of this paper is to *begin to* integrate … .' You may not want to be as tentative in everything you write, but this modulation may, in fact, be more accurate; if your work is at an early stage, it is appropriate to signal that explicitly in your writing. Moreover, this ensures that you will not overstate your achievements at this early stage. There are many ways of modulating your writing – many of which you will have noted in your reading.

As your research and thinking progress, you can begin to make explicit the difference between stronger statements, when you write about work you did some time ago, for example, and writing that is still tentative, when you deal with your more recent or proposed work, for example.

In fact, you may find that you want to modulate your writing much of the time, in many other ways, or your supervisors may encourage you to do so. This is often about learning how to write in a debate – which is what you are doing by writing a thesis – taking account of the fact that you have to evidence what you write, either in your research or with reference to others', and where evidence is contingent, assertions are modulated.

However, if, as is likely, you notice that you have, for example, written a general statement that, even with references, seems overstated, you can revise your style by adding modulators to the start of your sentences, thus modifying your assertions, as illustrated in the box.

REVISING YOUR STYLE

Asserting	*Modulating*
'There is a problem with…'	'Perhaps there is a problem with…'
'Existing policy/methods do not…'	'It could be argued that…'
'The literature is deficient in…'	'One interpretation of this is that…'
'The contribution will be…'	'The potential contribution is…'
'This is one way of…'	'This could/might be a way of…'
'This is an effective means of…'	'This can be of benefit…'
'It is a fact that…'	'Research suggests that…(references)'
'This is more likely to…'	'In this study…'
'This suggests…'	'At this stage, this could be an indication of'

You may begin to wonder how you can ever write with 'authority' if your writing is always so 'modulated', but what you write is always open to question, even open to debate. It is not just that your supervisors want to question everything you write; instead, they are helping you to develop your writing in this way, although there is nothing inherently wrong with asserting your point, particularly in your early writing. This is one way of finding out what you think, expressing your thoughts directly.

The verbs and modulators are useful for making the focus of your writing clear, making the 'moves' (Chapter 19) in your writing explicit, rather than leaving them implicit and expecting the reader to make connections exactly as you intend them to be made. Of course, your reader is an expert in the field, but your supervisors expect you to make your writing coherent, and this means making purpose and structure explicit.

Some students worry that this approach will make their writing too simplistic, arguing that they should not be 'spelling things out' for their supervisors. Another way of thinking about this is that by making the structure of your writing, for example, explicit, you demonstrate that you can manage and construct an academic text. Your supervisors may find this reassuring. It will certainly make your writing easier to read.

On the other hand, if you feel that you are getting into the habit of starting all your writing with 'The purpose of this text is to', think carefully, before you change it, about the relative value of change for change's sake in the context of thesis writing: many postgraduate writers report that, at some point in their education that they cannot precisely place, they learned that repetition in writing should be avoided. Yet repetition has its uses in academic writing, such as identifying priorities, establishing themes and signalling continuity. If your supervisors object to this use of repetition in your writing, you can make the case for it: say how useful you find it to make your purpose explicit. If need be, you can continue this discussion by weighing the pros and cons of using other forms for your opening sentences. Alternatively, perhaps you could negotiate to continue with this approach for this early stage, with the possibility of change in later drafts or final submission.

If you are reading this thinking that this overcomplicates writing tasks that are simply intended to help you 'get started', you may be right. Perhaps you were invited to 'write whatever's on your mind', or 'sketch your thinking' or 'just express yourself'. However, remember that, in the current climate, with its emphasis on timely submissions, writing simply to 'express your ideas' may be considered a luxury, even a rarity. In any case, these types of writing can, if repeated too often, mean that you take too long to find a focus.

Paradoxically, there is a place for unstructured writing, and for writing that has neither audience nor purpose: strategies such as freewriting (Elbow, 1973) have been found to have great value for thesis writers, both in the early and later stages (Murray, 2006). The rationale for using freewriting as part of a thesis-writing process is that it allows you to express your ideas freely. It offers a creative approach to developing your thinking in writing, and it is one of the best techniques for getting started.

The act of freewriting (see box below) is quite different from 'academic writing' – more like brainstorming in sentences, without plan, structure or continuity.

FREEWRITING

Write for 5 minutes
In sentences
Without stopping
Don't let anyone read it
Write about a subject related to your research
Keep your writing open – explore the topic from different angles
Let the sentences flow in any order. (Adapted from Elbow, 1973)

There are three main benefits in regular freewriting. The first is its 'non-stop' nature, which helps to silence your 'internal editor'. While audience is clearly critical, anticipating audiences' reactions can inhibit writing. Anxiety about readers' reactions can block writing altogether. Freewriting helps you to forget about those reactions and focus on expressing thoughts and ideas. The second benefit is the freedom to move from one sentence to another without worrying about how the two are linked. This often produces quite unpredictable solutions to thinking and writing problems. The third is that writing in sentences – rather than in note form or a list of bullet points – though these are useful – helps writers produce text, and knowing that they can produce text reassures them that they will not face blocks. Finally, Elbow (1973) has found that freewriting increases fluency, in the sense that it helps you put your thoughts into writing more easily, producing text quickly that you can then improve, revise and submit to your readers. At the very least, you can use freewriting as a 'warm-up' for other forms of writing.

Case Study: Becoming a Thesis Writer

There are many ways of describing the process of developing a high level of academic writing skills from the point you are at now, the start, to the endpoint, submitting your thesis. One way of finding out how research students experience this development process is to collect their observations and insights over a period of time, for example, collecting emails written over a year, which then form an 'email trail' of the thesis writer's developing competence.

Plotting and revealing the thesis-writing process in this way is a thought-provoking and motivational tool for research students. It shows solutions they develop to problems they face. Motivation is created by the recognition that while the thesis process seems to consist of a stream of problems, it is also a problem-solving process.

In one study, the email trail produced insights into a thesis writer's experience of the first stage of his research and early days in his thesis writing, showing changes in his perspective, behaviour and understanding (Murray, 2002). This student's email trail revealed three major phases in his development as a thesis writer, which can be characterised as (1) 'problematising', (2) 'personalising' and (3) 'professionalising'.

Problematising. In the very early stage of this student's research, the prospect of writing a thesis produced of a stream of questions for which he had no answers. Lack of definition and uncertainty about writing meant that it seemed more demanding than other academic or research tasks, where the writer felt he had more knowledge and experience and was therefore more comfortable. His emails at this time were full of questions to himself and recognition that he seemed to be producing more problems than solutions:

> I seem to be developing a habit of writing down my thoughts and listing problems. Could this be a way of externalizing my thought process? (Murray, 2002: 231)

What is interesting about this quotation is that the student was not only reflecting on how his involvement in research was changing his thinking, even at a very early stage, but also that he was reflecting *in writing.* What is important about this quotation is that it shows the writer 'developing a habit of writing', even if the writing produced, as yet, no more than 'thoughts' and 'problems'. This is one example of how writing can be used to solve what in this case were a range of inter-related problems: time management, knowledge of the field, motivation and writing skills. These are not inherently 'problems', but they were, at this stage in the thesis-writing process, from the thesis writer's perspective, problematised in the email trail.

Personalising. At this stage the writer was identifying specific problems with his writing strategies and was beginning to take responsibility for addressing them:

> I have been putting off sending you a message because I had achieved so little this week. I find that the e-mails are putting pressure on me to get on with research or ... reading just so that I have some progress to report to you. That is a good thing! (Murray, 2002: 232)

This phase involved not only identifying a problem with making progress in writing, but also creating a strategy for solving it, in writing. If this seems like an obvious solution, it should be pointed out that the demands of thesis writing often create complex problems, and one solution is writing for real audiences, with real deadlines. Again, this student's problem-solving occurred in the course of his writing. Perhaps, it could be argued, problem-solving was a result of writing, in the sense that writing replaced general anxiety with creative thinking.

Professionalising. Subsequently, the writer began to see writing as a professional task that had to be fitted into his professional time and integrated into his professional life, a process he saw as an on-going challenge:

> At last the exam papers are finished and I can concentrate on my research for the next couple of weeks.... It is now Tuesday night and I am surprised to find that I have beaten the targets set on Friday. (Murray, 2002: 233)

The use of 'targets' for writing, as for other tasks, is important here. This was a key strategy, which, in spite of its obvious value, took time for this student to develop. Subsequently, when he looked back, one year on, at the emails he had written during this first stage of his research, he realised he had made significant progress by taking a problem-solving approach to his writing. Without this collection of observations he might not have gained this perspective; in fact, even with these observations, he felt he had not captured the 'highs and lows' of the first phase of his research and writing.

What this case study shows is the combination of emotion, cognition and external factors that impinge on thesis writing, as well as the changes on all of these levels that may occur in the early stages of a research project, while a student is developing the skills and strategies required for writing a thesis.

Or did this student waste valuable time? One supervisor, reading extracts from this case study, was adamant that the student had wasted time that should have been spent 'writing the thesis' instead of 'writing about not writing it'. This supervisor's response attaches less value to discussion of thesis writing and, potentially, oversimplifies the complexities of becoming a thesis writer. You will have to judge for yourself how much and in what form you reflect on the challenges you face as a thesis writer, but doing so in writing can provide, at least, further writing practice and, at best, problem-solving for writing and, perhaps, for your research.

A strength of this case study is that it does not idealise the process of becoming a thesis writer, but describes, perhaps more frankly than is generally the case, its 'highs and lows'. You can now begin to recast these as challenges that writing your thesis may present.

This is not to say that all research students will go through these three phases; instead, it indicates that there is a development process to progress from a novice level to becoming an experienced thesis writer. That this includes confusion and frustration may indicate how much development occurs as you write a thesis. The point is not to ignore writing problems, but to take a problem-solving approach, using the strategies described in this chapter. In due course, starting now, you will create your own writing process, establishing which challenges you are likely to face and which strategies you will use to engage with them creatively.

Conclusion

This summary takes the form of questions, arising from points covered in this chapter, which you can use to initiate discussions of writing with your supervisors.

QUESTIONS TO CONSIDER

- Are there usually specific stages in research and thesis writing in your area?
- Or, what will they be, specific to your research project?
- Which forms of writing are expected of you now, and which forms will be expected of you in the next few months?
- How will the learning stages of your project be represented in different writing tasks that you will have to do?
- What types of feedback will your supervisors provide?
- Which type(s) of feedback would you find useful at this early stage, and which would be less useful?
- Can you get feedback from other people?
- Discuss your writing practices – do your supervisors have any suggestions?
- Can your writing process be more efficient (see Murray 2006, chapter 8)?

You can use the last item in this list to develop a programme for your writing, for the early stages and right through to completion of your thesis.

Bibliography

Bolker, J. (1998) *Writing Your Dissertation in Fifteen Minutes a Day: A Guide to Starting, Revising and Finishing Your Doctoral Thesis*. New York: Henry Holt. Gives excellent advice on good practice in planning and doing thesis writing, all tried and tested, positive in tone and motivational.

Elbow, P. (1973) *Writing without Teachers*. Oxford: Oxford University Press. Defines freewriting, an approach that has been shown to increase fluency. Research students and academics have used it to develop ideas and build confidence in writing.

Murray, R. (2002) 'Writing development for lecturers moving from further to higher education: A case study', *Journal of Further and Higher Education*, 26(3): 229–239.

An account of the journey of one thesis writer's development, learning to juggle teaching, research and writing. Detailed and frank account of some thesis-writing challenges.

Murray, R. (2004) *How to Survive Your Viva*. Maidenhead: Open University Press-McGraw-Hill. Describes all aspects of the oral defence of a thesis/dissertation, analyses recurring questions and describes strategies for answering them well.

Murray, R. (2004) 'What can I write about? The rhetorical question for PhD students and their supervisors', paper in 'Supervision', Vol. 8 of *Working Papers on the Web*, available at: www.extra.shu.ac.uk/wpw/supervision/Murray.htm (accessed 29 September 2007) Makes the case for research students learning a range of writing skills and strategies, and illustrating some of them.

Murray, R. (2005) *Writing for Academic Journals*. Maidenhead: Open University Press-McGraw-Hill.

Murray, R. (2006) *How to Write a Thesis*, 2nd edn. Maidenhead: Open University Press-McGraw-Hill. Covers the whole process of writing a thesis. Chapter 8 describes a 'fast-track' process for those who didn't start writing in the early stages.

Murray, R. and Moore, S. (2006) *The Handbook of Academic Writing: A Fresh Approach*. Maidenhead: Open University Press-McGraw-Hill. Draws on academic writing and organisational behaviour literatures to explore how institutions can enable and inhibit writing and what writers can do about it.

National Postgraduate Committee, www.npc.org.uk/ (accessed 29 September 2007) Provides guidance, codes of practice and runs conferences on postgraduate issues.

13 Plagiarism, Intellectual Property Rights and Copyright

Jude Carroll, Chris Luton and Laurence Bebbington

Introduction

This chapter discusses three broadly connected issues that may affect you during your research degree, Plagiarism, Intellectual Property Rights (IPR) and Copyright. By reading this chapter, you will be made aware of some key points in relation to each of these areas. The chapter has been presented as two separate sections; the first section deals with plagiarism whilst the second section deals with IPR and copyright.

Specifically the section on plagiarism will explain:

- the rules and academic conventions relating to plagiarism
- the application of those rules and conventions, especially with regards to referencing and citation.

Understanding these issues will enable you to avoid inadvertently plagiarising others' work and being clear on how to demonstrate professionalism in your academic writing.

The section dealing with IPR and copyright will explain the following:

- Why you should be aware of intellectual property?
- The different forms of intellectual property.
- How universities deal with intellectual property issues with respect to research students?
- The time limits associated with different types of copyright.
- Guidance regarding how to avoid infringing copyright.

This chapter will therefore give you a good initial insight into protecting the ideas that your own research may generate, whilst also respecting the ideas, work and knowledge that has been generated by others.

'Credit Where Credit's Due': Dealing with Issues of Attribution, Citation and Plagiarism in Postgraduate Research and Writing

Research students know they must stay within the rules of attribution and citation. They are much less sure about how to ensure they do so. Research students generally know there could be consequences if they stray, even inadvertently, over the line between acceptable and unacceptable writing practices. They are much less certain where the line might be. They are often unsure about how to find out where the line might be. A growing number of research students have encountered definitions of plagiarism. Most have little or no understanding of what the definitions might actually mean.

This section addresses the issues on the right and takes note of those of the left in the statements above. It tries to delve beneath the definitions you will find in most postgraduate handbooks about plagiarism to explore what the definition used in your university actually means. More importantly, it suggests how you might apply your understanding of plagiarism to decisions you make whilst writing up your research. How can you be sure that your thesis or dissertation is judged as an authentic expression of your own work? (Note: In this section, the term 'thesis' will be used in the section to denote all types of research degree written submissions.)

What This Section Does Not Cover

This section will not replicate the guidance you can find easily on citation and referencing in your own university or research setting. Your university's library probably publishes a guide to referencing practices and your university's website may do as well. Programme handbooks now routinely offer guidance on how you cite others' work and they often describe what will happen if you do not. You are strongly advised to consult these documents and guidance when writing and if you cannot find any local advice, then you should look further afield. Even a rudimentary online search will reveal dozens of guides to referencing systems as well as many sites about plagiarism. Some are listed at the end of the chapter.

This section will also not deal with all types of plagiarism, excluding in particular plagiarism arising from deliberate fraud and cheating. It also excludes plagiarism (often referred to as collusion) that happens when students copy each others' coursework or each other's solutions to class-wide assignments, as these situations are not encountered in research degrees. There are a growing number of ways that students can plagiarise through deliberate cheating such as paying ghost writers to write their thesis. It can happen when students submit another student's thesis or someone else's literature review. They can plagiarise by downloading whole documents from the internet and submitting them unchanged (usually as well without attribution) or by substituting a company report or professional document for an academic piece of coursework. This kind of activity does happen – I have met students who say they do it themselves or know of others who do. Newspapers describe such practices and record the worries expressed by academic managers as to their extent and frequency. However, there seems little point in addressing this kind of plagiarism in a book devoted to helping students who want to submit good work and from which they wish to receive authentic qualifications.

So instead, this section will look at plagiarism that happens when research student writers either do not understand the rules and assumptions that underpin academic regulations about plagiarism or (as is probably closer to the case) when research student writers are not sure how to apply those rules and conventions, especially but not exclusively those pertaining to citation and referencing.

Referencing Others' Work

Most academic writers find it useful to keep guidance on referencing and citation close at hand as they write. Many prefer looking up questions in a hardcopy version rather than relying on a website. Often, websites also offer a printable version and if you rely on one for your guidance, printing it out might be worthwhile as it means you do not need to toggle between screens. However they find the advice, academic writers (even experienced ones) find that they need to refer to the notes frequently. Rules are complex and wide ranging; there are always unusual circumstances or specialist sources ('How would one cite a radio programme?') that need a specific treatment. Novice writers will find themselves needing advice very often as they write up their efforts.

Early on in your research degree, it is advisable to identify which of the many possible formats you are expected to use for referring to others' work so you can answer the standard questions such as those below. Because formats vary, the answer to such questions will vary, too.

- What information about a source is recorded under the system you must use?
- How is information inserted into the text as you are writing – usually using a variation on what is referred to as an in-text citation?
- What is the format for an in-text citation (for example, '…..xxxx [*author's name, date of publication*])'? And when must the format include the page number?
- How sources are listed in reference lists and bibliographies, for example, Harvard author-date system or Vancouver system?[1]

Sometimes, academics and librarians assume that once you know the answers to these kinds of questions about referencing systems and therefore, know how to use referencing conventions (and this is no small task – even after decades of published writing, I still have questions) you will be able to avoid plagiarism. However, this is rarely the case. Writers who are relatively new to academic writing and those who are new to research degree level writing need many other skills to ensure their work is judged as their own and to meet the requirements for authenticity in research degree submissions.

There's More to Avoiding Plagiarism than Referencing

Plagiarism and its avoidance are complex issues. I was reminded of this complexity recently when, towards the end of a 2-hour workshop on plagiarism for 40 postgraduates from all over the world, I was interrupted by a student who put up his hand to ask a question. We had already covered referencing and how to paraphrase and then we had tried out exercises to see how they worked in practice. We had worked through a list of 10 statements, some of which needed a citation and some of which did not, and argued about the grounds for deciding which did and which statements did not need to refer to others' authority and could stand alone as 'common knowledge'. We had discussed why in-text citations were needed at all in academic writing and how a writer could weave others' ideas and words into their own text. We had defined plagiarism and done more exercises around the definition. Everyone had seemed busy and involved. Then this student asked his question:

> Would it be plagiarism if I collected all the data for my masters and analysed it all so I was sure what it meant. Then I gave the data and the analysis and the meaning to someone else and that person wrote it up and then handed it back to me and I handed it in. Would that be plagiarism?

I asked all 40 students for a show of hands. Half thought it would be plagiarism; half thought it would not. None were 100% sure. One who said it was not plagiarism said, 'Well, he did the work. The rest was only writing.'

These students (and many more, perhaps even including you, the reader) needed to work even harder than we had already done to understand what is meant by the term, plagiarism. They also needed to take steps to ensure their work did not inadvertently plagiarise – that is, did not submit others' work as their own. Research students, in particular, need to avoid plagiarism for a range of reasons.

Reasons for Avoiding Plagiarism

Some of the reasons for complying with academic writing conventions (and thereby, avoiding plagiarism) are positive and indeed, are central to the academic values and beliefs that underpin academic writing. If you follow the conventions,

- You show your skill as an academic writer.
- You ensure your examiners know how widely you have researched the topic and are convinced you have read and understood others' work. Neville (2006) in his extremely useful guide to references refers to this kind of citation as providing credibility.
- You show you can evaluate the authority and utility of sources you have encountered in your studies. Again, more credibility.
- You show you can weave an argument using others' ideas and discoveries to support your own findings and conclusions. Neville (2006) and many other authors refer to this kind of writing as evidence of authority. You enhance your own authority as a writer by explicitly using the authority of others and by reminding the reader that you are doing so.
- You show you are respectful to others in your field of study; you are mindful of their contributions. This is important because a research student writer is joining the discipline, albeit as a junior member, and uses citation to acknowledge the work of those who joined previously, carrying on the discussion within the discipline community.

Some of the reasons for understanding what is meant by plagiarism (and therefore avoiding it) are pragmatic.

- *You are less susceptible to unnecessary fears.* For example, you will not fall foul of the belief that an original idea might actually be a duplicate of one that is already in the public domain and by claiming it, you risk plagiarism. In fact a research student who claims an idea in ignorance of others' prior claim will, at most, be accused of faulty scholarship. So do feel free to have ideas without the need to spend weeks searching the library to see if anyone else had it before you. But when you write, make sure you claim the idea as your own.
- *You avoid over-citation.* Where writers cite too much, the result is awkward and can seem to lack confidence.
- *You are more likely to adopt practices during your collection of information that keep the link between an idea and the source.* This can save hours later on spent trying to rediscover who said this or wrote that when you come to write up.

Of course, some of the reasons for avoiding plagiarism are linked to the negative consequences of breaching academic regulations. Most research students know (or soon learn) what could happen if they plagiarise. Often such consequences are spelled out in some detail in induction courses or skills-training sessions. Consequences could include the following:

- *Your text being deemed unfit for an award* (or even in some cases, having credit that has already been awarded removed in the light of new evidence).
- *You are being asked to rewrite sections of text* if plagiarism is spotted before submission.

- *You are being referred to disciplinary processes* within the institution. In some cases, students are removed from the programme.
- If the plagiarism includes external publication or conference presentations, then there are *threats to personal reputation* and even denial of professional accreditation.

So, It Is Worth Avoiding Plagiarism – but How?

Here's a typical definition of plagiarism:

Plagiarism is defined as submitting someone else's work as your own.

Often the definition is followed by examples of the kinds of actions that might lead to plagiarism. Some have been listed already as cheating but others are more to do with carelessness or ignorance such as copying from the web and never noting the source then, weeks or months later, using the 'harvested' text in your own writing. That is plagiarism as is copying from other students, too close paraphrases, and including a good paraphrase but not saying where the idea came from in the text. So, the definition seems straightforward but the many ways it could happen and the many questions that soon arise when writers encounter the definition show it is not. Even those who say, 'Yes, I understand that definition' and note the examples will ask things like:

- 'So, is it plagiarism if you pay a copy editor to go over your thesis?'
- 'Is it plagiarism if you look at other dissertations covering the same ground as your own and follow that format and structure?'
- 'How many words can you copy from the original without it being plagiarism?'
- 'Is it plagiarism if you copy text from an open site on the internet?'

and so on.

In order to have any chance of answering your own questions about plagiarism, you will need to look below the words to the underpinning assumptions which drive academic writing in the UK and in many (but by no means all) other countries. You also need to remember that definitions of plagiarism are situation-specific so you cannot assume that the understanding you may have already gathered about plagiarism in your undergraduate study, or that derives from previous experiences in a non-UK academic setting, or in business, or in professional practice is accurate – you cannot assume that what you thought then about plagiarism will apply to your new UK postgraduate writing. You may need to set aside previous practices and adopt some new ones. Your new writing practices need to be rooted in the beliefs and expectations that underpin UK academic writing.

What Does It Mean – 'Work'?

This is the most important word in a definition of plagiarism. Plagiarism is when you submit someone else's work as your own. The word 'work' refers to the text of the thesis as if it were a thing (as in the phrase 'a work of art') and 'work' covers the effort that is required to bring your thesis into its final form. So the student in the story who said, 'the rest is just writing' had taken too narrow a view of the word 'work', assuming it only meant data collection and analysis. Plagiarism is interested in all the work that adds value to your thesis. Your reader, when they see your final draft, will be wondering, 'does this writer understand what she/he is writing? Has she/he learned anything from doing this work? Has she/he struggled to make sense of the data for himself/her self, to make his/her own version of the information?'

If your reader (i.e. usually your examiners but perhaps other readers, too) can see how you have changed what you found in your research, perhaps by writing what it means in your own words (a paraphrase) or by using ideas in a different situation or by commenting on what it means – if your reader sees this work, they will see the work that arises from it as your own.

Not all work matters when judging plagiarism. For example, the work of choosing the paper on which your thesis is written probably is not being judged (though it might be if, for example, if this was a thesis in fine art on creative publishing and the writer decided to submit it on handmade paper). Another example might be grammatical accuracy – the work of ensuring no grammar mistakes could be included in a thesis in English literature but not in one for computer science. If you are not sure what work will be judged by your examiners, you need to check with your supervisor. If you pass off others' work as part of your own claim that your thesis deserves a pass, you plagiarise.

Once you have decided what work is valuable, then you can ask others for help with all the rest. So, you could ask statisticians to make sense of your data – but only if the help is acknowledged in the methodology section and if the assessment criteria do not include judging your own ability to conduct such an analysis. Another example of legitimate help might be asking for help from library staff in locating texts and in using databases. This would not be passing off others' work as one's own. But if a student hired a researcher to identify all the sources needed in their literature review, this would be plagiarism because it creates a false impression about something that all research students are expected to show they can do – to select and evaluate useful sources. Using databases, on the other hand, is usually seen as a means to this valued work.

'Work' Expressed as Words

Writing is hard work. It requires the writer to choose words and put them together, even if the text that emerges says something that has been said many times before. The words are the writer's own because the writer has chosen them, even if some of the words are drawn from stock phrases and standard ways in which these things are discussed. In authentic work, a writer puts words together in such a way that the reader can tell that the writer has understood what the words said (a paraphrase). A paraphrase that is created as the last sentence states is the writer's own words and it is original. It is not 'original' in the sense of being novel or unique – it is not 'original' in the sense of never having been written before but it is 'original' in the sense of being created by the writer.

An analogy may help here: Suppose I wanted to know if you could cook so I visited your house for a meal. Suppose you pulled out a pie from the freezer, placed it in the microwave, heated it and served it to me. Would that be your own work? Would it be original? Would it show you could cook? Yes, but it would not be work that showed your understanding of cooking and it would not be 'original' in the sense that was just mentioned. But suppose instead of the cook-chill approach, you went to the market (i.e. the library) and selected vegetables (i.e. academic sources) and decided which were better and cut them up (i.e. took notes, not just highlighted bits) and put the ingredients together to make a pie (i.e. or a paragraph in your thesis). Would that be your own work? It is pretty clear it would be though, like academic writing, it is built on the work of others like the shopkeepers and farmers. The 'shop-chop-assemble-bake' pie would be original even if it (or the paragraph in your thesis on methodology) was like thousands that had already been cooked (or written). I would know you could cook in the second case though an excellent cook would add their own twist just as an excellent thesis adds the writer's own ideas and personal insights.

Plagiarism does concern itself with the words you use but it is much more interested in the work that went into writing them. Novice writers are often concerned to know how many words can be left from the original without plagiarism whereas they should be asking another question: Have I changed and altered others' words in ways that show I understand them? You cannot show your understanding by finding and including someone else's words, even if they say exactly what you want them to say. If the originals really are perfect, then quote them verbatim using any of the conventions suggested in your reference guide such as inverted commas ('.....'), or an indented paragraph or italics – whatever methods are suggested in your referencing system.

Your responsibility as a research student writer is to make sure at all times that the person reading your text is clear about whose work and whose words are being used. You cannot put the source in the reference list and assume the reader will guess where ideas come from.[2] Using others' exact words with suitable attribution is not plagiarism (though I have met people who mistakenly think it is if the writer cites too many others and does so too often).

If you create a false assumption in the assessor as to whose work is being assessed, they may well deem it plagiarism.

Someone Else's Work

In UK academic practice, some work has been claimed by named people. Some has not. If you are to avoid plagiarism, you will need to be sure of the difference. The distinction can be very difficult and even more so if you are new to the UK, new to your subject area and new to academic thinking. How, if you are really new, can you tell what is something that everybody knows on the one hand and something that belongs to someone else on the other?

Many research student writers find guidance useful on 'common knowledge' but this turns out to be very hard to provide. If in doubt, ask around and seek several views (*Does everyone know this?*). Common knowledge does not need a citation. It often refers to facts ('Columbus discovered America in 1492') but it can also include standard formulae ('the law of supply and demand') or can be simply the way that people in the discipline write about such things ('it was a win-win solution'). It may help to follow the adage, 'When in doubt, cite' though some writers have referred to this kind of writing as being 'like trying to walk with your shoelaces tied together' (de Lambert et al., 2006). The last sentence deliberately mixed citation requirements. I did not use a citation for the adage (*'when in doubt...'*) because I judge it to be not the work of any one person and not requiring the reader to be able to check on its veracity or provenance. I did use a citation for the phrase about shoelaces. I cited because the 'shoelaces' phrase itself was a direct quotation from an article in a refereed journal, because it is very distinctive and likely to have been created by the author, and because I wanted to show you, the reader, that I have credibility. My citation implies, 'See, I know about the topic and I can choose sources that are authoritative.'

Over-citing can make your writing seem lacking in confidence but it is generally easier to correct than under-citation. If you fail to include a citation at draft stage then find later that one is necessary, this can mean hours or even days of effort to plug the gap. Students who, from day one, use a system for collecting all the information on all the sources which they have consulted in their research, no matter how tiny or irrelevant,[3] usually avoid this scenario.

You must cite anything included in your thesis which is not common knowledge and which is not derived from your own efforts in such a way as to be original to you. You also cite if you think the reader will need to check on a statement's veracity. And you cite to add authority to a statement or acknowledge that others have different views. So, whereas in the earlier paragraph, the statement about when Columbus discovered America is offered as an example of common knowledge, in some contexts, it would be much better if you cited where this idea came from. You might do that, for example, when writing about whether the Vikings had a prior claim and when evaluating the relative authority of both sources. Once you decide a citation is needed, your referencing guide will show you how this is done.

How Does Work become 'Someone Else's'?

Work comes to be seen as 'someone else's' by some public act that links the work with the person. This is commonly publishing but it could be delivering a conference paper or creating a website. The work can be spoken, painted, sung or danced. I read not too long ago about the person who claimed that banoffee pie was his own work. Whatever the medium, the claimant draws upon the work of others but also adds something new or recasts old ideas. Then claims only the new, changed or additional bits.

Your own work, once it is published, will of necessity add to the knowledge and insights in your discipline. That additional bit will be 'your own work' for others to cite in their turn as they try and decide how much they need to change it to make it 'their own' and how best to cite your work.

Citing others' work does far more than protect you against charges of plagiarism. In a fundamental way, by citing others' ideas and by paraphrasing others words to show you understand them, you validate your claim to become a member of your disciplinary community. Your authentic thesis marks the legitimate start of this process and you contribute by ensuring the work and the words it contains are your own.

IPR and Copyright

Universities are epicentres for the knowledge economy: they work with knowledge on a daily basis and not only assess and compare knowledge, but, more importantly, they innovate and create it. It is that very same knowledge and ideas which drive the UK and world economy. However, to exploit or sell the ideas and innovative creativity of industry and artists, we need a framework within which to promote and protect those ideas. Without this framework others would simply copy the ideas and there would be no incentive available for the creators to maintain the distinctive identity of those ideas or to make income. So research students at a university need to be very mindful of the importance of protecting ideas and to know that it is not only the individual creator who may want to see those ideas properly protected, but also a sponsor of research that may need to be sure it can benefit from the ideas once they are created.

We have talked a lot about ideas, but let's try to put this in a legal context. Simple concepts of property such as a car, house or land that we see daily can be legally protected as property rights. If someone tries to steal them, you might phone for a police officer and have the thief arrested, charged and taken to court. IPRs, on the other hand, are a bundle of rights that protect applications of ideas and information that have commercial value. IPR confers a set of time-limited legal rights over the expression (such as graphic or literary ideas) and use of certain ideas, legal rights which prevent others from using those rights. These rights need to be put in place to prevent others copying or using ideas which inventors may have spent considerable time and income to create. Take for example a blockbuster film: it might cost millions of pounds to produce, but can easily be copied onto a CD. Likewise a drug which a pharmaceutical company may have taken over ten years to develop and to process through the necessary regulatory approvals, might easily be copied.

These bundles of legal rights take different forms: some come about automatically as soon as the work is created, others need to be registered or applied for before they have any effect. This is because some rights (such as for inventions) need to go through a complicated registration and searching process to ensure that no earlier rights have been granted for similar inventions. On the other hand, where someone produces a drawing or written work, unless it has been copied it is likely it is original and IPR is created automatically as soon as the author or artist completes the work. To complicate matters more, a simple item such as a bottle of medical tablets bearing a well-known brand, may have a number of IPRs associated with it, some of which may actually overlap: the shape of the bottle, wording on the label, a logo etc. – all can be legally protected as IPR.

This sounds like great news for someone trying to protect ideas you might think, however, protecting some ideas can be a very expensive process and this is because some rights, which can be granted worldwide for a single idea, can confer extremely valuable monopolies to individuals or companies. Therefore there needs to be some type of balance in terms of conferring rights to allow someone to make considerable wealth out of a monopoly right, against the public – such as you and I – interest in having access to those rights.

It is probably best at this stage to explain the different forms of IPR a research student may come across within a university, although identifying IPR can often be difficult for anyone non-experienced in the field.

Patents

Research students involved in the physical sciences are more likely to come across patents. An owner of a patent has a monopoly right granted to protect a novel invention which is capable of industrial application – such as a new device for measuring the pressure in a car tyre. They are not automatic and only come into being following the filing of an application. If the invention becomes public knowledge before it is filed, no rights can be granted. Patents can be granted for individual territories, groups of territories or worldwide. However, the monopoly right (to prevent others using it without permission) is normally limited to a maximum term of 20 years, after which time the grant comes to an end and anyone can use the invention.

Copyright

This is probably one of the most common rights a research student will come across in a university context. It is an automatic right conferred on the originator or author of original works. Copyright prevents a third party from copying or disseminating those works without the permission or agreement of the author. It protects the expression of works (i.e. the aesthetic look, appearance, etc.), as opposed to the inventive nature behind the works. The most likely form of copyright will be written text or drawings – in such things as journal articles, chapters in books and photographs. But copyright extends to other types of work that research students may use in their research – such as software, music, sound recordings, audio works etc. You should be aware that copyright extends to works whether they are published or unpublished and research students using unpublished materials protected by copyright (sources such as unpublished letters, diaries, manuscripts and similar materials in libraries and archives) will find that copyright protection for unpublished works is very strong and that use of or quotation from these sources will often require explicit permission from the rightsholder. The institution holding the item can advise on this. All unpublished literary works are protected by copyright until at least the year 2039!

Copyright allows the owner of copyright in a work to control, or allow, things like the copying of the work (e.g. by photocopying or scanning); publishing a work; renting or lending the work and other important activities like controlling the use of the work on platforms such as the internet. You can see from this that copyright is actually potentially quite restrictive.

Copyright protection does not last forever. However, the periods of protection given to different types of work are generally long. In brief, the main periods of copyright protection are as follows:

- *Literary Works*: These include textual works like articles, books, computer software etc. Copyright normally lasts for 70 years from the death of the author, although the periods of protection for unpublished works vary. Some older published works (between about 1925 and 1945) can also enjoy what is known as revived or extended copyright but this is a complex area and therefore not covered in this short discussion.
- *Dramatic, Musical and Artistic Works*: These include things like plays, music and artistic works such as photographs, graphic works, sculptures etc. They are also protected for 70 years from the death of the author.
- *Sound Recordings and Films*: Sound recordings are basically protected for 50 years from the date of their making or first publication; films for 70 years from the death of the last maker of the film.

Fortunately the rights of the copyright owner to control the copying, publishing, renting or lending, communicating a work on the Internet etc. are not unrestricted. If they were then every time you wanted to reproduce a copyright work, you would have to ask the copyright owner's permission! Certain limits are placed on the rights of a copyright owner to control the use of works. These exceptions are very important in research and academic work. They allow bona fide researchers to copy and use copyright works without having to get permission every time they use them although there are certain limits which you are advised to observe.

Exceptions to copyright allow you to copy works in the normal course of your research activities. Some of these exceptions involve the concept of 'fair dealing.' This is a legal concept which is a bit ambiguous but generally it means making a single copy for yourself in circumstances where the copying does not damage the commercial interests of the copyright owner. Your copying should be for non-commercial educational purposes and only of a reasonable amount of the source. So you can, for example, photocopy or scan one article from a periodical issue or one chapter from a book. Generally accepted guidelines suggest that the material copied must not be greater than 5% of any published work, or a single copy for personal use of the following:

1   In the case of a book, one whole chapter
2   In the case of an article in an issue of a serial publication or in a set of conference proceedings, one whole article
3   One illustration, diagram or map not exceeding A4 size as a separate item from any of the above
4   In the case of an anthology of short stories or poems one short story or poem not exceeding 10 pages in length
5   In the case of a published report of judicial proceedings, the entire report of one single case
6   Up to 10% of a pamphlet, report or standard, up to a maximum of 20 pages.

These guidelines are derived from the Copyright Licensing Agency's Photocopying and Scanning Licence and are likely to be regarded as fair amounts when copying from published works.

A second exception relevant to academic is one which allows you to reproduce the whole or a substantial part of a copyright work for the purposes of criticism or review. Criticism or review or both are integral to research and writing. Reliance on this exception, however, requires some care. You may freely quote or use reasonable extracts from any type of work where you are genuinely subjecting it to genuine criticism or review – criticising a work or another work, or criticising or reviewing underlying themes, philosophies or positions inherent in them. But, for example, to reproduce an art work and hardly refer to or criticise it – is not likely to be acceptable.

Another exception that may be relevant to students is copying for the purposes of examination. Briefly, this allows a student to copy material (e.g. by photocopying) for the purposes of answering examination questions – and this includes continuous or other assessments that will count towards a final examination mark. This only means that you can copy material (e.g. photographs or plates, tables, diagrams etc.) for incorporation in an essay, assignment etc. or as appendices to a dissertation or thesis, for example. It does not mean that you can copy anything merely because you are revising or studying for an examination. Only copying directly linked to the examination is permitted. Relying on this exception would not allow a university to make your work available in its e-dissertations or e-theses collections – the material would have to be removed. Any such copying must always clearly acknowledge the source. This exception can be helpful to students who want to enclose copyright materials as appendices to a thesis. Nevertheless, this exception is probably better used only if you have failed to get explicit permission from the copyright owner to include the works.

Although you could rely on the exceptions above if you are using certain types of copyright works (e.g. copying plates or photographs from books for inclusion in your thesis) you are strongly advised always to consider writing to the copyright owner and asking for explicit permission to reproduce works in your thesis. Look at the source publication to see if you can identify the copyright owner. If not, write to the publisher of the item or find them on the internet. Publishers will have Rights or Permissions departments which can give you permission to make good-quality copies of items that you might wish to include in your thesis. If you decide to write for permissions then these points are important:

- Clearly identify the works you want to use and their copyright owner(s)
- Write to them and explain that you wish to make copies of the works for inclusion in your thesis and that the copying is for non-commercial educational purposes for your higher degree
- State that you will make a suitable acknowledgement to the item and that permission to reproduce has been granted by the copyright owner
- Keep any permissions letters that you receive back from the copyright owner
- Request permission early and in good time – copyright owners may take months to respond.

If you do not get a reply or permission is refused you could consider using the works but only if you are certain that the use might fall within either (or both) of the criticism or review and examination exceptions mentioned above.

Be aware that many works on the Internet enjoy copyright protection. Merely because material is freely available on the Internet (or in print for that matter) it may not necessarily be copied and used at will. In using material on the Internet consider the following:

- Check to see if there is a copyright statement or policy on the website which provides guidance on use of materials from the site

- In the absence of clear copyright guidelines apply the copying limits above. Don't assume that in the absence of a clear policy that any website is consenting to all kinds of copying
- If in doubt look for an appropriate email link or contact on the site to clarify the position.

Remember that material may be placed on websites by those who have no authority to do so. Many pirated works (books, music, images etc.) are available. You should not copy, download or make hypertext links to any such infringing material.

In using electronic books, journals and databases made available through your university remember the following:

- Usernames and passwords are for your personal use only. Do not share them with anyone else
- All electronic resources are provided for non-commercial, personal educational purposes to support you in your research and study
- Material may be downloaded or emailed to your email address for your own personal use. Do not forward it to anyone else or post it on bulletin boards, the Internet etc.
- Do not remove, obscure or alter in any way any copyright information that appears on any materials that you download from a service.

Generally you can scan a single work for the purposes of non-commercial personal research or private study but must be aware of the following:

- Do not alter, edit, mutilate etc. a scanned or digitised copy
- Do not forward it by email, place it on an intranet or internet
- Store a scanned or copy on a non-networked drive for your own use
- Scan only within the limits outlined above (i.e. one article from a periodical issue etc.)
- Generally speaking single photographs, illustrations, charts, maps etc. should not be scanned (unless you are the copyright owner or have prior permission).

If you have teaching responsibilities as part of your research degree studies then your institution is likely to hold licences that permit you, in the course of teaching and learning, to copy or reproduce works for distribution to students in teaching. For example, your institution will have licences from societies such as the Copyright Licensing Agency, the Educational Recording Agency, the Newspaper Licensing Agency, the Design and Artists Copyright Society etc. that allow you to copy, distribute or use articles in journals, extracts from books, recordings made from television and radio, newspapers articles, artistic works etc. with students. Ask the person responsible for copyright in your institution for details and guidance on these licences.

Moral Rights

Moral rights refer to the unalienable right of an author or creator of copyright to be named or identified as the creator of that work. For research students, and in particular those who go on to become senior academics and/or researchers within a university, identifying themselves as a creator of copyright material is very important in terms of prestige and advancement in employment. Publishing research and teaching materials, in most cases, enables an academic to move up the academic ladder. Academics also gain notoriety through being identified as the creator of works; who has ever heard of so-called ghost writers of books gaining any form of prestige from their work without being identified!

Trademarks

Trademarks are 'signs' or marks which protect items such as logos, graphics, sounds, shapes and even smells. To be protectable as IPR the mark must create a link between a distinguishable mark and the owner of that mark. If there is any confusion created in the mind of a user of that mark, the owner will not be able to obtain a monopoly right to that mark. A good example is Kodak, which is a very distinguishable mark and everyone fairly knows the company as a producer of films and cameras – which gives the mark a real strength in law. It is unlikely research students will be involved with trademarks, unless they perhaps use a university logo (which would be a trade mark) or create their own brandname or logo.

Other less important IPRs are performance rights, database rights (these rights are normally covered by copyright), and design rights.

Ownership of IP

Having determined whether any form of inventive or creative material can be classified as IPR, the next important step for a university, a research sponsor, third party or research student is to determine who owns the IPR and/or is entitled to benefit from any commercialisation of the IPR. The very term 'ownership', especially of something with potentially a very high value, often invokes a secret distrust of the other party, as if one party is trying to out-do the other or one party's contributions will not be fully realised. This is why, from the outset, it is better all parties reach agreement on respective contributions and entitlements. Most universities have in place IPR policies and procedures which outline how IPR will be handled and apportioned within a university. This can be overridden by existing contracts with research sponsors or third parties – where the university and research student is bound by terms and conditions within that agreement. However, university policies and procedures often only relate to staff and normally research students and other students are not mentioned.

For the purposes of ownership, research students, those who are not members of university staff, need to determine the type of engagement they have with the university and, as mentioned above, whether any agreements exist which will bind them legally. Agreements such as these I should point out are normally put in place to protect the interests of the university and third parties (such as research sponsors); they are not there to protect the interests of research students!

If research students are paying their own fees in a personal capacity, they should be entitled to any IPR they generate (whether in their own or university time): in short they are consumers and should be treated as such. This includes their own studies or research. Some universities, possibly without legal justification, require research students to sign an agreement on enrolment that states the university will own any IPR they generate while enrolled with the university, most offering a share of revenue received from successful commercialisation of the research student-created IPR. It is not known whether this type of term within an agreement has been tested legally, however, it is probably unlikely a university could enforce such an agreement without showing it was legally entitled to claim rights to the IPR.

Where research students take up (third party) sponsored or research council-funded research, it is almost certain they will be bound by agreements with the university which require that all IPR belongs to the university and/or sponsor, although the university may allow the student to benefit from an incentives scheme through which normal members of staff can also benefit. The university will be under an obligation to a sponsor of research and could be sued for damages if IPR is not adequately protected. As such, a university with efficient IPR management processes is likely to be favoured by industrial sponsors who like to see robust IPR structures and processes in place to ensure IPR resulting from research is adequately safeguarded.

A Typical Example of How a University Handles Research Student IPR

Helen, who is a research student in science, enrolled at university X. She pays her own fees. During the course of her studies she discovers a novel inventive step – which is possibly protectable as a patent. She writes down the details and draws diagrams. Helen then discusses it with her supervisor, who feels the idea has merit but could be improved by making some minor changes which she agrees will improve the idea. Because of her excitement in making what she considers a scientific breakthrough, Helen decides to give a presentation at a forthcoming promotions event in her scientific field which is open to companies throughout the UK. She also comes up with a catchy new brandname which she intends to use should the idea get to the marketplace. Helen then decides to discuss the matter with her university's IPR team.

The IPR team will in most cases be impartial. They will be representing the university's best interests, but also looking for benefits for Helen. They will first make an assessment as to whether any protectable IPR exists and try to establish ownership: as Helen pays her own fees and is not bound by any legal agreements (there is no research sponsor) she can probably claim ownership of any resulting patent. However, the university will ask that the supervisor's ideas are accounted for and a percentage contribution may need to be agreed. To take the new invention forward and file a patent application will probably require advice from a patent agent, which will involve an expense.

The university is likely to agree to take the patent forward using their specialised IPR team, only after Helen has agreed to assign the patent application to the university. In this way Helen will be offered the normal staff revenue terms should the university successfully commercialise the idea. Costs for a patent filing over the first three years could be up to £20,000 (for which the university often has a budget) so there is a considerable cost involved. It is likely the university will require Helen to include the copyright in drawings and even the logo (which could be protected as a trademark) within the assignment, as it is better to keep all the IPR in one bundle. If the idea is sold or exploited commercially these IPR will add to the value and Helen will benefit in the revenue she receives from the university. Helen will be prevented from giving a presentation until the patent application is filed, as it is only from this time (the official filing date) that Helen can tell others about her new idea – which even includes friends down at the local pub! Most large universities in the UK lose one or two patents a year through early disclosure of the invention before a patent has been filed – often when talks are given at trade events.

Key Things to Remember regarding IPR

So one can see that IPRs, although a very specialised area of law, play an essential part in ensuring knowledge is protected and benefits accrue to those who generate ideas. Most successful scientists, even Nobel Prize winners, can be shown to have a series of patents or other IPRs which protect their ideas and inventions: by protecting the ideas as IPRs they are able to generate income which can then be reinvested in particular technologies to allow them and their research teams to continue to carry out research which benefits society.

Most universities in the UK work on preventative measures when it comes to protecting IPR; it is very unlikely a university will take legal action against a member of staff or third party over a breach of IPR, therefore putting in place clear legal agreements at an early stage will ensure they never arrive at a point where there is any misunderstanding or a ground for dispute. Conflicts between research students and universities will, from experience, normally be about any share (of an idea) a research student will be entitled to based on the level of their contribution. For this reason universities will first insist all parties sign a so-called revenue sharing agreement, which will outline contributions and apportionment of revenue for future successful commercialisation of ideas. A research student should always look to see this agreement is in place before assigning IPR to a university. That way their rights will be guaranteed.

Research students should not worry about talking to IPR teams within universities. They are there to help and provide guidance and ensure everyone benefits from successful exploitation of ideas. They can also help with identifying the IPR and advising whether the ideas have any substance. IPR teams have processes for handling IPR: identification, protection and exploitation. Where there are costs involved in protecting IPR, universities also have budgets for protecting IPR so there is no risk for the research student. Remember only one in a hundred ideas is successfully exploited, so it is better the university bears any risks involved.

Conclusion

This chapter has given you a broad survey of three issues that may affect you during the process of gaining your research degree. You should now know what plagiarism is and how to avoid it. Additionally you should now know how ideas, yours and others, are protected and exploited and how universities normally deal with the IPR generated by its research students. Having an understanding of these issues is all part of the process of becoming a professional researcher who operates with integrity and understands how others should also operate.

Notes

1 This endnote illustrates another convention that can be used to notify the reader that the author's point or statement is linked to the work of another source of information. Here, however, it serves another purpose. It is used to draw your, the reader's, attention to the difference between a reference list and a bibliography. I suggest you are clear as to which is required in your own thesis.

2 You need to do this explicitly. Some students new to the UK assume the reader will know the source of a statement or be familiar with a research study or finding because the reader is an expert. This does not work in UK citations. You must tell the reader even if you think he or she already knows you are quoting another source.

3 One example of such a tool is EndNote although there are others worth recommending and new ones are also developed regularly. Your supervisor might suggest a suitable tool or you could consult the librarians for guidance. Using a systematic repository will save hours of work and worry later on in your writing. It also lessens the risks of plagiarism. Anyone who followed up the citation would see that there is another complication as well. The citation in

fact refers to a secondary source because the phrase about shoelaces is imported into the cited text. The citation should say (xxx, xxx as cited in xxxx, xxx) and my version is plagiarism. I have created a false assumption in the reader about the actual breadth of my research efforts. I take the risk here to show the need for continuing care and attention in such matters.

Bibliography

de Lambert, K., Ellen, N. and Taylor, L. (2006) 'Chalkface Challenges: A Study of Academic Dishonesty amongst Students in New Zealand', *Assessment and Evaluation in Higher Education* 31(5): 485–503.

Neville, C. (2006) *References and Bibliographies, Effective Learning Service*, University of Bradford at: www.learnhigher.hope.ac.uk/ (accessed October, 2006)

Pears, R. and Shields, G. (2004), *Cite Them Right: The Essential Guide to Referencing and Plagiarism*, Newcastle upon Tyne, UK: Northumbria University Press.

14 Transferable Skills Training and Assessing Your Training Needs

Ellen Pearce[1]

Introduction

Did your pulse quicken when you read the title of this chapter? If so, you may not be a typical research student. What excites most such researchers, naturally, is the subject of their research. Their priority is to get on with the research itself. The topic of 'transferable skills training' and 'training needs' can, therefore, seem remote from the research student's concerns – perhaps even a distraction from them. The aim in this chapter, however, is to show the opposite, that seeing your research as part of a broader training or development programme can help you really get the most out of your research and help you maximise your efficiency and success as a research student. It can also help you become more aware of your personal preferences and strengths which can help you when considering what to do after your research degree, or back in the workplace. The career-related aspect of skills assessment and development is covered in Chapter 23, 'Identifying and Valuing Your Transferable Skills'.

This chapter will focus on the background to, and importance of, the skills agenda for researchers in the UK, and resources that support researchers' self-development. It aims to clarify what transferable skills and training needs are and to outline their relevance and value. We hope that by reading this chapter you will also have a clearer idea of the opportunities available for developing yourself and what may be gained from seeing your research degree as a way of trying, testing and honing your skills.

The UK Policy Context

When I did my PhD there was no skills training at all – just 3 years of isolated research. Skills training on methodologies, conference presentations, submitting work for publication and networking would have been useful.

(Former AHRC research student; AHRC, 2006)

Ten, or even five years ago, this former research student's experience was typical of many. The picture began to change in the late 1990s when a growing body of policy makers began challenging the accepted view of postgraduate research training. There was much agreement that it was of prime importance to retain the piece of original research as the PhD's key purpose. But evidence – such as variations in completion rates and research student surveys – showed that gaining the knowledge, skills and experience necessary to achieve a successful piece of research was, in the majority of universities, a rather hit-and-miss process. Learning all you needed 'on the job' – by doing your research degree – could work very well indeed, if the supervisory and departmental support was of high quality, or if you came to your research degree with a base of skills and strategies gained in previous work experience. Or it could work badly – sometimes very badly indeed. Even where departmental arrangements worked well, there were rarely incentives to help research students develop a broader awareness of the skills they were learning and an understanding of how those skills might be relevant in different career settings after the research. In questioning the prevailing tendency to a narrow emphasis on the *research,* rather than a broader focus on the trainee *researcher,* policy makers were concerned both to achieve higher rates of successful completion and to enable researchers to make better-informed transitions to future careers. Better-trained researchers, it was argued, would make swifter, more effective contributions to the economy and society, whether in a university role or while moving to jobs outside academia.

This shift in emphasis is marked by a number of policy 'landmarks'. This section briefly introduces those central to the development of integrated skills training:

- The Joint Skills Statement (JSS) – agreed by all the Research Councils in 2001 (see Appendix 2 in this volume). Its purpose is to give a common view of the skills and experience a typical research student should have. It forms the framework for transferable skills training for research students in the UK
- *SET for Success* – a report in 2002 for the Chancellor of the Exchequer of a review led by Sir Gareth Roberts into the supply of science, technology, engineering and mathematical skills in the UK (Roberts, 2002)
- The Quality Assurance Agency's (QAA's) revised Code of Practice for postgraduate research programmes (see Appendix 1 in this volume).

The Joint Skills Statement

In 2001, the Joint Statement of Skills Training Requirements of Research Postgraduates was produced as the result of a collaboration between a number of bodies including the UK Research Councils and the UK GRAD programme. This statement has become the most widely used taxonomy of such skills in this area. The JSS organises postgraduate researchers' skills under the following headings:

- Research Skills and Techniques
- Research Environment
- Research Management
- Personal Effectiveness
- Communication Skills
- Networking and Teamworking
- Career Management.

Its importance is that it not only provides a framework for individual research students, but also for higher education institutions in terms of the support that they should be providing to research students.

The JSS is reproduced in full in Appendix 2 of this volume.

SET for Success – Sir Gareth Roberts' Review

SET for Success arose from a concern with skill shortages in science, engineering and allied areas. Whilst demand for these skills has been increasing, it was argued, supply has fallen. Roberts' task was to suggest ways to improve the supply.

Roberts highlighted the development of broader skills as key to both academic and non-academic careers, regardless of discipline or sector. For research students, he recommended that any higher education institution should supply

at least two weeks of dedicated training a year, principally in transferable skills, for which additional funding should be provided and over which the student should be given some control. (Roberts, 2002, Para. 0.44)

The QAA Code of Practice

The revised Code of Practice for postgraduate research programmes was published by the QAA in 2004. It sets out a number of precepts defining the expectations that the QAA, research councils and funding councils have of higher education institutions regarding their provision for postgraduate research. Elements of the Code of Practice, including the precepts, are reproduced in Appendix 1 of this volume.

The influence of Sir Gareth Roberts' recommendations is clearly evident in the revised code.

What matters here about *SET for Success* and the QAA Code of Practice is not so much the detail as the broad implications. It is clear from these that

- the business of identifying research students' training needs and the development, recording and reviewing of their skills is important, and should not be left to chance
- the skills involved include not only research-specific ones but also skills of a more general kind
- there are expectations in varying degrees, of (a) research students themselves, (b) their supervisors and (c) their institutions.

Changing Practice in the UK

The good news is that the UK developments, particularly the Roberts Report *(SET for Success)* and the QAA Code of Practice, have resulted in more than just good intentions. In accepting the findings of the Roberts Report, the Chancellor allocated significant funds for its implementation. This included funds specifically for the development of research students' skills. The amount of money devoted to this particular initiative is substantial – approximately £13M per annum for postgraduate researchers. Much of this has been spent on the actual delivery of skills training, but over one third of it has been used to develop an infrastructure within institutions to ensure that such training is coordinated and sustained.[2] Monitoring by the Research Councils and by QAA is designed to ensure that resources are allocated appropriately and that institutions meet the requirements of the Code of Practice.

International Comparisons

European Union education ministers are getting closer to agreement on a common framework for doctoral programmes (the consultation and decision-making process known as 'The Bologna Process'[3]). Aspects of the UK research degree model that strengthen 'researcher employability', including transferable skills training, are widely recognised across Europe and are likely to be part of the final framework.[4]

In parallel to the Bologna Process, the drive to increase Europe's research competitiveness, known as the Lisbon Agenda, has led to fresh thinking on the support needed by early career researchers – beginning with research degree students. For example, The European Charter for Researchers[5] issued in 2005 by the European Commission, articulates researchers' entitlements to personal and professional development.

Developments in the UK are therefore part of a wider international shift in focus in research degree programmes: talk of 'transferable skills' is unlikely to fade away!

What Skills Do You Need to Be Successful in Your Research Degree?

When I started my PhD I thought that 'transferable skills' was just a buzz phrase, but after taking part in the UK GRAD programme and other smaller courses I have begun to realise just how important they are. It was especially useful to learn more about giving and receiving feedback in my group. This has improved communication with other members of my research group as well as my supervisors. The benefits of this were rapid assessment and improvement of projects throughout their lifecycle, ultimately resulting in a higher standard of research.

(Research Student)

It can be useful to think about the skills and competencies you have in terms of two distinct groups. First, there are subject and research-specific skills. These may include data collection and analysis skills for example.

Second, in order to be successful as a researcher, you will use a set of other general skills that you can use in any area of your life and that are common for all research students. For example, project management skills. These include being able to see the big picture, defining and setting goals, prioritising activities and working to deadlines.

These general skills also include skills of reflection. This is about making time to take a step back to consider how your research is going. What is working well? Where might there be gaps in your knowledge or skills, which slow your progress in your research?

Here is one way of doing a progress report for yourself. The JSS mentioned at the beginning of this chapter is written in the third person. To help you to apply it to your own situation it has been converted it into a first-person exercise, which you can find on the UK GRAD website. To do this, visit www.grad.ac.uk select 'Resources', then 'Just for Postgrads', then 'Managing Yourself' and finally 'Evaluate your skills'. The URL is www.grad.ac.uk/evaluateskills

You will see that broadly speaking the structure of the JSS is, to begin with, the most research-related skills (the first group of skills described above) and then it moves on to more generic (transferable) skills. The extract below illustrates one 'research-related' and one 'transferable' skill area from the seven areas of the JSS.

You can use the JSS exercise to help you (a) audit your skills, (b) assess your training needs and (c) prepare a development plan. Work gradually through the statements, thinking about the context of successfully completing your research degree. For each statement

- give yourself a rating based on your current competence
- note the best example you have achieved to date
- think of ways to improve.

It is useful to record your responses in writing – this will make it easier to track your development over time. The exercise on the UK GRAD website has columns for recording your responses.

EXTRACT FROM UK GRAD WEBSITE JSS EXERCISE

Research Environment

- I have a broad understanding of the context, at the national and international level, in which research takes place
- I am aware of issues relating to the rights of other researchers, of research subjects, and of others who may be affected by the research
- I appreciate and apply the standards of good research practice in my institution and/or discipline
- I understand relevant health and safety issues and demonstrate responsible working practices
- I understand the processes for funding and evaluation of research
- I can justify the principles and experimental techniques used in my own research
- I understand the process of academic or commercial exploitation of research results.

Communication Skills

- I can write clearly and in a style appropriate to purpose, e.g. progress reports, published documents, thesis
- I can construct coherent arguments and articulate ideas clearly to a range of audiences, formally and informally through a variety of techniques
- I can constructively defend research outcomes at seminars and viva examination
- I contribute to promoting the public understanding of my research field
- I effectively support the learning of others when involved in teaching, mentoring or demonstrating activities.

This section has been designed to help you understand the range of skills that you will benefit from developing and how they will help you to get the most out of your research project. Clearly, no research degree (or researcher) is the same – the skills and experience you bring to your research and the demands of the particular research project will make for limitless variations in individual's skill development needs.

Many research students' first reaction to the JSS exercise is to see the relevance of skills that they can relate immediately to their research in the 'here and now', but take more convincing that some of the more general skills are worth investing time in. To take the example of the quotation at the start of this section, the research student was surprised to find that developing 'giving and receiving feedback' skills could lead directly to better research.

Transferring Skills beyond the Research Degree

The best way to appreciate the transferability of the type of skills discussed here is to imagine the options for your development as a set of concentric circles (see Figure 14.1). In the centre is your current project, your research degree. Around this is a second circle, representing the option of continuing as a researcher within academia. Around this, moving further away from your research degree, is a third circle representing the option of becoming an academic. This is distinct from being purely a researcher, since many academics have responsibilities beyond researching, for example, teaching, supervising and managing. You may also decide that you want to use your research-specific skills or knowledge, but move out of the academic sector, perhaps working for a government agency or department, a private company, a not-for-profit organisation or in a self-employed capacity. The final circle represents the option least obviously related to your research degree: that is, working outside academia and in a non-research role (Section III – Chapter 26 – of this book considers such destinations in detail).

FIGURE 14.1   Development options

How the skills developed during your research degree apply to future jobs will depend on the nature of your research and the job or career you pursue. Most of those skills listed in the JSS are likely to be of immediate relevance to 'all' of the options within Figure 14.1.

For example, if you move into post-doctoral research after your research degree, you will use research management skills – defining the outcomes of projects, understanding the bigger picture and the research context, working well with others to achieve shared goals, managing resources, time and budgets.

If your next move is a research role outside academia you should be able to build very directly on the 'personal effectiveness' and communication skills that you developed during your research degree. These may include being flexible, creative and open-minded and constructively defending research outcomes. You will almost certainly need to 'own' your continuing professional development and take the initiative in order to progress.

In general, non-academic employers are looking for people who work well both independently and in teams, present themselves and their work professionally and effectively, can manage projects and deliver results. For example, managing the public relations of a small charity may need skills in developing creative approaches to achieve results, nurturing cooperative networks and key relationships, ensuring that published information is credible and reliable, constructing coherent arguments and articulating ideas to a range of audiences. These are all skills that you can develop during a research programme.

These examples show more clearly why there has been so much powerful advocacy for emphasising the development of research students' transferable skills. Support for the development of transferable skills is based on the view that such development achieves two desirable outcomes: it helps students to complete their doctorates successfully *and* prepares them to perform at a high level in their next roles, whatever and wherever they may be.

Who Is Responsible for Developing Your Transferable Skills?

Who is responsible for identifying your training needs and your skills development, recording and review? On the one hand, according to the QAA Code of Practice, your institution clearly has a number of responsibilities. These include ensuring that you are informed of the development opportunities available, and that your supervisor meets with you early on to agree your development needs and a plan for meeting them.

On the other hand, the code of practice also requires research students to take responsibility for their own development. You should work with your supervisor to identify training needs and then attend any development opportunities that have been agreed. You are also required to keep written records of your development. The taking of responsibility, moreover, is built into the JSS within the skills themselves – note in particular, the references to self-awareness, self-discipline and self-reliance.

In practice, of course, the responsibility is shared between you and the institution and works best when the two parties collaborate. The precise nature of that sharing varies a good deal between institutions.

What varies less, is the importance of postgraduate researchers' supervisors. The supervisor role is pivotal. Supervisors need to help their students to identify both their training needs and appropriate opportunities, linking the student to the institution as they do so. In turn the institution has responsibility for ensuring that supervisors are adequately briefed and are not overburdened. There is more on these aspects in Chapters 8 and 9 of this volume.

Your Personal Development

Integral to achieving the aims of the Roberts agenda and the essence of the QAA Code of Practice as discussed earlier in this chapter, is the process of Personal Development Planning or PDP as it is often referred to. It is through individual reflection on learning and development that you will really be able to take stock of your skills and abilities and plan further development.

The Code of Practice puts special emphasis on the importance of PDP. PDP is defined sector-wide as 'a structured and supported process undertaken by an individual to reflect upon their own learning, performance and/or achievement and to plan for their personal, educational and career development' (QAA, 2001 see 'What is a Progress File').

Research students very often make the point that

> It's very easy to get buried in the research and neglect personal development. Without a formal requirement (and reminders) to do so I would probably forget all about it. (UKGRAD, 2004: 5)

Your personal development plan (PDP) will include four main stages:

1 Assessing your skills, as they are at present, and your training needs
2 Formulating a plan for development
3 Implementing your plan and recording your development
4 Reflecting on the impact of the development.

This process is a cycle enabling you to take control of your development. Many institutions have developed or adapted PDP tools for their postgraduate researchers. Finding out about what your institution provides in the way of support for your personal development (if indeed it has not already been made clear to you) is the obvious first move.

There are also other tools available (the majority free of charge) to supplement what your institution offers and which may be extremely useful.

Tools for Auditing Your Skills and Analysing Your Needs

Chapter 23 in this volume looks at valuing your transferable skills in the context of career choice after completing your research degree. This section explores some tools available to support you to audit your skills and consider your training needs within the context of successfully completing your research degree. All these resources are referenced in the final section of this chapter.

As has already been suggested, the JSS (especially its reformulation earlier in this chapter) provides one tool for auditing your skills. One advantage of using this tool is that, because it has become incorporated into the QAA Code of Practice, it provides something of a common language among professionals tasked with providing training for postgraduates.

There are, however, other tools available. The Royal Society of Chemistry (see www.rsc.org), for example, has developed its own Postgraduate Skills Record (PSR). This divides postgraduate skills into six categories:

1   Handling information
2   Communication skills
3   Improving learning and performance
4   Planning and organisation
5   Working with others
6   Scientific skills.

Despite the different method used for classifying skills, there is in fact a good deal of overlap with the JSS in terms of content. It could provide the different perspective you need – whether or not you are a chemist.

UK GRAD has developed a series of searchable online databases to enable professionals to share practice relating to skills development and postgraduate researchers are welcome to also register to seek ideas and resources used in other institutions. The relevant databases here are the (specialised) PDP Database and the (broader) Database of Practice. From www.grad.ac.uk go to the Resources section.

In thinking about developing new skills, it can be helpful to assess the styles in which you learn. Assessing your learning style can help you to select those training and development opportunities most suitable for you. You can also, on the basis of your assessment, seek to become a more all-round learner by deliberately expanding the range of learning styles that you employ (see 'Sources of support' at the end of this chapter for some suggested websites for exploring learning styles).

Once you have assessed yourself and your needs, you can then see where the gaps are and begin to plan your development. Again, there are several resources to assist you. The Royal Society of Chemistry's PSR and many other frameworks seek to do this by encouraging you to think of your development in terms of a continuous cycle involving assessment, planning, implementation, recording, reflection and reassessment. London Metropolitan University, for example, has a log book which prompts you to consider skills according to what stage you are at in the research process, and the University of Sussex runs a reflective workshop programme for humanities researchers which leads to an online professional profile. It is important to check what is available at your own institution.

An additional resource for planning your self-development is available from the UK GRAD website. This resource, which you can use on its own or in combination with those outlined above, focuses on developing personal objectives. It does this by guiding you through four stages of thinking by identifying the following:

1 What is stopping you from achieving your goal?
2 What will help you to achieve your goal?
3 Resources available to help. And then,
4 Asking you to set yourself deadlines.

The website supplements this framework by supplying detailed advice on how to formulate objectives and also some worked examples. The URL is www.grad.ac.uk/setobjectives

Support to Implement Your Plan and Record Development

It is worth stressing that formal training courses are far from being the only means of developing skills offered by universities and national organisations. Skills may also be developed by, for example, practical experience (and reflection on that experience). As the QAA Code of Practice notes, involvement with such activities as, say, the organisation of a conference or the editing of a journal may provide useful opportunities for development. These may also be activities that you undertake outside of the research environment.

One key national provider of support for developing the skills of postgraduate researchers is the UK GRAD Programme. GRAD has helped to co-ordinate institutions' provision of postgraduate training by establishing eight regional 'hubs'. These are regional centres that aim to increase the provision, quality and choice of training for researchers.

One of the most popular training opportunities provided outside research students' own institutions are GRADschools. These are provided each year by UK GRAD. There are two types: national GRADschools attracting participants from across the country and regional or local GRADschools, both varying in length between three and five days. In addition, UK GRAD provides a number of shorter, more specialised courses at such as the Career in Focus programme providing an insight into careers in specific sectors.[6]

GRADschools are designed for postgraduate students of all disciplines. They provide intensive, broad-based development activities involving a mix of the following:

- Skills-development exercises (e.g. creativity, communication and presentations)
- Career sessions (e.g. improving your CV, defining your career goals and interview practice)
- Case studies (to practise skills while increasing your awareness of career options).

Many of the activities are conducted in groups or teams, always supported by tutors with extensive work experience.

GRADschools typically receive very positive evaluations. Almost all participants (93% in 2005) leave the course motivated to complete their research degree. Many people find that these events help them to manage their actual research better – and two thirds identify improvements in being flexible and adaptable in solving problems, while others develop innovative and creative approaches to their research.[7]

> What made the course so useful was how it allowed you to escape from the intricacies of PhD work and explore what you had to offer others . . . .In the job market personal qualities and transferable skills will be ranked in equal measure with specific technical expertise. The GRADschool course at Otterburn explicitly addressed these, drew them out of us through an astonishing array of curious, amusing, complex, and thought-provoking challenges. The schedule was packed with opportunities to stretch us every which way, and it worked. It was a truly outstanding programme which has given me the momentum I needed to continue. (Research Student)

You can find out more about GRADschools (including application details and information about funding) from the UK GRAD website (www.grad.ac.uk). Click first on 'GRAD courses' and then on the 'Postgraduate researchers' option. The URL is www.grad.ac.uk/GRADschools.

Recording Your Personal Development

Developing transferable skills (particularly when you are 'learning by experience') is often extremely enjoyable and there is a danger that the more routine business of recording and reflecting on what you have learned gets forgotten. Remember to think about the whole PDP cycle as outlined above, with four stages (assessing your skills and your training needs; formulating a plan for development; implementing your plan and recording your development; and reflecting on the impact of the development).

If you forget to analyse what exactly you have learned and fail to set yourself targets for applying those skills in your daily life (within your research project and other activities) the benefits of the skills development may soon be lost.

Others' Experiences: Why Personal Development Works!

Inevitably some of the discussion above has been generalised or abstract. To balance this, we would like to finish by providing real-life examples in boxes below. We hope that you will recognise in these accounts many of the themes that we have discussed above. It may be useful as you read, to consider the role of the following:

- Subject-specific, research-specific and more general skills
- Formal and informal development opportunities
- Ownership and responsibility.

The importance of personal development support alongside academic research:

I am currently studying towards a PhD in Molecular Plant Genetics at a UK University. You quickly realise that it is once you are in your lab that the 'on the job' training begins.

One aspect of the Graduate Training Programme (GTP) is a recognition that regular work should be completed that consolidates research findings. To do this we present our work in a seminar and as a poster. As a result of participating, one example of a transferable skill that I developed is being able to 'cherry pick' good data from what should be a wealth of experiments. In doing this, I began to realise where our good data comes from and how I might develop and improve upon this.

Organisational skills and personal development are encouraged by the GTP who provide a Personal Record of Achievement, in which you should log everything you partake in within the confines of your PhD or otherwise. I think this is really important as the faculty (not to mention potential employers) highly values students that manage their time well enough to incorporate activities which promote their personal development. I and several of my peers have found a good way to develop personal skills is to demonstrate in Undergraduate laboratory practicals. I was able to work on and improve my communication skills as we are challenged to explain conceptually advanced topics to students who are themselves challenged, and sometimes even a little apathetic.

As the vice-student rep on the GTP board, I have had the opportunity to discuss what we, as students, thought were our training needs. As a result myself and a colleague organised a PhD away day, focusing on 'increasing personal effectiveness'. The feedback was excellent because people went away equipped with techniques to manage their time and resources more effectively – which will have a direct impact on achieving their research goals.

I began my PhD as a mature student with a full range of administrative and secretarial qualifications, and all the skills I'd developed as a wife and mother.

Not all PhD students are white, middle-class, 21-year-olds moving straight on from an undergrad degree! In the History department at Teesside we have what is known as the 'LWL' – the 'Ladies Who Lunch'. This is a group which I set up with three other PhD students (all mature ladies, well, 47, 50, 52 and 57-years old) and our postgraduate Tutor. Once a month, come hell or high water, we arrange to meet for lunch, coffee or supper and just get things off our chests. It really does not matter if the other members of the group are not studying the same subject as you – they are under the same constraints and pressures, and an evening in the pub enables you to laugh, cry or just sympathise together.

I decided to go on a GRADschool because I am a great believer in life-long learning and that if you are offered a chance to try something different then you should take it. Competition for the right job now seems much more about branding yourself as a product – the right tool for the job! So I needed to see how to develop those new skills; how to present myself and my CV to the best advantage, whether my years of experience in offices was still relevant, and how to edit my experience into a list of positive assets which I could 'sell' to a future employer. I needed to see how other people perceived me. I was also interested to meet people who might be potential employers and discuss with them how to turn my very humdrum CV into the sort of document which would merit a second look.

When I got back I sat down with a cup of coffee and read my personal positive consequences, a game we played where we all wrote (anonymously) positive attributes we saw in our fellow team members, to be opened only when we got home. My team thanked me for being friendly, a team player, creative, funny, diplomatic and up for anything. Since then I used the skills I honed at GRADschool to take a good hard look at my thesis and also at where I wanted to go after my PhD was over.

First, I gave myself a rigorous overhaul and saw that I was treading water with my research. I actually had all the information I needed to write up the last chapter and the appendices, but I had been prevaricating, probably due to a lack of confidence in my own ability to succeed. I had to sit down and finish writing it, which I did.

Second, I arranged a career interview with the University Careers Office and gave my CV a completely new look. Following advice from the experts at the GRADschool, I opted for a skills-based CV which would concentrate on all my experience, my skills, both academic and transferable, and my strengths. This has enabled me to 'sell myself' and almost immediately after completing my PhD, I was asked if I would join, temporarily, the History staff at Teesside to teach a first-year undergraduate course. Since then I have been asked to teach the MA History course next academic year, and have been invited to do some freelance writing for an Arts Council sponsored travelling exhibition.

What I think I also learned at GRADschool was that being part of an elite – the UK PhDs – is a responsibility which one must act on. It is not enough just to say, 'I've got my PhD, so I deserve a good job'; what one should really say is 'Now I've got my PhD, where do I go with it?' If you change your attitude to see it as a springboard, then you may find yourself pursuing a whole range of wider options than you considered originally. As an Arts PhD, it is normal to go into an academic environment, either teaching or researching, but I have already found other outlets for my work with a local artist and with a local landowner who wants me to write a new guidebook for his property and a history of his family. While this is essentially academic, it gives me scope for using my research skills and my transferable skills in tandem, and then putting my finished work into the public domain for all to see.

The thing to remember about the process of undertaking a research degree is that it is primarily your responsibility. Universities and research institutes are committed to supporting your development, so do make the most of the opportunities available. Talk to your supervisor if you feel that you need more help in either identifying which skills you need to develop further, or how to develop the ones you have already identified. If you need further support, check who else in your institution is there to help: this should be clear from your postgraduate handbook.

Conclusion

This chapter has focused on the importance and relevance of the skills agenda for researchers in the UK, and has outlined some resources that support researchers' self-development. We hope that now you've read this chapter you will also have a clearer idea of the opportunities available for developing yourself and what may be gained from seeing your research degree as a way of trying, testing and honing your skills.

All our experiences in life can bring new insights, so however experienced or inexperienced you are when you embark on your research studies, there will always be opportunities to expand your self-knowledge, your understanding of how others relate to you and your effectiveness in carrying out the tasks in hand. Embrace them – often taking a risk can lead to a breakthrough in something you weren't expecting!

Notes

1   We gratefully acknowledge the assistance of The Professional and Higher Partnership in the preparation of this chapter.
2   Taken from the 'Career Development and Skills (Roberts) reporting 2005' rzport by RCUK for the UK GRAD Policy Forum, 11/12 January 2006, Aston www.grad.ac.uk/downloads/documents/Forums/Policy%20Forum%202006/Summary%20of%20Roberts%20reporting%202005.pdf
3   www.grad.ac.uk/europolicy
4   www.europe unit.ac.uk is the briefing service for universities on Higher Education developments in Europe
5   www.ec.europa.eu/eracareers/pdf/am509774CEE_EN_E4.pdf

6   www.grad.ac.uk/cif
7   All statistics based on 2005 student appraisals for national GRADschools. Available from the
     UK GRAD Programme.

SOURCES OF SUPPORT

UK GRAD Programme: www.grad.ac.uk

Tools to Help You Assess Your Own Skills

There are many web resources available to support you assess your skills. Here is just
a selection – explore your own Institution's websites and careers service.
University College London. Browse for postgraduates (visit www.ucl.ac.uk/keyskills/
grad/index.html). This is a useful site that presents Key Skills in a grid under the
headings of academic skills, self- management skills, communication skills and interpersonal skills with advice and links into resources to improve your skills.

The Shell Big Trip. The site (visit www.thebigtrip.co.uk/) includes a personal profile
that asks you to rate your 'key personal values' along with your transferable skills and
personal strengths.

The Royal Society of Chemistry. It has developed a *Postgraduate Skills Record*
(visit www.rsc.org/Education/HEstudents/PSR/index.asp) of continuing professional
development that covers various stages of the doctorate. It enables postgraduate
researchers to record, assess and identify skills which need developing during their
research degree programme. It is aimed at chemists, but it is applicable to any
experimental research and most of the sections are generic to all postgraduates.

Tools to Help You Assess Your Own Styles, Preferences and Goals

Some of these tools cost money to use, but your graduate school, staff development
department or careers service might have a licence and be able to offer advice, so
check first before paying for an individual online assessment.

Business Balls. The site includes Kolb's learning styles model and experiential learning theory (visit www.businessballs.com/kolblearningstyles.htm).

Learning Styles. The site provides free information and tools to help you understand
and use learning styles effectively (visit www.learning-styles-online.com/).

Belbin. Its te*am roles* section pick out the way we behave, contribute and inter-relate
when working in any team. They are used to assess your preferred behaviour when
working with others (visit www.belbin.com/).

MBTI (Myers Briggs Type Indicator). It identifies and describes personality types based
on personal preferences (visit www.myersbriggs.org/). Thinking about your preferences
can help you to work more effectively with others and to make good career choices.

Lifework Transitions. This is a valuable interactive resource that has exercises on
defining core competencies, your passions, preferences and purpose, and goal setting
(visit www.lifeworktransitions.com/exercises/exercs.html).

References

AHRC (December 2006) *Arts and Humanities Research Council Career Path Study of PhD Students*, available at: www.ahrc.ac.uk/images/PhD_Report.pdf (accessed 30 June 2007). The study tracked research students who began their PhD between 1997 and 2000.

QAA (2001) www.qaa.ac.uk/academicinfrastructure/progressFiles/guidelines/progfile 2001.asp (accessed 30 June 2007).

Roberts, G. (2002) *SET for Success: The Supply of People with Science, Technology, Engineering and Mathematics Skills,* www.hm-treasury.gov.uk./Documents/Enterprise_and_ Productivity/Research_and_Enterprise/ent_res_roberts.cfm (accessed 30 June 2007).

UKGRAD (2004) 'A national review of emerging practice on the use of Personal Development Planning for postgraduate researchers', *2004 UK GRAD Programme*, at www.grad.ac.uk/downloads/pdp_review.pdf (accessed 30 June 2007).

15 Presentation Skills
Dr Helen Lawrence

Introduction

Your research project may be the most exciting, cutting-edge investigation in your area but the reality is that if that research is not presented effectively, nobody will know about it. This chapter explores some of the issues surrounding giving presentations and, acknowledging that effective presentation does not come easily to everyone, aims to give some advice and guidance about the practicalities of planning, creating and giving presentations.

We have all seen some terrible presentations. I was astounded at the first academic conference I attended to see a well-known researcher presenting some findings whilst standing in front of his projector so that the screen showed a perfect silhouette. His diagrams were just about visible on his shirt. Handwritten overhead transparencies, PowerPoint™ presentations with every possible animation, presenters speaking too quietly, too quickly, with too much or too little variety in tone...the list is nearly endless. It seems that presentations are hazardous territory.

Be encouraged. This chapter is intended to provide a map to the territory. It will not take the hazards away, but it will identify them and give advice on how they can be avoided.

EXERCISE

Before reading further, take some time to make a list of all the habits you associate with poor presentations. What is it that irritates you as a member of the audience? What is likely to make you lose concentration and stop listening to the speaker? Make your list as comprehensive as possible, write down everything you can think of.
Now select the ten most dreadful habits from your list, ending with the worst:

10:————————————————

 9:————————————————

8:——————————————————
7:——————————————————
6:——————————————————
5:——————————————————
4:——————————————————
3:——————————————————
2:——————————————————
1:——————————————————

Refer to this list when you are preparing a presentation. If you can avoid these, you will be well on the way to giving a great performance.

Different Presentation Settings

There is a wide variety of different presentations research students may be called upon to give. The good practice described throughout this chapter applies to all these different settings.

Conference Presentations

As a research student, it is important to engage with the wider 'community of practice',[1] as described in Chapter 16. Attending academic conferences is an ideal way to meet other researchers in the field, and is the appropriate place to present work that is ready to be released into the public domain. Attendance at academic conferences is also excellent longer-term preparation for your viva (see Chapter 21).

Timing is crucial. A presentation will be designated a time slot, typically lasting somewhere between 10 and 30 minutes. It is important to note what the time allocation is; often it will be expressed in a form which clarifies question periods: for example, '20 minutes plus 10 minutes questions'. Do not let your presentation use up the question time, as this will result in losing the very valuable opportunity to field questions in a public setting. Time the presentation carefully so it fits the allocation.

Many conferences have parallel sessions, where two or more talks are ongoing at any one time. The delegates thus have a choice of which presentations to attend. In order to gauge the approximate size of the audience for your own presentation if you are delivering such a session, take the number of delegates and divide by the number of parallel sessions.

It is worth paying particular attention to who the audience will be. To get a general idea, talk to colleagues who have attended the conference in previous years. Studying the advertising material marketing the conference, looking at who this has been sent to and how the conference is marketed will also give a good idea of who may attend. Then look through the delegate list and the conference programme as soon as it is available, to see who is actually going to be there. It may be that researchers are present whose work is in a similar area, in which case it is wise to consider the impact of their work on the field. Does it raise issues which you should address? How will you refer to other people's research?

Poster Presentations

Giving a poster at a conference or other event is a valuable way of publicising research without giving a standard oral presentation. The presenter is encouraged to create a poster (to a specification provided by conference organisers) giving a flavour of the research. It is common for poster presenters to stand by their posters to answer questions. The good practice described throughout this chapter also relates to presenting a poster.

Departmental/School/Faculty Presentations

You may have the opportunity to present your research within a departmental, school or faculty seminar series within your own institution. This provides valuable experience in presenting research, in a less public arena than national or international conferences. Departmental seminars vary in formality, size and timing and it is important that research students attend these seminars in advance of having to present, in order to gain an appreciation of what is expected.

Media Interviews

If your research is of particular public interest, you may find you are asked for an interview by the media. If this is the case, ensure that the likely agenda of the interviewer (or their editor) is known in advance, and what the message is that the public need to hear. An under-prepared interviewee is at greater risk of being misquoted or misinterpreted. It is wise to contact a more senior academic with experience in this area for advice; they may then recommend talking to the university's communications office. Some institutions have clear policies on speaking to the media and staff who support academics with this.

Interview Presentations

Increasingly candidates for jobs are asked to give a presentation as part of the interview process. Read and follow the instructions carefully, as every aspect of your presentation will be assessed. For example, a candidate who had been asked for a 5-minute talk spoke for 18 minutes. Content aside, this gave a negative message about his attention to detail, ability to follow instructions and time management. It is also important to consider whether, in the context of the job applied for, it is the content of the presentation or presentation style which is of primary importance.

Size of Audience

Although the advice in this chapter about giving presentations applies regardless of the size or setting of a presentation, there are different issues to bear in mind if presenting to an audience of 500 than if there are 10 people in the room. Some people find it more intimidating to present to a small group where there is little opportunity to avoid interaction with individuals; others find an anonymous sea of faces more challenging.

In essence, the larger an audience becomes, the more formal a presentation is likely to be, with eye-contact and interaction becoming more difficult, the use of a microphone more likely and the need for visual aids to be based on projection (using traditional slide projectors, overhead projectors or data projectors). These are easier for a large audience to see than hand-held props, flipcharts or other visual aids. Think about what the size of the audience means for you in preparing for your presentation.

Preparing Your Presentation

Regardless of the type of presentation or the size of the audience, there are two questions which should always be at the forefront of the presenter's mind during preparation:

1   Who is the audience?
2   What do they need to know?

Answering these two questions will in turn provide two results: first, it will provide a focused idea of what the central message of the presentation is; and second, it will provide an insight into what the presentation will be like from the audience's perspective.

Remember, a presentation is not about the presenter and what that person can do or has learned. It is about the audience and what they need to know.

EXERCISE

Before reading further, take a moment to make some notes about the next presentation you will give.

- Who will be in the audience? What do they already know?
- What is the single most important thing that you want them to learn from your presentation? Write this down in no more than 25 words.

This single most important lesson is the central message. This is the reason why the presentation is being given. The central message should be the theme of a presentation; to use a musical analogy, it should be the refrain to which every point made refers back. Therefore it is useful to continually refer to it throughout your preparation.

Deciding on the Content

Once the central message is discerned, return to the two questions posed earlier.

1 Who is the audience?
2 What do they need to know?

The answers to these questions should provide what the audience already knows as well as what they need to be told in order to understand the central message. Remember that the answer to the second question will always include 'nothing that takes longer than the time allowed'.

With the answers to these questions in mind, the presenter is now in a position to decide on the content of the talk. It is useful to consider the whole area of knowledge surrounding the theme of the presentation and then, with the central message firmly in the forefront of your mind, to decide:

1 What is essential to include?
2 What would be good to include?
3 What is dispensable?

Everything which could possibly be included in the presentation should be prioritised according to these criteria. This will help immensely when structuring the presentation.

Different Presentation Structures

When preparing a presentation, spend time considering the best structure to use. This is because clear structure aids understanding, supporting the audience's learning and engagement, and clear structuring also aids memory. While lectures are a particular kind of presentation, referring to Brown and Atkins' (1988) descriptions of structures of lectures (based on the work of Bligh, 1972) may be helpful. Various options are open, some of which are detailed below.

Classic or Sequential

This structure starts with an introduction which outlines what is going to be covered, generally setting the scene, then moves on to one piece of material after another, leading the audience step by step through the development of an idea. It ends with a conclusion which outlines the main points again. This structure in itself does not provide strength or direction to an argument.

Comparative

If the subject matter involves setting one argument or interpretation against another, it may be useful to structure a presentation in a comparative style, as laid out here:

Introduction	Interpretation X and Interpretation Y
Feature 1	Interpretation X and Interpretation Y
Feature 2	Interpretation X and Interpretation Y
Feature 3	Interpretation X and Interpretation Y
Summary	

Although this structure looks straightforward, it is demanding for both the presenter and the audience. The potential for confusion is considerable, so if this structure is chosen, do ensure that clear signals are given as to which interpretation is under discussion. Visual aids (to be discussed in detail later in this chapter) may well be key to the success of this method.

Problem-based

This may mirror the way that the research itself was approached. It begins with a statement of the research problem and then progresses through possible solutions tested before finally reaching the favoured solution of the problem. This is an engaging method as it carries the audience through the research process. As with the comparative approach, there is a possibility of confusion between potential solutions, especially when cross-references are made. Another potential hazard here is that if an audience member misses one stage of the process they may lose the whole flow of the argument. A good handout with the stages clearly laid out may help to guard against these pitfalls.

Question-based (In Conjunction with Others)

Using questions to move from one part of a presentation to another, regardless of which structure is employed, is a useful tool to connect with the audience.

It is likely that the audience is forming questions in their minds as they listen; and it is possible, with some thought, to anticipate some of these questions and to articulate them as the answer is about to be revealed. This demonstrates a presenter's empathy with the audience. For example:

> The next step was to look at a wider selection of data. How was this wider sample to be identified? I decided to follow Jones (2005) and take a random selection....

EXCERCISE

Before reading further, consider structure in relation to your own presentation material. What are the pros and cons for each with regard to your content? Is there an accepted structure within your discipline? Which structures have you seen in presentations you felt were particularly effective?

Visual Aids

Review your list of poor presentation habits. Frequently these relate to the use of visual aids. It can also be the case that a lack of visual aids in itself can present a problem for the audience. So how can the right balance be achieved?

To return to the central theme of this chapter, remember the two questions which should be kept in mind when preparing a presentation:

1   Who is the audience?
2   What do they need to know?

Considering visual aids from the audience's perspective will make it easier to produce useful, rather than distracting, materials.

Why Use Visual Aids At All?

A presentation is usually characterised by an individual speaking to a group of people. However, it is hard to concentrate on a presentation which uses solely the voice as a medium for communication. Without some variety, some opportunity to employ another of the five senses, most people will lose attention after a short period of time, regardless of how interested they may be in the topic.

Visual aids provide that opportunity. They give the audience an alternative focus and can often enable the presenter to describe more complex concepts with the assistance of diagrams or other illustrations.

Another benefit of visual aids is that they can make a presentation more memorable, as many people are more likely to remember what they see than what they hear. Handouts, of course, provide the ultimate in this function as they serve as both a visual aid during a presentation and an aide memoire afterwards. This does emphasise the importance of getting the visual aids right, as no one will want to be remembered for creating a poor impression.

Who Is the Audience?

Answering this question with visual aids in mind will often inform the presenter of what is possible. Will the audience be used to seeing PowerPoint™ presentations? Will they be expecting an overhead projector to be used? Are they more comfortable with simply following a presentation with a handout?

Do remember to find out at the earliest opportunity what facilities are available. Do not be like the interview candidate who invested a great deal of time in creating a beautiful PowerPoint™ presentation to accompany his job talk, only to check facilities the day before his interview and discover that the only equipment available was a chalkboard.

It is also important to be aware of people in your audience with particular needs: particularly those with sight or hearing impairments. There are often fairly straightforward measures which can be taken to ensure these members of your audience are catered for. There is helpful advice and guidance on how to use various technologies responsibly at the Techdis website.[2]

What Do They Need to Know?

At the most basic level, the audience needs to hear the central message. It is wise to ask:

1   How does this visual aid help convey my message?

Do be honest in your response to this. If the answer to this question is 'It doesn't add anything, but it looks great!', consider carefully whether the visual aid should be included.

Having made those general points, what follows is more specific.

Using PowerPoint™

Technology can be an extremely useful tool, however, it is important to remember it is *only* a tool. Make sure that it does not drive the presentation.

Text on a PowerPoint™ slide should only ever be key points, never the unedited text of a presentation to be read from the screen. A good guide is: maximum six lines of text per slide, each with a maximum of six words (the '6x6' rule).

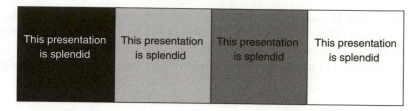

FIGURE 15.1 Examples of contrast between text and background

It is also wise to limit the number of slides in the presentation. Work on the principle of 2–3 minutes per slide.[3]

It may be tempting to use complex patterns or pictures as a background to a PowerPoint™ presentation, perhaps with the motivation of making it more interesting. Do remember your audience. The clarity of the presentation should take priority. Ensure that there is a good contrast between background and text. Look at the examples in Figure 15.1 and consider which ones are easiest to look at?

If it is important to have a logo or design device on a presentation (perhaps a university or research group logo), make sure it is in the same place on every slide. If it moves or changes size or colour, the moving motif will become a distraction for the audience, detracting from the presentation's message.

In order to keep the slides easy to read, choose a simple 'sans serif' font (without decorative fine lines at the top and bottom) like 'Arial' or 'Tahoma', and use between 30 and 40 point font size.

Before employing text effects, take a moment to ask:

1 How does this moving text/sound effect/animation help convey my message?

It may be that revealing text one point at a time helps your audience focus on the item under discussion; this can be very useful, but too much of this (or other animation) can be distracting.

One of the benefits of presentation technology is its versatility. Rather than using additional sound equipment to play an excerpt of data, for example, it is possible to have the item digitally recorded and then inserted into the presentation to be played by simply clicking an icon. Likewise it is possible to link to the Internet. All of these resources can be helpful.

However, every link is a potential hazard. Assess the risk of links not working. What can be done to minimise this risk? It may be worth forwarding a presentation to conference organisers in advance with a request that they test the links. How bad would it be if they didn't work? Is the link necessary, or could the point be made by using screen shots incorporated into the presentation? Is the desired effect worth the risk of technology failing?

Ensure that graphics and images are labelled carefully and that all text is to the side of images rather than superimposed over them. With all graphics, as with fonts, make sure that clarity and relevance take precedence over beauty.

What looks acceptable on a computer screen can often look very different projected onto a presentation screen and viewed from a distance, so try to view your presentation in advance whenever possible.

Be aware that whilst the Internet can provide an array of images, cartoons and pictures that can enhance presentations, some of them are copyright and so a charge is payable before they can be shown in public. Do read the small print on websites to establish the legal position before using images taken from them.

Summary – using PowerPoint™:

- Limit the amount of text on each slide
- Choose your background carefully
- Keep motifs or designs constant
- Use a simple font and large font size
- Use text effects and animation sparingly
- Use links to other software with caution
- Use graphics and images with care.

And while addressing all these points remember the question:

1 How will this help to convey the central message?

Just because something is possible, doesn't mean that it is advisable!

Overhead Projectors

Much of the guidance for using PowerPoint™ also applies to overhead projectors (OHPs). The key to success in using OHPs is to consider your transparencies, imagining you were part of the audience.

When creating transparencies, before printing them, look at them first on screen in Print Preview. If they can't be read easily without magnifying the image, the font is not large enough. Use 16 point as a minimum, many slides will look more effective at 24 point.

In some image-oriented disciplines it is common practice to use traditional slide projectors. If this applies to you, then practise and become familiar with projectors. Do not load the slide tray or carousel in a hurry and, time permitting, double-check them to ensure that they are the right way up and the right way around, that the lens is focused and that the projector is at the right height for the screen. The last two are particularly important when dealing with non-fixed projectors. Also make sure that the remote works, or that that there is someone who can forward the slides on request.

Handouts

Handouts can be used to great effect as both a visual aid and a record of a presentation. As such, make sure that any handouts provided include the title and date of the presentation as well as your name and your contact details. Give some thought to how a handout can best be used. Will it be sufficient for someone not at the presentation to gain an insight into the work presented? Or does it contain supplementary material useful only to those who hear the talk? Answering these questions will assist in deciding on the content and structure of a handout. It will also impact on whether the handout should be given out at the beginning of the talk (providing supplementary information, but will people read the handout rather than listening to the presentation?) or available at the end.

And of course, how will the handout help to convey the central message?

Props

A model, piece of equipment, relevant object etc. can make what is being said more tangible and more memorable. This is particularly useful with small groups (see above section on audience size) where a prop could perhaps be passed around, and will almost certainly be seen by the whole audience.

One Final Note of Caution

Almost any visual aid can go wrong, or for some reason be unavailable on the day. It is worthwhile spending some time working out contingency plans. What could be done if some or all of a presentation could not be staged with the planned visual aids? Could an alternative method be used? What could be done to prepare for the unthinkable?

Practising Your Presentation

The conference, interview or other presentation event should not be the first time that a talk is delivered. It is always a good idea to practise a presentation, if at all possible with a friendly and constructively critical audience. If there is a group going to a conference together, organising a practise session of all presentations to give feedback to each other would be a valuable experience. This will help to assure all participants that they are fully prepared, the material is familiar, that the visual aids are appropriate and that the timing fits the allocated slot. If it is not possible to practise with an audience, do make sure at least to talk through the presentation aloud. Sometimes it is only by hearing the words out loud that an awkward phrase can be noticed.

If possible, do be sure to become familiar with the presentation venue. This includes being familiar with the size, shape and layout of the room, and with any technology that must be used. There is little more disconcerting than expecting a seminar room with moveable chairs and suddenly being faced with a large lecture theatre filled with serried ranks of people, their faces obscured by the spotlight shining onto the podium. It is often the case that a presenter has no choice over a venue, but being prepared is the next best thing.

Finally: prepare until you know you are ready and then stop. Over-preparation can make you feel more nervous.

Dealing with Nervousness and Anxiety before and during a Presentation

Some people find that nervousness provides the adrenaline they need to focus and give a good performance; and some people find the mere thought of standing up in front of an audience positively crippling.

Read this section and then judge for yourself whether your fear is nervousness which may be helped by some of the techniques suggested, or a genuine and debilitating phobia. If the latter is the case, contacting your university's counselling service is a sensible step. However, if nervous reaction is simply an inconvenience, the advice below may help improve performance.

Prepare

Preparation (including practising), as discussed above, is the key to a successful presentation. If your material is familiar and the practicalities of your presentation thought through, the likelihood of anything going wrong is considerably lessened, and the 'fear of the unknown' reduced.

What Is the Truth about This Situation?

Stress reactions are only very occasionally about what is actually happening; usually they are a result of thinking about a situation. When the physical symptoms of anxiety are experienced, for example, 'butterflies' in the stomach, perspiration, increased heart rate, the body is responding to what the mind is telling it – that is, there is a dangerous situation here from which the body should be prepared to run. The good news is that each person can master their own thoughts, so ignore the mind for a few moments and focus instead on what is physically true about the situation.

Breathe!

Notice your breathing. Is it fast and shallow? Or are you breathing deep, slow breaths which are filling your lungs with oxygen and allowing your body to function as it was intended to? Full, deep breaths will increase a physical sensation of calm and you will find yourself more able to relax both before and during your presentation, and while you are talking, a deep breath will ensure that you can keep going until the end of your sentence.

Stand Up, Shoulders Down, Open Your Mouth Properly

Your vocal tract, the parts of your body designed for speech, is created to allow sound to be produced with natural ease. However, if you stand with your shoulders curving forwards and you speak with your mouth barely opening at all, the vocal tract is deprived of the space needed to be effective.

Know Yourself and Your Own Reactions

People respond differently to nervousness and it is important that each person knows their own reactions as this allows you to plan in advance. If your hands shake, avoid holding paper that will rustle and draw attention to the tremor. Avoid drinking coffee in the couple of hours before your presentation, but it is important to keep the voice lubricated by sipping water. If prone to breathlessness, find a way to give yourself a moment at intervals through your presentation to refocus on filling your lungs effectively. This could be by pausing each time you change a slide. No one will notice if you take a three-second break and that may well be sufficient.

EXCERCISE

How do you deal with your own anxiety in other, similar, stressful situations? Canvass opinions from your supervisor/colleagues/friends. How do they combat nerves? Which of these might work for you?

Practicalities of Giving Presentations

Reading from a Script or Speaking from Notes?

While politicians making speeches almost always do so by reading from a prepared script, most academic disciplines favour the more personal style which results from speaking from notes. A supervisor is a valuable source of information and advice about what is appropriate in your discipline.

If speaking from notes is expected, then you could try speaking from the handout if using one; or using the notes function of PowerPoint™; or using cue cards (small cards with one or two notes on each), which act as a prompt to the speaker and can be held discretely without rustling.

If the audience expects a presentation to be read from a script, as is the case in some disciplines (e.g. English Literature), ensure that the text is written as a script rather than what could be part of your thesis. Remember the audience. Make notes in the script to prompt a pause or change in tone. Rehearse so that the text is familiar, as this will help in maintaining connection with the audience.

Humour

Using humour within a presentation is sometimes recommended as a method of connecting with the audience. Laughter creates positive feelings and so it can be a way to enliven the proceedings and to engage with the audience on a personal level. However, do use humour with caution.

Be yourself. If humour does not come naturally to you, it is unwise to tell jokes within a presentation as it may be interpreted as insincere or false.

Remember the questions which should be central to preparing a presentation: how does this joke/quip help to convey the central message?

Allow for the fact that a multicultural audience will have a range of thresholds for what is acceptable and appropriate.

Appearance

People will notice the appearance of a presenter before the presentation even begins. Do spend a moment thinking about what is appropriate in the setting, as well as what you will feel comfortable and confident in.

Individuals have different styles and approaches. Some people feel confident in smart clothes; others will feel uncomfortable wearing clothes they would not usually wear. Do avoid clothes which will restrict breathing or which will reveal perspiration marks. Notice what the effect is of particular clothes on you: do you feel more or less confident when wearing a jacket in your presentation setting? Do you stand differently according to which shoes you are wearing, and if so, what is the impact on your voice?

Once it is established what is appropriate for the specific presentation setting, find an outfit in which you feel good; and make sure there is nothing about it which will either cause you to fidget or distract the audience from your message.

Eye-contact

Do try and communicate naturally with the audience. The level to which eye-contact is appropriate is culturally defined and it is important to establish what the expectation is within the culture in which the presentation will take place. In the UK, the norm is that there should be some eye-contact between people who are communicating with one another; this is also the case between presenter and audience. Do avoid staring at one person for extended periods of time, both the presenter and the audience member will feel more comfortable if eye-contact is made, held for a second or two and then broken as the presenter moves on to connect with another member of the audience.

Use of English

There is a large number of research students in the UK whose first language is not English, and yet English is the language in which they study and present. The challenge of this should not be underestimated. The more practice these researchers can get in speaking English in formal and informal contexts, the better.

If this applies to you, make an effort to use English in social settings, with colleagues or friends. When you practise your presentation, ask for specific feedback on the language from native English speakers. And primarily, be encouraged. Many native speakers will be in awe of your ability to present in English at all.

Conclusion

This chapter aimed to explore some of the issues surrounding giving presentations and to give advice and guidance about the practicalities of planning, creating and giving presentations.

To summarise, then, an effective presentation is one which

- is prepared with the audience in the forefront of the presenter's mind
- has a clear central message; everything else in the presentation is there to aid the conveying of that message
- has visual aids which have been selected to provide a helpful focus for the audience
- is given by a presenter who is calm and confident in the expression of the material.

And remember:

Who is the audience? What do they need to know?

Acknowledgements

It is essential to acknowledge the unwitting contributions of Steve Hutchinson, David Howard and Francis Newton. Between them they have taught me so much about presentation skills that writing this would have been impossible had I not been privileged to have worked with them. Many thanks are also due to Eleanor Loughlin and Karen Clegg for their comments and input.

Notes

1 This concept is discussed in the next chapter, and is based on the work of Wenger (1998).

2 www.techdis.ac.uk

3 If your talk is on a particularly visual topic, involving many images, it is common practice to have a dual projection, that is, showing an image on one screen and text on another. If you are doing this, remember that it takes longer to take in this information. Work on a minimum of three minutes per slide in this case. If complex equations are shown, it may take longer than two to three minutes for the audience to digest, so it is important either to present the information in an alternative and more easily accessible way, or to show the slide for sufficient time.

SOURCES OF SUPPORT

For those who are serious about enhancing presentation skills, it is worthwhile asking for feedback on presentations from people in the audience. Select people who will be direct and constructive. If possible, an extension to this exercise is to watch yourself on video. Whilst this is not necessarily a comfortable process, it is often an invaluable learning tool.

The best way to learn presentation skills is to practise. Many research students have found valuable opportunities on UK GRADschools (described in more detail in Chapter 14 of this volume), where a supportive environment makes it easier to try new skills. Find more details of these at: www.grad.ac.uk/GRADschools. It is also highly likely that your own institution offers courses on presentation skills for research students – ask your supervisor about this.

Andrew Bradbury (2000) *Successful Presentation Skills (2nd edn)*. London: Kogan Page Ltd.

This book is not written specifically for research students but for people doing presentations in a wide variety of contexts, and this is its strength. The points Bradbury makes are applicable to any presentation, and his style is accessible and informed.

Joan van Emden and Lucinda Becker (2004) *Presentation Skills for Students*. Basingstoke: Palgrave Macmillan.

This is aimed at people using presentation skills within a further or higher education environment. The readers are not assumed to have a great deal of experience. It is worth reading for the context-specific content.

Andy Hunt (2005) *Your Research Project: How to Manage It*. Oxford: Routledge.

This is an excellent resource for researchers, which covers many aspects of the postgraduate experience. It has a valuable section on communicating with others, including some useful tips on presentations.

References

Bligh, D. (1972) *What's the Use of Lectures?* Harmondsworth, UK: Penguin Books.

Brown, B. and Atkins, M. (1988) *Effective Teaching in Higher Education*. London: Routledge.

Wenger, E. (1998) *Communities of Practice: Learning, Meaning and Identity*. Cambridge: Cambridge University Press.

16 Academic Conferences
Dr Martyn Kingsbury and
Dr Roberto Di Napoli

Introduction

In this chapter we aim to alert readers to the importance of conferences for scholarly development both in terms of knowledge enhancement and of joining a group working in a particular discipline or specialism, and becoming part of a 'community of practice' (Wenger, 1998). This is followed by some practical issues for you to consider when thinking of attending a conference and, briefly, how to organise a conference of your own. The chapter starts with an excerpt from an interview with a postgraduate student, who was in the latter stages of her research, giving her initial impressions of attending academic conferences. This student was from a research group comprising medics and biomedical scientists, where international conference attendance and presentation was routine. While this may not be the norm for all, the excerpt helps to set the scene and raises some issues that are discussed later in the chapter.

There can be a great deal of variation in conference practices both within and between disciplines. Your supervisor, and, perhaps, more senior postgraduate colleagues, will play an important role in guiding you and introducing you to academic conferences. This chapter aims to facilitate this process by providing both background information and practical advice.

The world of conferences is evolving with the introduction of new technologies that allow virtual conferencing; however, we focus on traditional conferences, where groups of scholars gather together to consider a specific theme, as these remain the most common. Also, it is especially at these traditional conferences that you will have the advantage of meeting other researchers face-to-face and getting an overall sense of a particular community of practice.

Case Study

An excerpt from an interview with a postgraduate research student (FC) in the final stages of her research degree in biomedical science:

MK: What do you remember about your first conference experience?

FC: My first conference or my first proper conference?

MK: What do you mean?

FC: Well, my first conference was a local one given by (a local group) and while it was interesting and I didn't feel nervous about my poster, it didn't really feel like a real conference compared to the next one (an international conference).

MK: What was that like?

FC: It was exciting; I 'saved' work and put in two abstracts - I was nervous 'cos it's quite competitive, but both got accepted. I didn't really expect that. It was a real event, five of us (from the department) went and there was a real build-up of excitement as we all got money, organised hotels and travel and practising our 'stuff'. When we got there (Strasbourg) it was great, loads of interesting stuff.

...I got a question from somebody from Maastricht and I bumped into him at the reception and what he said really helped with the extraction (a methodological) problem.

...The dinner was good we all got dressed-up, we had (a senior academic) on our table and I thought it might be awful but it was great after a wine or two and he seemed really interested in what I was saying.

...I think the next one is in Oslo, I might see if I can get stuff together for that, it's about time I had a look at what I've got as I'll be finishing off soon.

Academic Conferences as Learning Experiences

Knowledge Development and 'Communities of Practice'

Academic conferences are truly *learning experiences* where scholars and professionals go to present their own data and ideas, and/or to learn something new from their peers, within a given knowledge field.

The word knowledge is a contested one. Usually, people intuitively reify it; they see it as a 'thing', often synonymous with information. However, the more contemporary view is to understand knowledge not just as a static, 'objective' collection of data that resides in the mind of an individual but rather as an ever-developing entity that is constructed in the interaction among people. As Davenport and Prusak (1998: 5) put it:

> [K]nowledge is a flux mix of framed experiences, values, contextual information, and expert insight that provides a framework for evaluating and incorporating new experiences and information. It originates and is applied in the minds of knowers. In organizations, it often becomes embedded not only in documents or repositories but also in organizational routines, processes, practices, and norms.

Early in your academic career, as a student, it is normal that you see knowledge as 'something to study'. However, as you start postgraduate research, you increasingly become involved in work that produces or tests the knowledge in a discipline and conferences become an important arena for presenting and discussing that knowledge. Data gains new meaning when it is talked about (Mercer, 1995: 13) and conclusions are tested against the minds of others; conferences are optimal arenas for this.

The learning, however, does not stop at the subject knowledge level; conferences are also social experiences that offer individuals the opportunity to become part of a *community of practice* (Wenger, 1998). A community of practice entails the idea of the mutual engagement that, over time, binds members together into a social entity, through a shared repertoire of communal resources (knowledge, methods of investigation, routines, vocabulary, styles etc.). In other words, communities of practice are joint enterprises that are understood and continually renegotiated by their members. Conferences are events that assist their members in starting and/or strengthening their membership in a given community of practice (for instance, doctors, sociologists, historians etc.) and/or its sub-communities (cardiologists within medicine, or medievalists within history, for example). Furthermore, as you increasingly participate you become an 'insider' and get *encultured* into the community, acquiring not only explicit formal expert knowledge but also the embodied ability to behave as a full community member (Brown et al., 1989; Brown and Duguid, 1991). Thus, not only are conferences important venues for postgraduates to gain, and ultimately present data, they also allow postgraduates to contribute to knowledge enhancement, and are important for disciplinary 'membership'.

Seen in this light, conferences have at least two dimensions: a knowledge-related one, in that they promote and spread new knowledge in a given disciplinary area; and a personal development one, in that they act as hubs for the formation and growth of the professional identities of those who participate in them through their contact with colleagues. This is clearly described by the student in our case study above. Because of their double nature, conferences constitute an integral part of the life of any academic and/or professional, and they are particularly important for postgraduate students. Not only do conferences put students in touch with current research and thinking within their own specialism, but, as importantly, with members of a particular community they aspire to be a part of. Conferences help students to realise the passage from student status to professional status.

Conferences as Gateways to 'Communities of Practice'

Having established how knowledge development and social interaction are strictly intertwined in this section, we have some suggestions of how best to take part in a conference community, although these are to raise awareness and are not hard and fast rules. Different people will have different preferred ways of interacting with communities of practice when at a conference.

When entering a new group, it can help to picture yourself as an anthropologist looking at how the community sees itself and works together. To achieve this, you should consider questions like: what are the priorities of this particular community? What do these say about the ethos of the community and its practices? Is the community hierarchical or inclusive, that is, open to the contribution of many of its members? Can one easily find a voice in it or is space mainly granted to established members? How is this reflected in its conference structures? Is there a dedicated space for postgraduates? If so, what are the rules to follow in order to access such a space? In other words, 'study' the way a specific conference reflects the norms and values of its community, especially in terms of granting space to its (new) members. A good supervisor will be an invaluable source of information about, and guide to, your particular community of practice and will help with the process of gaining 'membership' and acceptance. However, there are things you can do independently – visiting websites and/or obtaining printed materials are often the quickest and most economical ways to gain information, but if you are lucky, you may be able to visit a conference to observe, although this is likely to be a small local (and therefore cheap) conference.

Once you have a sense of how a conference reflects the group it serves, the group's ethos, values and behaviours, you then have to decide at what level to participate in a conference. If you manage to obtain funding (and this might be difficult), is it possible to take part as an observer, just to get a sense of how a certain group works and listen to possible novelties in terms of knowledge development? Or is a more active role, presenting your research/thinking preferable? A gradual immersion within a new community is often preferable and more fruitful than a head-on one. In this sense, it may be good practice to take part in local events (organised by your department or institution for instance) before launching into national and international conferences. It is recommended that, over time, you experience as many different conferences and conference contexts as possible, as they add important knowledge to the sense you may have of a given community of practice, and are an opportunity to meet some of the community's key members. The 'exposure' you choose will depend on your experience, needs and confidence.

There are a number of reasons why conferences can be excellent opportunities for postgraduates to become better situated within a community of practice:

- Conferences help to *map knowledge and identify gaps* – this is especially useful as a research student, when you are attempting to position your own research within wider contexts and capitalise on any innovation you can bring. This is particularly true in the UK, where the *viva* is not a public event (see Chapters 2 and 21 in this volume) and conferences offer other means to present your work to your academic peers.
- Mixing with colleagues at a conference is also an opportunity to *seek experience* and *request information* about questions and doubts arising from your own research and thinking – this often happens in the interstices

of a conference, over coffee or lunch, when socialising helps dialogue at different levels with other participants.

- Similarly, you can use conferences both to *find synergies* with other colleagues with a common interest, and/or to *explore possibilities* for application of ideas and results, as they emerge during a conference – this can be important for a postgraduate seeking to define the focus, scope and possible applicability of their own thinking and research. A good supervisor will facilitate such synergies *in situ*, by introducing you to other researchers who share your interests during the conference.

- Finally, conferences are places where you can *discuss developments* of a possible novel project and *plan visits* to take initial ideas further. It is often at conferences that new projects are born, through informal discussions with colleagues. Setting such projects in motion is one of the best ways to start being fully part of a community and acquiring a voice of one's own in it. Acquiring a voice is one of the most challenging tasks for research students, as they are new to the game, so to speak. Taking part in conferences is one of the best ways to achieve this. They are excellent arenas to try out your ideas and facilitate their development, and can be important in your academic and professional development well beyond the postgraduate stage.

The activities described above could be superficially described as networking, but there is more to conference attendance than simply networking. Becoming an academic (and a professional) entails joining a community of practice where you share the responsibility for the pursuit of knowledge in your particular subject area, which requires an attitude of open and honest co-operation with your peer community, and the conference is often the forum for this interaction.

Features and Practices of Academic Conferences

We have discussed academic conferences as communities of practice and shown the important part they play in forming and disseminating the knowledge base of any discipline, both in terms of substantive subject knowledge and of the implicit 'social' knowledge that allows you to both absorb and be absorbed into the culture of the community of practice. In this section, we will consider the more practical aspects of academic conferences and give some generic advice that will help fuller understanding and participation.

A Conference Life Cycle

There is considerable variation in what constitutes an academic conference both between and within disciplines; they can range from large international gatherings with multiple parallel sessions to small gatherings of those with a commonly shared specific interest. There are, however, some generalities, common to most academic conferences, which constitute a conference life-cycle:

Organisation: A conference is often organised by an academic society or group of academics or professionals with a common interest. Prior to the conference these people come together and decide on the general structure of the conference, the number and type of contributions, sources of financing the event etc.

Announcement: The conference is announced by a call for papers which lists the main topics, an outline timetable and invites contributions; normally, specifying that work should not have been previously published. This announcement can be made in journals, academic websites, at other related conferences and/or via targeted email distribution lists.

Submissions: Prospective contributors submit an abstract of their contribution, often online, and this is reviewed by members of the conference committee or other experts before acceptance. When submitting, it is important to carefully consider submission guidance, as the format (number of words, style etc.) of your abstract will help decide whether your submission is successful or not. A clear abstract, with a crisp title relevant to the theme of the conference usually increases chances of success. If submitting work with other colleagues check that everybody has read the abstract and supports its submission. It is also useful to clearly establish who will do what with regards to preparing and presenting the work. In some conferences the mode of presentation is decided by the review committee; if you have a choice, this is normally indicated on the submission form.

Presentations: Once accepted, work is normally presented as concise oral presentations (10–30 minutes) or as a poster presentation. A poster display can also require the authors to give a short explanatory presentation and/or the authors may have to be present for discussion at set times. More rarely, work may be presented as a demonstration of techniques and one or more time slots will allocated for the demonstration and for the presenters to answer questions. The choice of presentation mode is often between the 'low' stress, good audience interaction but low profile of a poster presentation and the 'high' stress but higher-profile oral presentation. Again, when presenting, by whatever method, it is important to follow the advice given by the organisers and the chair of the session in which you are participating; timing and specific details of presentations are especially important (see Chapter 15 in this volume).

In addition to these presentations conference organisers will usually invite scholars of high standing and profile to give longer keynote presentations or chair discussion sessions. Such sessions are normally closely linked with the main topic(s) of the conference and help to form the conference structure.

Other activities: Workshops where participants split into groups to actively study or discuss topics may also form part of the conference, as can meetings of learned societies. Publishers can be central in a conference; they may contribute to financing and publish conference contributions, and, usually, have stands featuring relevant publications. There is also, normally, a significant social and entertainment component to facilitate contacts among participants in a less formal environment.

Publication: In addition to the abstract submitted before the conference, speakers are sometimes asked to submit a short paper on their presentation. Such papers and the successful abstracts are usually edited into a volume of proceedings for distribution to conference participants and the wider community of practice.

Further conferences: Conferences are also a source of information on further and/or similar events. This can be useful information for future planning and while organising academic events, perhaps later in your career, can be a good way of distributing information to a target audience. In this case, it is useful to alert the conference organisers about your intentions to advertise and let them have possible materials for distribution in advance.

Some Practical Benefits of Attending Conferences

The practical benefits of attending conferences will, to some extent, depend both on the stage of your research work and on your academic development. The following attempts to capture the relevance and importance of academic conferences throughout the student 'life-cycle'.

Before Becoming a Postgraduate Research Student

- *Deciding direction:* A conference can aid the process of deciding to take an academic path; it is a good opportunity to observe the academic community and decide if you would like to be a part of it.
- *Choosing research areas:* An academic conference can highlight which areas of work are considered 'hot' topics by those within the discipline; this can be useful in choosing potential research areas.
- *Looking for supervisors:* If you are fortunate to attend conferences as an undergraduate or masters student, they can also be a way of investigating research groups and identifying potential supervisors; you can then meet group members and find out more about the group under consideration.

As a New Postgraduate Research Student

- *Appreciating context:* Attending a conference can help you appreciate the field and contextualise your work; they give context to the established literature and show 'cutting edge' work before it enters the literature and thus are invaluable in deciding future direction.

- *Useful information:* You can get information about different methodologies, the data they produce and its possible interpretation. This can reveal new directions and possibilities for your own work and suggest options for collaboration.
- *Shopping:* Trade stands, publishers, learned societies etc. are often present at conferences and can provide an opportunity to buy equipment, books and services (sometimes at reduced rates), or at least to see what's available and get advice.
- *Advice:* Conferences offer an opportunity to ask established academics for their views and guidance. Whilst it takes confidence to ask a question in front of a large audience, those presenting posters are often less senior and may be more approachable. They are a valuable source of information, particularly regarding methodology as they are often actively engaged in research and willing to share their experience.
- *Seeing the great and the good:* Conferences provide an opportunity to look at the work of, and meet members of leading research groups.
- *Building a network:* Conference networking opportunities can help to form a wider group of friends and colleagues and help you feel part of your academic community. The coffee breaks, conference dinners and social events often lead to more useful exchanges and interactions than the conference proceedings themselves, as our case study at the start of this chapter suggests. Academic research can sometimes be a lonely and frustrating business and the support network provided by friends and colleagues can be a real help (see Chapter 18 in this volume).

As an Established Postgraduate Research Student

As your work advances the emphasis often shifts away from methodology to presenting your own data. Presenting new work gives a sense of ownership of both your data and ideas and is vital in academic development.

- *Motivation:* Presenting at a conference can be an incentive to complete work to an abstract deadline. Moreover, writing the abstract is a useful incentive to think about what it means and attempt to draw some (preliminary) conclusions. A large international conference in some exotic location can be a milestone to work towards and presents its own reward once achieved.
- *Review and feedback:* Presenting even preliminary work to the wider academic community for review and feedback helps immensely with interpretation and deciding direction. The amount and quality of feedback will depend on the conference. The submitted abstract is usually competitively reviewed before acceptance; if it is allocated to an appropriate session and the conference attracts a quality audience, it is likely to attract interest and receive informed feedback. Furthermore, the abstract may be published after the meeting where it may receive a wider audience and possibly further feedback. However, even at conferences without a high degree of formal review, informal feedback on work can be tremendously helpful and is sometimes more focused.

- *Reflection:* Preparing the presentation helps you think about your work from a different perspective, putting it into a wider disciplinary context and gaining ownership of the data and ideas.
- *Confidence:* As you become familiar with and absorbed into a disciplinary community, you are better able to communicate ideas and understand feedback. This helps to further contextualise work and tends to increase your confidence in it and yourself; this is often accompanied by an increased sense of belonging to the community.
- *Awards and rewards:* As your research advances and develops into a body of work, you may be entered for awards sometimes offered by academic societies at conferences. Even being entered for something like a 'young investigator' award is a positive affirmation and can raise your profile within the community; winning such awards more so.
- *Funding experience:* As you become more established, you may attend more conferences, possibly involving international travel and significant expense. There are many sources of funding for such academically related trips and all but those in the wealthiest departments will need to apply for funding to attend. Funding can come from academic and professional societies, the research councils, industry and sometimes from multiple sources. Obtaining conference funding is good practice for the process of funding applications and is a relatively low risk way of getting a track record with funding bodies. Supervisors should be able to give advice on likely sources of funding, and departments sometimes have lists of sources and their contact details.
- *Furthering participation in a community of practice:* Conferences are a valuable chance to build on your links within your academic community; they can provide opportunities for collaborative work and a welcome chance to renew friendships. It is therefore important to maximise your participation – this can be as simple as wearing your own conference name-badge and using the badges to identify and talk to others. It is also helpful to get your supervisor and other contacts to introduce you to new people. Staying at the conference venue can also help as you meet people around the hotel and make the most of the less formal opportunities for interaction such as coffee-breaks and conference dinners.

As You Complete Your Postgraduate Research

As your work nears completion the emphasis may shift again, towards discussion and the defence of your work and ideas in the wider academic community. It is also a time for looking at the wider context and deciding future direction.

- *Reflection and feedback:* A good conference with a wide and expert audience with which to engage in a robust discussion of your data and ideas can be invaluable in writing your thesis and rehearsing its defence in the viva (see Chapters 19 and 21 in this volume).

- *Supportive evidence:* Ultimately the award of a research degree depends on the production of a suitable thesis and defending it in a *viva voce* exam (see Chapter 21 in this volume). Prior presentation of your work at peer-reviewed meetings and subsequent publication, even in abstract form, not only builds a body of supporting evidence but also helps confidence.
- *Investigating external examiners:* Conferences can give a chance to look for potential external examiners; while this is the supervisor's responsibility you can also make suggestions. If an examiner has been appointed, conferences can offer a chance to meet, and find out more about them.
- *Reconsidering direction:* On completion of a research degree you arrive at a point in your career where it is possible to change direction. A conference can be an opportunity to examine what options are interesting and available.
- *Looking for post-doctoral positions:* Becoming an active and visible contributor at conferences can attract interest, potentially leading to offers of the next job; at least you can investigate what post-doctoral positions may be available (see Chapter 24 in this volume).
- *Becoming established:* Continued conference participation is important in maintaining and extending your position in an academic community. This, together with your publication record, is evidence of expertise and a good academic reputation and is important in obtaining funding and furthering your career. Eventually, conferences may become an important source of your future postgraduate students.

How to Choose Academic Conferences

Normally a supervisor will discuss options and help choose which academic conferences to attend. Although it is impossible to offer definitive advice, we suggest below some questions you may ask to help in this decision process.

Is the Conference Relevant?

What is the title; is it in an area of general/ specific interest?
Are the planned contents and section titles interesting?
Is there a section suitable for my work?
Are the invited speakers relevant and interesting?
What sort of audience is a presentation likely to have?
Is there anybody who I would particularly like to meet attending?

What Sort of Conference Is It?

Local/national/ international?
Small and focused or large with parallel sessions?
Low or high profile?
Competitive or inclusive and open to all?
Short (day) or longer?

What Are the Logistical Considerations?

Are the deadlines reasonable and achievable?
Does the timing fit with my schedule/needs?
What are the transport/accommodation requirements?
What does it cost and who can be approached for funding?
What are the regulations/rules for the abstract and presentation?

What Are the Particular Attractions?

Are the conference proceedings published and if so where?
Are there people at the conference I particularly want to meet/hear?
Is there particular information I want to get from the conference?
Does the conference have a good reputation?
Would I be eligible for any particular support and/or prizes?
Are any friends/colleagues going?
Is the conference in an attractive location?
Can the conference be combined with other beneficial activities?

Am I Ready to Attend?

Is there appropriate work ready to present?
Is the work suitable for the conference?
Are there any issues of confidentiality or patents to consider?
What is the likely mode of presentation – is this acceptable?
Do I feel comfortable/confident about presenting work?
How much of the conference am I likely to understand/benefit from?

The answers to the questions above are obviously often related. A long international conference is often expensive and relatively difficult to attend, but it may be worth going if funding is available and or participation will bring sufficient benefit. Often, the decision comes down to balancing the costs of attending (in terms of both time and money) with the potential benefits. Consideration of the questions above, in light of all the previous information and discussion, will help make the cost/benefit analysis more straightforward.

Finally, it is worth noting that there are conferences specifically organised for research students; the Research Councils and UK Grad are active in this area.

Moving On – Organising Student Conferences

Having looked at various aspects of conference attendance, it is useful to briefly consider the other side of the coin: conference organisation.

Organising a conference is a complex business requiring many skills (organisation, communication, budgeting etc.), and much work; they are there-fore usually organised by a team of people who share expertise, resources and the actual work. Helping with conference organisation is a useful experience to add to your curriculum vitae and more importantly, it helps develop your skills and puts you at the centre of your community of practice.

A good way of gaining this experience is to promote a student conference. This could be organised within your department, or be a wider across discipline/department event within a whole institution. Student-organised conferences are enjoying increasing success in many universities, as they act as hubs for sharing work and experience among students and academics in a given institution, while giving less established scholars some useful visibility beyond their own department.

Student conferences are, by definition, student-driven, with academic assistance in the organisational logistics, and the search for funding. However, student input is vital and therefore, before becoming involved you should think about the time involved in relation to the progress of your studies and other commitments.

The following are some sets of fundamental questions (and sub-questions) one should ask oneself when thinking of organising such an event:

- Why should we do this? What are the main aims?
- Is there a perceived need among fellow students and in the institution at large?

'Why' questions are always important and should be answered within the realities of your own institutional context. For example, if there is a need for students to get exposure to different research methodologies, you may want to launch a conference to expose participants to the research in different disciplinary areas, and assist them in finding mutual assistance and synergies.

- How should we go about this? What are the main organisational stages?

Having established the 'why', there is a lot of work to do about the 'how'. In the first instance, it is good to form a provisional committee and write a short rationale for the conference (this rationale should contain a provisional title, the aims and benefits both to students and the wider institution, along some idea of the costing and, possibly, a 'sketchy' conference structure). This can be presented to more senior academics for feedback and to ask them about potential resources needed and sources of funding.

Questions about its structure would follow: when should it take place? How long should it last? Should just local students and/or academics present, or should external guests be invited? What kind of presentations? Individual or group ones? A mixture? How is the event to be publicised, and to whom? What logistical considerations are there (space, technology and audiovisual equipment, catering, entertainment)? Should the proceedings be published? How – in paper format and/or on the web? For each of these questions, it is useful to ask yourself 'why' all the time in order to clarify thinking.

After the conference, it is advisable to 'take stock' of the event and start thinking about future planning. It is good practice to hand over organisation of any subsequent events to a new group of colleagues in order to allow others to gain experience.

Conclusion

In this chapter we have considered the role of academic conferences in the formation and development of professional identity and as vital elements of communities of practice. They are essential in the formation and dissemination of disciplinary knowledge, both in terms of substantive subject knowledge and of the implicit social knowledge required to become encultured into a discipline or community of practice. We have discussed how the importance of conferences changes during your personal and professional development, introduced the idea and process of organising student conferences and given some practical advice on conference attendance.

THE KEY POINTS

Conferences are important for scholarly development in terms of both knowledge enhancement and of becoming part of your academic community. They are gateways to your participation within your academic community and participation is important. Although there is variation both between and within subject areas, in general there are several things to consider:

- The first stage of participation is choosing a conference that best suits your needs and time frame (these may change as you progress)
- Submit an abstract for consideration, paying careful attention to submission rules/ guidance and deadlines
- If appropriate choose a presentation format that best suits your work, needs and experience
- Once accepted, prepare your presentation carefully and practise until confident, especially if timing is important
- Make the most of conference facilities, have a look at the trade stands and publications available
- Interact with as many people as possible – the exchange of information and ideas is often the key to a successful conference and can be a real boost to your work and enthusiasm
- Wear your conference badge and stay at the conference venue or associated accommodation. This not only makes the logistics easier, but also maximises your opportunities to participate
- Enjoy yourself, but be careful not to overdo things; whilst the conference should not be a 'holiday', take advantage of social opportunities.

Despite their importance in academic life, relatively little has been written about conferences, the references we have used are given below, as are some websites that may provide further information on conferences or offer possible sources of financial support. We would also direct the reader to investigate their own academic/learned societies and the websites of any particular conferences relevant to their own interests.

SOURCES OF SUPPORT

Some Websites That Offer Data Bases of Possible Conferences

These can be searched and browsed by subject and location, some are aimed at particular disciplinary areas while others are more general.

All Conferences: www.allconferences.com/
Conference Alerts: www.conferencealerts.com/
H-Net Academic Announcements: www.h-net.org/announce/
Humbul Humanities Hub: www.humbul.ac.uk
Papers Invited: www.papersinvited.com/
Resource Discovery Network: www.rdn.ac.uk/
Social Science Grapevine: www.sosig.ac.uk/gv/

Some Websites That Offer Conference Abstract Services

These services range from those providing free software to help manage the abstract review and proceedings publication in conferences to companies that offer full conference management services.

Atlas Conferences: www.atlas-conferences.com/about.htm
Cyber Chair: www.borbala.com/cyberchair/
Easy Chair: www.easychair.org/
Oxford abstracts: www.oxfordabstracts.com/

Websites of the Trade Bodies for Professional Conference Organisers

These can help in finding well-established professional help in conference management and organisation.

The Association of British Professional Conference Organisers: www.abpco.org/
Meetings Industry Association – UK: www.mia-uk.org/
International Association of Professional Conference Organisers: www.iapco.org/
International Congress and Convention Association: www.iccaworld.com/

Other Potentially Useful Websites

British Academy: www.britac.ac.uk

The national academy for the humanities and the social sciences in the UK.

Community of Science: www.cos.com/

Global resource for scientific information including conferences, funding and publications.

The British Council: www.britcoun.org

Supports worldwide learning opportunities and creative ideas aiming to build lasting relationships between the UK and other countries.

The National Postgraduate Committee: www.npc.org.uk/

A charity to advance postgraduate education in the UK that publishes various guidelines.

The Research Councils: www.rcuk.ac.uk/

The core site of the UK's eight Research Councils.

The Royal Society: www.royalsoc.ac.uk/

The independent scientific academy of the UK dedicated to promoting excellence in science.

UK GRAD Programme: www.grad.ac.uk/

Site offering training and advice for postgraduate students.

References

Brown, J.S., Collins, A. and Duguid, P. (1989) 'Situated cognition and the new culture of learning', *Educational Researcher*, 18, 32–42.

Brown, J.S. and Duguid, P. (1991) 'Organizational learning and communities-of-practice. Toward a unified view of working, learning and innovation', *Organization Science*, 2, 40–57.

Davenport, T.H. and Prusak, L. (1998) Working Knowledge: How Organizations Manage What They Know. Boston, MA: Harvard Business School Press.

Mercer, N. (1995) *The Guided Construction of Knowledge: Talk amongst Teachers and Learners.* Cleveden: Multilingual Matters.

Wenger, E. (1998) *Communities of Practice: Learning, Meaning and Identity*, Cambridge: Cambridge University Press.

Wenger, E. (2006) 'Communities of practice', available at: www.ewenger.com/theory/ (accessed on 20 July 2006).

17 Teaching as Part of Your Professional Development

Dr Kate Exley

Introduction

Increasingly research students are both being encouraged to contribute to the teaching in their department or school and are themselves wishing to gain teaching experience to help them improve their career prospects and supplement incomes.

This chapter aims to provide research students, new to teaching, with confidence to begin teaching. It does not aim to be comprehensive but rather to give a sound starting point and some initial guidance for good practice. The chapter will also suggest follow-up resources for those wishing to develop their teaching skills further.

The chapter begins by considering the varied motivations for research students teaching in today's higher education system. It then identifies ways in which higher education institutions are providing support for research students who are new to teaching, before going on to consider the approaches a new teacher can employ themselves to develop their skills. This section includes discussion of the 'professionalisation' of teaching and considers ways in which a new teacher can seek accreditation for their own teaching development.

The most substantial section of the chapter (Getting Going with Your Teaching) provides clear guidance on teaching and learning activities in five common teaching contexts, namely:

1 Demonstrating in laboratories and practical classes
2 Tutoring in seminars and tutorials
3 Supervising and supporting project students
4 Preparing to give a first lecture
5 Marking coursework essays and reports.

The chapter concludes by providing a range of text and online 'Further reading' resources.

Key Issues

Why Do Research Students Want to Teach?

For some research students teaching is a formal part of their scholarly role within the institution. Graduate Teaching Assistant posts, for example, require research students to undertake teaching activities as part of their contract with the institution. This is a very common approach to Graduate Training in North America and is growing in the UK. However, for the majority of research students in Europe and the UK teaching is seen as an extra-curricular activity and actively limited by funders (such as the Research Councils) and institutions, in their policies and good practice codes, to around six hours per week.

It is generally accepted that postgraduate students should have access to teaching experience as part of their professional development. Research students are clearly seeing great benefits in undertaking teaching during their higher degrees although motives do vary. Some common drivers are included in Table 17.1.

Higher education institutions in the UK are adopting formal systems to support research students in both recognising and recording the skills development they attain during their studies (see also Chapter 14 in this volume). In May 2000, Universities UK, the Standing Conference of Principals, the Committee of Scottish Higher Education Principals and the Quality Assurance Agency issued a joint policy statement on the use of 'progress files' in Higher Education (UUK, SCoP, CoSHEP and QAA, 2000). It states that institutions should, from 2005/06, have in place a transcript mechanism for all students (including research students) for recording student achievement, and a means by which students can explicitly monitor, plan and reflect on their personal development. Such 'progress files' (which have many names including Personal Development Plans – see Chapter 14 in this volume) therefore serve as a reminder of the broader skill set that can be developed through activities such as teaching and may well encourage research students to seek out opportunities to teach.

Additionally, in 2002, Sir Gareth Roberts' 'SET for Success' review (Roberts, 2002) established the principle that research students should have two weeks' dedicated training a year focusing primarily on transferable skills development.

TABLE 17.1 Common drivers for postgraduate research students to teach

Skills development	both teaching skills and professional skills
Career focus	for those seeking an academic career particularly but skills also transferable to other work environments
Extra income	for an activity that is often related to their research
And some little extras	understanding something better if you have explained it to somebody else, keeping in touch with the fundamentals of the discipline or broadening knowledge and understanding etc.

Training in teaching skills is included in this and as a result many institutions now provide a wide and varied menu of teacher-training opportunities.

Why Do Higher Education Institutions Want Research Students to Teach?

There has been a long tradition in UK universities of research students contributing to undergraduate teaching. In the sciences, research students 'demonstrate' in laboratories and in the humanities, lead tutorials and seminars. However, this relatively low level of contribution is set to increase to mirror the situation more commonly observed in North American universities and colleges where research students are significant providers of teaching. There is no doubt that academic staff value and gain from research students undertaking teaching as this allows them more time for their own research and other activities such as consultancy. All of which are very important for the reputation and standing of the institution.

There is also a growing body of work that shows how effectively 'seniors and peers' can support learning (Falchikov, 2001). Proctoring schemes, in which more senior/advanced students guide the learning of students at an earlier stage in their studies, have been shown to be effective and this is believed to be because somebody who has recently learnt something themselves is able to pitch the level of an explanation and see what a new learner may find difficult more easily than somebody who has known/understood for a long time. There is no doubt that many undergraduate students find their postgraduate tutors easier to approach and are therefore more likely to ask them questions and admit that they don't understand something.

A managed and supported opportunity to teach appears to be, for both research students and institutions, a beneficial activity. It is, however, clear that this does require safeguards and quality checks to ensure that undergraduate students do get the teaching and learning experience that they have the right to expect.

Institutional Support for Developing Research Students as Teachers

The support and training of new teachers has risen in importance in many universities, not only for new academic staff but also, increasingly, for research students beginning to teach. However, the extent to which research students are able and indeed, encouraged to undertake formal training leading to teaching qualifications, remains quite variable from institution to institution.

Once they are employed to teach, some research students gain access to well-developed academic Staff Development provision and attend an array of teaching, learning, assessment, supervision and student-support workshops and classes. Increasingly, individual schools and departments are requiring their research students to attend training before they are allowed to teach undergraduate students. Some schools design and run specialised teaching courses whilst others stipulate a minimum engagement with university-wide provision, for example, a research student must attend three teaching-related workshops run by the Staff Development Unit or the Graduate School.

Programmes have been supplemented and expanded in recent years, not in small part due to the injection of funding flowing from the 'SET for Success' review (see above) which has given substantial sums to support skills training for research students (see also Chapter 14 in this volume).

Over the last decade, there has been a growth in the development of accredited teaching programmes and teaching qualifications such as 'Postgraduate Certificates in Teaching and Learning or Academic Practice'. The Higher Education Academy in the UK provides a mechanism that enables institutions to have their own teacher-training programmes accredited nationally. The Academy uses the national framework for professional standards in teaching and support (Higher Education Academy, 2006) to benchmark the provision of locally provided training courses and programmes. This means that teaching experience and qualifications gained in one UK higher education institution are more readily understood and credited in another. There is also growing understanding of the framework worldwide enabling international research students to return home with a recognised teaching qualification if they wish.

The Academy also holds a register of practitioners that gives status and recognition to teachers in UK higher education institutions. Those who complete an accredited programme are eligible to join this register as either a Registered Practitioner or a Registered Associate Practitioner – the former being the level expected of a full-time member of academic staff and the latter being more appropriate for somebody for whom teaching is an important but limited aspect of their role, for example, research students who teach.

Developing Yourself as a Teacher

Opportunities to Teach

The clear objective of any research student is to achieve the qualification, for example, PhD they set out to within the period they are registered and funded for. This must remain the focus and take precedence over other interests and goals. It is therefore, vitally important that any teaching activities and development opportunities are balanced with the demands of the research endeavour. It is common practice that any commitment to undertake teaching requires the approval and signature of the research supervisor.

Many institutions and funders of research studentships stipulate a maximum amount of time that students can spend teaching, which usually means no more than six hours per week averaged out over the academic year. Graduate

Teaching Assistant contracts do vary and commonly give an amount of teaching in hours per year, for example, 120 hours per year. There is of course a wide range of contractual arrangements that can be entered into. For example, at Birmingham University in the UK, Teaching Assistants are appointed on contracts that stipulate 25% of the time is allocated for teaching duties leaving 75% for research. Research students with this kind of contract are expected to complete their research in four years rather than three years. This 25% of time is approximately 300 hours per year and is equivalent to 12–14 hours teaching per week during two semesters.

Note

1   If you want to teach you should check your school or department's policy – some do not let first-year or final-year research students teach. You should then speak with your research supervisor(s) to check that they would be willing to support your case. Your supervisor may also be able to guide you on how to find out about local opportunities to teach. Research students often teach on courses and modules for which their own supervisor is the convenor as subject specialisms can provide obvious choices for matching teaching topics and tutors/demonstrators.

2   Once teaching has been allocated to you find out as much as you can about what is expected. A useful checklist is given below.

PREPARATION FOR TEACHING CHECKLIST

- Meet with the module convenor to discuss aims and objectives of the teaching session(s)
- Check you fully understand your job/ role and how it relates to others
  (e.g. technical staff, convenor etc.)
- Check you fully understand your duties and responsibilities
  (e.g. are you expected to provide additional support to the students in 'office hours' or mark work and give feedback etc.?)
- Check you know what the expected standards of job performance are and how you will be monitored
- Find out something about your students
  (e.g. level, background, experience, disability issues etc.)
- Talk to somebody who did it last year
  (e.g. what were common student questions or problems etc.?)
- Familiarise yourself with health and safety procedures
  (e.g. who are the local 'First Aiders'?)
- Familiarise yourself with the teaching environment
  (e.g. audio-visual equipment, laboratory layout etc.)
- Familiarise yourself with the reporting structures
  (e.g. if a student is not turning up to class who do you tell?)
- Reflect on your own training needs (are there any skills you need to update such as hands on laboratory skills?)

Evaluating and Developing Teaching Skills

The evaluation of teaching and learning is now built into university systems and structures through course review, student evaluation mechanisms and peer-review schemes. As a new teacher there may also be further informal evaluation processes such as teaching observation by course convenors or Heads of School who are keen to check that quality standards are being maintained in teaching, and identifying and responding to any arising training needs of their new teachers.

When considering evaluation it is useful to consider the two faces of evaluation, first, evaluation for quality assurance (checking you are a competent teacher) and second, evaluation for development (how can I improve what I am doing in my teaching?). The first feels like something done to the teacher whilst the second is something the teacher has control over and can focus and direct to help them develop specific aspects of teaching.

There are several sources of evidence that teachers can use to develop their teaching practices in the form of feedback from

- Supervisors and course convenors
- Students
- Colleagues, peers and other new teachers
- Personal reflection.

Both formal and informal mechanisms can yield helpful data. Formal approaches such as the use of student questionnaire surveys at the end of the year tend to be used for quality assurance purposes whilst many informal mechanisms are in place such as the ones listed below.

- Conversations with students
- Anonymous feedback at the end of teaching sessions, for example, getting your students to use post-it notes of 'things to start doing', 'things to keep doing' and 'things to try and stop doing'
- Observation and discussion with colleagues
- Recording or videoing teaching sessions
- Keeping a teaching diary of critical incidents in teaching etc.

These tend to provide more instant evaluation feedback for developmental purposes. However, at the end of the day it is the teachers themselves who must reflect upon the different points of feedback and consider how best to use them.

It is important not to respond impulsively or unthinkingly to feedback, as it is often contradictory and incomplete. Different methods of evaluation represent a whole series of 'different voices' that in turn are representing a wide range of different perspectives and values. For example, students want to pass the course exam so will give feedback from this perspective whereas the course convenor is likely to want the students to develop their cognitive skills and abilities to think critically and will give you feedback from this viewpoint. The new teacher needs to think of their own 'teaching goals' and use the feedback to help them meet these. It is an on-going process just as valuable to the experienced teacher engaging in Continuing Professional Development as the researcher beginning to grow their teaching skills.

Logging and Evidencing Teaching

For a new teacher it is now sensible to begin to log teaching experiences and to nurture the habit of reflecting on teaching experiences and critically appraising them in order to enhance teaching skills and performance. Many initial teacher qualification programmes include the requirement to put together a personal 'Teaching Portfolio' that seeks to document and evidence the process of development. Reflection on practice (Schon, 1983) is frequently used as the underlying philosophy and this asks teachers to select elements or activities of their teaching and closely review those experiences. This may involve identifying and challenging initial assumptions, collecting evaluative evidence on effectiveness and relating experiences to theory and personal values and teaching philosophies

If a researcher intends to pursue an academic/teaching-related career in the future, it can be helpful to begin to compile teaching evidence from their experiences. This could be the beginning of a personal teaching portfolio or form a useful basis of material for future job applications. It might include the following:

- A statement of teaching responsibilities, including course titles, numbers, enrolments, student group etc.
- A reflective statement by the teacher, describing their personal teaching philosophy, strategies and objectives, methodologies etc.
- Examples of course syllabi, lesson plans/notes detailing course content and learning outcomes, teaching methods, readings, homework assignments etc.
- Records of participation in teaching workshops and events
- Notes on any articles and books about teaching that have been influential
- Copies of any feedback received through both formal and informal means
- Details of teaching changes or innovations together with any evaluation of their effectiveness
- A description of steps taken to evaluate and improve one's teaching, including changes resulting from self-evaluation
- Thoughts on future developments to be taken.

(Adapted from 'The Teaching Portfolio', Seldin, P., 1991)

For those who are encouraged to seek a more formal accreditation of their teaching and charged with building a teaching portfolio for a qualification pathway, it is important to remember that such 'evidence' requires explanation. In a teaching portfolio it is important that the evidence is introduced and contextualised for the reader. Why has this example been selected, which features have particular meaning for the teacher and what are they drawing from the experience that they are including in the portfolio? It is not sufficient to simply say 'I have done this'. The portfolio is a place to discuss experience and attempt to make the processes of development open to the portfolio assessor. For example, when presenting student feedback in a portfolio it is important to indicate how the teacher is using the feedback, how they are interpreting the information and what future direction they intend to take. Therefore, 'reflective commentaries' on the evidence included in a teaching portfolio are probably more important than the evidence itself.

Reflection and Writing Reflectively about Teaching

Reflection is a form of thinking that is used to make sense of complicated experiences and unstructured thoughts. It is a process of 'making sense of and distilling meaning'. The process of writing it down, 'reflective writing', is primarily so that others can see it. However, the very act of writing it down is likely to shape the reflection itself as reflective writing is not 'stream of consciousness writing' but is planned and constructed in order to provide a reader with access to processes which would otherwise be hidden from them. In a teaching portfolio there are usually several clear purposes and intended outcomes to the processes of reflection. These may include the improvement of specific teaching activities, demonstrating competence to others, linking theory with practice, showing development in action etc.

Most reflective writing includes the following:

- An initial description of the context, the purpose, the subject matter, the teaching activity etc.
- A recognition of personal reactions and emotions related to the experiences recorded
- An analysis of key factors that influenced the experience and the outcomes
- Explicit links to other learning (such as literature, research, theory etc.)
- An exploration of ways forward and an 'internal dialogue' that shows self-questioning and personal debate
- A meta-cognitive element – that is, a critical awareness of one's own mental processes, being able to stand outside and comment on one's own thinking
- An action plan based on the above.

Many new teachers do find reflective writing quite a challenge. It differs from many other styles of writing in that it is personal and requires the inclusion of the author and writing to be in the first person. Using 'I' in academic writing is very unusual and may take practice to adopt with comfort.

The use of personal questioning can be a helpful tactic to adopt, for example, try asking the following questions:

- What did I do, what did I experience?
- Why was it important?
- What meaning(s) am I attaching to this experience?
- What did I feel? How do I feel now?
- Why did it happen? What factors were influential?
- How do I know – what sources, data, evidence do I have?
- How does this experience link with other things I know? (e.g. readings)
- How do I improve, develop, change etc.?
- What should I do next?
- How do I know?

The literature on reflective practice in teaching and learning provides further definitions, and discussion of the purpose and nature of reflection. Jenny Moon, for example, provides excellent guidance in her *Handbook of Reflective and Experiential Learning: Theory and Practice* (2004).

Getting Going with Your Teaching: Practical Suggestions

This section does not aim to be comprehensive but rather to give a good insight into effective teaching practice (hints and tips and good ideas) and to further identify reading and follow-up resources.

Five very common teaching situations are explored using a case-study approach in which a fictitious new teacher is followed in their initial teaching experiences. Practical pointers and teaching suggestions will be highlighted.

Five Teaching Situations: Guidance for Good Practice

The five teaching contexts considered are as follows:

1 Demonstrating in laboratories and practical classes
2 Tutoring in seminars and tutorials
3 Supervising and supporting project students
4 Preparing to give a first lecture
5 Marking coursework essays and reports.

Readers are encouraged to take a quick look at all five contexts as much of the advice and suggested good practice are applicable in a wide range of teaching situations.

Demonstrating in Laboratories and Practical Classes

Tom is a second-year postgraduate student doing biology laboratory demonstrating for the first time this year. He will be working with two other demonstrators to look after a three-hour laboratory session with 60 first-year students. The practical classes run for 10 weeks in the second semester, and are organised and led by Tom's colleague Dr Clark.

Tom first attends a briefing event with Dr Clark who talks about the following:

- The purposes of the laboratory classes – what she wants the students to gain from the session (learning aims) and the specific knowledge and skills she wants them to attain (learning outcomes)
- The health and safety arrangements and procedures
- The technical details of the practical work including equipment checks
- Common problems the students have and likely question areas.

Dr Clark also talks about the role of the demonstrator. She says:

- The demonstrator is there to support the students' learning and not to do their thinking for them. So the demonstrator should try to help the students find answers for themselves by commenting, prompting and suggesting rather than giving all the explanations.
- The demonstrator is there to make sure the students are working safely, so should focus on their practical skills, use of equipment and adherence to laboratory rules and regulations – including tidying up at the end of the session.
- The demonstrator is 'pro-active' and should not wait to be asked questions but move around the class checking the progress of the students and antici-pating problems.

The preparation Tom does includes making sure that he can use all the equipment and confidently carry out the technical procedures and techniques required in the practical class. He does this over a lunch time with the help of the laboratory technician who sets up the practical work for the students. Tom reads through the experimental schedule and guidance provided to the students and checks he knows who are the trained first aiders in the depart-ment. Tom also chats to Sam, who demonstrated in the practical last year, to get the demonstrator's view of the practical course. With Sam, Tom finds out the common difficulties with the first experiment the students carry out, and checks he has understood the questions that the students are asked to answer in their experimental reports and log books. Although not expected to formally assess the log books in this practical course, the demonstrators are expected to 'sign off' the logs during the class. This means that students' progress can be informally checked each week and the students are encouraged to develop good laboratory practice by recording findings as they go rather than writing them up at the end.

In the practical itself Tom finds that he really enjoys working with the students. He sees that students find it easier to talk to him than to the course convenor and are more willing to express doubt or ask questions. Some do try and get him to do the work for them but he finds it quite easy to encourage them to think it through for a couple of minutes by highlighting a couple of key points and using questioning to help them see their own solutions. Only twice did he have to intervene when he observed unsafe practice and students responded well when he brought their attention to correct procedure. Two groups of students struggled with the experiment for very different reasons.

Group One appeared very under-confident and they constantly looked to Tom for reassurance and seemed to need to keep checking that they were doing the right things. With these students encouragement and praise seemed to be all that was needed. In chatting to the group Tom discovered that they had done very little of this kind of experimental work before and so he spent 10 minutes running through the experimental protocol with them, checking that they understood the terminology and could answer basic questions about how they would do the next couple of steps in the experiment. Through such questioning Tom was assured that the students were understanding the work. He also took time to comment positively when they did something well. Promising to check back with them in quarter of an hour he left the group confident that they were progressing well and that they knew they were on the right track.

Group Two seemed to be taking a very relaxed attitude in class and were wasting time gossiping. He tried a couple of times to speed them up with gentle comments but this was only marginally successful. Half way through the class Tom decided a more directive approach was necessary. He approached the group and asked them to summarise where they had got to in the protocol. He then said that they would need to work extremely efficiently if they were going to complete the work in the remaining time and he needed to know who was doing what next. He strongly encouraged the group to explicitly allocate tasks and ascertained when these would be completed for him to check. His direct and constructive guidance had an immediate impact on the group. He wished he had tackled the situation much earlier and recognised that he had felt a little shy/uncomfortable himself in approaching the group and being so firm. He wanted the students to like him but he also wanted them to respect the role he had.

Tom realised that with just these two groups he was using a whole range of facilitation skills to coach and encourage the students whilst also trying to manage and structure their learning activities. He decided that he would attend one of the university's teaching workshops to help him hone these skills.

Towards the end of the practical Tom was asked by the course leader to check the experimental logbooks of all the students working in his section of the laboratory and to sign them before they left the class. The vast majority of students had completed the data collection and had begun to tackle the questions posed by the course leader. He was able to give feedback to the students and help them if they were feeling stuck. Group Two were behind with their work and hadn't completed the data collection when other students began leaving the laboratory. Tom watched them carefully and insisted that they complete their work. This did involve him staying in the laboratory for 20 minutes at the end of the session. When the students were finished he told them that each week they would need to get their work checked before leaving and that in future weeks he wouldn't be prepared to stay later with them so they would need to work more efficiently in the session.

The laboratory, quiet at the end of the session, looked tidy but Tom did a quick check and made sure equipment was safe and the laboratory was being left in good order. Sitting down for a moment to collect his thoughts Tom considered his first demonstrating experience.

Tutoring in Seminars and Tutorials

Jen is an MPhil student leading tutorials in History. She has done this for the last two years and has grown in confidence in the role. She has experimented with a number of different ways of organising the classes and now has a range of tried and tested strategies for dealing with the common difficulties she faces in her 'discussion-based' seminars.

She recognises the importance of 'starting off as you mean to go on' and now begins her tutorials with a clear outline of the session, that includes explicit mention of the main aims of the class and the specific themes she wishes to address. She also outlines the expected process of the class indicating how she will expect the students to work and what she sees as being her role and responsibilities. For example,

> Today we will begin by looking at the three questions on the board. Please can you work with your neighbour to discuss your views. I think this will take about twenty minutes and we will then bring the discussion together and collect the most important ideas and issues.

This year Jen spent the first 10 minutes of her first class asking her students to talk about how they would work together in the seminar and she also clarified her role as tutor describing herself as a 'facilitator' and a 'guide'. This seems to have been very useful with the students seeing, more clearly, why and how the seminar differed from the lecture. Next session she is going to experiment further by asking her students to draw up some 'ground-rules' or a 'seminar agreement' in the opening class. Her plan is to ask the students to work in threes to list out the important features of a productive seminar class, for example, arrive on time and do the preparation reading, and then to ask them to turn them into a list of points that they all feel they can agree to.

Jen's seminars rely on the fact that the students will have done some reading and some preparation ahead of the class. This has caused problems for her, as often some have done this whilst others haven't and she has found herself giving a 'mini-lecture' about the readings at the start of the session just to give the unprepared students a way into the session. Frustrated by this she has tried a number of things to make it more difficult for students to turn up having done nothing. She now allocates a specific task or reading to each pair of students and asks them to bring a written note of five bullet points about the readings to the seminar. She has also asked the students to write three questions or to produce a list of priority areas to class. These small but directive tasks have helped students focus more on their preparation and come ready for discussion. Jen's colleague, Sarah, requires her students to email a summarising page of notes to her on the Friday before her tutorials on the Monday. She circulates these to all the students in the group so everyone benefits when the time comes to revise. She intends to use the Blackboard virtual learning environment (VLE) to do this next year. She will set up a discussion board and ask students to post their pre-class summaries to this but she needs to find out how to do this and will attend a university course next term to learn how.

Jen's tutorials run this year with 16 students and she finds this a really good number to work with. It is easy to split the class into working groups of about four and to give them a number of discussion questions before bringing the whole group back together to summarise and clarify learning points. This way nearly all the students take part very easily. She likes assigning different topics or foci to different groups and then having a whole group discussion that can become a debate between different perspectives.

She has found getting discussion going to be difficult in the past, especially if the group members were naturally quiet or shy. Her two students from China were very quiet in her classes initially. Jen is very approachable and tries hard to make the seminars welcoming and comfortable. She pays attention to seating arrangements and likes to run the class with students sitting in small groupings. She has found that asking students to write down their initial thoughts about a discussion question or talking in pairs about it, before asking them to comment or answer in front of the whole group, has particularly helped the non-native speakers in her group to gain the confidence to speak out. The Chinese students do need lots of encouragement to do this and Jen realises that 'discussion-based learning' is something very new to them.

Two other approaches she has just started experimenting with are assigning roles to individual students when they are working in a small group. For example, having a note-taker, a spokesperson and a discusser etc. Rotating these roles from task to task and mixing up the membership of the working groups has also helped to bring new energy to the discussion. A second approach involved Jen's more strategic use of the white board in the classroom. She divided the board into three columns, 'positive', 'negative' and 'neutral' and as the class continued and students made contributions she wrote up the points in the appropriate column. She used the board in her closing remarks and found it very helpful in summing up important points from the seminar. Two students came up to her at the end of the class and said how helpful they had found this approach saying that they sometimes found it difficult to identify the most important points from a wide-ranging discussion. Having the board structure had helped Jen to show the students how to begin to structure, interpret and analyse the information and ideas the students had collectively contributed. She intends to use a similar approach next week when she leads a class comparing and contrasting two different historical accounts of the same event.

Jen has very much enjoyed her teaching but acknowledges that she has spent a lot of time preparing for classes, especially for new classes, and she needs to keep this in balance with her other workloads.

Supervising and Supporting Project Students

Phil is a post-doctoral researcher supervising a final-year project student in material sciences. His student, Matt, has an academic supervisor, Dr Chen, who oversees his project work but Phil is the 'hands-on' and 'day-to-day' supervisor of the project. In fact, Phil hopes that the pilot study Matt is tackling will yield some useful results to complement his own research. As a senior researcher in the group Phil has informally helped a number of students in the department but this is the first time that the arrangement has been made 'official' and Phil is called an 'associate supervisor'.

Although Phil sees Matt most days around the workshop or laboratory he schedules a regular and more formal meeting once a week. This usually lasts about half an hour and is the time in which progress is reviewed. Phil currently keeps a hand-written note of the main outcomes and points raised in these formal meetings and gives a copy to Matt. However, he has recently attended a workshop on supervision and one idea he picked up was about 'developing the student's ownership of and responsibility for the project'. He intends trying a new approach for the second half of the project in which Matt is expected to produce the record of the supervisory meeting. He may even use email rather than paper to do this, asking Matt to email him a paragraph of notes after the weekly meeting, that contains a note of what had been agreed and any plans or actions arising. He can reply to this email with any additional comments he feels are useful and show his 'agreement' with the student's record.

Working day by day with Matt, Phil has seen him grow in confidence and observed a change in their working pattern. At the start of the project, Matt asked Phil everything and wanted his direction, but now, halfway through the project, Matt is coming to Phil with ideas of what he wants to do and Phil is helping him think critically about his choices and to double check things. So initially Phil was trying to give really clear instructions and 'train' Matt in safe working practices. Phil has found a helpful strategy which is to ask Matt to explain things back to him so that he can be assured that he has really understood. Asking Matt to draw diagrams to explain a procedure or concept has also been useful.

In giving clear explanations Phil has found it really important to check his starting level, as once or twice it became clear that he had over-estimated Matt's previous knowledge. So starting simple and moving forward quickly seems to work best. Starting with an explanation of why this or that procedure is relevant or important is key to help Matt gain a more holistic understanding too. Littering his explanations with examples and analogies has also improved Phil's clarity.

Increasingly Phil is finding himself coaching Matt by asking him questions. The questions can be open or divergent questions, like 'how?' and 'why?' that can invite a range of possible responses and can instigate a discussion. Or they can be closed and convergent, for example, 'what is the cost of that?' or 'when will you take your sample?', yielding specific and narrow responses. Such questions close down a discussion and tend to focus on factual rather than interpretive answers. Phil has also noticed that asking questions can put Matt on the defensive and he has worked hard to try to reduce this by thinking about how he asks questions, and has adjusted his body language, for example, trying to remember to sit down next to Matt to ask questions rather than standing over him etc.

A key part of the supervisory role in the laboratory has been training Matt in a range of quite technical and 'hands-on' skills and techniques. Phil has found using the 5-step skills teaching protocol (George and Dotto, 2001 reported in Exley and Dennick, 2004) a useful prompt.

Step 1. First introduce and contextualise the skill being taught, for example,

So this is the lathe, you will be using this to shape several of your metal samples. Your metal samples need to be cylindrical and to fit snugly into the processor so you need to be accurate and careful. It is a key piece of equipment for you in your project and it will take you quite a bit of practise to use properly.

Step 2. Demonstrate the skill in real time – showing how it looks when you can do it well. This gives the student a realistic goal to aim for.

Step 3. Repeat the demonstration but this time doing it slowly and explaining what is being done, and why. Keep pausing and encouraging the student to ask questions about what is going on in the different stages of the skill/procedure.

Step 4. Ask the student to provide the explanation of the skill whilst you follow their instructions. Ask the student questions like 'what should I do next', 'why is it important that I do this first?' etc.

Step 5. Then the student is encouraged to have a go. Watch a few times to check the student is working safely and give them any detailed suggestions and feedback. Then the student has to practise by him/herself.

An aspect of the supervisory role that Phil thinks is very important is to stress the importance of planning and reviewing the plan as the project progresses. Having a realistic and written plan, which includes timescales and measurable outcomes, has been very beneficial for Matt in conducting the project and for Phil in enabling him to tailor his help and support. Reviewing the plan is a key agenda item in the formal supervisory meetings every two or three weeks; 'are we on track? and do we need to make any changes?' being core questions to be addressed regularly.

Phil feels that this is also helping Matt to develop good practices that will see him through into employment when he will need to work independently. It may be that a sign of successful supervision is getting a student to the point where they don't really need you much anymore.

Preparing to Give a First Lecture

Eva is a final year research student in the School of Archaeology getting ready to give her first lecture to the first years in the 'Introduction to Archaeology' course. She has given three research seminars to colleagues in the department and one at a national conference. She found these talks quite nerve wracking to give and is quite anxious about the forthcoming lecture. Her supervisor has offered some help and she has scheduled a meeting with him next week to discuss her plan for the lecture.

Her approach so far has involved the following:

1 Thinking of the needs and level of understanding the students currently have
2 Thinking about the focus of the topic and some possible lecture structures
3 Thinking about facilities and resources

1 Thinking of the needs and level of understanding the students currently have

The student group is large and of very mixed ability and background. She will have 85 students and this will be only about the tenth lecture they have attended at university. Eva is keen to make sure that her lecture has appeal and interest for all the students so she is planning to try to grab their attention with some provocative questions at the start of her lecture which she hopes her lecture will go on to address. She plans to use some photographs and images to illustrate important points she wants to make and has started collecting these together. She is also thinking how to stretch the more able students in the group by providing some follow-up resources and references and to show them how this lecture topic will link forward and be useful to them in their own mini-project work towards the end of the semester.

Eva has also read the course documentation for the module in which her lecture sits, to check what the students had been told already. Here, she found course aims and learning outcomes. The former being a holistic statement about the learning goals of the course, that is, what the module convenor intended the students to gain from the module overall. The latter being a set of five bullet points describing in detail what the students would be able to do at the end of the module, for example, 'At the end of this module students will be able to describe, using examples, the important social and ethical issues impacting on modern Archaeology.' There was also a module outline document that gave a brief synopsis for the content and themes of each lecture. This was helpful as it showed what the students could be expected to have some familiarity with from earlier lectures and also gave an indication of what the rest of the module would go on to look at. This background and context could be woven into the lecture to help give the students a more coherent experience and a clearer framework to interconnect themes across different lectures.

2   Thinking about the focus of the topic and some possible lecture structures

The working title for the lecture is 'Origins of Farming' which, as a subject, is very broad. Eva has decided to focus on three important topics, namely: why did farming develop?, when and where did it develop first? and finally some examples of the effects of early farming practices on the development of plant and animals species. Deciding on these topics took a bit of time and to help prioritise she consulted a handful of general textbooks to see which were the common chapter headings and themes that their authors had taken.

The next step was to plan out the best way of using the time she had with the students and to do this Eva drew a vertical line on a page representing the hour she had and began to divide the time between the main topics (see Figure 17.1).

This felt like she had the 'map' of the lecture and a firm foundation to plan the detail. She began using PowerPoint™ presentation software and remembered guidance offered on an earlier presentation skills course about keeping her slides simple and clear. She used the font 'Arial', because the Disability Office had suggested that this font is more easily read by students with dyslexia and she used size 24 point and larger to ensure visibility. Eva limited the lines of text on a slide to 8 and tried to use images and photographs to add a bit of visual interest.

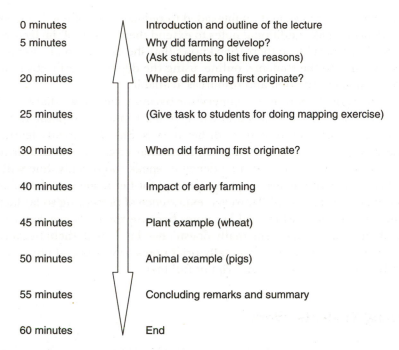

0 minutes		Introduction and outline of the lecture
5 minutes		Why did farming develop? (Ask students to list five reasons)
20 minutes		Where did farming first originate?
25 minutes		(Give task to students for doing mapping exercise)
30 minutes		When did farming first originate?
40 minutes		Impact of early farming
45 minutes		Plant example (wheat)
50 minutes		Animal example (pigs)
55 minutes		Concluding remarks and summary
60 minutes		End

FIGURE 17.1 Planned structure of Eva's lecture

Eva is also interested to explore how to get a bit more student involvement or interaction in the lecture and is wondering about trying setting a 5-minute task in the middle to revive attention and help the students relate to the topic. She intends to discuss this with her supervisor but her ideas include asking students, at the beginning of the lecture, to list five reasons why they think farming originally developed. This would hopefully get the students oriented towards the topic and develop some interest. Then about 20 minutes in, she will show them a world map with regions marked on it and she will provide them with a list of names and archaeological dig sites where evidence of early farming has been studied and ask them to match up the sites with the marked regions and to do this in pairs. She will then show them the correct answers and let them see if they were right or not. These ideas need further clarification and talking it through with her supervisor will help to do this.

3   Thinking about facilities and resources

The modern lecture theatre that Eva will work in is tiered and well equipped. She intends to go down to the room before her lecture and ensure that she can use all the technical equipment.

Remembering the better lectures she attended as an undergraduate Eva is also keen to provide the students with a clear handout for her lecture and has decided to provide them with a copy of her PowerPoint™ presentation with

6 slides copied per page and double-sided to reduce costs. She will encourage the students to make additional notes to extend their record of the lecture in a way that is memorable to them. She knows that she can also make her lecture notes available to the students, online, using the departmental website which carries course information and resources available.

Eva values the help from her supervisor because she knows that he will be constructive with his feedback and will give her some useful pointers to help her present clearly and to cope with her nerves. She has already learnt that taking in a glass of water to drink helps with her croaky voice and drinking slows her down when she has a tendency to speak too quickly. She will produce her own lecture notes to act as a prompt for her if she loses her place or forgets an important detail. However, experience of presenting so far has also taught her that she mustn't read her notes because she loses eye contact with her audience and actually, she really doesn't need to look at them because she does know her subject well – so really brief notes or words and phrases work much better than a lecture transcript or full text.

Marking Students' Work

Mohammed is a research student in economics. He teaches on two very different level one, first-year courses and marks some of the course assessments for both of them.

In the first course, the students are asked to answer a set of three short problems each week. These usually involve doing brief calculations, plotting graphs and analysing figures according to standard models and protocols that have been introduced and discussed in that week's lecture and seminar classes. These assessments are required components of the course and must be handed in each week but do not form part of the final course mark. This course is assessed 100% in a final examination.

Mohammed finds these problem sets straightforward to mark as he is provided with a set of 'model answers' and a mark sheet that gives a specified number of marks for particular elements of the answers. He simply works through the students' problems and grades each according to the criteria that the course leader has provided for him.

He makes a note of 'common mistakes' and points of misunderstanding as he works through the students' work and makes a decision about how to address these. If only a small number of students have made these errors, he produces a corrections sheet, that includes the problem solutions together with accompanying explanations and staples this to their work when he returns it. If a larger number of students have made similar mistakes he allocates 10 minutes of the next class to going through the solutions with them.

He feels this is an appropriate use of his teaching time as the assessment is clearly trying to provide the students with an opportunity to practise their skills and deepen their understanding and also to facilitate tutor–student communication and feedback. Assessment is clearly part of how the students are learning and is formative in nature.

The second course is very different in focus and form. Here the students are asked to produce two essays over the course of the module. The first does not count for their final assessment grade but the second does (to a value of 25%). Mohammed marks both essays but the second is also second-marked by the course convenor to help ensure the reliability of this assessment.

The first essay is likely to be one of the first essays that these first-year students will have attempted at university and so represents a significant experience for them. Mohammed realises that for many it is a huge learning curve to adapt to university-level work with stringent demands on such things as referencing, development of a coherent argument, balanced use of evidence etc. He bears this in mind when he sits down to mark these essays. His instincts tell him to be kind and encouraging in his observations and comments. However, he is also very aware of the need to be honest and clear in his marking, as the students will use his feedback to help them judge the value of their work against the quality standards expected, and will use his comments in preparing for the second essay which does count towards their final assessment grade.

Mohammed thinks that marking essays is much more difficult than assessing quantitative problems. It feels more subjective and he is less confident in giving an absolute mark. He has no difficulty in determining whether an essay is weak, middling or strong when he reads the work holistically. He then uses a marking sheet to further interrogate his reactions and judgement. The marking sheet ask him to allocate proportions of marks to specific criteria such as structure, quality of argument, use of evidence and sources, presentation etc. This further deconstruction allows him to assign marks systematically but it still feels unscientific and far from certain. He has therefore agreed to work alongside a fellow research student, also involved in tutoring on this course, to double check a sample of marked essays. Very reassuringly he has found that their marks have actually been in close accord despite his concerns. This checking approach has meant that he feels secure that his views are in line with others in the school and the marking sheet helps him to apply consistent standards for all his students.

Mohammed also found that some of the students seemed to be struggling to use an appropriate style and structure, and he realised that this was because they were so new to writing essays at undergraduate level. He decided that next time he would ask the students to come to his seminar with a plan for their essay including a fully written introduction. He thought that the seminar could then very usefully include a discussion amongst the students about what makes a good essay at undergraduate level, where he could impart some essential study skills to them and tell them about the university's study skills support services.

One other point of interest has been the marking of work from two students who are registered as being dyslexic. At the start of the year Mohammed was not sure what the term 'dyslexic' really meant and he certainly wasn't clear what the implications were for him as a teacher or assessor. He took advice. He attended a university seminar on supporting the learning of students who have a disability, dyslexia and/or a long-term medical condition, and picked up some useful ideas about presenting information clearly for all students. He also became more aware of the difficulties that the speed-reading he had been expecting of his students in class might be causing his dyslexic students. However, he was still uncertain about his responsibilities in marking their work and so he spoke with the course convenor. Together they confirmed that all the students would be required to submit a word-processed essay that would be spell-and-grammar checked before submission. They also reviewed the assessment criteria to determine the impact that poor spelling or structure could have on course grading and realised that this was a very minor part of the assessment and would not disadvantage dyslexic students. As the students had three weeks to work on each essay it was decided that additional time should not be needed although the dyslexic students would be entitled to extra time in the end-of-year examinations. With this reassurance and clarity Mohammed found no difficulty in assessing the essays and kept their dyslexia in mind in the tone and manner of his feedback comments to them.

Conclusion

This chapter has provided an overview of why you might want to consider teaching during your research degree, and what kind of support you might expect from your institution including how you might get accreditation of the new skills you develop by teaching. The chapter has also explored a range of contexts for the teaching role in higher education and has provided some practical advice for good practice. However, in many ways it has just touched the surface of many of the topics included and therefore this final section includes a range of suggestions for follow-up reading and further exploration of teaching.

SOURCES OF SUPPORT

Further Reading Suggestions for Developing Teaching Skills

Exley, K. and Dennick, R. (2004) *Giving a Lecture: From Presenting to Teaching*. Series 'Key Guides for Effective Teaching in Higher Education' Routledge Press: London
This guide provides the new teacher with straightforward and practical advice on lecturing that includes preparing and presenting clear explanations, involving students and producing accessible learning resources. It will give a boost to ideas and inspiration.

Exley, K. and Dennick, R. (2004) *Small Group Teaching: Tutorials, Seminars and Beyond*. Series 'Key Guides for Effective Teaching in Higher Education' Routledge Press: London

This guide provides the new teacher with straightforward and practical advice on small group teaching that includes the role of the tutor, teaching methods and techniques, inclusive practices and the incorporation of teaching aids and tools.

Haines, C. (2004) *Assessing Students' Written Work: Marking Essays and Reports*. Series 'Key Guides for Effective Teaching in Higher Education' Routledge Press: London

This guide provides the new teacher with straightforward and practical advice on one of the most powerful tools in teaching, namely assessment. This book clarifies the concepts and issues that make assessment difficult before going on to provide clear and practical advice and guidance.

Kahn, P. and Walsh, L. (2006*) Developing Your Teaching: Ideas, Insight and Action* Series 'Key Guides for Effective Teaching in Higher Education' Routledge Press: London

This guide gives advice on choosing effective teaching methods and approaches, using student and peer feedback, working with others and developing teaching practice.

Moon, J.A. (2004) *A Handbook of Reflective and Experiential Learning: Theory and Practice*, Routledge-Falmer: London.

Writing reflectively about teaching may not be a natural or an easy thing to do for some new teachers and this book provides both the theoretical underpinnings and the practical guidance for those wishing to reflect upon their teaching experiences either for personal or professional development.

Morss, K. and Murray, R. (2005) *Teaching at University*. Sage: London

Includes background theory of teaching and learning, and guidance on using electronic media for working with students.

Park C (2004) 'The graduate teaching assistant (GTA): Lessons from the North American experience', *Teaching in Higher Education*, Vol. 9 (3)

The use of GTAs is well established in the US and this paper provides an analysis of the issues involved and references to other studies in this field. The paper draws a distinction between the GTA employee who provides teaching support and is training for a career as an academic (common in the US) and the graduate student who teaches (more common in the UK).

Savin-Baden, M. (2004) *Foundations of Problem-based Learning*. (Society for Research in Higher Education) Open University Press

Useful Websites and Links

The UK GRAD website provides information and guidance on teaching
www.grad.ac.uk/cms/ShowPage/Home_page/Resources/Just_for_Postgrads/
Managing_your_research/Teaching_and_demonstrating/p!empFlde
Problem-based Learning – Online Resources
www.pbl.cqu.edu.au/content/online_resources.htm

Conditions and Research Student Charters

AUT (now UCU) A good practice guide for the employment of postgraduate students who teach www.aut.org.uk/media/html/postgradgoodpractice11.html and the

National Postgraduate Committee (NPC) Employment charter (2000)
www.npc.org.uk/page/1003802201?format=print
These outline what postgraduates are entitled to expect from institutions in terms of
support, information, training, pay and representation.

Development and Recognition – Professional Standards in Teaching

The professional standards framework and its implications for institutions and
teachers is explained on the Higher Education Academy's pages
www.heacademy.ac.uk/4260.htm

Subject-centre Networks

Twenty-four subject centres providing discipline-based support in teaching, learning,
course design and assessment together with a range of networking opportunities that
can be accessed from the HEA subject network page.
www.heacademy.ac.uk/SubjectNetwork.htm

References

Exley, K. and Dennick, R. (2004) *Small Group Teaching*, London: Routledge-Falmer.

Falchikov, N. (2001) *Learning Together: Peer Tutoring in Higher Education*. London:
Routledge-Falmer.

George, J.H. and Dotto, F.X. (2001) 'A Simple Five-step Method for Teaching Clinical
Skills', *Family Medicine* 33: 577–578.

Higher Education Academy (2006) *National Framework for Professional Standards*. www.
heacademy.ac.uk/ourwork/policy/framework (accessed 1 January 2008).

Moon, J.A. (2004) *Handbook of Reflective and Experiential Learning: Theory and Practice*,
London: Routledge-Falmer.

Roberts, G. (2002) *SET for Success: The Supply of People with Science, Technology,
Engineering and Mathematic Skills*, available at: www.hm-treasury.gov.uk/Documents/
Enterprise_and_Productivity/Research_and_Enterprise/ent_res_roberts.cfm (accessed
27 August 2007).

Schon, D. (1983) *The Reflective Practitioner*. New York: Basic Books.

Seldin, P. (1991) *The Teaching Portfolio – A Practical Guide to Improved Performance and
Promotion/Tenure Decisions*, 2nd edn. Bolton, MA: Anker.

UUK, SCoP, CoSHEP and QAA (2000) *Joint Policy Statement on the Use of 'Progress Files'
in Higher Education*. www.qaa.ac.uk/academicinfrastructure/progressFiles/default.asp
and click on Policy Statement (accessed 1 January 2008).

18 Beating the Research Blues
Dr Steve Hutchinson

I woke up this morning, got my thesis to write
Said I woke up this morning, got my thesis to write
Oh, my supervisor gone and left me
And there ain't no end in sight

Introduction

The research blues are those times when you just can't find the motivation to keep going with your work. The research blues are when you can't see the point in what you do. The research blues are when you can't bring yourself to see your supervisor. The research blues are when you feel like an unworthy fraud.

All research students get the blues.

Reading this chapter at the start of your research degree will go a long way to stopping the blues from striking. If, however, they've already taken hold, this chapter offers some practical advice to help you dispel them.

Starting at the Very Beginning...

Before you start reading this chapter, there are just a few clarifiers and a question for you to answer.

KEY CONSIDERATIONS

- You're working on a research degree...
- This is a subject that you are passionate about (if not, then why not?) and based in a discipline that you enjoy.
- You're working on a project that is all for you, and you're becoming the world expert in an area that you love (again, if not then why not?)...

- You're spending quality productive time indulging your curiosity, and are unfettered by piles of administration and many of the other distractions that impact on your supervisor (let alone the world outside of academia)...
- If nothing more, this is something that you *chose* to do.

So, the question is:

'How Can You Possibly Be *Anything* Other Than Supremely Motivated All the Time?'

This seems like a ridiculous and slightly naive way to start a chapter about being blue and demotivated; yet essentially these are *the* only really important facts about being a research student. (Add to these the facts that (a) in all likelihood no one is forcing you to do a research degree and (b) you can quit anytime, and the question is even stronger.)

However, ask any academic, post-doctoral researcher, completed doctoral candidate or final-year student who is writing up and they'll tell you in graphic detail about the horrors of the research blues (also known as the 'second-year slump') or the times when (to quote an anonymous research student I met recently) they need a break 'so badly they could die'.

Also in addition to these uncharted terrors, there are a host of more specific reasons why research students become demotivated and down. This is no small problem for researchers. Without breaking any confidences, I recently worked on a course with a group of eight researchers; four of whom had sought counselling and two who revealed that they were taking antidepressants. This story *is* shocking, but hasn't surprised too many people who've been around research for a while.

This chapter explores a few of the reasons why researchers get the blues and offers insight on what people do to get through. It then asks some questions and might provide a framework to beat your blues. Maybe *you* won't actually get depressed, but you'll certainly know when things aren't right for you. This might be in part due to your lack of understanding about what it means to be a researcher (though if you've read this book, then you'll be fairly well clued up!).

FURTHER CONSIDERATIONS

Bear in mind that being a research student is *meant to be hard work*, but also remember that you always have the right to be happy and fulfilled, to have an opinion, to ask questions and give and receive feedback. (The *right to be happy* is not the same as being happy all the time.)

And, most importantly, *at all times* you have the right to ask for what you want (but of course you might not get it!).

Here are some initial questions that 'blue' students often find helpful:

Do you *know* what you are actually entitled to (help, support, facilities) as a registered research student at your institution?

Do you *know* what is feasible in three years (or two or six or whatever your normal period of candidature is – without a 'writing-up' year) of study?

Do you *know* what the processes are at your institution for when things go astray?

And while the tone is all militant and reactionary, the following are a few other things that as a human being and a researcher you have the *right* to.

- Respect – make sure you know your entitlements and have a clear understanding of what to do when things go awry.
- Make mistakes – a higher degree is a process of training!
- Make decisions – whose thesis is it anyway?
- Be successful – but this is not the same as your experiments 'working' or you having the insight that will win you a Nobel Prize…
- Say 'No' (again, whose thesis is it anyway?) and change your mind – provided that your objectives are measurable, realistic, specific and clear.
- Independence – you're training to become an independent expert in your field. How are you going to achieve this if your supervisor is still telling you what to do a week before the viva?
- You have the right to contact with other researchers – but don't expect this to be automatically organised for you.

Life as a researcher will become far more tolerable if you keep these things in mind, however bad you may at first feel.

For more information on your rights and entitlements as a research student you might wish to look at the Code of Practice for Postgraduate Research Programs (amended 2004) as set out by the Quality Assurance Agency for Higher Education or QAA (www.QAA.ac.uk) to which British Universities adhere (see Appendix 1 in this volume). In addition, the National Postgraduate Committee (www.npc.org.uk) is the representative body for postgraduate students in the UK and is available to give advice on all postgraduate issues.

Why Might You Get 'the Blues'?

This section will examine many of the reasons for the 'blues' and consider some strategies for dealing with them.

A Lack of Progress?

Starting with the 'big one'; the fundamental reason why research students get the blues is because the degree is a big piece of work. More specifically, it is a big piece of work with only one real deliverable – the thesis/viva examination at the end. (Of course, many institutions have a formal upgrade process from initial registration to full doctoral candidature. If your institution does this – then consider this to be a *good* thing, not a needless hurdle. Any official progress-check mechanism will help you to plan your time, set objectives and stay focused.) At the very least, it is a three-year project, and is often carried out in some degree of isolation.

Experience and anecdotes show that many researchers start and set about working with great diligence and they produce plenty of work which their supervisor praises. Then they find that they like the reading/fieldwork/bench-work so much that they lose sight of what their actual purpose is. (Clue: your purpose should be to pass the exam!) Despite a great deal of initial success they leave university to work/practice in their research-specific industry and never complete their theses.

So, ask yourself:
'In one sentence, what is the purpose of my time at this university?'
What does this answer tell you about the amount of time you spend on activities that are not related to the important things (like producing a thesis)?

If your day is spent in a library, office, laboratory or archive combing through the data or running endless repetitions of an experimental process, then it is easy to see how this can become demotivating – especially if the vital breakthrough is elusive. Many research students when commencing their research have little idea of what is feasible during their normal period of candidature, and as such become very disillusioned when they realise how slowly research often actually moves.

In addition, some students have little or no idea about what is actually required in a research thesis (how much, what quality, how long the normal period of candidature is, how it will be examined etc.) and so have little idea what they are working towards. Crudely, this is the often-seen *'I'll do random studies until my supervisor says I have enough.'* approach. This however, as a strategy, is deeply flawed.

Recently, I spent some time working with an Engineering student at a UK university who had arranged to see a student advisor when she had been in some distress and very demotivated because of negative feedback from her supervisor. After a bit of discussion we realised that the real issue was not with the feedback on her practical work (which was always good) but with the feedback on her upgrade/transfer report. With a little more talk it became clear that she had vastly underestimated what was required in a doctoral-level thesis, but had never discussed this with her supervisor. This only came to light when she revealed that her literature search strategy was 'using Google' and that after over a year's work, she had only accumulated twelve references. Her engineering work was sound enough, but she had never had a 'big picture' conversation with her supervisor.

While this story may seem extreme, it does show how easy it is to lose sight (or never have sight in the first place) of the big picture. It's reasonably easy to get a feel for what is actually required, but you do need to think through the process backwards, as illustrated here.

QUESTIONS TO CONSIDER

Ask yourself: 'What is actually expected from me in order to pass?' (Do you actually know, or are you guessing?)

Have you read a few theses from your discipline? These will give you real insight into what level of thinking/reading/working is expected.

What does a completed (and successfully examined) thesis look like in your discipline? What structure does it have? How many references does it have? What does the quality feel like?

So, at least, if you know how much work is required and have a feel for a suitable structure, this will give you a framework around which you can set yourself some deadlines.

Many researchers run out of enthusiasm, patience, funds and workspace because they are under the misapprehension that a research degree can go on forever. It is a scandal that many within the academic sector do nothing to dispel this notion. So, have you considered what will be the non-negotiable date of submission? (Asking yourself 'what date does my funding stop on?' will be more help to you here than 'what date will the university forcibly eject me for taking too long?'.)

When you have done this, then you can start building a realistic project plan backwards from this point/date (see Chapter 20 for more advice on this topic). You may be surprised how quickly the time seems to vanish. This focus can be very motivating to some researchers.

The bottom line is that if you have no deadlines, milestones or progress markers of any sort – it will be very difficult to chart the evolution of your thesis.

What are *your* progress checks, milestones and devices that you use to break a huge project down into smaller, more manageable tasks?

In short, a research degree is an enormous undertaking with few natural progress markers and no clear endpoint. Unless you build meaningful progress checks in your process, you'll sooner or later get the 'Oh, what's the point?' sort of feelings that are only natural under such circumstances.

What's the Point of It All?

So, what 'is' the point? Why are you doing a research degree? What will it give you if you are successful? What won't you be able to do if you fail?

Remind yourself why you are doing the degree. Perhaps this motivation will be about status, or career progression, or even simply to prove that you can do it, or maybe just for the sheer love of the subject. Whatever your initial driver is, write it out and stick it somewhere prominent. Read it every day. *Keep sight of the big picture.*

And finally, if it's all so bad, then why don't you quit and do something else?

List your reactions to this question, and use them as fuel to get things moving and change your motivational state.

Researchers who are undertaking a research degree simply for the love of the subject often find it hardest to project manage to a deadline and as a result sometimes don't submit at all. If this is you – be very careful and go and reread Chapter 20 in this volume!

What Motivates You?

The great but capricious thing about motivation is that it is different for everyone. So, what is it about research that you find motivating? Or conversely, what is missing that is causing you to be demotivated? Is your motivation or lack thereof, tied to your creativity and circumstances? Many students (especially overseas students) have huge pressure placed upon them from funding bodies, families and sponsors. Such pressures are not helpful when it comes to dealing with creative blocks, and in scenarios such as this it is often helpful simply for the candidate to tell the stakeholders that it is an issue.

Academic autonomy is very important to most researchers and frequently students tell a '*I know I should go to the office, and my thesis is important to me, but I just don't do it*' story. When discussing this, they often say that creativity is more important to them than structure. Often they then find it helpful to go to 'work' only when they feel like it and stop feeling bad about thinking '*must go to work, must go to work*'. What previously seems like a chore then becomes an opportunity to discover, which tends to fit in better with what is important to them and their genuine motivation returns.

So, what motivates you? If your supervisor shouted at you, would that motivate you? What about if you were in danger of letting yourself down? What about if you had a deadline? What about if there was a risk that someone would be 'very disappointed' in you?

Think for a moment about a time when you were 'really' motivated. Write down five bullet points about that motivation. (These can be anything – for example family, sunshine, holiday, money, applause etc.)

How can you use these personal motivators (however obscure they might seem), and build them into your thesis plan?

A nice little trick (that I and many of my colleagues use) is to keep a collection of all of the positive feedback and nice comments that people make about you. This is known by a variety of names including 'Fuzzy File', 'Feel-Good Folder' and 'Love Tray'. On the days when you feel like an unworthy fraud, look at these positive and sometimes emotional reinforcements of what a talented and fantastic person you actually are!

A question that can link emotion and motivation and helps a lot of research students climb out of a slump is 'what are your carrots and what are your sticks?' In other words, what are your rewards and punishments – or your incentives?

When Did You Last Reward Yourself?

If you work hard, and your thesis is on track (because you've got a plan – haven't you?!) then you should feel free to reward yourself. This could take the form of a cup of tea at the end of page, or an afternoon off to go shopping when you finish a chapter; whatever would motivate you to keep going. The promise of a weekend away or a holiday is a great incentive to keep going when all seems bleak!

QUESTIONS TO CONSIDER

When did you last set a goal, meet it and then – importantly – reward yourself?
What did you do and what effect did it have?
From today set yourself small, measurable and timed targets, and *reward yourself* when you meet them.

The write-up period is often said to be a particularly challenging time, but some students love it. The obvious signs of progress can be very motivating, especially if you print out each page as you write it and file it in a way that you can see the pile grow: progress that can be literally measured with a ruler! If this act is reinforced with regular rewards and 'punishments' (if progress is not on schedule) then the whole process seems far more manageable.

At the end of each day, plan the next one. At the end of each week plan the next one. Always focus on smaller goals with a clear view of how these fit onto the grand project plan. You'll find *progress is very motivating.*

For some people, the simple act of sticking to a plan is all the motivation they need to keep going. Motivation is of course much more than just about rewarding yourself. There is a whole other flipside to things that you can use to your advantage.

Who Else Cares about Your Work?

Think about the times as a 'taught' student when you *really* worked hard, and consider how often those times were related to occasions when you were going to be assessed. As an independent author and authority you no longer have this regular luxury (!) and if your supervisor likes you to work independently from him/her you might find the need for someone to simply take an interest.

In 'what motivates you?' earlier in the chapter, you may have noticed that other people often contribute to your motivation (and, even if not, contact with other researchers is still a good idea). If this was the case, how could you find someone else to (reciprocally) keep your motivation up?

If you share your goals so that someone else knows what you're doing and *not doing*, it can help to keep you focused on what needs to be done. For obvious reasons, not least of which it gives you a chance to let off steam, this person should not always be your supervisor!

Get someone to check on your progress. Make your goals accountable to an external party and make it harder for you to put things off *'because there's always next week.'* This can be on whatever basis you like, but doing this every one to two weeks is probably sensible.

A sound piece of advice often given by performance and life coaches is 'design your alliances'. In this context you need to figure out how you want your significant other to 'be' with you if you meet your goals (happy, challenging, congratulatory or pushing) or if you don't (angry, sad, disappointed etc.) and *then tell them*. Again, this will be a personal thing that will be down to you and your buddy. Proactively design your relationships so you *both* get the most from them in order to ensure that your personal motivators are also kept active in the equation.

However, none of these measures can overcome the frustrating monotony that may make up a large part of your research!

Does It Have to Be Boring?

A great deal of in-depth research is boring. It should be said that this does *not* mean the end product of research itself (though as a researcher you will hear some *monumentally* boring conference papers), but the sheer act of futile digging down into the sources or the data looking for another minute clue, and for weeks at a time, can be quite daunting. So, notwithstanding everything else that has been written in this chapter so far, how do you stop getting overcome at times by the sheer tedium of it all?

Your current answer to this question may be *MySpace* marathons, playing *Tetris* or winding up the gullible post-doc, but these are hardly long-term solutions. A productive strategy for shrewd researchers is that they use the things that they *do* find interesting to keep them going through the bits that they dislike.

QUESTIONS TO CONSIDER

Which parts of the research/thesis work do you 'love'? (Don't say 'none of it' – you're not being forced to do it!) So, *use your passion* and make jobs you *do* like the reward for yourself after you've completed stuff you *don't* like. The great thing about this approach is that *it's all work!*

Work out how much of your life you spend on *non-productive tasks* (like checking your email) and *displacement behaviour* (like desk-tidying). When you find yourself wasting time, watching daytime TV one full working day each week, then that should be all the motivation that you need to actually change your behaviours.

Too Much to Do, Too Little Time?

If you are having a problem motivating yourself to deal with the sheer enormity of the project then remember that the government, 'research councils' and universities acknowledge that a PhD is a piece of work which a competent and capable student, if properly supported and supervised, can submit in *three years* of full-time study. There are also similar time-bound caveats surrounding all higher degrees.

In other words, the process of a higher degree is now acknowledged to be scholarship and apprenticeship (learning to be an *independent* academic) and training. The sooner that you sit down and work out exactly what your project is (and conversely what it is not) the easier it will seem.

Remember that in the early stages, such feelings of an overwhelming project are entirely natural. However, by the end of the first year you should have a good idea of where you are going to say 'stop'. Remember, it's your thesis and it should be neither too big nor too small!

Revisit the earlier part of this chapter and produce a thesis plan. Arrange a meeting with your supervisor(s) and share this plan. If nothing else, this will help you to have a 'big picture' conversation.

Some research supervisors completed their research degrees before the time constraints now placed upon you were set in place, and as a result took (much) longer to complete their theses. As such, it's probably worth remembering this and seeking different opinions if you're still slaving away after seven years and your supervisor is urging you to 'just do a little more...'. The sooner you resolve this issue and possible tension, the easier life will be – leaving you free to actually get on with getting some meaningful insights or results. Or maybe not.

No Findings or Negative Results?

A surprisingly common cause of the blues for research students is the 'my-experiment/study-*hasn't-worked*' complaint. (This is far more likely for scientists and social scientists, and so just for the record can I say for perpetuity that your experiments *always* do what they were set up to do. There, I feel better now.) However, students from all disciplines are frequently confronted with the reality that for all of their project-managed hard work, they have little or none of the good stuff that is going to win them a Nobel Prize.

But does this actually matter? In some ways (especially for your career development) it certainly does – as it's obviously difficult to publish non-findings. However, the research degree is not all about the end product. Remember that it is a process of training and apprenticeship as well as 'pure' research. This is a tough concept to get your head around if you feel like you're wasting your time without an 'answer', but it is important to remember this when it comes to transfer/upgrade and the final viva.

A post-doctoral researcher recently told me that in his thesis there was little in the way of 'publishable results' and he had felt very uncomfortable about submitting a thesis that was largely based on negative results and what he 'hadn't discovered (!)'. He then spoke of his viva which he had found to be very challenging, but ultimately rewarding because the examiners had appreciated the methodology, resolve, valuable insights and foundations that he had made for future workings. He was, however, a very eloquent researcher and had a clear idea of the *value* of what he had done.

If you are to get anything at all from your higher degree, you need to bear in mind what your 'significant and original contribution' to the field actually is (see Chapter 19 in this volume for more on the concept of 'originality').

QUESTIONS TO CONSIDER

Ask yourself 'what is original about my work?' (and your answer should be no more than a short paragraph).

The answer here could be your methodology, your research philosophy, your subject matter, your standpoint, your analysis or a host of other things. Be very, very clear about this and it will help you enormously to focus, and to convince the examiners of the value of your work! If you are unsure, arrange a meeting with your supervisor as soon as possible. As a counterpoint to this, it is well worth asking yourself the opposite question.

What is not original about my work? (again, your answer should be no more than a short paragraph).

Your answer to this question may be any of the things listed above, and with this in mind it is easier to understand the value of your work to the researchers who'll follow you. You took great insight from the successes and failures before you, and so they will do the same with your work. Or in other words if you 'see a little further it is because [you] have stood on the shoulders of giants'. (Thanks to the gigantic Sir Isaac Newton for that one!)

Again, this notion is a tough pill to swallow, and if you really have doubts about the value of your work, this is a conversation to have with *several* academics as well as your supervisor. Finally, know that the thesis does not have to include everything that you've done, and so some selective pruning is expected.

How Can I Deal with Research Setbacks and Failures?

Maybe you couldn't get the visa to go to the prestigious archives. Maybe your funding was not approved. Maybe a team from another university beat you to 'the answer'. Maybe your laboratory burned down. Maybe your laptop got stolen.

These are things that have happened to plenty of research students and might happen to you too. So, before these can strike, and the blues can attack, what is your contingency plan, or your safety devices to minimise the impact.

KEY CONSIDERATIONS

List all of the things that might go wrong.
What is the probability of any one of these things happening?
What would the impact on your project be of any one of these things happening?
Those things that are both catastrophic and pretty likely are well worth dealing with in advance! (So back up all of your files daily and keep copies in two locations. You've been warned!)

While we all know that hindsight is a wonderful thing, it is your foresight that may well save your research one day. However, if the worst has already happened, what can you do?

The first thing that you must, must do is to let your supervisor know. If you already have a plan to deal with problem then even better (supervisors *like* proactive thinking and proposed solutions, not just an endless list of problems). You must *not* keep your supervisor in the dark.

QUESTIONS TO CONSIDER

If you have a research problem, consider at least three different alternative solutions before you go to see your supervisor.

The next thing is to consider the impact on the big picture. Will this setback affect the viability of the thesis? (Your supervisor's objectivity will help to answer this question). Will this setback affect the final deadline for submission?

If collectively (between you and your supervisor) you decide that the setback will impact on the 'passable' viability of the thesis (not the same as the ultimate academic quality of it) it is important that you raise this issue with the other project stakeholders as soon as possible. You might also want to investigate the feasibility of appealing to suspend your registration. This would mean you could sort the problem out without piling undue time pressure on yourself at the end of the process.

Whatever you do, it is vital that you enlist as much help as you possibly can. Research problems like this are best dealt with using all the support networks and contacts that you have. Setbacks are not just about research progress though, and some can be related to actual process of candidature.

Academic 'Failures'

Some researchers (quite understandably) receive a confidence knock and a big setback if they fail to make it through either of two of the major hurdles *en route* to a higher degree. These are of course, temporary failure to upgrade/transfer, and a referral at the final viva.

The 'real' problem here is that because your work is so important to you, you might view setbacks like these in an emotive and subjective way. If these happen to you then clear your head, take a day or two off and make every effort to look at these setbacks with the objectivity that a research degree is supposed to train you to have.

Also remember that while there are one or two examiners with an axe to grind, the vast majority are good people and have at heart two central questions.

QUESTIONS TO CONSIDER

1 Is this thesis/report the best that it can be with the conditions imposed?
2 What help does this candidate need to ensure that the thesis/report is the best that they can do, so that the standards of academe and this university are maintained?

Failure to Upgrade/Transfer Registration

If you are unfortunate enough to have not got through the transfer then bear in mind that the purpose of this process is to safeguard the standard of the degree, to ensure that the project is 'do-able', to check that your progress is on track (which is where your planning and management would have been helpful), to check that you are the right candidate for the task and that you are receiving appropriate and sufficient training and support.

The principal thing to know is that even if your upgrade has been deferred then you are still a player in the research game. You should have been given the information which will help you to make the transition to full doctoral status, and you've had the benefit of two academic experts (maybe not in your exact field, but hopefully close enough) who have helped you move closer to your goal.

Also, you should consider the notion that the transfer is like a training ground for the final viva. It should be fair (if you believe otherwise, you should say something straight away), but expect it to be tough. Ultimately it should be a helpful process so ask your supervisor what you can expect.

If you 'fail' outright at this stage, it is probably for a good reason, and it's better that you know *now* rather than potentially waste another two or more years. Of course, you can usually appeal against the decision at this stage. Finally know that candidates, who meet regularly with their supervisor, are competent and conscientious, have a feasible project plan and are undertaking appropriate training, sometimes have their transfer deferred for six months but almost never fail at this stage. This process is almost nothing to do with how 'clever' you are.

The very fact that you're a registered research student means that your institution, department and supervisor think you are clever enough to be enrolled. Students who struggle are generally those who don't get the big picture of what a thesis is and is for; can't projectmanage or lose their motivation.

Referral/Corrections at the Final Viva

Did you pass your driving test first time? Some people do, and some people don't. It (usually) doesn't mean they're any less of a driver when they finally pass.

It's nearly the same with the research degree viva, but you probably only get one extra attempt at it. The important thing is that, even with a referral you're still a player in the game with one life left! (see Chapter 22 for more insight on the viva and examination process).

The vast majority of candidates are expected to make corrections and some *do* have to refer. It's probable that less than 10% of candidates at your university will pass with no corrections at all.

Find out the percentage of candidates who pass outright, receive corrections, are referred or fail at your institution (your Graduate School or Research Office should hold this information).

You still have a chance even if after the viva you find yourself with a referral:

KEY POINTS

- Don't Panic – you've got another chance
- Find out *exactly* what they want from you
- Swallow your pride and do what they ask (you might not agree, but this way you live to fight another day)
- Remember, their job is to help you to produce the 'best' thesis that you possibly can.

Research shows that many of these problems could have been entirely avoided if the candidate had received appropriate and timely supervisory feedback. Usually, in this scenario both parties are equally culpable.

Academic Appeals

If you feel that you have been treated unfairly (even before the worst-case scenario) you should know your entitlements regarding your university's appeals procedure. Many candidates are anxious about even asking the question (for fear of being seen to be causing trouble) but it is vital that you understand what you can and cannot appeal for. For instance, you may find after a candidate has submitted their thesis your institution will not accept appeals on the grounds of inadequate facilities or supervision. If you are at all concerned about this as an issue you should immediately consult the academic within your department who has responsibility for postgraduate researchers.

Currently, appeals procedures are thankfully very rare. This might illustrate that, for all of its flaws, the system gets it right most of the time. If the examination panel is well-chosen and free of bias and if the candidate has had frequent, appropriate and constructive feedback from their supervisor and has taken their advice this is an issue that is unlikely to be problematic. However, feedback (or more usually, the lack of it) is, for some, another reason for the blues to strike.

Feedback – Are You Getting Enough?

Are you getting enough feedback on your work? As an objectivity check it is also worth realising that *'Because my supervisor says so!'* is *not* the right answer to the question 'How do you know your work is good enough?'

List all the sources of feedback that you use to build a picture of academic competence and quality

Consider the strengths, weaknesses, opportunities and threats inherent to getting feedback from each of these sources

Now add some potential new ones.

Remember that this is *your* thesis, and you should take responsibility for *objectively* measuring the quality of what you produce.

To be more objective about the quality of your work, when you've finished writing something, put it in a drawer and leave it for at least two days; then re-read it; then seek feedback.

However, (and this is a big-as-in-'BIG' however) before you seek feedback from anyone (especially outside of your department) you should always consider how you are protecting your intellectual property. This is particularly the case in Arts and Humanities disciplines, or if you are sharing *ideas* as opposed to *results*. Once an idea is out in the public domain it is hard to prove it was yours. Seek advice from your supervisor, and be very clear what your institution's policy is regarding protecting intellectual property (see Chapter 13 in this volume).

For most research students the primary source of feedback will always be the supervisor, but this relationship in itself can sometimes be a cause for the 'research blues'.

The Student–Supervisor Relationship – How Can It Possibly Cause the Blues?

Before you read this section, go and reread Chapters 9 and 10. Take a long, hard look at your relationship and then repeat. If your relationship with your supervisor(s) is causing you stress then there is more than one person with responsibility for that malfunction. (That means *you* too!!)

Many research students realise that they are in a very privileged position, and get into a vicious circle of self-talk as their internal dialogue tells them that they should be loving their research and working brilliantly with their supervisor and that there must be something wrong with them because its hard, and infuriating and isolating and frustrating and not everything they hoped it would be.

Combine this with a 'sink or swim' mentality that is still ingrained in many research supervisors, who themselves often had little in the way of skills training or pastoral support and it is easy to see why relationships can go astray. After dialogue with colleagues and years of working with hundreds of research students, it became clear to me that there are two reasons why productive supervisory relationships are so successful.

The first is that some relationships are naturally open, and both parties are able to say exactly what needs to be said. Unfortunately this is not much use if your relationship is not like this.

The second is that both parties (even more if there are joint supervisors) have an ongoing dialogue about their relationship. Problems are steered towards, not away from, and all involved are clear about what the relationship is for and where the boundaries lay.

KEY CONSIDERATIONS

List all of the things you expect from your supervisor
Share this list with a final-year student or a post-doc or new academic

Amend it and temper it with a note of realism

Draw up another list of what you think a supervisor expects from you. (You'll probably find this quite difficult!)

Use these two lists as the basis of a 'designed alliance' meeting with your supervisor.

Student–Supervisor Relationship – What Can Go Wrong?

Research students often list the following common problems with their supervisor (Many of these points are adapted from Philips and Pugh (2000) but thanks to Dr. Sara Shinton and many others for additional insight):

- The supervisor pays no attention to the 'whole person' – just the project
- The supervisor does not offer enough support with the process of research (techniques, data analysis)
- The supervisor does not offer enough guidance on direction
- The supervisor is not available for discussions
- The supervisor only indulges in 'fault-finding' and is not constructive with the criticism given
- The supervisor has unreasonable expectations of the student
- The supervisor is not interested in the project
- The supervisors disagree with each other and the student is caught in the middle.

The final one is a stupidly common problem, and one that I encounter on a weekly basis. My advice is usually that life is too short and just to err towards the one whose views most closely align with yours and who you think will give better supervision.

And at the same time, supervisors cite the following problems with their research students:

- The student is oversensitive and doesn't accept the challenges set
- The student lacks passion and enthusiasm
- The student doesn't follow advice
- The student lacks independence
- The student is not honest about their progress
- The student lacks commitment
- The student doesn't realise how much work is actually involved.

Do you notice how many of these problems are the flip-sides of each other (i.e. the same problem from two sides)? Do you recall the open lines of communication that good relationships all have? Isn't it obvious where the problems start?

In spite of all of the emotions that can surround this relationship and the power dynamic at play (for some students this is as extreme as a '*my supervisor is the omniscient master and I am the unworthy pupil'* viewpoint), it is *vital* that you raise these issues before they get too large.

If you are ducking behind shelves in the library to avoid your supervisor, this is a good sign that things have gone too far and you need to sort them out. If you need more advice on assertiveness and 'asking for what you want' you may find that your Staff Development or Student Training departments provide useful courses on Assertiveness.

If your relationship between you and your supervisor is less than perfect, write down all of the reasons why. For example:

My supervisor is constantly criticising me

Then reframe each issue and state it in 3 different ways (or get a friend to do it). Thus 'my supervisor is constantly criticising me' might become any or all of the following:

1 My supervisor wants me to be able to handle criticism at the viva and is training me
2 My supervisor wants me to push myself as hard as I can to achieve my full potential
3 My supervisor knows how I can improve my work.

All of these are far healthier points at which to renew discussions with the supervisor.

However, the only way to ensure that you and your supervisor have a productive working relationship is regular, meaningful contact. This does not have to be face to face, but it should be one to one. Regardless of the policy of your institution and your personal circumstances, you should be meeting your supervisor at least once a month for an hour or two. This meeting should have a structure so that you get what you need from it, and so both of you feel able to discuss the process of your research as well as the products. In fact, if you're campus based, then try to see them more often. Simply putting your head around the door to say hello and 'How's that grant application coming along?' is a great foundation to a more productive relationship.

Who has the most to lose if the relationship goes awry? (If you've not been paying attention, the answer is 'the student'.) So, with that in mind, who should take responsibility for ensuring the relationship runs smoothly? (Answer: 'the student').

On the other hand, put yourself in supervisorial shoes. Supervisors share your long-term vision of success – good quality research and a completed thesis. If you need a solid foundation to build from, this is a pretty good one. Supervisors are busy, busy people. (You wouldn't want one that wasn't!) Make sure that you get the most from them by being honest and organised and being fully prepared for each meeting.

If it helps, remember that the feedback they offer should be on actions and work, not on you as a person. If the feedback is too general ask for specifics. A piece of work that is returned to you with red pen all over it and the words 'this section is too untidy' may not help you at all. If you want feedback on the general direction of the thesis, then feedback on your commas and full stops will be equally useless. Don't be afraid to ask for what would be helpful.

Don't expect to be best friends with your supervisor. You are professional colleagues first and foremost. Anything more is a great bonus, but only a bonus. So be professional. (And at a fundamental level, this means managing your project properly!) Part of this professionalism means open dialogue. All research students expect their supervisors to give them feedback, but it's very rare that feedback flows the other way. Supervisors (as committed academic professionals) should welcome constructive feedback!

I know a research student whose supervisor gave praise very scarcely. One day after a departmental seminar she came to our office in a state of great excitement. The presentation had gone really well but, more importantly, her supervisor had given her praise. This praise was more motivating to her than any number of good insights or results. 'That's great,' we told her 'and did you tell your supervisor that it was motivating for you to receive praise?'

She thought for a moment, and simply replied 'Well... No.'. 'Then, how' we all exclaimed 'will he know to do it again!!'

She left our office to have a much-needed chat with her supervisor!

Supervisors are human beings too. Give them feedback and praise (on specific actions and behaviours) in just the same way you'd expect to receive it. And if it's in this form:

'When you did X, I found it really helpful because Y.'

You'll find the relationship improves noticeably and quickly.

Do all of this while the problems are small and manageable. Every university will have a procedure for changing supervisors, but (if you chose your supervisor wisely at the start) this measure should be the very last resort.

And finally, never forget in the seriousness of academic discourse, to show your enthusiasm. Your supervisor must be enthusiastic about his/her discipline, and one of the reasons for supervisors working with research students is to surround themselves with bright young passionate minds. A lack of enthusiasm on your part is almost an insult to their vocation! (This counts in your viva voce too!)

Isolation – How Can I Deal with the Downsides of Being a Lone Scholar?

However well you work with your supervisor, and however well you project manage and reward yourself, it can still be enormously frustrating and soul-destroying to work day after day by yourself. Some researchers relish being a lone scholar, but most don't, and sooner or later you'll need a support network.

List all of the people who are in your support network, and potential research network (both face to face and virtual) and who can act as resources to help you on the way to success

List all of the ways that you can reciprocate.

Having a healthy support network is not the same as being in a thriving academic community. Friends and family have a key part to play (which is why you should include rest, recuperation, friends and family into your project plans) but there is no real substitute for other junior and more senior researchers with whom you can exchange ideas and thoughts.

If your research is in the sciences you may be fortunate enough to be part of a large research group, but in other disciplines you may have to work a little harder. Don't expect your department or university to hand networks to you on a plate.

If you want to develop your networks, ask yourself the following questions.

QUESTIONS TO CONSIDER

Who is in your supervisor's network, and are there any introductions they could make on your behalf?

How well is your face known in your department?

If your department provides you with a workspace, do you use it?

Do you use the coffee area/staff common room on a regular basis?

Do you attend seminars, talks and other research-related activities in your department? (If they don't exist, could you help set something up?)

Is there a writers' group you could join (see Chapter 12 in this volume for more information on this)?

How well are you known around your faculty (i.e. in related but different departments)?

How well is your face and name known within the wider academic community? (What could you do to enhance your profile?)

Does your university have any web-based virtual research networks? (If your university has a research office, they'll be able to advise.)

Which web-based networking and academic sites do you use (e.g. JISCmail, ResearchResearch etc.)?

Do you know what other related research activity is going on within your part of the country? (Regional subject centres, hubs and consortia for example)

Does your university have a postgraduate centre, or does the students' union have a postgraduate students association?

What system do you have in place for managing and keeping track of your contacts and networks?

The answers to these questions and the actions that you take as a result may well be all you need to combat the isolation of being a lone scholar. In fact you may find that your real problem lies in keeping from being disturbed. In this case, I find a big pair of headphones and a very rude sign informing people not to disturb me help enormously.

If you still find that you are isolated, you could build in contact with other researchers as a reward to yourself. This is particularly important if you do research on a part-time basis. Meeting for coffee/lunch once a week on campus is a great incentive to actually go in and develop other networks.

Is (Lack of) Money the Problem?

Most candidates suffer from financial hardship whilst being researchers. Although this situation has improved over the past few years, it still is an issue that is a significant cause of distress.

From the very beginning of the project, understand that money is a finite resource and if you have three years of funding then the project should be three years from start to submission. Be extremely careful of taking a scholarship or bursary for one year with a view to finding more money for subsequent years as you go along.

If you are seeking further funding then your university's research support mechanisms may be able to advise you on sources of income. You should also talk this problem through with your supervisor and the academic within your department who oversees all research students. They will be able to advise you on what sources of funding may be available to you (supervisors are surprisingly resourceful if presented with this sort of problem).

Many full-time students are finding that the only way to continue is to work part-time at the same time as being a full-time researcher. Sometimes this is by means of an increased teaching load, but often it is by waiting tables or pulling pints. If this is the case for you, consider how much paid work you are *allowed* to do (there was probably a limit in the contract you signed at the start of your candidature) and whether the extra income is really worth the late nights and days away from your research.

If you find that you are massively overstretched financially then your university's Student Welfare service may be able to advise you. Ultimately, you may find that your only solution here is to suspend your registration while you recharge your bank balance.

The bottom line here, before it's too late, is to get the following right:

- Understand how long your research candidature actually is
- Get the money for that amount of time
- Acquire and hone your project management skills to finish on time.

Could Over-enthusiasm Be a Problem?

To coin an old cliché, a higher degree is a marathon, not a sprint. Many researchers work horrendously long hours and burn out because they can't maintain that effort for a long period of time. After a certain point, there is a very real trade-off between the quantity and quality of work that you can do.

Also, it is vital that you make the distinction between 'working' (i.e. the original contribution to knowledge) and 'being at work' (photocopying, emails, *Tetris* etc.). To combat this problem, and the ultimate frustration that it brings, work out when your most productive times of day are, and save your 'work' for then. Work out when your lull periods are (i.e. after lunch) and use that time to do your filing etc.

Are You Looking after Yourself Properly?

How much holiday are you entitled to take as a research student at your institution? How many weekends have you worked in the last month? How many days last week did you eat lunch at your desk? When did you last do any light exercise? Do your social activities and family tend to get shunted to one side as the work piles up?

It is incredibly all-consuming to be a professional researcher. It is a *wonderful* thing to do for a living, but no matter how inspired and busy you are there is no excuse for not eating healthily, exercising (a bit) and taking proper breaks. Build them into your daily plan.

Getting the Balance Right

Assuming that all these pearls of wisdom have dragged you out of the depths, and you are now back and raring to go, there are three more very important words for you: *Work*, *Life* and *Balance*.

Much is written on this subject, and there are no end of seminars you could attend or books on 'self-help' you could read. However, unlike most, you are in an enviable position of, in effect, being your own boss. It is your decision how to strike a balance between researching and everything else in your life. Make the choice wisely, and remember that if you don't build 'life' into your 'work' plans, it will be the first thing to be displaced.

Friends and family are the things that get shunted by the thesis as the work piles up, but in the grand scheme of things, these are the things that are actually important. You must ring-fence time to recharge your batteries and spend time with important people – otherwise they'll disappear.

Who Else Might Be Able to Help?

If you find that your problems have not been addressed by this chapter then all is not lost as there are many, many sources of support for you. These might be the following:

- Other research students and research staff (but remember to focus on action and not just on whinging!)
- Your supervisor (95% of all problems can be solved here, if the lines of communication are working properly)
- Other academics (but be careful that your approaches are not read as disloyalty…)
- Your Postgraduate Research Tutor (or whatever device your department has in place to act on behalf of all research students)
- University welfare services and professionals in your student union.

Despite having access to all of these external sources I found the most useful thing that helped me beat the research blues was a good friend with a willing ear, a Chinese meal and a packet of Jaffa Cakes.

However, What If It Goes Beyond 'the Blues'?

Of course, you will know if things get really bad and your situation goes beyond the things that are dealt with in this chapter.

It is essential that you remember that *you are not alone*. Dealing with issues as serious and as 'close' to you as a constant state of distress, misery or depression is not something that you should even try and handle by yourself. This is difficult, but you must consider the ramifications of *not* dealing with these issues.

A starting point might be to talk to other professionals in the sector whose views you respect. Tell them about what is going on. Unless they are qualified to officially listen to you they are likely to refer you on to someone who is;

but training providers, other academics, careers advisors and members of your graduate school can still be a safe and comforting person with which to start to air your feelings. They may advise that you take a holiday from your project to gain some perspective, or they may suggest that you look into suspending your registration for the same reason. Both pieces of advice are good, and may (but similarly may not) be appropriate to your needs and state.

Generally, universities have a 'student counselling' service as well as anonymous free call lines that you can ring at any time of day or night. (Also, *The Samaritans* (www.samaritans.org) offer confidential and emotional support and while people may believe that they are a last resort, this is certainly not the case.)

These services will all have qualified professionals who can anonymously listen to you and either help you productively work through whatever is in your mind or see that you get more specialised help. Seek these services out, even before it gets serious. *They are there to help you.* Many research projects and individuals' professional and personal sanities have been rescued by a timely intervention from a trained counselling professional.

If these measures sound insufficient then you can of course visit your institution's 'student health' facility or your doctor (a GP – you know, a 'proper' doctor). If your research blues have become clinical depression (you'll know) then you *must* treat it as seriously as if you had broken your leg. Your brain gets poorly just like the rest of your body. Don't be afraid to seek help, and certainly don't keep fruitlessly blaming yourself for how you feel.

And Finally... a Short Action Plan to Help

Ultimately, the only person that can really do anything if you've got the 'research blues' is 'you'. So, if you've got the blues – what can you do? The last part of this chapter is a six-step recipe for ridding yourself of the usual blues. These steps are not original and are adapted from a variety of motivators, coaches and gurus, most especially the work of Anthony Robbins (1994).

STEP ONE

Ask yourself 'what is getting in the way of my being happy and my research being successful?'

Note: This is a *very* different question to 'why am I blue?' as it allows you to isolate the causes (the 'what's') and deal with them. 'Why' questions tend to provoke introspective thought, and not actions.

STEP TWO

Focus on what you *want* to happen – not what you *don't want*. For example:

'I don't want to be isolated' is far less achievable and tangible than 'I want to meet my supervisor for one hour, once a week.'

Ensure that your goals are positive, precise and within the realms of feasibility...

STEP THREE

Ensure that this is what you *really* want.
Ensure that this really is the cause of what is causing things to be 'not right'.

In other words make sure that you're not just putting a plaster over a gaping wound.

STEP FOUR

Take a big step forward. Do *something* towards your goal. As a researcher you should know that you need to change something significant so you can identify its effect on reaching your goal.

Do it now, do it now, do it now!

STEP FIVE

Know whether things are improving:

Is the course of action that you took working for you or not?
Is it moving you closer to what you want?

STEP SIX

Repeat steps one to five until you get what you want!

Conclusion: 'and Finally, Finally ... '

Being a research student is a great opportunity, and there are far too many students who drop by the wayside for want of a bit of motivation. Don't let one of those students be you. Good luck!

Acknowledgements

The tone and examples in this chapter have been influenced by my friends and colleagues Helen Lawrence, Heather Sears, Jamie McDonald, Odette Dewhurst and Sara Shinton.

Bibliography

Some of the references provided here are citations from the chapter. Some of them are the readings and thoughts that have influenced the general direction of this chapter. All of them are useful. However, if you immediately rush out with a desire to read all of them you may just want to question whether this is a productive strategy or non-thesis displacement behaviour!

Brown, S., McDowell, L. and Race, P. (1995) *500 Tips for Research Students*. London: Kogan Page

Cryer, P. (2006) *The Research Student's Guide to Success*, (3rd edition). Maidenhead: Open University Press

Edworthy, A. (2000) *Managing Stress*. Maidenhead: Open University Press

Gaskell, C. (2001) *Your Pocket Life Coach*. New York: Element/Harper Collins

Graves, N. and Varma, V. (1998) *Working for a Doctorate*. London: Routledge

Greenfield, N. (ed.) (2000) *How I Got My Postgraduate Degree Part Time*. The Independent Study Series. Published in collaboration with *The Guardian*. (out of print but a few copies available from www.johnwakeford.com)

Phillips, E.M. and Pugh, D. (2006) *How to Get a PhD: A Handbook for Students and Their Supervisors*, 4th edition. Maidenhead: Open University Press

Robbins, A. (1994) *Giant Steps: Small Changes to Make a Big Difference*. New York: Pocket Books/Simon & Schuster

Rugg, G. and Petre, M. (2004) *The Unwritten Rules of PhD Research*. Maidenhead: Open University Press

Salmon, P. (1992) *Achieving a PhD – Ten Students' Experiences*. Stoke-on-Trent: Trentam Books

Wellington, J. et al. (2005) *Succeeding with Your Doctorate*. London: Sage

Whisker, G. (2001) *The Postgraduate Research Handbook*. Basingstoke: Palgrave

19 Writing Your Thesis
Dr Joanna Channell

'What I find difficult is writing in a suitable style.'
'My difficulty is knowing when to stop in the lab to allow myself enough time to write up.'
'What I am finding difficult is determining what and how much should go into each chapter.'

(Research students at a writing workshop)

Introduction

This chapter is designed to be of maximum use to research students who are between 12 and 9 months (full-time, or part-time equivalent) away from their planned submission date. At this stage, most research students will be getting on well with their research, have some interesting findings (and maybe some not so interesting), and they may have given a couple of conference papers or had a journal article accepted. While it is important to write from early on in your research, this is the time to get going on planning and managing the creation of the final version of the thesis. This means working on the following areas:

KEY CONSIDERATIONS

- Academic requirements, styles and conventions
- The 'building blocks' for the thesis: essential content and sections
- Choices about structuring
- Planning and managing the writing project and getting the most from your supervisor(s)
- Motivation and looking after yourself.

Thus this chapter is about both the product (the pile of A4 sheets which form the eventual thesis); and the process of creating it.

We begin with the product.

UK Research Degree Thesis Requirements, Styles and Conventions

---

'What are the examiners looking for?'
'I want to know more about the assessment and marking process.'
'How original is original?'

You will find specific and detailed information to help you to answer these questions in two places:

- Your university's regulations for higher degrees (there will be specific regulations for each degree for example EdD, MPhil, PhD etc.)
- Its guidance for supervisors and examiners of higher degrees (often in its quality manual).

To give a general idea, Table 19.1 has a compilation of typical requirements for the PhD, taken from the regulations and guidance of several different UK universities:

TABLE 19.1   Compilation of the typical requirements for the PhD

Evidence of general skills and knowledge	Evidence of research achievement	Presentation
• 'Evidence of the candidate's ability to relate the subject matter of the thesis to the existing body of knowledge with the field' • Critical judgement in a particular subject • Appropriate analysis of previous and new findings • A broad knowledge and understanding of his/her discipline and of appropriate cognate subjects	• A knowledge of the research techniques appropriate to his/her discipline • Successful application of research techniques to the issues investigated • 'A distinct contribution to the knowledge of the subject • Evidence of originality	• Well-organised thesis • Conforming to all University requirements, including the word limit • In English • Spelling, punctuation, grammar, paragraphing, formatting to be corrected to a high standard

The baseline instruction about the PhD thesis at many universities is that there is a maximum length: often 100,000 words plus appendices. It is important to conform to this and to be clear that, as one university so nicely puts it 'this figure is a limit, *not* a target.' Examiners are looking for quality and clarity, not quantity, so do not make the mistake of padding out your thesis to make it longer.

What Makes a Piece of Academic Writing 'Good'?

While readers often use the word 'good' as a shorthand to describe a particular piece of writing, what they mean is more like 'effective for its purpose and appropriate for its readers'; that is to say, writing quality is always dependent on context. For academic writing, four overarching variables can help to assess quality, see Table 19.2.

These headings often form the basis of feedback about research writing, from supervisors, for example, such as 'this chapter contains interesting material but it is not explained clearly' or 'reads well but not enough evidence to make your case'. Use the four headings to assess your own writing, and to interpret feedback about it.

Contribution to Knowledge

At the heart of higher degrees at doctoral level is the need for originality and, more specifically, the concept of making a contribution to knowledge (CTK). The requirement to demonstrate the contribution through the writing in the thesis is what drives everything about the content, organisation and style conventions of the various sections. The thesis as a whole needs to contain evidence to convince the examiners, by the end, that there is a sufficient CTK to merit award of the degree. Figure 19.1 shows the possible logic of a thesis argument.

TABLE 19.2   A framework for assessment of academic writing

Topic	Interesting, timely, academically valuable, leading to an original contribution to the area
Content	Focused, justified, sound research described in sufficient detail that someone else could replicate it
Organisation	Logical, telling the 'story' so that it is easy to follow and in a conventional pattern for a thesis
Presentation	Appropriate writing style/choices of words and phrases; grammar, spelling, punctuation all correct Visually – does it look good on the page? Typography, layout, clear diagrams

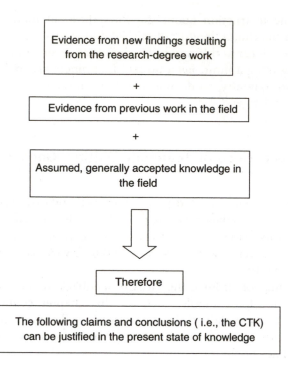

FIGURE 19.1   The possible logic flow for a thesis

It is therefore key to writing success that candidates work out, before undertaking much drafting, what the main claims and conclusions of their thesis are likely to be. Exercise 1 provides a template for this. The argument diagram above can be used as a template to make notes about the findings, previous work, assumptions and claims and conclusions of any piece of research.

EXERCISE 1: THE CONTRIBUTION TO KNOWLEDGE OF YOUR DOCTORAL WORK

This exercise is designed to help you to clarify the contribution to knowledge and think about how to explain it convincingly in your thesis (and at the viva).
   Write one sentence which summarises the main goal of your research:

'The aim of my research is to...'
What is the value of this research – importance? interest? timeliness?
'This research is valuable because...'
Write down up to four main findings so far
Write down at least two contributions to knowledge or conclusions from your work

> Tip: Talk over what you have written with someone who is not close to your subject area. Non-specialists often ask really useful 'naïve questions' ('what's the point of this work?' 'why did you do it this way?' for example) which challenge you to find the best ways of explaining how and why your research is important

So far, we have seen some of the overall principles which guide the writing of the thesis. The next section outlines the writing styles and content for the main sections a thesis will normally include: introduction, approaches and methods, discussion, conclusions. Reviewing prior literature is not described as a separate section, since in many theses prior literature is discussed in several different places, and there may not be a specific review chapter (for detailed information on how to tackle reviewing the literature and writing about it, see Murray, 2002; Chapter 3). The sections below are described in the order in which they will probably appear in the final thesis, but this might not be the order in which you draft them; for example, many thesis writers leave the introduction until last.

Writing Style (1) the Introduction

Although readers do not see the conclusions until the final chapter, the writing in the first chapter creates the context for the CTK evidence and argument, and sets up expectations of what the thesis will contain. The following is an example from a successful PhD.

TEXT EXAMPLE A

Thesis title: Privatising Britain's passenger railway
(Paragraph 3 of the introduction. First two paragraphs describe the UK government policy which led to the privatisation)

Academic interest in the British Rail sell-off has been widespread. Various studies have traced the evolution of policy from empirical and theoretical perspectives, whilst others have provided generalised policy analyses or focused upon specifics such as the economics of rail privatisation. [description of prior work omitted]

But despite the rapidly expanding literature on rail privatisation, there remain omissions and considerable scope for original investigation into the subject. This is particularly true with regard to railway competition, and there is certainly a need to further augment academic understanding of the policy adopted to promote it. Although the above studies have contributed significantly to current knowledge, they have tended to be narrow in focus, assessing the policy either in terms of economic theory or without extending their analyses much beyond the bounds of the railway industry. Little attempt has been made to examine the evolution of railway competition policy, or to discuss it in the wider context of political economy. Moreover, none of the studies has examined the outcome of the policy in any significant detail. Concern has instead revolved around general concepts rather than comprehensive reviews of specifics. Finally, those studies which review the policy's prospects of promoting competition in the future are now somewhat dated and need revisiting in the light of recent events.

This study therefore focuses on the policy adopted to promote competition in the British railway industry at the time of privatisation. [continues] (Shaw, 1999)

This candidate sets the context for his research by summarising existing work in the field. He then claims a space in the field for his own work by specifying what is *not* known, and the need for up-to-date work. Before reading any of his results, therefore, readers already have a clear expectation that there will be contributions to knowledge, and original work, and that those contributions are valuable and relevant.

The writing in the first chapter needs to accomplish the following goals:

- Grab the readers' attention
- Establish the interest and importance of the work
- Specify the wider context in which the work has taken place
- Create the expectation of original contributions to the field
- Tell the reader what is coming next.

A possible schematic structure for the thesis introductory chapter therefore consists of four 'moves', as described in Table 19.3.

TABLE 19.3   Schematic structure for a thesis first chapter (after Swales 1990)

Move 1	Introduce the broad topic area, alluding to its interest and importance
Move 2	Focus onto the specific area and create a context for your work by giving a summary of the state of knowledge in the area *before* your work was started
Move 3	Create a space for the present research, either by identifying a specific gap or gaps, or by suggesting an extension to, or questions about, existing work
Move 4	State the focus and aims of the thesis and summarise what is in each chapter.

Writing Style (2) Approaches and Methods

Careful writing of this section is critically important because the cornerstone of scientific method requires that your results, to be of scientific merit, must be reproducible.

(Day, 1995: 36)

Any higher degree thesis, whatever its topic, must provide clear evidence that the research in it has been carried out using appropriate approaches and methods and it is expected that these will be described in detail. The examiners will want to know exactly what you did, and why you adopted the approaches and methods used.

Some tips to get these right are provided below:

- Be precise
- Be concise and clear
- Use subheadings to help the reader
- Description of statistical methods is required but details are not usually necessary if using standard approaches
- Give references to previously used methods, or methods adapted from others' work, for example:

  'Cell samples were taken from the ear of each donkey according to the method described by Bloggs (1994).'

- If your approach and/or methods are all new, ensure that the introduction to the thesis makes clear that part of its contribution (CTK) is to the development of methods and approaches.

Language Hints

- Use the simple past to report what was done:

  'A commercial extruded dry food *was fed* to 15 adult donkeys...'
  'These data sets *included* values for...'
  'Subjects *were assigned* randomly to two groups...'
  ... 'Each donkey *underwent* a thorough oral examination and...'

- Use the present for a currently accepted method or approach:

  'The development of Alzheimer's *can be classified* into five stages.'
  'Because of growing evidence suggesting that evidence from tick-box patient satisfaction forms is at best inadequate, and at worst, misleading, in-depth exit interviews, which allowed patients to "tell the story" of their hospital stay, were carried out.'

Writing Style (3) Discussions of Findings

Discussions of findings usually occur in sections of several different chapters, rather than in one chapter entitled 'discussion'. The aim of discussing findings is to show that you understand the value and importance of what you have done, and how it fits into the wider context of your field of study, so what you write here again serves to highlight the CTK and originality of your research. Remember from Table 19.1 that a specific requirement of the PhD is that you provide evidence that you can relate your work to the field in general. Through discussion of findings, thesis writers also demonstrate their analytical skills.

To be specific, discussion of research findings will involve some or all of the following strategies or moves:

1   Summarising results or findings
2   Interpreting results, that is to say what results show/imply
3   Comparing sections/parts of your own results
4   Comparing or contrasting your findings with findings or conclusions of previous published work
5   Accounting for differences in present findings from previous work
6   Accounting for why present results occurred
7   Critically evaluating present work
8   Critically evaluating previous work
9   Commenting on methodology of own work
10   Commenting on methodology of previous work.

Two short examples from successful PhDs show how some of these can be expressed.

TEXT EXAMPLE B

Topic: (Economics) Loyalty cards and their use in UK retailing

Text	Move
In this chapter, the Dick and Basu (1994) Relative attitude – Repeat patronage Matrix has been critically examined. Specifically, the discussion in this chapter suggests that 'loyalty' in marketing terms is not a personal characteristic of the individual. Only when both attitudes and behaviours are related to a named store or object is it possible to talk of loyalty. This suggests great care needs to be taken when attempting to classify consumers according to their 'loyalty'. Loyalty to what needs to be carefully specified. A number of circumstances that the Dick and Basu (1994) matrix cannot display, such as proportion of purchase, behavioural and attitudinal change over time and identifying choice set were also identified. (Hartley, 1999)	Summarise work, relate to previous research Interpret results Compare with previous work, critically evaluate previous and present work.

TEXT EXAMPLE C

Topic: Accurate estimation of rainfall using microwave attenuation and mathematical modelling

Text	Move
Careful examination of attenuation levels for specific events confirmed that even when baseline levels were calibrated manually, the link recorded considerably greater attenuation than that suggested	Critically evaluate present work
by the amounts of rain at the path gauges. Since both urban links pass over similar terrain, operate at identical frequencies and are	Compare different part of results
compared with data from a similar set of raingauges, the reasons for the overestimation apparent on the shorter path remain a subject for investigation. While equipment fault is a possibility, no potential explanation has been suggested	Critically evaluate present work (point to shortcomings)
by the equipment assemblers ... . (Rahimi, 2004)	Comment on methodology

Writing Style (4) Conclusions

The final chapter of the thesis is often quite short (less than ten pages), and it benefits from being short, as this creates a positive impression of overview and overall mastery of the topic area on the part of the writer.

The three main types of content in the conclusion chapter are:

- summaries of findings
- overall conclusions
- implications for future work and speculations of what may happen next, including potential practical applications.

This means that many of the discourse moves found in discussions are also present in conclusions. The difference is that in the final chapter, the main task is to bring the argument about the originality and contribution to knowledge to a successful conclusion. So, while it is important to mention any shortcomings, and to consider and dismiss competing explanations of findings, the drive of the argument is always towards the positive exposition of CTK. Leave the examiners with a clear sense of what has been achieved and of your confidence in the validity of your conclusions. Here are two extracts from the final chapter of a PhD. The first extract, the opening of the final chapter (9) sets out the content and organisation of the chapter, and creates expectations for the reader of what they are going to read next.

TEXT EXAMPLE D (EXAMPLE – CONCLUSION CHAPTER TO SHOW STYLE AND CONTENT)

Thesis title: Factors influencing household attitudes and behaviours towards waste management in Exeter, Devon

9.1 Introduction

This final chapter deals with the salient conclusions derived from the preceding three data chapters and discussion chapter. A review of the salient conclusions is given (section 9.2) and these are used to construct the fundamental thesis that underlies the findings of this research. This review of the findings is then set in context by an examination of the policy recommendations for the local authority of Exeter City Council which emanate from this study (section 9.3). Based on the results from this research, policies are recommended which would make a difference in attempting to encourage pro-environmental waste behaviour in Exeter. The implications of the current research for future work are then considered and developments in theory and methodology are considered (section 9.4). (Barr, 2001)

Next, the candidate summarises the key findings, indicating his confidence that the findings support his claims and conclusions:

TEXT EXAMPLE E

9.2 Salient conclusions of this research

9.2.1 Principal results

The principal outcome of this research is to state that minimisation, reuse and recycling behaviour are fundamentally different. The descriptive statistics in Chapter Five show that waste minimisation is undertaken less often than reuse of waste, which in turn is done

Opens with a strong simple statement of the main finding.

Signposts where the evidence for this conclusion can be found.

---

less often than waste recycling. The bivariate statistics in Chapter Six demonstrated that this descriptive difference was reflected in the diversity of the predictors of the three behaviours. This was confirmed later in Chapter Six when analysis of the significant predictors of each behaviour was examined. Reference to Tables 6.33 and 6.34 as well as Figures 6.6 and 6.8 shows that recycling intentions and behaviours are predicted by fundamentally different sets of variables than minimisation and reuse intentions and behaviours. [continues] (Barr, 2001).

Indicates how readers need to link different parts of the results to build the argument for the conclusions.

Overall, the candidate writes to create the impression of someone who is in control of their material, well able to take an overview at the same time as holding a clear picture of the detail. You can almost picture the examiners ticking boxes as you read it and, indeed, this thesis (like all those used here as examples) was suggested by its home department as one that would serve as a good example for future candidates.

Thus far, we have been looking at the expected contents and writing styles of different sections of the finished thesis. Now we need to turn to the task of fitting those different building blocks together into a complete and well-structured thesis.

Choosing a Fitting Structure for the Thesis

Something I find helpful is reading other people's theses from our lab and similar fields.

(Research student at a writing workshop)

Guides to writing theses often assume that there is only one standard pattern for theses chapters (described here as the 'classical' pattern). However, many do not conform to it. The classical pattern works well if the researcher has employed just one or two analytical approaches, and not too many different kinds of data or findings. If the research is interdisciplinary, if it is applied, if it is in a creative discipline, if it involves different kinds of data, for example, qualitative and quantitative findings, or if it used diverse methodological procedures at different phases of the work, then the work may not fit easily into the classical pattern.

Here, therefore, are two other patterns which you could use, or adapt. These are the 'mini-thesis in each chapter' model, and the two-part model, shown in Table 19.4 next to the classical model for comparison.

TABLE 19.4 Chapter pattern organisations

Pattern 1: The classical model	Pattern 2: The mini-thesis in each chapter model	Pattern 3: The two-part model
Title page	Chapter 1: Introduction and review of previous literature, in sections	Chapter 1: Introduction to the whole thesis
Acknowledgements		
List of contents		
List of tables and figures		Part 1: Methane recovery in mines (example)
	Chapter 2: General approach	Chapter 2: Review of literature on part 1
		Chapter 3: Methods and approaches for part 1
Chapters:	Several chapters as needed for each group of data / findings:	Chapters as needed + Results and discussion for part 1 findings
Introduction	Introduction	
Review of the literature	Methods	
Approaches, methods and materials	Results	Part 2: Ventilation in mines (example)
Data and results	Discussion	Chapter n: Review of literature on part 2
(usually several chapters)		Chapter n: Methods and approaches for part 2
Discussion and conclusions		Chapters as needed + Results and discussion for part 2 findings
	Final chapter: General discussion of all the results and conclusions	
References		Final chapter overall discussion bringing together the two parts and conclusions

The mini-thesis pattern could be used if you have several groups of results or findings, each of which needs to be described and discussed separately. Make one chapter for each group of findings. This model is often used in bio- and medical work. It is also used in agriculture, where you have both labora- tory and field experiments, or in education where you have observation work in different types of schools.

The two-part pattern is often used where the research falls into two clear parts. With this pattern, make sure that the introduction shows how the two parts fit together and why there are two parts. Then write an overall conclu- sion at the end.

The best starting point for working out a structure and chapter plan for a particular thesis is to analyse the contents of several recent theses which are close to its topic area and see how they have been organised.

Focussing on the Process

So far in this chapter, we have been considering the thesis as a product and thinking about what it needs to look like in terms of content and writing styles for the various sections. Now we need to move on to looking at the process of preparing to write, drafting and editing, in order to achieve that product.

Developing the Chapter Plan for Your Thesis

Part of the excitement of higher degree work is that as the researcher pro- gresses, their conceptual model of the research area becomes more and more complex: about two (full-time) years in they are likely to be seeing new ques- tions, new angles on old questions, links no-one else has noticed, new angles on data and arguments, new possibilities for further research. At that point the higher degree student faces what can feel like an almost impossible task of translating that multidimensional complexity into the narrow restrictions of the one-dimensional linear form of the written thesis.

Here are two exercises designed to facilitate this task:

1 Making a conceptual map of all the potential content for the thesis; and then
2 Reworking the conceptual map into a linear chapter structure.

EXERCISE 2: MAKING A CONCEPTUAL MAP

1 Take two large sheets of paper. Get coloured pens, sticky notes; whatever suits you to work creatively
2 Think over all the material you have collected, read or thought about in connection with your research. Include: physical material (photocopies, notes about previous research, reports, results, any articles or drafts you have already written); and concepts and ideas you've thought of but not got onto paper yet
3 Note it all down on the first sheet without attempting to impose any order or organisation
4 Then take the second sheet and create the conceptual map. Start the conceptual map by putting in notes of the main claims and conclusions, and contribution to knowledge you expect to make. Think creatively about where things belong and which things need to be connected to each other to support the argument of your thesis. Don't worry at all about how the text will be organised at this stage.

Some people find it helpful to show this map to a friendly colleague. Describing what you are trying to do to someone else can help you to clarify your ideas.

EXERCISE 3: MAKING A CHAPTER PLAN

Now use the conceptual plan and the possible thesis structures to work out the best way to organise your material into chapters.

Try making a horizontal plan for your chapters and their contents (Cutts, 2004: 127–8). Set your next large sheet out (sideways) like Table 19.5.

TABLE 19.5   Content plan for chapters

Chapters	Chapter 1	Chapter 2	Chapter 3	Chapter n (+ as many as you need)
Content required and where that might already exist				

Give each chapter a number and a working title. Then list down the columns all the content which needs to be in each one. Show where existing text (first-year report, article) can be pasted in and edited. Progressively find a place to fit in everything from the conceptual plan. Keep adding detail to the horizontal plan as you refine it, then re-order each chapter and move the content around, so that the whole makes sense.

Once you have a draft chapter plan, you will want to show it to your supervisor for comment and approval. And once you have that, you will be ready to make a timeplan for the write up. This is the topic of the next section.

Planning Your Writing Up

What I found helpful was coming out of the lab for a month to step back from experiments and thus being able to organise a good thesis plan.

Deadlines – breaking things up into smaller chunks and having to have that part finished by a certain time.

Something which helps is a plan of action with a strict timetable.
(Research students at a writing workshop)

Completing research students generally agree that having a writing plan is essential. Many researchers will be writing text daily or weekly throughout their registration and this is a good habit (as discussed in Chapter 12 in this volume). Others (and this is more likely for laboratory-based work) may have written little continuous text apart from their laboratory notebook records. Whatever the case, there is a need to plan carefully the closing stages of creating the final text and I suggest this means having a detailed project plan for the last six to twelve months of work (or part-time equivalent). Working back from the end is a good tip. So the first step is to give yourself a target handing-in date and then work backwards. Be aware that the final polishing will include a wide range of tasks: editing, checking headings, making it look nice, chasing down incomplete references, running it off the printer and copying the resulting pile of pages; these usually take longer than candidates expect. Remember also that there will be non-academic constraints: births, marriages and deaths, families, public holidays, supervisor's holidays and work commitments will continue without reference to your research degree thesis.

EXERCISE 4: MAKE A PROJECT PLAN FOR WRITING UP YOUR THESIS

1   Set a realistic target submission date
2   Set a date when you will stop reading new articles, collecting new data or adding to your analyses
3   Make a month-by-month plan covering the time up until your target hand-in date. For each month state: specific activities and milestones you want to reach and any constraints or dependencies which could affect the plan
4   Indicate on the plan when your supervisor will get each draft chapter, when you would like it back and when you will be making the resulting revisions
5   Make more detailed week-by-week plans for the first and final months.

Once you have your draft plan, you need to discuss it with your supervisors, and give them copies. Is it realistic? Are they going to be available when you hope they will be reading your drafts?

Revisit your plan each month and be prepared to modify it in light of progress. Read Chapter 20 in this volume for more detail on using a project management approach to writing up your thesis.

Managing Yourself, Your Supervisor and the Writing

Writing a thesis is a lonely business; however much support you may get from your supervisor, colleagues and your family and friends, when it comes down to it, only you can put the words on the pages which are going to be bound together as your eventual thesis. Meeting this challenge is made easier if you follow some well-recognised strategies for writers of all kinds.

1   Create the time periods and the psychological space to concentrate on writing.
2   Work out your best ways of working, for example, when during the day is best for writing? What environment is best? Total quiet, music, other people working around you?
3   Writing regularly is more important than writing for long periods at a time – however, doing both, that is writing regularly *and* writing for long periods at a time may well be the most productive thing to do.

An Engineering Doctorate graduate described how her housemates helped her to create a 'writing room' in their house: empty apart from her computer and materials necessary for her write-up. Each day as the others set off for work, she 'set off' to work in her writing room. And each day when the others returned, they asked her to debrief about her writing progress that day.

Here are some more ideas from successful writers about what helped them to work effectively:

Not trying to work at home – working alongside people writing up has been very motivating.

When I need to keep going I promise to reward myself (e.g. with a take-away).

Its helpful to have some regular period during the day to devote to it.

First thing in the morning, when I'm shaving, and ideas start loosening up…

What I find helps is to divide time spent writing into small chunks and to do something different between those chunks, e.g. sport.

Working on different chapters so you can swap when it gets boring or difficult.

The support of supervisor(s) during the write-up period is crucial and well recognised by successful candidates:

Something I find helpful is knowing my supervisor is "supportive".

Supervisor pushing me on to start submitting chapters to him.

Research students have needs and expectations of supervisors which are specific to these closing stages of the research degree. Candidates at my workshops have listed the following as some of the main things they hope for from their supervisors.

Tell me what you expect
Be available and willing to arrange regular consultations
Constructive criticism of writing, not a spell check
Resources support and guidance on relevant reading
Consultation between the two supervisors so that they know each other's approach
And, be able to see each supervisor separately on some occasions
Be approachable – I want to be able to drop in on you
Help me with structure
Tell me what is not clear
Tell me if and where I am waffling
Tell me how to improve: identify what is wrong and suggest how to change
Ask me questions about my ideas
Recommend some previous theses I can look to as models
Be truthful about how thoroughly (or not) you have read my drafts
Be interested in my work
However, please...
DON'T rephrase for the sake of it
DON'T keep making a note of the same mistake if it is repeated
DON'T tell me about grammar or spelling *unless I ask you to,* I can take care of it later.

I suggest using this list to think about what you would like from your own supervisor, and about how to negotiate so that you get what you need. Not surprisingly, supervisors have their own ideas about what works best during the closing stages of the degree, and the next box shows their suggestions about how candidates can get the best from their supervisors.

The most important thing, though, from supervisors' point of view, is that supervisees keep in touch. This is because the prime danger signal that something is going wrong for a particular supervisee is lack of contact and communication. Even if your preference is to hide out in a remote Scottish croft to write up your thesis, you need to keep in regular touch with your supervisor and report briefly whether or not you are on track with your writing, and approximately when the next chapter is going to appear. See Chapter 9 in this volume for further discussion on managing this relationship.

Supervisors would like their supervisees to do the following:

Communicate regularly
Let them know if there is a problem.

Be honest:

At least so we know you are making progress or not.

For meetings provide an agenda:

What do you want covered?
What have you done since we last met?
How do you want me to comment on your writing?
Is this a finished draft, or do you want comment on the ideas, or the structure before
  you polish up the grammar and spelling?

  Report regularly via:

Email
Lab book
Journal of work.

Come with constructive suggestions:

  If we aren't doing what you need, please tell us!

Agree a timetable for your writing up:

So we know when to plan to have time to read your work
So you know when we are not here.

'Being Able to See the End'

Now you can see the end of this chapter, and I hope that you are also beginning
to formulate your plans for seeing the end of your own thesis process. The end
of the process is, of course, the product, the completed thesis ready for submission, and I hope also that you now have a good sense of the general principles
of what the thesis needs to look like as well as some ideas of how to map your
own material into a suitable thesis plan. Remember also to plan actively how
you will look after yourself during this challenging time, and how you will get
support from relevant people. Finally, a round-up of top tips from those who
know best, research students who are about to submit:

  Get your own copies of your university's regulations for higher degrees,
  thesis presentation instructions, guidance for supervisors and instructions
  for examiners of PhDs.
    What I find helpful is a detailed thesis plan.
    I ask myself "do I really need this in my thesis – what will it do for it?" –
  in order to maintain focus and be selective.

Making sure you write everything down, good records and reference structure.

What I found helpful was to write up my experiments – I could see how my work fits together and where I have gaps still to fill in.

Being able to see the end.

And a fitting last word is this reminder from a former research student of one of the key things for research students to keep in mind as they work towards a successful conclusion:

Another thing I find helps is to remind myself that I've been studying this for 3 years, and so I *do* know something about the subject.

Theses

Barr, S. W. (2001) Factors Influencing Household Attitudes and Behaviours towards Waste Management in Exeter, Devon, PhD, Geography, University of Exeter

Hartley, M. (1999) Reward Cards and Customer Loyalty in UK Supermarkets, PhD, Economics, University of Nottingham

Rahimi, A.R. (2004) Statistical Validation of Rainfall Estimates Obtained from Microwave Attenuation, PhD, Department of Mathematical Sciences, University of Essex

Shaw, J. (1999) Privatising Britain's Passenger Railway: Expectations and Outcomes of the 'Free' Market Approach, PhD, Department of Geographical Sciences, University of Plymouth

Acknowledgements

Many people have contributed to the development of the material in this chapter. Some of the material comes from two modules of the University of Nottingham Graduate School Programme: 'Getting going on your thesis and Getting your work published', developed by Jo Longman and Joanna Channell, and 'Finishing your thesis and preparing for the viva' developed by Jo Longman and Claire O'Malley. A key role was played by postgraduates at the University of Plymouth who attended pilot sessions, tried out activities and gave evaluations and suggestions for the course 'Writing up and completing your PhD'. Ideas and feedback from students and staff at the universities of Exeter, Essex and Surrey is also included. Robert Day's *How to Write and Publish a Scientific Paper* has been a valuable source of wisdom, as has been the continuing work of John Swales on all aspects of academic texts. The examples from completed theses are particularly valuable so there is a special debt of gratitude to former research students whose successful theses are used as examples.

Bibliography

Books about the Process of Getting a Research Degree

Burton, S. and Steane, P. (eds) (2004) *Surviving Your Thesis*. London: Routledge

Cryer, P. (2006) *The Research Students' Guide to Success*, 3rd edition. Maidenhead: Open University Press

Holtom, D. and Fisher, E. (1999) *Enjoy Writing Your Science Thesis or Dissertation! A Step-by-step Guide to Planning and Writing Dissertations and Theses for Undergraduate and Graduate Science Students*. London: Imperial College Press

Murray, R. (2002) *How to Write a Thesis*. Maidenhead: Open University Press

Partington, J. Brown, G. and Gordon, G. (1993) *Handbook for External Examiners in Higher Education*. Sheffield: UKUSDU

Phillips, E.M. and Pugh, D.S. (2006) *How to Get a PhD*, 4th edition. Maidenhead: Open University Press

Rugg, G. and Petre, M. (2004) *The Unwritten Rules of PhD Research*. Maidenhead: Open University Press

Books about Research

Blaxter, L. Hughes, C. and Tight, M. (1996) *How to Research*. Buckingham: Open University Press

Howard, K. and Sharp, J. (1983) The *Management of a Student Research Project*. Aldershot: Gower (very useful handbook on the design, execution and reporting of research)

Books about Language and Writing

Barras, R. (1978) *Scientists Must Write*. London: Chapman and Hall (some idiosyncratic ideas, but plenty of hints on what not to do)

Cutts, M. (1999) *The Plain English Guide*. Oxford: OUP

Day, Robert A. (1995) *How to Write and Publish a Scientific Paper*. Cambridge: CUP (useful for most disciplines, not restricted to scientists)

Swales, J. (1981) 'Aspects of Article Introductions', Aston ESP Research Reports 1.

Swales, J. (1990) *Genre Analysis: English in Academic and Research Settings*. Cambridge: CUP.

Woods, Peter (1999) *Successful Writing for Qualitative Researchers*. London: Routledge.

Books about Creativity and Ideas

Ayan, J. (1997) *Aha! 10 Ways to Free Your Creative Spirit and Find Your Great Ideas*. New York: Crown Publications

Michalko, M. (2001) *Cracking Creativity*. Berkeley, CA: Ten Speed Press

Pegg, M. (1995) *The Positive Workbook*. Leamington Spa: Enhance Ltd

Web-based Sources

www.ukgrad.ac.uk (the UK GRAD Programme) (accessed 12 January 2008)

www.clearest.co.uk (the website of the Plain Language Commission) (accessed 12 January 2008)

20 Submission and Completion
Dr Fiona Denney

Introduction

Chapter 19 has already dealt with the detail of writing the thesis but a written thesis does not constitute a completed research degree. You still have to submit your thesis to the awarding institution for the purposes of examination, and make any amendments required from the examination process before your degree can be awarded. It is this process of submitting and completing that is explored here. The chapter is aimed at research students who are about to start writing up and need to consider what lies ahead of them. It is focused on helping you to apply project management techniques to the wider process of submitting and completing.

By the end of the chapter you should:

- Be able to apply project management techniques to the submission and completion process
- Have considered factors such as regulations
- Have considered some of the barriers to submission and completion you might face.

Although some aspects of writing the thesis are also discussed here, this chapter is not intended to be a detailed exposition of writing the thesis. You should refer to Chapter 19 for specific guidance in this area.

What Submitting and Completing Means

Submission and completion represent the culmination of a period of transformation: transformation from being a novice researcher to a more experienced one and transformation in terms of the development of research skills, generic skills and the ability to advance a field of knowledge. Completion of your research degree also represents an ability to write effectively and appropriately, and to communicate the findings and implications of research to the wider academic community. A research degree is seen as a professional qualification, admitting you to academia and scholarship, and demonstrating your ability to do research. Submitting your thesis and completing your research degree indicates that you have reached the required standard to become a professional in this area.

By implication, the end of this process also means that you will have demonstrated the ability to conceive, plan and execute a project. This is one of the most important generic skills that research students can develop and transfer to their future career. Good project managers are in high demand in all areas of industry and other sectors. Applying those project management skills to the process of submission and completion is explored later in this chapter. It is important first, however, to identify the differences between submitting and completing and this is discussed in the following section.

The Difference between Submission and Completion

One of the problems with a discussion about submission and completion is to recognise and understand the difference between the two terms. It is therefore important to be clear about what is being measured and what is meant by these expressions.

Submission generally refers to the date on which you hand in your thesis to the awarding institution for it to be processed for the viva, or oral examination, then to take place. This does not signify the successful completion of the research degree or the award of the degree. Depending on the outcome of the viva, the award of the actual degree may be up to a year from the date of the examination.

Completion is usually the term that refers to the date that you are awarded the degree. This date can, however, vary from institution to institution depending on what is recorded, that is the date on which the letter goes out to the student, the date on which the relevant committee meets and agrees the award, the date on which the degree-awarding ceremony or the date the certificate is sent to the student.

Question: How do I know what my university does in terms of submission and completion dates and procedures?

Answer: You need to obtain a copy of your university's regulations for research degrees and check the processes with your supervisor and/or postgraduate degree administrator. Very often this information is available on the university's webpages along with a postgraduate student handbook. If you are still unsure after reading this material then do ask your supervisor about dates and procedures.

This information is important on two levels; first, to you the student, it is necessary to know when to expect the award of the degree (completion) and to have a deadline to work towards (submission). Second, to the institution, submission and completion rates are monitored by various bodies nationally and form part of funding requirements, as discussed below.

Completion Rates

Both the Higher Education Statistics Agency (HESA) and the Research Councils (RCs) are now collecting and analysing data on submission and completion rates. Many research degrees in the UK are funded by the British taxpayer via Research Council awards, and there is now growing pressure on the government to demonstrate the returns on research degree funding. This increases the pressure on institutions to reach targets that have been set by external agencies for submission and completion rates. The four main funding bodies in the UK consulted with higher education institutions and the Research Councils in May 2003 and established targets of 70% completion within four years for a full-time PhD and eight years for a part-time PhD (Improving standards in postgraduate research degree programmes, May 2003/23, Department for Employment and Learning, Northern Ireland; Higher Education Funding Council for England; Higher Education Funding Council for Wales; Scottish Higher Education Funding Council[1] (2003). Completion rates at individual institutional level are now monitored in HESA statistics and the RCs and other funding bodies are taking note of these when allocating studentships.

One of the reasons for this approach has been described by the Science and Technology Facilities Council:

> [A]t the end of the three years it is true to say that a substantial portion of the successful research training of a student lies in ensuring that they have the ability to write an extended and coherent report on the work that has been done, and in many cases the writing of the PhD thesis is the one single unaided piece of work that a student undertakes....
>
> There are then three clear reasons why a student should submit a thesis within the three years:
> Almost by definition a student who does not complete within the three years or takes longer or does not complete at all is deficient in the aspect of their training described above. The Science and Technology Facilities Council believes that this alone is a strong argument for trying to achieve a reasonable completion rate.
> For students funded on a three year studentship, extensions are unlikely and their personal situation is very difficult if they have to balance the demands of completing the thesis and looking for a job without any funding.

Finally many students in astronomy and particle physics have been funded by the Science and Technology Facilities Council, which is accountable to Government for the use of its funds, and the completion rate clearly affects the ease with which this particular use of funds can be defended. (Science and Technology Facilities Council Website at: www.scitech.ac.uk [accessed 22 June 2007])

It is important to note that the Science and Technology Facilities Council, in this statement, is referring to three years as the main deadline for submitting a thesis, whereas the 2003 consultation document refers to completion within four years. This again, highlights the confusion between submission and completion rates. Completion can occur as much as one year after submission due to amendments after the viva.

This confusion is reflected in a study conducted by HEFCE (the Higher Education Funding Council for England) in 2005, where the rates measured differed considerably from those recorded by the RCs.

In January 2005, HEFCE published the findings from the study which had followed students who registered for a PhD (or MPhil to PhD) in 1996–1997 in the UK. This report was entitled 'PhD Research Degrees Entry and Completion' and defined a student as having completed:

> [when the student has] been awarded a PhD and the 'qualification obtained' has been returned through the individualised HESA student record. This will typically be up to a year after the student submitted their thesis for assessment. (HEFCE 2005: 3)

The progress of these students was monitored for seven years and the findings from this study make for interesting, if worrying, reading. The following summarises the key points:

- In terms of completion, within the seven year period that HEFCE looked at full-time (FT) students with financial backing e.g. from Research Councils (RCs), charities or the British Academy had the best rate of completion.
- FT students in biological and physical sciences had highest rates of completion (in terms of subject area).
- For part-time (PT) students the subject area with the highest rates of completion was medicine/veterinary sciences.
- 71% of full-time PhD students in this cohort completed within 7 years, but only 34% of those on a part-time programme completed within 7 years.
- HEFCE data demonstrated that only around 36% of FT, funded students completed within four years. The statistic is broadly similar for non-Research Council-funded, FT students. The Research Councils (some of the primary funders of research degrees) calculate their own submission and completion rates and

quote their four year submission rate as being approximately 75% for FT students. Due to the fact that the HEFCE study examined completion rates, some of those students recorded by the RCs as having submitted within 4 years, fell into a 5 year completion statistic in the HEFCE study. This clearly highlights the confusion between submission rates and completion rates in measurement terms.

- Impact of change of mode from FT to PT decreases chances of completing a PhD (around 20% changed) and vice versa from PT to FT (around 3% changed).
- For PT students, the overseas students had the best rate of completion.
- Age was found to have a significant impact on completion – the older the student, the lower the probability of completion.

What is clear is that starting a part-time PhD is a high-risk venture: we can estimate that only one in three students is likely to submit a thesis within six years. (HEFCE 2005: 32)

This is not meant to discourage anyone reading this chapter who is an older, part-time UK/EU student working in the humanities and social sciences, but it is intended to inform you about issues that may exist in your particular discipline and mode of registration.

There are of course, many complex individual reasons for not completing a research degree (remembering too that there are students who submit but never complete). One common reason, starting a new job before your research degree is finished, is explored in more detail towards the end of this chapter. There are also some possible discipline-specific reasons.

The sciences (including biological and medical sciences, chemistry, physics, mathematical sciences and engineering) do have more of a tradition of project-based research degrees which are often developed as part of a wider project owned by a Principal Investigator. These research degrees have usually been developed with the three- or four-year deadline in mind and are therefore more tightly scoped than those in other disciplines. Prospective science students often apply to research on a specific question or area, whereas applications in the arts, humanities and social sciences may be to research in a broader subject area. The first year of a humanities research degree is therefore typically spent in narrowing the topic down and defining the research question. This is not something that science research degree students typically have to do. These discipline-based features may provide a partial explanation of the figures from the HEFCE report presented above.

In addition the team-working environment in the laboratory, where there may be several research students and post-doctoral researchers working on aspects of the same, wider project, can be helpful to those who are just starting out in research. This environment does not tend to exist in the arts, humanities and social sciences: isolation is common as students tend to work on individual research projects rather than a wider team project (see Chapter 18 in this volume).

In spite of the fact that the project approach is less common in humanities and social science disciplines, all students can benefit from adopting a project management approach to their research degree. The process of submission and completion is a particular phase which lends itself well to project management techniques. The following section takes you through project management and its application to the final phases of your research degree.

Managing the Process of Submission and Completion

Using a Project Management Approach

Regardless of discipline, it is important for all research students to consider their research degree as a discrete project. If you apply project management tools and techniques to your degree then you will find it easier to scope out, write up and therefore submit and complete.

This is reflected in the QAA framework (2001), which states that doctorates are awarded to students who have demonstrated:

> [t]he general ability to conceptualise, design and implement a project for the generation of new knowledge, applications or understanding at the forefront of the discipline, and to adjust the project design in the light of unforeseen problems (QAA 2001, Annex 1: Qualification descriptors)

So what is meant by the terms 'project' and 'project management'? Project management as a discipline has emanated from the software development industry and as a result, textbooks on project management often define it according to the norms of that sector. The following are just some of the definitions from project management books:

> The most obvious characteristic of a project is that it has to achieve some particular purpose…[it is] *an instrument of change*. (Brown 1998: 7, italics as in original)

> A project is usually temporary and carried out for a specific purpose within defined timescales and resource limits. (Irwin 1999: 85)

> A project is a collection of tasks that is carried out by a team to meet an objective as defined by a sponsor. It has a beginning and end date, a budget and risk. No two projects are ever the same. (Elbeik and Thomas 1998: 17)

The Association of Project Management (APM) is the professional body in the UK which exists to develop and promote project management throughout industry and other sectors. The definition of project management that APM uses is as follows:

> Project management is the process by which projects are defined, planned, monitored, controlled and delivered such that the agreed benefits are realised. Projects are unique, transient endeavours undertaken to achieve a desired outcome. Projects bring about change and project management is recognised as the most efficient way of managing such change. (APM 2006: 3)

In spite of the industrial bias to these definitions, there are several common elements that are relevant to research degree projects:

- *Something changes*: In the case of a research degree it is about managing the process of change from a position of knowing relatively little about a specific topic to becoming an expert in that field.
- *There are defined time limits and resource constraints*: It is important to recognise these and their impact on the project. The deadline in particular is key in the context of submitting and completing on time, as already discussed in this chapter. The tradition in research degrees has been to see this as a 'moveable feast' but this is now no longer the case.
- *The project involves a collection of tasks which need to be managed efficiently and effectively*: Your research degree project will have already involved a wide variety of tasks ranging from scoping out the area under investigation, finding and reviewing the literature, constructing and conducting the data collection/experimental techniques, analysing the data and having regular review meetings with your supervisor. The final stages of submission and completion have other tasks but these still need to be managed efficiently and effectively in order for you to meet your deadline.

Hopefully you have already been applying some project management techniques throughout the process of your research degree. The deadline for submission, however, provides the most important focus for the project; project management techniques can be employed to manage this phase of your research degree more effectively. The following sections take you through this process stage by stage.

Stage 1: Agree a Deadline, Stick to It and Try to Engage Your Supervisor's Commitment to It as Well

Unfortunately, research students often regard the deadline for their research degree as highly flexible, and supervisors are sometimes complicit in this approach. Failure to meet the deadline is therefore a problem with the generic learning aspects of the research degree on the parts of both supervisor and student. The factors that contribute to this include the supervisory relationship, recruitment of appropriate and able students and a regular and rigorous monitoring process throughout. Although the two latter factors are outside of your control as a student, you do have some control over the supervisory relationship (see Chapter 9 in this volume for more help on this) and you can take time to learn and apply project management techniques which will help you to meet the deadline for submission.

Q: How do I know what the submission deadline is for my research degree?
A: Most of the funding bodies in the UK require the institutions which receive the funding to work towards a four-year completion deadline for full-time doctoral students and seven or eight years for part-time doctoral students. You should also refer to your institution's own guidelines on this. For example, the Academic Regulations for Research Degrees at King's College London states that the expected submission deadlines are as follows:

a "for PhD, MPhil, MPhilStud, or MD (Res) programmes – within four years of registration for full-time students or within eight years for part-time students;"

b "for extended MPhil/PhD programmes which include a preliminary research training course leading to a separate award at Masters level – within five years of registration for full time students of within ten years for part time students;"

c "for specialist doctorate programmes – within four years of satisfying the examiners in the practical and/or taught elements of the programme. The maximum period of study for undertaking the practical/taught elements of the programme is four years."
(*Academic Regulations for Research Degrees*, King's College London: a68)

Stage 2: Identify the Tasks That Have to Be Completed before You Can Submit the Thesis

One of the most important aspects of project management is that it requires you to plan backwards *from* the deadline, incorporating all the activities that need to be done in order to complete your project.

EXERCISE 1

Write a list of all of the activities that you have to complete in order to submit your thesis. For example, finish amendments to Chapter 2 of the thesis; compile Appendix A; complete pre-submission form and get supervisor's signature etc.

Try to estimate some timings for these activities. A good rule of thumb is to estimate what seems to be a reasonable length of time for each activity and then double it! Things always take longer than you think!

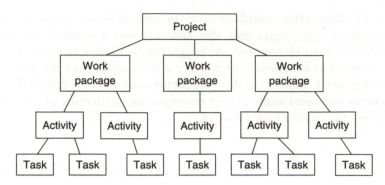

FIGURE 20.1   Work breakdown structure

In project management 'speak', this list of activities is often referred to as a work breakdown structure. It requires you to identify the key work areas (or packages) that need to be completed, and then each and every individual task that has to be conducted. The idea is to continue identifying these tasks right down to the level at which the work is actually done. If you find this confusing, for each task that you identify ask yourself the question: 'what needs to be done in order to achieve this?' If you can still answer the question with additional tasks then you need to add in another layer. It can be drawn up to look like a family tree, illustrated in Figure 20.1.

Stage 3: Once You've Identified the Tasks and Estimated Timescales, You Can Plan the Order in Which They Need to Be Done, Working Backwards from the Deadline

You've probably realised by this stage that you've got a large number of tasks to complete and a deadline that is looking hugely unrealistic in their shadow. If you've been using project management techniques throughout your research degree process then you will have realised that one of the keys to progress is managing to do several tasks concurrently rather than linearly. There are several project management tools that will help you to plan this out visually including Gantt charts, network diagrams and PERT charts. Good project management books explain these in more detail see, for example, Brown (1998), Eibeik and Thomas (1998) and Irwin (1999). Gantt charts are the most simple to use and are usually adequate for research degree projects and are therefore described in the following paragraphs.

Gantt charts are named after an American engineer, Henry Gantt, who first developed them. A Gantt chart is basically a linked bar chart, which shows the beginning and end of a project, the tasks that have to be completed and the dates at which these tasks should start and end. Gantt charts have a number of advantages including being simple to read and draw, usually included in project management software and being widely used.

Figure 20.2 is a sample Gantt chart for the submission of a research degree project. It assumes that some of the research has already been written up as you've been going along, that the literature review is more or less up to date and the data analysis is complete.

Figure 20.2 illustrates the point that a project management approach to completing and submitting a thesis enables you to manage several tasks that have to run in parallel to each other. This is a key factor in being able to meet the deadline that you have set yourself.

Figure 20.2 also highlights the importance of review meetings with your supervisor.

Stage 4: Make Sure You Agree Dates for Review Meetings with Your Supervisor When Planning Your Work and Stick to Them!

Review meetings are absolutely critical to the success of any project. It is easy to assume, when reading the definitions of projects given earlier in this chapter, that you are not working in a team and anything that refers to a 'team' is therefore not relevant to you. It is important, however, that you recognise that you and your supervisor constitute a team. A lot of institutions now support supervisory teams whereby the student has more than one supervisor, but even in the (now relatively unusual) situation where the student has just one supervisor, those two individuals still constitute the 'project team'. As such, good communication between both parties is essential for the successful outcome of the project. Regular review meetings in the final stages of the research degree process are key contributors to good communication.

Often students feel that their supervisors are not interested when they come to the final stages, or they find the writing-up stages so difficult that they do not want to admit to the supervisor that they are struggling. This is a stage when the student often loses touch with the supervisor. An experienced and good supervisor will recognise this as a warning sign – no contact is bad contact! You, the student, need to recognise that it is your responsibility to stay in touch with your supervisor during this time and that regular review meetings will help the process of submitting and completing your thesis. You may not want to admit that you are struggling, but it is far better to engage your supervisor in discussions about the difficulties you are having than just carrying on trying to cope on your own. Be honest,

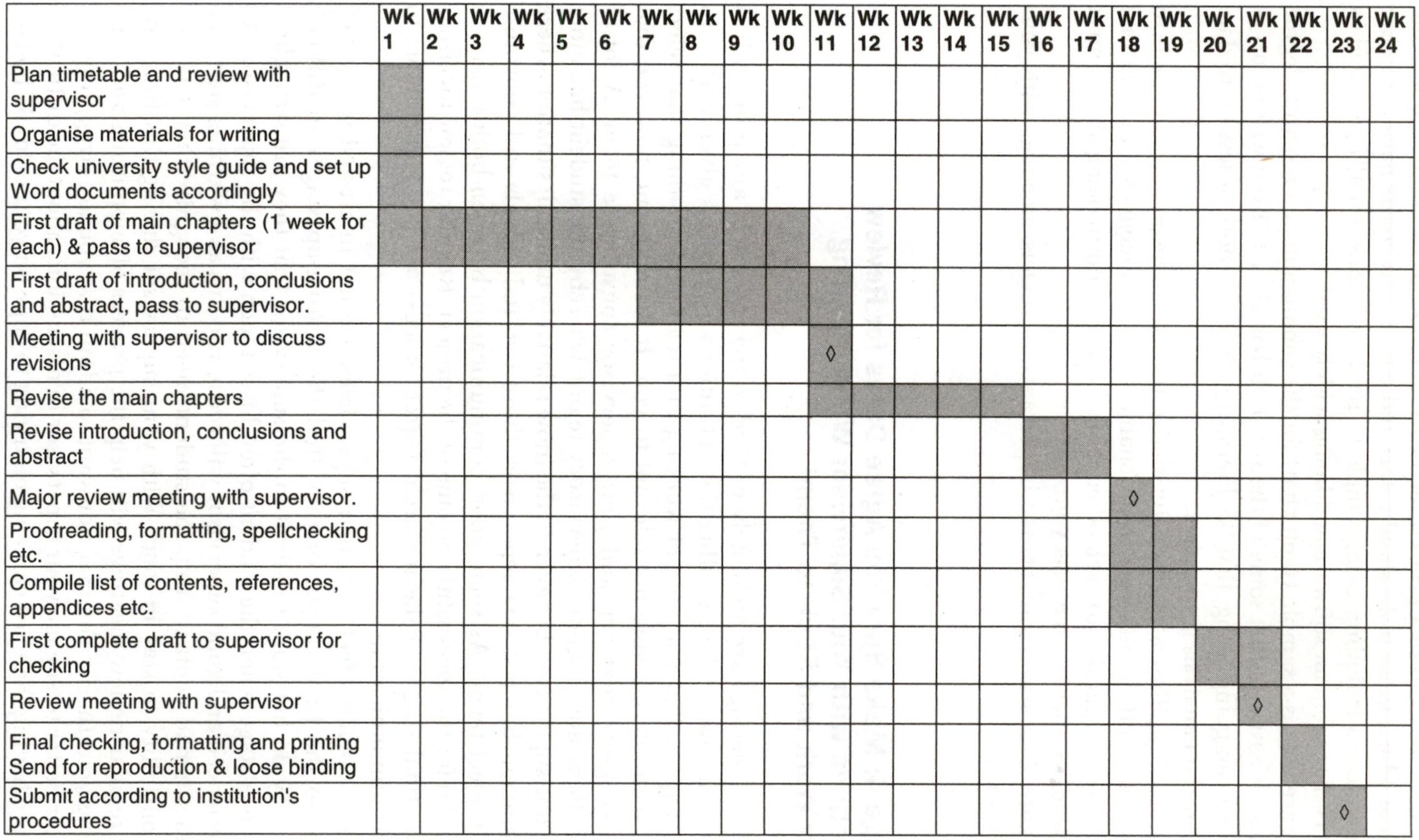

	Wk 1	Wk 2	Wk 3	Wk 4	Wk 5	Wk 6	Wk 7	Wk 8	Wk 9	Wk 10	Wk 11	Wk 12	Wk 13	Wk 14	Wk 15	Wk 16	Wk 17	Wk 18	Wk 19	Wk 20	Wk 21	Wk 22	Wk 23	Wk 24
Plan timetable and review with supervisor	▓	▓																						
Organise materials for writing		▓																						
Check university style guide and set up Word documents accordingly																								
First draft of main chapters (1 week for each) & pass to supervisor				▓	▓	▓	▓	▓	▓	▓														
First draft of introduction, conclusions and abstract, pass to supervisor.							▓	▓	▓	▓	▓													
Meeting with supervisor to discuss revisions											◇													
Revise the main chapters															▓	▓								
Revise introduction, conclusions and abstract																▓	▓							
Major review meeting with supervisor.																		◇						
Proofreading, formatting, spellchecking etc.																		▓	▓					
Compile list of contents, references, appendices etc.																			▓	▓				
First complete draft to supervisor for checking																				▓	▓			
Review meeting with supervisor																					◇			
Final checking, formatting and printing																						▓		
Send for reproduction & loose binding																						▓		
Submit according to institution's procedures																							◇	

◇ indicates a milestone

FIGURE 20.2   An illustrative Gantt chart

make regular contact and meet with your supervisor to review your work together. Team work helps!

Stage 5: Allow PLENTY of Time for Proper Proofreading

Mullins and Kiley (2002), in asking examiners to identify what made a good thesis, were also able to characterise those aspects which make a bad thesis. Amongst those characteristics was 'sloppiness', identified by typographical errors, errors or gaps in referencing and footnotes and mistakes in calculation, all of which could be remedied by more attention to detail in the final stages of the research degree project. One of the problems is that students rarely realise how long it will take them to proofread their thesis properly and fail to factor that into their plan for the final stages.

EXERCISE 2

Figure 20.2 was drawn up using *Microsoft Excel*™ but you can use whatever software package suits you best. Using the list of tasks and timings that you identified in Exercise 1, plan the final stages of your research degree to take you up to your submission deadline. When you've done this, find an old piece of your writing – it could be a conference paper, journal article or chapter of your thesis – and proofread it thoroughly, correcting every mistake. How long did it take you? Estimate from that how much time you need to leave for proper proofreading at the end of your writing-up period.

Tip: There are lots of software tools available to help you plan your research project. *Microsoft Project*™ is the most commonly used but there are freeware alternatives available over the internet. The most important thing is that you find a method of identifying and viewing tasks and their appropriate timeframes, combined with an overview of milestones and goals that have to be met.

Proofreading the thesis also means applying the institution's regulations for layout and formatting. These are discussed in the following section.

Regulations

All institutions will have specific regulations relating to the process of submission. It is important that you familiarise yourself with what is required. Here are the regulations from Queen Mary, University of London as an example:

Length of thesis:

'A thesis must not normally exceed 100,000 words (including footnotes, but excluding bibliography and appendices) for the PhD, and 60,000 words for the MPhil. Individual Graduate Studies Committees shall have discretion to specify a lower maximum limit for theses submitted in their particular discipline.' (*Academic Regulations*, Queen Mary, University of London 2002–2003: 125)

Binding:

'In the first instance candidates should submit three copies of their theses, **either**
Three which are soft-bound, or
Two which are soft-bound and one which is hard-bound
All theses (whether soft or hard-bound) must
Be covered in medium blue cloth (e.g. water resistant material);
Be lettered in gold up the spine with Degree, Year and Name and Initials in the same form as the College records, with letters 16 or 18 point (.25 inch).
[The date on the copies of the thesis submitted for examination in November and December should be that of the following year.]
Hard-bound theses must have the pages sown in (not punched).
Soft-bound theses should have the pages glued in.
Theses submitted in any other form of binding will not be accepted.
After the examination is complete, students must make sure that the Research Degrees Office has one hard-bound copy and one soft-bound copy of the thesis with any required corrections completed. The University will not issue the result of the examination to successful candidates until it has received one final hard-bound and one soft-bound copy, and the examiners have confirmed that any amendments to the thesis required by them have been made.'

Number of copies:

'Three copies must be submitted to the University Research Degree Examinations Office, Room 261, Senate House…and each candidate is required to bring one additional copy to the oral examination, paginated in the same way as the copies submitted to the University, and adequately bound.'

Layout:

'Margins at the binding edge must be no less than 40mm (1.5 inches) and other margins no less than 20mm (.75 inches). Double or one-and-a-half spacing should be used in typescripts, except for indented quotations or footnotes where single spacing may be used.' (Instructions and Notes on the Submission, Format and Binding of Theses submitted for the degrees of MPhil and PhD, Queen Mary, University of London)

Entry for the Examination:

'A student shall submit an examination entry form not more than four months before the expected date for the submission of the thesis. The entry form must be accompanied by an abstract of the thesis to assist in the appointment of suitable examiners.' (*Academic Regulations*, Queen Mary, University of London 2002–2003: 126)

If you look carefully at the regulations given in the box above, you will notice that they come from two different documents: the Academic Regulations *and* the Instructions and Notes on the Submission, Format and Binding of Theses submitted for the degrees of MPhil and PhD. Do make sure that you find all the relevant documents in your institution, as there may be more than one and some may provide more information than others.

Making the Decision to Submit

The regulations will also usually emphasise the fact that the decision to submit is regarded as being that of the individual student. It is generally recommended, however, that you submit only on your supervisor's advice. This does not mean that you are guaranteed to pass, but your supervisor is (usually) more experienced than you are and will, hopefully, have supervised to completion more than one student in the past. They will, therefore, have more idea of when your thesis is ready than you will have. There are, however, two notable exceptions to this rule.

First, occasions do exist where the supervisor has an alternative agenda and set of priorities than to ensure that the student completes on time. This occasionally happens when the student is working on one aspect of a larger project of which the supervisor him/herself is the grant holder. On occasions such as these, the student is asked to do more experiments or data collection than is necessary for the research degree because they are important for the wider project.

Although this situation is by no means common, it does occur and can cause conflict between the student and supervisor. If this happens to you it is critical that you remember that 'your' priority is to complete your research degree. On rare occasions this may necessitate having your thesis read by another member of staff to assess whether it is of the required standard and should be submitted.

The second circumstance occurs when the supervisor does not, him/herself, have a research degree, or is inexperienced at supervision and misjudges what is required. In this situation, the supervisor will usually again require the student to do too much rather than too little. The majority of UK institutions now specify that students should be supervised by a team, in line with the QAA Code of Practice (see Appendix 1), and that the first supervisor should have supervised at least one previous student successfully to completion. In practice, however, this does not always happen.

It is always best, wherever possible, to maintain a good relationship with your supervisor, and should you find yourself in this situation then it would be worth discussing the problem with him/her first. It may well be the case that you will still need to find someone else to read your thesis but it is always better if this can be done with your supervisor's agreement and help.

If you do find yourself in disagreement with your supervisor over the amount that needs doing, it is worth remembering that it is a doctorate you are aiming for, not a Nobel Prize (at least at this stage!). The thesis is still, essentially, a work in progress when you submit it. It has to undergo review by the examiners and this often entails further revisions. It should also reflect the learning that you have undergone during the process – the research training and knowledge that you have developed as a result of doing it.

One further benchmark you can use to guide you as to whether you are ready to submit is that of publishing your work.

Publishing before Submitting

There are differing views on whether it is good or bad to publish before the research degree is finished. On the one hand, it does indicate that the thesis is of publishable quality (a measure that your institution may use as part of the assessment criteria for the research degree you are registered for). On the other hand, some examiners may wonder if it is the supervisor's work rather than the student's (Mullins and Kiley 2002), and there is always a risk that the novelty of your work may be compromised by someone else publishing work based on your ideas before your degree is complete. These aspects tend to be discipline-specific and you will need the advice of someone more experienced in research in your field to guide you in this.

One potential way round this minefield is to submit a paper or poster to a conference that requires double-blind peer-reviewing before it is accepted. Through this process you will not have demonstrated that it is directly of publishable quality, but rather that it is of comparable publishable quality due to the peer-review process. It is also advisable to use aspects of your work rather than the entire central idea, if only for issues of brevity and clarity than anything else.

The process of making the work ready for submission can be stressful and is time-consuming. It is also a time when students are often under financial pressures and may be thinking about their next career move. The following section in this chapter examines the difficulties of balancing employment with submission and completion.

Taking on Other Commitments (Employment)

It is very difficult to balance looking for a job/working full- or part-time and the demands of completing the thesis. The Research Councils' national training programme, UK GRAD (www.grad.ac.uk), makes the point that searching for/starting a job can slow down, or stop thesis writing, in the last critical stages. Of course if you are registered for your degree part-time then you are already more than used to the difficulties of juggling competing priorities. The project management techniques discussed earlier in this chapter will certainly help you to manage your time and work load more effectively.

If it is possible for you, you might find it best to leave finding a job (or a new job) until after you have completed the thesis properly. This is, however, often unrealistic for research students who have not finished their degree by the time their funding runs out. If you are financed then it may be worth seeing if you can get an extension on the funding for six months or so in order to be able to submit without having to take on additional paid work.

The reason that paid work is discouraged is because it takes up valuable time that you could be devoting to completing your research degree. If the job is new to you, it will also take time for you to adjust to balancing both activities, which in itself causes an inevitable delay to completion.

If you are forced by circumstances to take on paid employment then you might consider working part-time and remaining within the academic environment if at all possible. For example, additional teaching or demonstrating opportunities may occur, exam invigilations or paid part-time work in the library or on the computing services help desk may be available.

There are a number of reasons why it is better to stay in the academic environment if possible. First, you won't have additional travel and commuting in terms of time and money to worry about. Second, it makes it easier to fit completing the research degree in because you are usually on the same campus as the library, laboratory or office that you need. And third, you remain within an environment where the people you come into daily contact with understand what a research degree is and what completing it entails. This understanding is not guaranteed outside of academia. Completing a research degree is hard anyway – taking on paid employment and removing yourself from the academic environment in order to do so may make it considerably more difficult.

Taking on other commitments before the thesis is completed is not impossible and doesn't necessarily mean that you won't get the research degree. It does, however, require a mindset of commitment and hard work as the following case study of Xena (based on a real person's experiences) demonstrates.

Case Study

Xena was researching for a PhD in business management part-time. Whilst in the completion phase of her PhD, she worked full-time as a university administrator and found that staying in the academic environment was critical to finishing.

Although she was supported to complete the PhD by her bosses and colleagues, her full-time job meant that she didn't have time during the normal working day to dedicate to writing-up her thesis.

Xena's first stage was to make her mind up about whether she really wanted the qualification because without that level of commitment she wouldn't have been prepared to make the temporary sacrifices that were necessary in order to achieve it.

So, do you really want it? If you do, then carry on reading. If you're not sure, then take some time out to consider this issue carefully. A research degree is not always going to be the most important thing in your life – life will continue without one, so what does it mean personally to you?

After making the commitment to wanting the PhD, Xena then had to evaluate every aspect of her life – both home and work. She had to work out what needed to be done so that she could write most efficiently and effectively.

Xena made the decision to work on her PhD after work in the evenings. She disciplined herself to stay in the office after 5 pm for an extra two hours. She took a quick break at 5 pm to get something to eat and would then work through until 7 pm on the thesis before going home.

It was exhausting but aiming to do that three nights a week helped to assuage her guilt that she wasn't doing anything on it during the week, and meant that she was making steady progress. She also committed one day at the weekends to writing the thesis, but only one day. This was because she found that regular time-off from all kinds of work was essential for her physical and mental well being. This meant adjusting her timescale for completion but she decided it was better to end the process alive and well, rather than in a hospital because she had made herself ill.

Xena wrote out a list of all the things that needed to be done in order to complete the thesis, estimated times for each task and then allocated slots to them. Although she didn't recognise the technique as a project management one, she used a bar chart to view these slots visually. Where she thought there would be a problem in fitting them into the timescale based on evenings and weekend working, she arranged to take some holiday from work so that she could dedicate additional time to the PhD.

Xena negotiated with her boss that if she took one week's annual leave, he would then match that by giving her one week's study leave, which enabled her to spend a fortnight dedicated to her thesis. Undoubtedly working in academia made this easier to negotiate.

Other things needed to be balanced as well – household chores, visiting family and friends, exercise and so on. Xena chose to pay for a cleaner once a week, even though at first she wasn't sure that she could afford it. She recognised, however, that doing so freed up more time to spend finishing the thesis. In addition, it reduced the number of things she had to worry about. She also found a yoga class to attend at work during one lunch hour per week to help with her fitness and stress levels.

Ultimately Xena submitted her thesis within the timescale she had been allotted. Although she was asked to make some minor amendments at the viva, she passed, and ultimately successfully completed her PhD.

Conclusion

On a final note: the submission and completion phases of the research degree process may seem like light at the end of the tunnel which, when examined more closely, is actually only the headlights of an oncoming train! Be prepared for stress; be prepared to take responsibility for project managing the final stages; be prepared to find out your institution's requirements for thesis layout and submission procedures. In short, as the Guides and Scouts used to say 'Be prepared!'

Acknowledgements

I would like to thank Dr Steve Ketteridge of Queen Mary, University of London, Professor Ron Denney and the editors for their helpful and insightful comments on earlier drafts of this chapter.

Note

1   See the relevant website at www.hefce.ac.uk/pubs/hefce/2003/03_23.htm

---

SOURCES OF SUPPORT

www.grad.ac.uk – The UK GRAD's website dedicated to realising postgraduate talent.
Cryer, P. (2000) *The Research Students Guide to Success*, (2nd edition), Buckingham: Open University Press.
Murray, R. (2002) *How to Write a Thesis*, Maidenhead: Open University Press.
Phillips, E.M. and Pugh, D.S. (2005) *How to Get a PhD*, (4th edition), Maidenhead: Open University Press.

References

Association for Project Management (APM) (2006) *Body of Knowledge Definitions*, 5th edition, High Wycombe: APM Publishing.
Brown, Mark (1998) *Successful Project Management in a Week* (2nd edition), London: Hodder and Stoughton.

Department for Employment and Learning, Northern Ireland; Higher Education Funding Council for England; Higher Education Funding Council for Wales; Scottish Higher Education Funding Council (2003) *Improving Standards in Postgraduate Research Degree Programmes Formal Consultation*, May 2003/23. www.hefce.ac.uk/pubs/hefce/2003/03_23/03_23.pdf (accessed 22 July 2007).

Elbeik, Sam and Thomas, Mark (1998) *Project Skills*, Oxford: Butterworth Heinemann.

HEFCE (2005) *PhD Research Degrees Entry and Completion*, January 2005/02. www.hefce.ac.uk/pubs/HEFCE/2005/05_02/ (accessed 6 October 2007).

Irwin, D. (ed.) (1999) *Managing Projects and Operations*, London: Thorogood Ltd.

King's College, *Academic Regulations for Research Degrees*, London: King's College.

Mullins, G. and Kiley, M. (2002) '"It's a PhD, not a Nobel Prize": How experienced examiners assess research theses', *Studies in Higher Education*, 27(4): 369–386.

Quality Assurance Agency (QAA) (2001) *The Framework for Higher Education Qualifications in England, Wales and Northern Ireland*, Gloucester: Quality Assurance Agency.

Queen Mary, University of London (2002–2003) *Academic Regulations*, University of London.

Queen Mary, University of London (September 2006) *Handbook for Research Students*, University of London.

Queen Mary, University of London *Instructions and Notes on the Submission, Format and Binding of Theses Submitted for the Degrees of MPhil and PhD*, University of London. www.studentadmin.qmul.ac.uk/students/theses.pdf

Science and Technology Facilities Council Website www.scitech.ac.uk/Grants/Studs/Supervision/Thesis.aspx (accessed 22 June 2007)

University of London (2003) *Regulations for the Degrees of MPhil and PhD with Effect from September 2003*, University of London.

21 The Viva
Dr Penny Tinkler and
Dr Carolyn Jackson

The viva, or oral examination, is a compulsory part of doctoral examinations in Britain (albeit with some exceptions where an alternative examination is arranged alongside the assessment of the thesis). The fact that many institutions stipulate that one cannot fail a doctorate outright without undertaking a viva or alternative examination is evidence that the viva is an important part of the assessment process. But what are vivas for and how can research students prepare for them? These are the key questions that we tackle in this chapter. The answers, however, are far from straightforward. To understand vivas we need to know what purposes they can serve and the ways they work; knowing these things is essential for effective viva preparation.

In this chapter we start by exploring the purposes of the viva, dividing these into examination, development and ritual. We then take a look at the key components of the viva, and the factors that shape them. The rest of the chapter considers viva preparation strategies that can be undertaken at various points of the doctoral process. Our discussion is underpinned and informed by the empirical research that we have undertaken over the last six years; this involved policy analysis, questionnaire surveys to academics and doctoral candidates, pre- and post-viva interviews with doctoral candidates and interviews with a variety of experts on PhD examining. This research has spanned a range of disciplines, and interested readers can find out more about it by consulting our other publications (Tinkler and Jackson, 2000 and 2004; Jackson and Tinkler, 2000, 2001 and 2002). In particular, we direct readers to our book '*The Doctoral Examination Process: A Handbook for Students, Examiners and Supervisors*' (Tinkler and Jackson, 2004) in which we explore all aspects of the examination process. In our book we discuss in detail points presented in this chapter and offer a wider range of examples, exercises and tips on preparing for the viva using long-term, short-term and final-stage strategies.

The Purposes of a Viva

Institutions vary in terms of the criteria candidates must meet in order to satisfy examiners in the viva. It is very important, therefore, that you check the criteria of the institution where your examination will take place. However, whilst this is an essential first stage, institutional guidance about the viva is usually very brief, and so you are unlikely to have all your questions about vivas answered by consulting these policy documents. In practice, the examiners are most important in determining the purposes of a viva, and for this reason we focus largely on their perspectives in this section.

According to the academics in our questionnaire survey, the viva serves a range of purposes. There is no consensus about the key purposes of a viva: no single purpose was mentioned by more than 36% of academics. Overall, the purposes divide into three categories:

1   Examination
2   Development of the candidate and her/his work
3   Ritual.

We now look briefly at each of these in turn.

Examination

There are a variety of viva purposes that fall under the 'examination umbrella'. These purposes, along with brief illustrations of what they mean, are listed below.

Authentication. The viva should always be a site for authenticating the thesis; that is, ensuring that the candidate is the author of the thesis and has undertaken the work presented in it. This role is especially important when the candidate has been working as part of a team, which is common in the natural sciences.

Locating the research in the broader context. A senior lecturer from Music explained, this means: 'To allow the examiners to question issues arising from the submission and for the candidate to support the thesis in a broader context than is normally possible within the submission (i.e. to discuss and respond to questions and the relevant work of others in the same field)'. However, the 'broader context' is difficult to define, and can be conceptualised very differently by different people.

Check understanding. Vivas are used to check that candidates understand what they have written. As Dan (Chemistry) recalled about his viva: 'Well, pretty much it [the viva] was all to show that I understood, that I had a clear understanding of what my research was about, where it could potentially go, rather than just getting examined on things which I could have looked up in a library book.' Checking understanding is, however, a two-way process. It is important to remember that the viva also serves as an opportunity for you to check that the examiners have understood your intended meanings.

Defend the thesis. The viva provides examiners with an opportunity to question, probe and explore the candidate's thesis. The notion that students should 'defend' their thesis suggests that it will be 'attacked'; this is not always the case and many examiners (although not all) try very hard to make the viva as non-confrontational as possible. As the following examples demonstrate, examiners often equate the 'defence' with being able to respond to criticism and justifying the decisions made in the course of the research.

> To provide the student with an opportunity to defend his or her thesis; to respond to criticism; and to discuss what he or she sees as 'problems' with interested experts. (Senior Lecturer, Social Policy and Social Work)

> To clarify problems arising in the text; to test the student's ability to justify (where there was any doubt in the text) arguments. To vindicate/salvage the thesis if in doubt in the text. To defend the thesis presented in the text, in general and particular (Lecturer, Religions and Theology).

Many candidates in our research found the opportunity to 'defend' and discuss their work extremely beneficial. Indeed, after investing so much time and effort in the thesis, some candidates were frustrated and disappointed if they were not required to defend their work. The examiners' conduct and tone is, however, crucial to whether questions are experienced as acceptably demanding or unacceptably confrontational.

Site of final decision making in borderline cases. Our research suggests that in the majority of cases (74% amongst our sample) a viva serves to confirm an examiner's decision about the outcome of the examination process that was made (provisionally) on the basis of reading the thesis. However, in cases where the thesis is judged to be borderline – for example, it may sit on the borderline between being referred and being awarded an MPhil – the viva has a very important examination role. A professor in Arts and Humanities summed this up: 'in one case where the thesis was referred a good performance helped convince the examiners that the candidate was indeed capable of achieving doctorate standard through [thesis] revisions.'

Development

Vivas can serve two developmental roles: basic and advanced.

Basic development. In cases where the thesis is *not* judged to be at doctoral standard, but where the examiners feel that it could be raised to the required standard by extra work, the viva can play a very important role in working out and discussing how the thesis can be improved.

Advanced development. When examiners judge a thesis to meet PhD standards, advanced developmental roles often come to the fore. These include guidance on publications, future research and careers. A number of candidates in our research referred to the value of this advanced developmental discussion: 'I think it's good '[be]cause it can give you good ideas about future development and future work' (Silvo, Economics).

Ritual

Doctoral examination, including the viva, is one of the most formal and explicit gatekeeping processes operating within academia. It can keep aspiring academics out of the academy, or it can welcome them in. While academics mentioned the celebratory or 'reward' aspects of the viva as a rite of passage, candidates occasionally experienced the viva as a more painful ritual.

An individual examiner's views about purposes will shape the way that she/he approaches a viva. Whilst in *general*, examiners see vivas as serving a blend of examination, development and ritual purposes, the purposes that *predominate in any individual viva* will be determined by five main factors:

1   The examiners' assessments of the thesis – whether it is judged to be strong, borderline, or weak/failed
2   The examiners' knowledge expectations – the depth and breadth of knowledge examiners expect candidates to demonstrate about their research topic and its context
3   The examining style – the type of academic exchange examiners expect candidates to manage. For example, some examiners aim to promote relaxed discussion, others aim for fierce, fiery debate
4   The examiners' personal/political agendas including discriminatory beliefs, personal grudges, favouritism, self-promotion and jealousy
5   The interpersonal dynamics between the participants in the oral examination.

In combination, these five factors shape the *components* of the viva.

Viva Components

Vivas have three main components: skills, content and conduct. To be successful in vivas candidates need to match their training and preparation to the different viva components, rather like the way in which a triathlete trains for the particular elements of a triathlon. If triathletes do not identify correctly and understand the different elements involved (running, swimming and cycling), they may train inappropriately and so find themselves unprepared for the specific demands on the day. The same applies to the viva. We will introduce each of the viva components briefly before suggesting how you can use this information to plan your viva preparation.

The 'skills' element is determined largely by the structural requirements of the viva and is probably the least variable element of it. By structural requirements, we mean that the viva is always an oral examination. As such, your verbal skills are explicitly or implicitly crucial to the examiners' assessments of you. Fundamentally, in a viva you must be able to understand the examiners' questions and points, and be able to communicate your answers clearly in spoken English. The 'skills' component also requires you to 'think on your feet'; perform/communicate clearly whilst under pressure; explain and justify/defend your work, interpretations and ideas during the viva.

The 'content' component of the viva is shaped by the examiners' assessment of the thesis and their knowledge expectations. The 'content' component of the viva is likely to require you to: authenticate your thesis; locate your research in the broader context; clarify aspects of your thesis; develop ideas; justify/defend aspects of the thesis; reflect critically on your work.

'Conduct' refers to how the examiners behave in the viva and how the group – examiners, candidate and possibly other participants – interact. The conduct of the viva is potentially the most variable aspect; it is also the least regulated. There are three sets of factors that shape the conduct of the viva: examining styles; examiners' personal/political agendas; and interpersonal dynamics.

Viva Preparation

Although many students assume that viva preparation is covered by rereading the thesis prior to the viva, this is misguided. Preparation for the different components of the viva is a long-term process and needs to be planned in the early stages of your research degree. A long-term preparation strategy will maximise your chances of: being successful in the viva; feeling positive about your performance and, as a result, more confident about your research and future prospects; impressing your examiners who, as a result, may be enthusiastic sponsors of your career.

The first step in viva preparation involves identification of your strengths and weaknesses in relation to each of the viva components, see box.

TASK – STAR RATINGS

Identify your strengths and weaknesses in terms of:
thinking on your feet;
performing and communicating clearly whilst under pressure;
explaining, justifying and defending your PhD work with different audiences;
knowing the 'broader context' of your thesis;
coping with different styles of academic exchange;
dealing with complex interpersonal dynamics.

Try using the following scale:
4 – I'm very strong on this
3 – I'm quite strong on this
2 – I'm not strong on this
1 – I'm very weak on this

For all areas where you score below 4, plan a strategy for improvement, ideally, in consultation with your supervisor.
You should revisit this activity at different stages of your PhD – at the beginning, middle, and towards the end. (Source: Reproduced from Tinkler and Jackson, 2004: 44 with permission from Open University Press)

This information can then be used to plan a (long-term) strategy for improvement, ideally in consultation with your supervisor.

Long-term Preparation

PhD training with presentations at conferences is the best way [to prepare for the viva], to talk to academics in your field as well as outside.

(Candidate, Biology)

Access to academic research cultures is a key way in which you can prepare for the different components of the viva. According to Deem and Brehony, academic research cultures include:

disciplinary and interdisciplinary ideas and values, particular kinds of expert knowledge and knowledge production, cultural practices and narratives (for instance, how research is done, and how peer review is exercised), departmental sociability, other internal and external intellectual networks and learned societies. (Deem and Brehony, 2000: 158)

Access to academic research cultures can enable you to acquire discipline-specific proficiencies that may equip you to handle the skills, content and conduct requirements of the viva. In other words, academic research cultures facilitate the build-up of department and discipline 'know-how' that can be crucial for the viva and, for those who want one, an academic career after it. For example, through access to academic research cultures you can acquire discipline-appropriate ways of speaking, experience of engaging in different types of academic verbal exchanges, and confidence to present and defend your ideas with different groups of established academics.

A range of activities make up academic research cultures such as teaching, attending and presenting at conferences, upgradings and publishing. Each activity can contribute to viva preparation, but they do this in different ways. In order to assess the value of different activities for your long-term preparation strategy it is helpful to think of what they offer in terms of the skills, content and conduct components of the viva. In this section we will consider the value of attending and presenting at conferences as a form of viva preparation (for discussion of a range of other examples see Tinkler and Jackson, 2004).

Conference Attendance and Presentation

> In retrospect, further experience of fielding questions following the oral delivery of a paper would have helped my viva performance.
>
> (Candidate, English and American Studies)

There are many benefits attached to presenting your work at, and attending, conferences – networking, publicity and so on. In this section we focus on how conferences may be useful long-term viva preparation in terms of skills, content, and finally, conduct. There are different benefits attached to attending *and* presenting at conferences than are attached to attending only. As such, the discussion below makes the distinction explicit.

Presenting at a conference is an excellent way to rehearse and develop the types of *skills* required for the viva. There are a number of different presentation formats at conferences. For example, verbal presentation followed by questions from the audience; poster presentations with questions from the audience; roundtable discussions (see Chapter 16 in this volume). However, all of the different presentation formats require you to do the following:

- Explain and present ideas clearly
- Think on your feet – particularly when responding to questions
- Perform under pressure – presenting to an audience of peers always adds a certain amount of pressure
- Justify and defend your work and ideas verbally.

Other aspects of conference attendance can also be useful for the skills component of the viva. Simply by attending and taking part in the conference as a non-presenter you can do the following:

- Be exposed to a range of different presentation styles and consider which are the most effective and why. This reflection is helpful when preparing your own presentations
- See how a range of people react and respond to questions
- Ask questions at other people's papers. This can be daunting initially; working out and asking clear questions takes practice
- Engage in discussions with people about your own and their work. Sometimes, you might need to provide a quick summary of key aspects of your work – clear, succinct responses can be difficult, so again, this sort of practice is very useful viva preparation
- Justify and defend your work in casual conversation – many of the best discussions at conferences take place in the bar or over coffee.

Presenting your work at a conference can also be useful preparation for the *content* component of the viva. It is interesting and useful to get feedback on work-in-progress and to be prompted to reflect critically on your work by more experienced colleagues. Presenting work and getting feedback on it can also help you to develop your ideas. In terms of preparation for the content component of the viva then, presenting work at conferences has many advantages. It does, however, also have limitations. The main limitation is that you will only be able to present, and hence be questioned on, a small part of your research at a conference, whereas in the viva the examiners will have access to the whole thesis. Because of this key difference and, of course, the different audiences, you cannot predict the content of the viva on the basis of questions that you are asked at conferences. It can be useful though, to make a note of the questions that you are asked in conferences, seminars and other presentations and to use some of these in your final-stage preparation.

Regardless of whether you present or just attend, being at a conference and listening to other people's papers can be very useful for getting to know the work in your field. It can take a long time for work presented at conferences to get published in journals or books, and so conference attendance is the best way of keeping up-to-date with work that is at the 'cutting-edge'. The value of this aspect of conference attendance should not be underestimated – it can be very important in the viva when demonstrating knowledge of your field and locating your work within the broader context.

Presenting a paper at a conference and fielding questions from the audience can be excellent preparation for the *conduct* component of the viva. Your audience is likely to consist of academics (and non-academics) with a wide spectrum of questioning styles, and it is good to get used to these different styles – although it can be daunting. The questions asked at conferences sometimes reflect the questioner's personal/political agendas – these questions are sometimes way beyond the scope of your paper but are asked because they relate to the questioner's individual interest. Getting used to handling these sorts of questions is useful, because examiners can also have individual interests that extend beyond the scope of your thesis. There can also be interesting interpersonal dynamics amongst the audience – all good preparation for the viva! If attending only rather than presenting, you can still observe the different styles of academic conduct in the sessions that you attend, although it is not nearly the same as being on the receiving end of it.

Overall, presenting your work at conferences is excellent preparation for the viva, particularly the skills and conduct components. However, presenting at conferences can be daunting, and so below are some suggestions to help those who feel they need 'breaking in gently'.

- Start off by presenting your work in your department, first to other research students and then to staff. Sometimes, there are research student conferences attached to main conferences, these can be a good venue for first-time presenters
- Try asking questions at conferences even if you are not presenting a paper. Just getting used to speaking in conference sessions is an important first step
- If you want to present work at a main conference, but don't want to do it alone, ask your supervisor or another student if you can present together. Presenting part of a paper is less daunting than presenting a whole one; there is then also someone else to share the questions with
- First-time presenters may find poster presentations less threatening than oral deliveries. Usually, this format involves presenting your work on a poster and being available at a set time to answer questions about it.

Short-term Preparation: 'Mock' Vivas

Some academics use mock vivas as a means of preparing students for their oral examination. Mock vivas take a variety of forms depending on who is being given the mock examination; what text is being examined; who the 'examiners' are; the audience; the timing of the mock examination relative to submission of the thesis and the actual viva (a range of types of mock viva, including public vivas, is discussed in Tinkler and Jackson, 2004). If you want a mock viva, ask yourself why? What do you want it to do? What do you need to practise? Re-do the exercise in the box captioned Task – Star Ratings: what are you least confident about? For example, do you need experience of different styles of questioning? Do you want to practise engaging with questions on a particular topic? Do you need general practice of 'thinking on your feet'? The format of your mock viva should be determined by what you most need to practise. Once you have worked out your objectives you can work out a package with your supervisor that will most readily meet them – use Table 21.1 to help you do this.

While mocks can be useful they have many limitations. In this section we consider the advantages and limitations of mock vivas by reflecting on some of

TABLE 21.1 The relationship between specific objectives and the organisation of a mock viva

Objectives of a mock viva with student as 'candidate'	Organisation of mock viva
Refine aspects of the thesis	Schedule – before submission Text – whole, or key parts of, thesis 'Examiners' – academic staff other than supervisor(s); peer group.
Foster skills useful in the viva – *viva basic skills*	Schedule – before or after submission Text – whole, or part of, thesis; published piece not written by 'candidate' 'Examiners' – ideally other academic staff, although members of the peer group can also be very effective. Supervisor(s) can be very helpful but they may be too familiar and/or 'safe' so that the 'candidate' does not gain experience of working under stress
Provide experience of thinking deeply about, focussing upon and answering different types of questions about the thesis – *viva content*	Schedule – before or after submission Text – ideally whole of thesis, although using part(s) of the thesis is still very useful 'Examiners' – ideally academic staff other than supervisor(s); members of peer group can also be very effective; supervisor(s) may be too predictable, and/or reinforce a particular approach to the candidate's work
Provide experience of managing different types of behaviour –*viva conduct*	Schedule – before or after submission Text – thesis or other published piece. However, this objective is most likely to be achieved if the 'candidate' is examined on their thesis, or aspects of it because the exam is experienced as far more personal (this is, of course, an important feature of the actual viva which encourages some candidates to be defensive) 'Examiners' – some supervisors can be very adept at playing a different character in a mock viva, but not all supervisors are born thespians. To foster a student's skills at managing viva conduct it is best to expose them to the different styles of questioning and behaviour of other academic staff and peer-group members

Note
Reproduced from Tinkler and Jackson, 2004: 132 with permission from Open University Press.

the main questions that students and supervisors ask about them. Answers to these questions are not straightforward. In our discussion we adopt a question and answer format. The answers highlight the positive features – the 'YES' features – as well as the important 'BUT' features. We urge you to heed both sets of responses.

Does Participation in, or Observation of, a Mock Viva Help to Demystify the Oral Examination?

YES – candidates usually approach their viva with a certain amount of trepidation. Mock vivas can be an important way for you to see, and sometimes experience, what is regarded as usual and/or professional examining practice in your department. A mock viva modelled on the format of an actual viva also provides you with information about the usual procedures and roles of participants.

BUT – in order for a mock viva to fulfil these purposes it must be organised in accordance with the policy on research degree examining in place at the institution where your viva will take place. Further, unless there is someone in the actual viva to monitor it, perhaps an independent chair, it cannot be assumed that the conduct of the actual viva will conform to institutional guidelines.

When Candidates Receive a Mock Viva That Addresses Their Thesis (Whole or Part) Does This Prepare Them to Answer Questions about Their Work in the Actual Oral Examination?

YES – opportunities to talk about your thesis and to explain and justify your approach are valuable preparation for the viva. A mock viva can also alert you to different, and unexpected, perspectives on your work, particularly if the mock examiners are not your supervisors: 'The mock viva was ... a good experience to discuss the work in detail with an "outsider", i.e., not my supervisor, who had a different take on the issues raised' (Hartley and Fox, 2004: 733). If the supervisor acts the part of 'examiner' she/he may be able, if she/he is familiar with the approaches of the actual examiners, to ask questions that are similar to those that may be asked in the actual viva, but this cannot be taken for granted.

BUT – mock vivas are not a good substitute for long-term preparation. Further, and most importantly, you should not regard a mock viva that examines the whole, or part, of the thesis as a trial run for the content of the actual oral examination. The specific questions asked in mock vivas and actual vivas are frequently very different (see also Hartley and Fox, 2004; Wallace and Marsh, 2001). Vivas can also have diverse content depending on the examiners' views of the standard of the thesis being examined, and about what types of knowledge a candidate should possess. So, for example, a candidate whose thesis is judged to be borderline may receive a very different type of viva in terms of content to a candidate whose thesis is judged as strong. Further, a candidate who has submitted an excellent thesis may be examined very differently by two examiners depending on the ideas that they each have about what contextual knowledge the candidate should possess; this is, of course, linked to the examiners' different approaches and interests.

When Candidates Are Given, or Observe, a Mock Viva Apparently Modelled on the Structure of the Actual Examination, Does This Provide Them with Insight into the Way That Examiners Behave and Give Them Practice at Managing Conduct?

YES – when you are the 'candidate' a mock viva can contribute to your experience of managing different kinds of academic exchange. This type of experience is always valuable in preparing for the viva. Similarly, observing a public performance of a mock viva does contribute to your knowledge of how academics engage in intellectual exchange. Also, where supervisors are familiar with the examining styles of the actual examiners, they may be able to conduct a mock viva that is similar in conduct to the 'real thing', but this cannot be taken for granted.

BUT – this aspect of mock vivas is only valuable if you regard it as *an example* of an academic exchange; it does not provide illustration of the way that your actual examiners will behave. A History student recalled 'My supervisor's mock viva was rather intense and made me unnecessarily defensive.' Whereas he expected his actual viva to be 'a grilling', 'formal', 'exhaustive' and preoccupied with 'specifics', it was actually 'relaxed', and focused on themes. Viva conduct varies according to examiners' personal/political agendas and interpersonal dynamics. It also varies depending on the examiners' views about what candidates should be able to cope with (their examining style).

Does a Mock Viva, in Which the Candidate Is Examined, Offer an Opportunity to Rehearse Skills That Are Key to the Viva Performance?

YES – irrespective of the content and conduct of a mock viva, experience of undergoing a mock viva can provide an important contribution to the development of skills required in the actual viva – being able to think under pressure, managing demanding questions, debating a point, communicating clearly, asking for clarification and so on. As one respondent in Hartley and Fox's study commented: 'It was a good preparation as this was the first time that I had "spoken" the answers. This allowed me to listen to myself and to see the effect of my answer on someone else' (personal communication). This type of mock viva is most useful if you receive feedback on your performance. Feedback can help you to see ways of communicating your ideas more clearly, think of ways of handling difficult questions or situations and confront aspects of preparation that you have previously avoided.

BUT – one mock viva is no substitute for longer-term preparation. You can equip yourself best for the skills demands of the viva by regular practice of talking about, and debating aspects of, your work. Be they conference and seminar presentations, or upgrading and conversion panels, as well as mock-viva-style exchanges, all are ways in which you can develop crucial skills and confidence. Mock vivas are the cherry on the icing on the cake.

Mock vivas can make an important contribution to viva preparation, although their limitations must be kept in mind and discussed with your supervisor. You should not think of your mock viva as a trial run for the real thing. A mock viva will not, indeed cannot, be the same as the actual viva in terms of content or conduct. Vivas are like interviews and driving tests – you can have a pretty good idea of what is likely to happen, but neither the content nor the conduct of the real examination can be expected to be the same as or similar to what you go through during your mock viva.

Final-stage Preparation

Re-reading the thesis is a vital form of final-stage preparation for all doctoral candidates. But though re-reading is valuable, it is *not* advisable to keep re-reading your thesis – once, possibly twice, should be sufficient. It is also *not* usually advisable to re-read the thesis a day or two before the viva. Re-reading should not be a last-minute activity because: it can lead to overload; it does not allow you time to reflect on how to manage questions; it can in fact lead to panic.

The main purpose of re-reading the thesis is to 'know your thesis'. But what does this mean? What should you be able to do at the end of the final stage of academic preparation? We have identified seven objectives that you should work towards when re-reading your thesis (see Tinkler and Jackson, 2004, for re-reading exercises).

- Know what is written in the thesis
- Know the layout of the thesis
- Understand what is presented in the thesis
- Justify and 'defend' the thesis
- Identify, and be prepared to discuss, weak areas, gaps and mistakes
- Identify the originality, contribution to knowledge and implications of the thesis
- Reflect on what could be done differently if starting again.

You can (and should) take your thesis into the viva so you do not need to learn your thesis 'off by heart'. But you do need to know what you have written, and be able to locate specific sections of your thesis quickly in the viva. 'Knowing your thesis' is not the same as knowing what the examiners will make of it because people read in different ways and for different purposes. Moreover, the content of the viva can vary considerably. Nevertheless, it is sensible to consider how your work relates to your examiners' interests and relevant literature written by them. Ideally this literature should be cited in the thesis because, as Delamont et al. (1997: 145) point out, 'if the external is relevant enough to the thesis to examine it, then his or her work should probably be cited.'

Alongside getting to 'know your thesis', re-reading often involves predicting the questions that examiners will ask and preparing to respond to them. It is likely that examiners will address key topics in a viva: originality; contribution to knowledge; methods chosen; theoretical framework; results, conclusions, implications and weaknesses. However, it is *not* possible to *predict* the following: *the specific detail or angle* of questions, the *importance* the examiners' attach to different questions, or *how far the examiners will probe* on particular points. This unpredictability at the level of specific questions is because of several factors (mentioned earlier). Most importantly, the questions examiners will pose will depend on: what they think of your thesis, and this, of course, cannot be assumed; their own intellectual preoccupations; and their views about the breadth and depth of knowledge a candidate for this particular research degree should possess. Additionally, questions can feel very different depending on how the viva is conducted. Answering a series of questions posed in a relaxed discussion is very different from answering the same set of questions fired off like a round of bullets.

Reflecting on the thesis from different perspectives, gaining practice at answering questions, rehearsing ways of answering demanding and/or unexpected questions are all excellent forms of viva preparation. It is also a good idea to ask yourself the questions you most fear an examiner asking you, and to work through responses to these. Second-guessing the specific interests of your examiners provides good practice at answering questions, but this strategy is not a reliable guide to the questions you will be asked in the viva. Although it is extremely useful to think about the questions examiners may ask, it is advisable *not* to allow your re-reading of the thesis to be constrained by this.

Conclusion

In this chapter we have considered the key purposes of the viva, the components of vivas and viva preparation. By breaking down the viva we have shown how you can identify what aspects of it you are likely to find most challenging, and how you can use this information to tailor your viva preparation. Overall, good preparation should mean that by the time you approach your viva you are experienced at engaging in various forms of academic exchange, flexible, and confident that in the exam you can 'think on your feet' and draw on your knowledge of your thesis and the broader field to address the examiners' questions. Long-term preparation, in combination with tailored short-term and final-stage strategies, will give you the best chance of performing well in the viva. Such preparations are an investment both for your viva and your future career.

Suggested Further Reading

The most comprehensive guide to the doctoral examination process, including the viva, is by Penny Tinkler and Carolyn Jackson (2004) *The Doctoral Examination Process: A Handbook for Students, Examiners and Supervisors*, Maidenhead: Open University Press. Based on extensive research, and illustrated with accounts from PhD candidates, their supervisors and examiners, the book guides students through all stages of the examination process including: what the viva is for and how it works; selecting examiners; viva preparation; the viva; and the post-viva period.

Guidebooks written exclusively for supervisors and examiners also offer students interesting insights into research degree examining. See, Sara Delamont, Paul Atkinson, Odette Parry (1997) *Supervising the PhD: A Guide to Success*, Buckingham: Open University Press; also, Lynne Pearce (2005) *How To Examine A Thesis*, Maidenhead: Open University Press.

Acknowledgement

We are grateful to Open University Press, and in particular to Shona Mullen, for permission to reproduce Table 21.1 and the 'Task – Star Ratings' box.

SOURCES OF SUPPORT

Society for Research into Higher Education (SRHE), especially the Postgraduate Issues Network – www.srhe.ac.uk

UK Council for Graduate Education (UKCGE) – www.ukcge.ac.uk

UK GRAD – is supported by the Research Councils and has regional 'hubs' that support a range of local postgraduate initiatives – www.grad.ac.uk

---

References

Deem, R. and Brehony, K.J. (2000) Doctoral students' access to research cultures – are some more unequal than others? *Studies in Higher Education*, 25(2): 149–165.

Delamont, S., Atkinson, P. and Parry, O. (1997) *Supervising the PhD: A Guide to Success*. Buckingham: Open University Press.

Hartley, J. and Fox, C. (2004) Assessing the mock viva: The experiences of British doctoral students, *Studies in Higher Education*, 29(6): 727–738.

Jackson, C. and Tinkler, P. (2000) The PhD examination: An exercise in community building and gatekeeping? in I. McNay (ed.) *Higher Education and Its Communities*, pp. 38–50, Buckingham: Society for Research into Higher Education and Open University Press.

Jackson, C. and Tinkler, P. (2001) Back to basics: A consideration of the purposes of the PhD viva, *Assessment and Evaluation in Higher Education*, 26(4): 355–366.

Jackson, C. and Tinkler, P. (2002) In the dark? Preparing for the PhD viva, *Quality Assurance in Education* (special issue – Quality and Standards in Doctoral Awards), 10(2): 86–97.

Tinkler, P. and Jackson, C. (2000) Examining the doctorate: Institutional policy and the PhD examination process in the UK, *Studies in Higher Education*, 25(2): 167–180.

Tinkler, P. and Jackson, C. (2004) *The Doctoral Examination Process: A Handbook for Students, Examiners and Supervisors*. Maidenhead: SRHE/Open University Press.

Wallace, S. and Marsh, C. (2001) Trial by ordeal or the chummy game? Six case studies in the conduct of the British PhD viva examination, *Higher Education Review*, 34(1): 35–59.

Moving on from Your Research Degree

22 What Can Research Students Do?

Dr Sara Shinton

Introduction

After the substantial hurdle of the thesis and viva lies the final challenge facing research students – moving on to the next stage of your career. This chapter will summarise what is known about the labour market for researchers and look at how you can work out which direction to take. For those of you with more clearly defined career plans, the final section will explore how to convince employers in any sector that you are ready to make an impact and how to impress them with your application.

The chapter will address three questions:

1 What can I do with my degree? – destinations of previous students will be examined and the main employment sectors which attract researchers will be summarised
2 How do I know what to do? – looking at how to make a career choice and information about further support
3 How do I get into the job I want? – considers the employers' perspectives of job applicants and suggests ways to convince employers that a researcher can bring something special to their organisation.

What Can I Do with My Degree?

Until a few years ago, any discussions about the careers of research students were based on anecdotes, assumptions and small surveys conducted by professional bodies or individual universities. Although bachelor-level graduates had been surveyed for many years, masters and doctoral graduates were overlooked and many myths about the value of a research qualification persisted. In 2004, to address this gap and as part of the wider reaction to the Roberts' review (Roberts 2002), discussed in Chapter 14 of this book, UK GRAD commissioned a report in partnership with Graduate Prospects. Graduate Prospects is the commercial subsidiary of the Higher Education Careers Services Unit (HECSU), a registered charity that supports the work of higher education careers services in the UK and Republic of Ireland and funds major research projects that benefit the higher education careers sector.

'*What Do PhDs Do?*' (UK GRAD 2004) was produced and is the UK's primary source of information on the employment of doctoral graduates currently available. The data in '*What Do PhDs Do?*' is based on the results of the 'Destinations of Leavers from Higher Education' (DLHE) survey conducted in 2004 with the 2003 graduates.[1] In the year 2003 alone, 12,520 people were awarded doctorates from UK universities. Of these, 7270 were UK citizens, and the analysis discussed in this chapter is based on those individuals (1525 EU citizens from countries outside the UK were awarded doctorates but are not included in the analysis). At the time of the survey, the data collection and analysis methodology made it impossible to identify numbers of research masters students, so all data presented represents doctoral graduates only. The 3725 non-EU citizens awarded with doctorates in 2003 were not surveyed by DLHE. Non-EU graduates are not surveyed by any other organisation and no information about their employment postgraduation is available. Despite this, there are programmes such as the International Graduates Scheme and the Scottish Fresh Talent Initiative (details of both can be found on www. workingintheuk.gov.uk) which have been developed to help retain the skills and expertise of international students following their graduation from higher degrees. The International Office in your institution should have the latest information available.

Of the 7270 UK citizens covered by the survey, 4695 replied – a 65% response. These responses are used in the figures below.

Of the 4695 respondents to the survey, 81% are in employment in the UK. The unemployment rate is at 3% – significantly below the rate for bachelor-level graduates (which stands at 7%) and for masters graduates (which is 4%). A total 8% of doctoral graduates choose to further their careers outside the UK. Although only 3% of respondents to this survey reported that they were either self-employed or freelance, this is a slightly higher figure than for first-degree graduates (Ball 2004). Chapter 27 provides additional information on the steps to take if you are considering starting your own company.

This chapter will not only present the key findings of *What Do PhDs Do?* but also point to other surveys and information and look behind the figures to give you a clear picture of the career *possibilities* that a research qualification opens up. These are only 'possibilities' because one of the key messages of this chapter is that the statistics are there to stimulate your own opinions, to show what others have done, but career choice should be based on your own skills, interests, working style and the opportunities available to you. The information in this chapter should be read in conjunction with Chapter 23 which will help you understand your interests and skills.

Who Employs Research Graduates?

Fifty two per cent of doctoral graduates surveyed in 2004, six months after their graduation were working outside academia. This demonstrates the transferability of a doctorate. Data for all masters graduates (not just research masters for whom specific data is not available) shows that they work in a wide range of employment sectors.

Wherever your career interests lie, it is positive to hear that a research degree opens doors to many different occupational areas. If you want to leave academia, it means that researchers can successfully move into different areas. If you want to remain, it means that the concerns you have about competition for academic posts as student numbers expand can be partly countered. Specific careers will be discussed in more detail in the next chapters, but here we will look at the overview and balance between different career areas.

Table 22.1 illustrates the main sectors which attracted the 2004 doctoral graduates – education, finance, health and manufacturing, with business and public administration also popular.

The subject of study has a clear influence on some of these sectors. People with research degrees in psychology, clinical medicine, nursing, biomedical sciences and social sciences have employment in the health and social work sector. Natural and physical scientists and engineers dominate manufacturing. Elsewhere though, the subjects are varied with sciences, social sciences, arts and humanities in the public sector. The business sector recruits a wide range of graduates with most from the sciences rather than economic and business-related subjects. The 'other' employers include publishing, retailing, cultural and recreational activities and attract a diverse mix of researchers.

Who Do I Want to Work for?

Although it only paints part of the picture, sector information is a good starting point as it addresses a key concern of researchers – do employers other

TABLE 22.1 Employment sectors entered by UK-domiciled doctoral graduates, based on standard industrial classifications

Employment Sector	%
Education	48
Manufacturing	16
Health and social work	15
Finance, business and IT	9
Public Administration and Defence	6
Other	6

Source: *What Do PhDs Do?* (UK GRAD 2004).

than universities want the skills developed through a research degree? The answer is clearly 'yes'. It also offers a starting point for your own career choice. What kind of wider activity interests you? In what context do you feel motivated to work? How do you define each of these sectors and what do you know about each of them?

- Education might appeal if you want to make a contribution to learning, teaching or novel research
- Manufacturing needs research skills or knowledge to develop and improve products for consumers or medical treatments
- Health and social work offers careers in which you could make a more direct impact on individuals
- The finance sector will give you a chance to apply your skills to commercial problems and generally offers higher earning potential
- The public sector might allow you to contribute to society by improving security, policy or government.

There are a few stereotypes in these 'sketches' of the sectors, but you can start to investigate them in more detail using the Prospects website which includes an overview of almost thirty areas of the labour market. As well as describing typical vacancies, these profiles also give an overview of recent, current and future issues and describe the key employers in each sector – see www. prospects.ac.uk/ and select 'Explore Job Sectors': from the 'Jobs and Work' pull-down menu.

Case Study 1 Liz

I started a PhD in Chemistry knowing I wouldn't stay in academia. I'd spent a summer working for a large consumer products manufacturer and noticed that most of the managers had PhDs. Although the company didn't hold people back who didn't have doctorates, it seemed to me that having a PhD would improve my prospects and for the first time I looked at it as a qualification which had value outside universities. Now I'm nearing the end of my PhD I'm starting to see why those managers were so good at their jobs. I've had to manage my own time, take control of the research and go to conferences to speak about my work on my own. Doing a PhD has made me much more resilient and effective. During my second year I started to think seriously about what I would do next, as my placement made me realise I didn't want to work in industry – it's hard to say why, but I wasn't that interested in the products and wanted more freedom with my work. I have really enjoyed demonstrating to undergraduates and my supervisor let me run a couple of tutorials for him. I realised I want a job which involved teaching or supporting people. At first I thought about personnel, but a trip to the Careers Service quickly dispelled that idea – to me it appeared largely administrative and not what I wanted. The Careers Adviser I saw suggested I think about teaching, so I went on a 2 day visit to a local school, but it seemed to be largely about crowd control and I realised I would find it frustrating to teach chemistry (which I'm still very interested in!) at a really basic level. With only a few months to go to the end of my funding I was starting to worry about getting a job, but finally the hours of browsing websites and papers paid off when I saw a job for an assistant in the education department of a large professional body. The job involves science promotion, representing the society at conferences and writing articles on education. The Careers Service helped me with my application and an academic in my department put me in touch with someone in a similar role in our professional body – they really helped me understand what the job involved. The advert didn't ask for a PhD, but I was able to demonstrate that I had skills they were looking for and lots of 'added value'. They offered me the job. The pay is much lower than I'd be getting in industry, but for me this is a first step in the right direction. I've managed to combine my scientific knowledge with my preference for a more 'people-based' job.

The values and culture of an organisation can have a huge impact on the quality of your life – if you feel a general agreement and shared vision, this can seem invisible, but if values clash you might feel demotivated or undervalued. The culture will affect the structure of the organisation, the way people are managed, individual levels of responsibility, workloads and career progression. As you investigate career options, consider the impact of these on your choice and look for evidence of culture in recruitment literature (websites and job adverts) and when talking to people. You can investigate your own values using the exercises in Chapters 23 and 26. University careers service staff will be able to point you to specific information sources, or may have their own insights into companies.

What Do Research Graduates Do?

The employment sector figures demonstrate the transfer of research skills and knowledge into all parts of the economy. The next level of detail to look at is the occupations entered by research-degree graduates at this early stage of their careers. All the figures reported here are from *What Do PhDs Do?* and refer to 2004 doctoral graduates who are working in the UK.

Many research students are understandably drawn to careers in research which allow them to apply their training in specific skills and draw upon the knowledge developed during their degrees. Unfortunately, it is not straight forward to identify 'researchers' using the available data as individuals use a range of job titles and these are classified in different ways. Some describe themselves according to their subject (i.e. physicist), whether they work in academia, industry or the public sector. Others refer to themselves as 'researchers', but don't define their subject area – although it seems likely that they are working in the same subjects as they were trained, we can't say for sure. It is therefore complicated to present general trends over the whole subject range and for specific information you are recommended to visit your careers service where they will hold information on the destinations of graduates from your degree programme, probably going back several years.

With these health warnings in place, we can look at the headlines. The most popular destinations are summarised in below. Academic and industrial research positions will be looked at in detail in subsequent chapters.

MAIN OCCUPATIONS ENTERED BY DOCTORAL GRADUATES IN 2004

Teachers: In this category 22% work in teaching roles, predominantly as university or higher education lecturers (15%) with secondary-school teachers accounting for small numbers (2%). Others range from professors to teaching assistants.

Researchers or scientists: In this category 37% describe themselves as 'researchers', according to their discipline (i.e. physicists) or as 'scientists' and work in education, the health sector and industry. This category includes all the post-doctoral researchers.

Engineers: In this category 8% work in engineering and IT occupations in all sectors, including education. IT professions attract graduates from all disciplines.

Managers and professional roles: In this category 17% are employed as managers (in commercial, industrial, public and educational sectors) or in professional roles in law, accountancy, architecture, public service and other areas.

Health professionals: In this category 13% work as doctors, nurses, psychologists and in other medical professions. (*What Do PhDs Do?* (UK GRAD, 2004))

If you can't see an occupational area that appeals to you on this list, don't be discouraged, these are headline figures. Graduates were found in 150 different occupations from the survey described in *What Do PhDs Do?* including sales, conservation, media, management consultancy, administration, patents and library work.

As we have seen, doctoral graduates from some subjects are more likely to enter certain employment sectors and the same is true for occupational areas. The figures below show the occupational areas entered by doctoral graduates from five different subject areas. To allow for easier comparison, the same categories are used for each chart, but in the social science and education and arts and humanities, the category of 'Scientists and other researchers' is predominantly university researchers or unspecified disciplines (but presumably in these subject areas) in both cases.

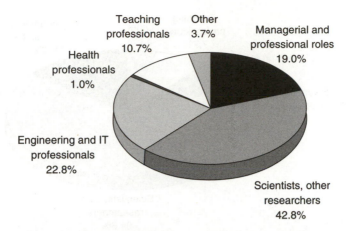

FIGURE 22.1 Types of work being undertaken in the UK on 1 January 2004 by UK-domiciled PhD graduates in physical sciences and engineering from UK universities in 2003

What Do Physical Science and Engineering Doctoral Graduates Do?

As can be seen from Figure 22.1, doctoral graduates from the physical sciences and engineering are predominantly employed as researchers and engineers in both the academic and manufacturing sectors. Managerial and other professions accounted for the first destinations of around a fifth of doctoral graduates and just over 10% were employed in teaching roles – mostly in higher education.

What Do Biological and Biomedical Science Doctoral Graduates Do?

Figure 22.2 shows that scientific and research roles dominate the destinations information for doctoral graduates from the biological and biomedical sciences. They are employed in both the academic and manufacturing sectors, with the pharmaceutical industry accounting for most industrial research and scientific roles. Managerial and other professions accounted for the first destinations of around 15% of doctoral graduates. Other occupational areas are relatively less common and the teaching roles are mostly in higher education.

What Do Doctorates in Clinical and Related Subjects Do?

In Figure 22.3, it is not surprising to see that doctoral graduates from the clinical sciences are predominantly employed as health professionals although

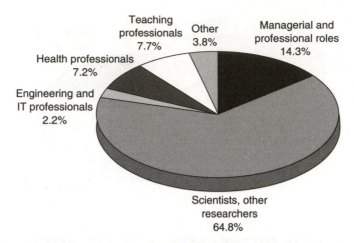

FIGURE 22.2   Types of work being undertaken in the UK on 1 January 2004 by UK-domiciled PhD graduates in biological and biomedical sciences from UK universities in 2003

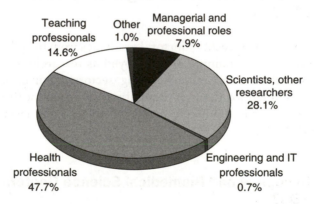

FIGURE 22.3   Types of work being undertaken in the UK on 1 January 2004 by UK-domiciled PhD graduates in clinical sciences and related subjects from UK universities in 2003

close to a third continue as researchers after completing their doctorates. Others remain in academia as university lecturers, making up most of the 15% in teaching roles.

What Do Social Science and Education Doctoral Graduates Do?

Figure 22.4 shows that doctoral graduates from the social sciences and education are most likely to be employed in academic teaching roles (52.5%) or

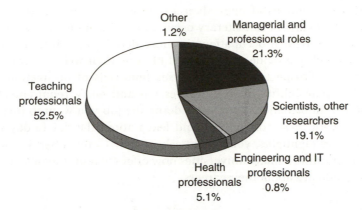

FIGURE 22.4   Types of work being undertaken in the UK on 1 January 2004 by
UK-domiciled PhD graduates in social sciences and education from UK
universities in 2003

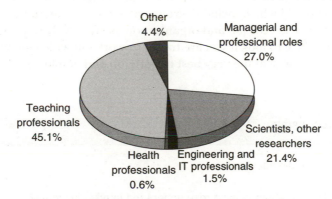

FIGURE 22.5   Types of work being undertaken in the UK on 1 January 2004 by
UK-domiciled PhD graduates in arts and humanities from UK
universities in 2003

employed as researchers mainly in the academic sector. Managerial and other
professions accounted for the first destinations of around a fifth of doctoral
graduates with this category including public service roles, social welfare and
business roles (as this group of subjects includes management and finance).

What Do Arts and Humanities Doctoral Graduates Do?

Figure 22.5 shows how doctoral graduates from the arts and humanities are predominantly employed in teaching roles (largely lecturing) and researchers in the
academic sector. Managerial and other professions are popular and accounted

for the first destinations of more than a quarter of doctoral graduates. This category includes artistic and literary occupations and public service roles.

To look at individual occupations in more detail you will find that many professional bodies provide career case studies on their websites or in careers literature. The Prospects website analyses hundreds of occupations giving details of responsibilities, career progression and entry requirements. The best source of information is someone doing the job you want to investigate. To connect with these role models and learn about the day-to-day routine, challenges and highlights, you should ask in your Careers Service about an alumni programme – many universities now offer current students the chance to talk to graduates about their careers.

How Do I Decide between All These Careers?

The first step to making a career decision is to understand your skills, interests and personality, so as you investigate different occupations you can decide how compatible these are with your potential. There is much more advice on this in Chapter 23 which includes a range of exercises. Recruitment literature is written to market the job and organisation as effectively as possible, so it is not the best place to look if you are trying to work out which job will suit you, as they tend to present the very best of both job and employer.

QUESTIONS TO CONSIDER

Start with some simple questions.

What do you like best about being a researcher (and in previous jobs)?
What don't you enjoy about research (or previous jobs)?
What would be your ideal job if there were no constraints?

Your answers will get you thinking about your motivations – at this stage you don't need to share these with anyone. In addition to noting down answers to these questions, think about what lies behind them. If you have identified an ideal job, why haven't you pursued it? Is this a thwarted ambition which is going to tarnish any other jobs you consider? Or are you happy to set it aside? It is important to address this early on in your career planning.

Doing research involves a range of activities, most of which have been described in earlier chapters. Think about which of these are most enjoyable: Teaching? Writing? Speaking to other researchers at conferences? Planning and managing your research? Coming up with new ideas? Or implementing them and finding practical solutions to problems? A useful tool for analysing your personal highs as a researcher is the 'Personal Development Portfolio' (it may be called something else in your institution) which you will have been encouraged to complete with your supervisor and other key staff during your degree. This is discussed in more detail in Chapter 14 of this book. If you look back over your portfolio, add a sheet which summarises what you actually like about being a researcher.

Case Study 2 Pat

I first started to consider staying in academia when I was doing my degree in History. I really enjoyed the extended dissertations that we had to produce and couldn't imagine finding another job which would allow me to continue to learn about History! I mentioned this to my tutor and he explained the reality of life as a lecturer. It was very different from the view I had – very long hours, lots of pressure to publish and to find funding (which is near impossible in our field) and lots of administrative duties and 'hours in pointless meetings' as he rather cynically put it. Despite this, he encouraged me to talk to other people in our department – particularly a PhD student and a temporary lecturer. Both confirmed his views about the pressures to publish, but they also told me how difficult it would be to get an academic position – neither of them were particularly optimistic about getting a permanent position.

Although at the time I was a bit put off, I asked them all if they could imagine doing anything else – and they all said 'no'! So, once they felt they had done their public duty in warning me about the pitfalls, we then had a long conversation about the benefits – and these convinced me to give academia my best shot. I can't imagine another career which would allow me to indulge in my interests, see my name in print, share my enthusiasm with students and to talk to other equally interested people at conferences and meetings.

During my PhD (which I had to partly fund through working) I got some teaching experience and also helped to organise a conference which really boosted my visibility and network. I spoke to all the key speakers at the conference and asked them if they knew of any positions or funding that would help me to start my post-PhD career. Through this, I found out about and was appointed on a temporary lectureship in another university. At the end of the one year contract the post was given full funding, so I applied but didn't get it. I was gutted! And really angry as I thought I was the best candidate and had worked hard during the year to do a lot more for the department than was expected. Unfortunately, the department felt they had to appoint the candidate with most publications. As my contract drew to a close I saw a research job advertised overseas (in southern Europe) in my general area (but not in a university) so I took it. I was abroad for two years and in that time I worked REALLY hard on my publications and managed to turn my thesis in to a book and to write a couple of monographs. I kept in touch with my former colleagues and others in the UK with email and by attending conferences, and was told about a lectureship coming up in a similar university to my last one. This time I was successful – my publications, the chance to build up my research

> interests and a glowing reference from my last head of department being the factors which worked for me.
>
> I'm glad I went into academia with my eyes open – there are many demands on my time and I have to be very disciplined to retain the focus on my research, but it is the only job I can imagine doing and it's been worth the sacrifices.

Similarly, the elements that you struggle to be inspired by are useful in making an effective career choice. Unless you are really lucky, there will be things about every career that aren't enjoyable, but you don't want these to dominate your time and energy. Again, your Personal Development Portfolio can help you to identify your dislikes and to take these into account when weighing up your alternatives.

Armed with this information, you can now begin to look at your options. The section on 'Sources of support' provides useful resources to allow you to investigate the occupational areas mentioned earlier and many more.

What Do Research Graduates Offer Employers?

UK research degrees require high levels of independence and initiative, which gives graduates from these programmes a very different skills-set from those developed through taught studies. Although it was developed to identify the skills needs of researchers, the Joint Skills Statement (see Appendix 2) of the Research Councils can be used to give a useful snapshot of the value that researchers can offer to employers, but you should again use your own records of your progress to produce a tailored list.

Some skills and attitudes you may have to offer are presented below along with online skills audits and resources.

SKILLS RESEARCH STUDENTS CAN OFFER EMPLOYERS AND RESOURCES TO HELP YOU IDENTIFY YOUR OWN SKILLS

Project and time management: Within the research project, you will have had to identify and stick to your own deadlines and to monitor your own progress.

Initiative: By definition, research requires a new approach to a question and the development of new ideas and solutions.

Tenacity: Research rarely runs smoothly, so most researchers can demonstrate their ability to rise to a challenge and work towards a solution without always having a clear idea of what that might be.

Critical judgment: Whether reading dozens, if not hundreds, of primary sources or developing your own arguments and hypotheses, researchers develop expertise at looking beyond the obvious and testing information they are presented with.

Professionalism: The level of intellectual challenge presented by a research degree and the independence of thought and action required to successfully complete a thesis, gives research graduates 'proven' abilities rather than potential.

Skill spotting: Your personal development portfolio should have helped you to monitor your skills development throughout your research.

The Occupational Competences of Researchers were developed by the Researchers' Lead Body and published by SEMTA, science, technology and engineering skills council. These break down the research cycle into eight stages and give detailed descriptions of the skills and knowledge which must be demonstrated by an effective researcher; visit their website at: www.ukstandards.org.uk/ and browse standards by 'Suites' using the pull-down menu, then scroll down to 'Research'.

There are also resources which focus on academic success.

The Research Career Builder is aimed at research staff, but is useful for research students as it not only lists the relevant skills and gives you a structure for recording them, but also breaks down each skills-set into different levels (from 'foundation' to 'expert'), available online at: http://gmpcrs.group.shef.ac.uk/

'Making the Right Moves' is aimed at scientific subjects in the US, but contains a lot of advice and skills descriptions that can be applied internationally and across many subjects; available online at: www.hhmi.org/resources/labmanagement

These audits are based on your own evidence and give you a chance to organise and analyse the skills you have used as a researcher. There are also a number of analysis tools available which look at other elements of your personality, such as motivations and personal preferences. Some of these are used in the recruitment process particularly by larger companies, so it is useful to familiarise yourself with these. They are also useful in giving you a broader perspective on your own skills, interests and personality which can be invaluable as you contemplate your career options. Most are based on well-researched questionnaires and can be costly to access as an individual. However, most Careers Services or Graduate Centres will hold licences and employ qualified staff to conduct these either with individuals or through training workshops. Some of those most widely available include the following:

The Myers–Briggs-Type Indicator is widely used in organisations across all sectors to help people work more effectively together and to help individuals reach their potential. The background to the tool and an introductory overview are available at www.personalitypathways.com/ Many careers services will offer feedback on your personality type and help you relate this to career choice.

Most careers services will also offer mock aptitude tests which can give you insights into fundamental skills such as literacy and numeracy. Some psychometric tests are available online from companies such as SHL; browse their website at www.shldirect.com/ For more information you can also browse the Prospects website at www.prospects.ac.uk

Questionnaires and tests should be seen as ways to gain useful insights for recognising your strengths and addressing any weaknesses. They are not intended to put you into a 'box' and prevent you from pursuing careers if you have a different profile to that suggested in careers literature, but they can help you to identify jobs which will play to your strengths and natural tendencies.

An excellent way to improve your skills and your awareness of your own tendencies and preferences is to go on a GRADschool or equivalent intensive course which will put you in a team of research students, give you a range of tasks to work on and offer many opportunities to get feedback on your performance and to discuss differences between your approach and those of other students. The national programme of GRADschools [www.grad.ac.uk/gradschools] is open to doctoral students. Many institutions also offer their own 'equivalent' GRADschool.

What Do Employers Want?

Once you have built up a clearer picture of what you want from a potential job and what you feel you have to offer, you now need to start sharpening a new set of career tools – your marketing skills. You need to work out how you will convince an employer that you have the ideal combination of skills, personal attributes and knowledge to make an impact in their organisation. In order to do this in a compelling and convincing way, you clearly need to know what they need from potential employees and what challenges you may face once you start work.

Employers will market themselves and their vacancies in a range of ways. Don't be frustrated if the organisation you want to work in gives little away about itself and you struggle to answer some of the questions raised in this section. Look on this as a challenge and apply those research skills so carefully honed during your project!

All employers will have a list of requirements in mind as they sift through applications. If you can build an accurate picture of what these requirements are *and* reflect these in all aspects of your application, you will dramatically increase your chance of success. To work out what is likely to appear on the 'shopping list' of your chosen employer, it is helpful to look at the different questions they will have in mind.

Can You Do the Job?

The minimum requirement for most employers will be that you are capable of doing the job and they will usually set out their needs explicitly in an advert. These include technical capabilities or familiarity with particular equipment, computer packages or methodological approaches. This list also includes specific skills such as problem solving or leadership which may be mentioned in vacancy statements of general recruitment information.

ACTION POINT

As a research student you may develop skills or knowledge that are in short supply, but never assume that an employer (even an academic one) will take it for granted that you have these – always echo the language and phraseology of the recruitment literature in your application. If they ask for familiarity with a specific computer package, for example, mention it by name and describe your level of expertise. If you are in the early or mid-stages of your research project, start to talk to potential employers about their skills and knowledge requirements, as it may be possible to integrate these into your degree.

Will You Fit into the Team or Group?

If you appear to 'theoretically' fit the demands of the job, employers (including academics) will next look at how you will interact with others in the existing team or group. They will want to see evidence that you have worked with other people and developed good working relationships. Employers outside academia sometimes have misconceptions about the academic working environment, although these can be addressed in applications and during interviews. They will want to see that you have an awareness of your own approach in a team (from previous work experience if you have worked in isolation as a researcher), particular strengths that you have and any areas of weakness. Admitting to weaknesses won't prevent you from getting a job, but this obviously needs to be handled carefully!

ACTION POINT

Use your Personal Development Portfolio and any associated discussions with your supervisor or others that you work with to help you understand your own approach when working with others and to collect evidence which illustrates this for future applications. If your day-to-day research is done independently, look for opportunities to engage with other researchers through local meetings of professional or learned societies, research student associations or engage with other stakeholders in your research through conferences or meetings. If you have worked part-time during your research or been involved in student societies, voluntary work or other responsibilities, ask for feedback from your colleagues.

Are You Serious about Development?

Employers usually invest heavily in the development of their staff and often spend many thousands of pounds on training, mentoring and reviewing their staff. They will look for evidence that you take your own development seriously and will make a real commitment to gaining new skills as they are required. Having undertaken further study you have obvious evidence of commitment to your own learning and development, so you should market this as a real strength. Whilst studying for your research degree, you should have had access to additional training in related skills including project management, writing, presentation skills and time management (see Chapter 14 in this book for more detail). You need to be ready to explain how you have identified your own development needs and found ways to address these. The training programmes put together by universities are a great opportunity for research students to tailor their skills to the needs of future employers. As employer awareness of these programmes grows, your attitude towards them and your own development will indicate to employers what your attitude to future training might be.

ACTION POINT

Make sure that you maximise the value of training available to you as a research student and engage with the graduate school or office which puts together the provision if you have identified a skills area which isn't covered. Most are keen to expand their programmes, particularly at the suggestions of students, and they may be willing to fund an event or workshop you want to organise if you can convince them of the value to other students.

Do You Understand What We Do and Where We Are Going?

In a recent survey of employers conducted by the University of Leeds (Souter 2005) the main concerns about the employment of researchers outside of an academic setting were associated with perceived lack of commercial awareness, overspecialisation and difficulty in making a transition out of the academic environment. If a non-academic employer receives an application from a research graduate which is written in very academic language and focuses on achievements which may mean little to them (journal articles and conference proceedings), as well as finding it difficult to extract value from these achievements, they may struggle to understand what your motivation is to leave the academic sector and doubt that you really understand the job they are offering and what it will involve.

ACTION POINT

The website of the organisation you are interested in should provide some information about their activities – if they produce an annual report it may be online and will give you a picture of current and future challenges. You should also familiarise yourself with the wider context in which your potential employer operates. If it is a university, familiarise yourself with issues such as research-funding strategies and the Research Assessment Exercise (RAE). The RAE is an assessment of the quality of research in UK universities and is used to allocate money from the public funding bodies. It is a major topic of discussion in academia, so if you are interested in remaining in the sector, ensure you have sufficient understanding of this and any other issues. In the health or social sector, you should be familiar with current changes (the NHS Modernisation Agency website www.wise.nhs.uk/ might help you research these). For commercial organisations, look at the markets they operate in – their competitors, which products or services they are currently offering and again, be ready to offer opinions. Although these insights aren't going to carry the same weight as having the right skills or abilities, they will help to address any concerns about your commitment to a long-term career, particularly if you are changing direction from your research degree.

Are You Going to Help Us Realise Our Future Aims?

The cost of recruiting a new staff member is such, that most employers will take a long-term view when they appoint someone. They will want to see the potential you have to solve future problems, generate new directions for their activities and hopefully, they will be looking for your potential to lead and manage in a more senior position.

ACTION POINT

Research career paths by talking to people in jobs that interest you and ask the Careers Service for advice or contacts. Think about the strengths you have and how you might build on these as your career develops.

Where Do I Fit?

Once you have pieced together your career jigsaw, you need to identify how you are going to position yourself. If you are planning a career change after your research degree, you need to be realistic about the level at which you are likely to enter an organisation. If you are competing with first-degree graduates for a job, your research qualification may not pay an immediate dividend in terms of a more senior appointment or more pay, but it should help you to succeed in a competitive recruitment process. If you have more extensive experience or a very specific set of skills to offer and have applied for a defined position rather than a generic graduate or mass entry position, you will need to do careful research into the structure of the organisation you aim to move into in order to justify being appointed at a particular level on the career path. You will need to explore the responsibilities and activities associated with different roles and salaries to ensure you can 'sell yourself' in these specific roles more effectively. This kind of information is most likely to come from personal contacts. Don't undersell the added value of your research degree, but at the same time, accept the employer's perspective if they want to be convinced by your performance after you've joined them. If a graduate-level position is the only point of entry into an organisation, don't reject the opportunity. Instead, ask the employer if career paths are flexible and allow people with talent to progress more quickly once they have proved themselves.

Conclusion

What Can Research Students Do?

This chapter was written to convince you that your career options with a research qualification are diverse and exciting. If you have enjoyed working in research you can continue your career in academia, industry and other sectors – some of these options will be described in more detail in the following chapters.

If you decide to leave research and find a new challenge, then the data and suggestions in this chapter should have encouraged you to look with confidence at careers that appeal. Your choice of degree and research topic is only part of the contribution you will make to a potential employer and with the right attitude and awareness of opportunities, a research degree should allow you to pursue any career.

Acknowledgements

Thanks to Dr Keith Morgan of Shinton Consulting Ltd for producing the figures on doctoral destinations and to Dr Charlie Ball of Graduate Prospects for discussions about postgraduate employment.

Note

1 'All data presented in this chapter is derived from the *HESA Destinations of Leavers from Higher Education Survey 2002/3*. Copyright Higher Education Statistics Agency Limited/Graduate Prospects'.

SOURCES OF SUPPORT

General Websites

www.grad.ac.uk – the 'Just for Postgrads' section includes career planning, details of Careers in Focus events and Ask the Experts archives.

www.prospects.ac.uk – occupational profiles of hundreds of occupations, links to employers and overviews of employment sectors

www.sciencecareers.sciencemag.org/ – written for scientists, but much with more general appeal

Face-to-face Advice

University Careers Services should be your first port of call as a research student. They will hold information on occupations, employers, the destinations of graduates with your qualification and will organise a range of events to help your career choice.

Many professional bodies are aware of the value of career support and employ careers advisers with whom you can discuss your options. Some also run careers events for employers in specific disciplines or will connect their members through mentoring programmes or to offer career insights.

Conferences are great places for informal careers discussions, but some now have formal careers provision and can offer delegates short appointments with an adviser.

Employers recognise that they also need to take a proactive approach to finding the best people.

Larger companies and organisations may run short placement courses or business games, whilst those with smaller recruitment needs will visit universities or specialist careers fairs so ask at your institution's Careers Service for details of events involving employers.

References

Ball, C. (2004) *The Changing Nature of Graduate Destinations*. Graduate Prospects available online at: www.prospects.ac.uk/cms/ShowPage/p!eXefmmp (accessed 30 June 2007)

Roberts, G. (2002) *SET for Success: The Supply of People with Science, Technology, Engineering and Mathematics Skills*. Available online at: www.hm-treasury.gov.uk./ Documents/Enterprise_and_Productivity/Research_and_Enterprise/ent_res_ roberts.cfm (accessed 30 June 2007)

Souter, C. (2005) EMPRESS (*Employers' Perceptions of Recruiting Research Staff and Students*). University of Leeds

The UK GRAD Programme (2004, 2006, 2007). *What Do PhDs Do?* Available online at: www.grad.ac.uk/wdpd/ (accessed 5 October 2007)

23 Identifying and Valuing Your Transferable Skills

Clare Jones

It is absolutely crucial to see oneself as a set of skills and not simply as an academic researcher. Many of the skills we use and develop are directly transferable to other careers and it is important to get to the point where you see that. If you can convince yourself, you can convince a potential employer.

(Rosemary, Geochemistry Researcher [a case study from HESDA's online resource Career Paths of Academic Researchers' – Physical Sciences Section])

Introduction

This chapter sets out the case for identifying and valuing the skills you will develop and use during your research degree, and that by doing this you will also recognise how you will be able to use these skills in a variety of contexts in the future.

Transferable skills training and development is an integral part of a research degree with the Joint Skills Statement of the UK Research Councils' Training Requirements for Research Students, outlined in Chapter 14 and contained in Appendix 2 of this volume, providing the foundation for this. Whatever you do after your research degree, you will need to employ a wide range of skills and be able to demonstrate to employers that you have the skills they need. It is also likely that you will change your career direction a number of times in your working life and therefore understanding the skills you have and appreciating how skills can be transferred will help throughout your career. Arnold (1997) in his book *Managing Careers into the 21st Century* says:

people will be working . . . in jobs with frequently changing skill requirements . . . spanning different organisations. (1997: 28)

Researchers and Transferable Skills

A simple definition of transferable skills is: 'those skills acquired in one context which can be transferred and used in another'. All working environments require skills: information management, decision making and the ability to defend judgements and decisions etc., and researchers developing these skills in an academic context will also be able to utilise them in other situations.

In the Joint Skills Statement the skills obtained from a research degree are listed as Research Skills and Techniques, Research Environment, Research Management, Personal Effectiveness, Communication, Networking and Team-working, and Career Management. Some of these, such as research management, are specific to a research degree whilst others are more generic in nature, for example, communication and team working. Other transferable skills include interpersonal skills, information technology and numeracy skills. All of these can be transferred to contexts outside academia, for example, one of the research management skills is being able to 'apply effective project management through the setting of research goals, intermediate milestones and prioritisation of activities'. The transferable element is the ability to manage a project, to set and achieve goals and to prioritise work. You will, of course, develop this skill through your research but could also use it in managing projects in other situations. The important thing is to recognise that project management skills can be used in different contexts and then be able to convince others of how you can use your skills and experience in the work they want you to undertake.

Identifying your own skills can be a difficult task to undertake; we often take these skills for granted, either because we know we can use them, or they are part of our 'routine work'. This can be exacerbated for research students, as they are less likely to be asked specifically about their transferable skills, and more likely to be asked about the progress of their research. You may need to take the initiative to ensure that your wider skills development is discussed; using the Joint Skills Statement as a framework for this purpose may help you and your supervisor to have such a discussion. It is often after they have completed their degree that researchers appreciate all the skills they have developed. The two quotes below are from researchers who contributed to UK GRAD's '*What Do PhDs Do?* 2004 Analysis of first destinations for PhD graduates' (discussed at length in the previous chapter), and they serve to illustrate the breadth of personal development which can be gained from a research degree:

> I realised I didn't have to be defined in terms of the research topic I was working on. Instead I should be thinking about what skills I had ... . UK GRAD (2004: 28)

> It was not the specifics of the research that helped, more the total acquired information, techniques and skills. UK GRAD (2004: 31)

In order to value your transferable skills, it may help to identify their importance to your work *now*. After all such skills as being able to effectively write about your findings, explain ideas clearly and concisely, and manage a project are central to being an effective researcher (refer to Chapter 20 on submission and completion).

You can place greater emphasis on your current development of transferable skills by undertaking a regular and structured review of your progress using a personal development planning approach as outlined earlier in this book (see Chapter 14). This helps to give recognition and value to all your skills as you move through the different phases of your research, and enables you to become more effective in your current work. The progress and impact of your research may be hindered if you do not understand both the research process skills you use and the knowledge you acquire in the process.

There are a number of tools available which can assist in analysing and assessing skills and in the final section of this chapter some of them will be discussed.

Even though you may regularly review your progress as you undertake your research, it may still be difficult to recognise how much you need to know about yourself and what information others may ask you to provide in the future. It may be that this lack of a detailed context for transferable skills is why some researchers are reluctant to give time to fully reviewing and analysing their skills. The next sections of this chapter will concentrate on providing you with this context as well as practical methods for undertaking this type of self-assessment.

How Much Do You Need to Know and Why?

The quotation at the start of the chapter talked of convincing yourself of the transferability of your skills before you could convince others, and as has already been suggested, it is common to assess yourself solely in terms of the progress of your research. This can mean that you undervalue tasks considered to be those that every researcher undertakes. Yet it is often the analysis of these everyday experiences, which not only provides the confidence to convince yourself of your progress but also allows you to see how transferable your skills are.

It is also worth noting at this point that you will also develop and use skills in other environments and situations and it is equally necessary, and valid, for you to analyse and use these in developing a comprehensive profile. In fact employers will often welcome evidence of your ability to adapt to different situations, therefore using your outside interests, voluntary work or life experiences can be very beneficial. Your personal analysis may also provide insights into your values, interests or types of work or situations that you enjoy being involved in. This information will also be useful when you are preparing to move on after your research degree (see Chapters 24–27 in this volume).

One example of analysing a 'routine' task is set out below, but there are many other situations you could use to provide examples of your transferable skills such as the preparation of an abstract, progress report or journal article. You could also analyse such activities as the planning and organisation of your work, running a seminar series or local conference or liaising with colleagues or research collaborators.

Case Study A poster presentation (an example from a Chemistry PhD)

Antoine, a chemistry PhD, has recently presented a poster of his work at a conference and is now analysing this activity by considering what it involved, the skills he used and their transferability to other situations. His detailed analysis shows the depth, and potential value, of such an experience.

Main Task – Preparation and Presentation of Poster for Conference

Sub-tasks

1 Reviewed and analysed of research material to identify key information to meet conference themes
2 Discussed and agreed ideas and approaches with supervisor
3 Sought advice from post doc researcher on effective poster styles to allow for a clear and concise presentation of material
4 Prepared draft poster and presentation for research group meeting and received feedback from colleagues
5 Acted on feedback and informal advice from other researchers to improve poster and presentation
6 Liaised with print department, agreed deadlines for printing and costs
7 At the conference – attended poster session and presented research to delegates from … .

Skills Used/Level of Competence/Outcomes and Achievements

Analytical Skills to Identify Key Themes

Communication skills – able to rationalise material in order to convey a clear and concise overview of research. Needed also to be able to capture interest of audience quickly. At conference used good oral presentation skills to provide further information by answering questions confidently and knowledgeably.

Teamwork/collaborative skills – Able to use feedback and advice from colleagues to improve work. Liaison and negotiation skills used with supervisor and with print staff in order meet deadlines.

> *Networking skills* – made a number of specific contacts with researchers working in similar areas.
>
> *IT skills* – improved IT design skills in order to produce poster with good visual impact – now feel more competent with ... software package.
>
> *Achievements* – awarded conference commendation for poster, invited to attend conference in ... next year as a direct result of contact made. Complimented on clear nature of presentation by ... .
>
> *Own assessment* – have significantly improved written and oral communication skills. Know that I can identify and analyse information to convey complex ideas in a clear and concise way. Can talk confidently and enthusiastically to a range of people – senior academics and industrialists to fellow researchers – which has made me feel more confident about defending my work at my viva. Felt more confident to discuss my approach with my supervisor and defend my ideas.

This detailed approach is time consuming, especially as only one example has been offered and Antoine will need to analyse other experiences. However, by regularly reviewing his development and keeping notes in this style he can, in fact, save time. Many researchers nearing the end of their degrees are under great pressure as they complete their research but this may also be the time when they see their ideal next move advertised, perhaps a post-doctoral research post or a job outside academia. Preparing an effective application takes time yet, recording and reviewing experiences using the methods described may mean that much of the groundwork will have been done and so the time needed to refine and complete an application could be achievable.

Convincing Others – Analysing for Transferability

Continuing with this case study researchers need to consider the transferable skills acquired in this activity and using job-related documents such as person specifications and job descriptions can assist this part of the process. Table 23.1 uses person specification and job description statements taken from real jobs to demonstrate the transferability of skills.

Analysing for transferability in this way means concentrating on the process and steps taken and not the outcome. It is also worth remembering that some familiar academic terminology may conjure up a very different image than the one you intend as evidence of your skill, and 'poster' is a good example of this. Outside academia someone may think of an advertising billboard or a poster in a teenager's room and so not be aware of the work and skills which go into the production of an academic poster. Other examples of this might be 'demonstrator' and even 'thesis'. Consider whether someone outside academia would have a clear understanding of these terms, and use your analysis to explain clearly the competencies acquired rather than assume that they know.

TABLE 23.1 The transferability of skills

Employer information	Evidence from self-analysis
Able to relate confidently and positively to people inside and outside the organisation	Worked with colleagues in research group to develop ideas, have to show confidence in own ideas. Talked confidently about research to delegates at international conference. Initiated approach to researchers from other organisations which have led to further collaboration
Articulates views/proposals clearly, concisely and logically verbally and in writing	Oral presentation of research work to research group members and able to discuss results and approaches Rationalised main points of work in a clear and concise academic poster with the aim of generating interest in the work achieved
Influencing others by expressing point of view persuasively	Have to be able to discuss ideas and approaches persuasively with supervisor, good example of this was poster presentation where I was able to use this to include specific points in the poster
Excellent written communication skills and the ability to write in a variety of ways	Preparation of poster demonstrates this Also prepared abstract and contributed to journal articles Have also had to prepare regular written reports for research group meetings

EXERCISES

Below are more statements from advertised jobs, identify examples for each one from your research work, or other activities, which you could use to convince yourself and others of your skills.

- *Teamworking*
  Build collaborative relationships with key internal and external stakeholders
  Able to evaluate others' strengths and weaknesses
- *Management and organisation*
  Able to co-ordinate and manage different project tasks
  Able to set timetables and monitor progress
- *Independent working*
  Able to work independently with conflicting demands in a high-pressured environment
  Able to perform job responsibilities without close supervision
- *Creativity and problem solving*
  Create new and imaginative approaches to work-related issues
  Make systematic and rational judgements based on relevant information
- *Research*
  Able to demonstrate research management skills
  Ability to devise robust research methodologies
- *Inter-personal*
  Clear desire to achieve results
  To be flexible/adaptable and able to cope with changing priorities and ambiguities.

Remember you can also use other aspects of your life to provide examples of your skills, for example, interests, voluntary activities etc. In fact, if you can provide evidence of skills from other contexts outside your research degree, then you are already showing how you are able to transfer your skills.

What and Who Can Help You?

The previous sections of this chapter have offered a context and approach to analysing and valuing your transferable skills but it is often difficult to obtain real benefits from this process without further help and support. This can be in the form of tools and frameworks to assist with the process of recording and reviewing, or using people to provide feedback and comment on the results of your analysis. There are also a number of career management books which can provide further information on skills and self-analysis. This is not an exhaustive list but identifies resources and support readily available to research students

Diagnostic Tools

UK GRAD – www.grad.ac.uk

Many of you may already be familiar with the UK GRAD website and the 'Just For Postgrads' section. Within this there is a useful section on career planning and management and it offers an analysis tool using the descriptors from the Joint Skills Statement. It allows users to rate their performance against the descriptors and also to identify an example to demonstrate this competency. This tool will help in examining your current role as a researcher. You should also explore the Doctoral Planner at www.grad.ac.uk/planner which will help you to review your progress in your research degree.

Royal Society of Chemistry – www.rsc.org/Education/ HEstudents/PSR/resources.asp

This resource has been developed for Chemistry PhD researchers although it is relevant for non-chemists too. It offers an approach to skills auditing and profiling and provides a timescale for review and the opportunity to identify targets for further development.

Prospects – www.prospects.ac.uk

Offers a personal-profiling tool entitled 'What Jobs Would Suit Me?' which allows you to identify your skills as well as other factors which may influence your career choices. It also offers career ideas for you to explore further using a comprehensive set of occupational profiles. Be aware that the tool generates a comprehensive list of career possibilities it does not 'match' you to a specific career. There will be occupations shown which you may immediately dismiss but you can use the list to identify occupational trends and to consider possibilities you may not have been aware of.

Windmills Programme – www.windmillsprogramme.com

This tool offers a structured approach to skills analysis and is not solely aimed at university researchers. As a consequence it provides a broad skills vocabulary and encourages the user to identify their strongest skills. It also provides a strong link to CV development by the building of a skills portfolio which uses language styles which are suited for use in non-academic CVs.

Research Career Builder – www.gmpcrs. group.shef.ac.uk/rcb.html

This tool has been developed for research staff but it offers a comprehensive review of the skills developed through research and may be of particular value to anyone considering the development of an academic career.

Swansea University Research Career Planner – www.swan. ac.uk/crs/career.htm

Again developed for research staff but provides a framework for a skills analysis.

Other diagnostic tools are available on a range of websites and your university careers service may also provide analysis tools. There is no 'one' best format and you will need to identify one that you find most comfortable to work with.

Career Management and Self-analysis Books

There are also a number of books that can assist in identifying and analysing transferable skills:

Ali, L. and Graham, B. (2000) *Moving on in Your Academic Career: A Guide for Academic Researchers and Postgraduates.* Routledge Farmer (Part II Focus on Yourself – Self-Assessment)

Lees, J. (2005) *How to Get a Job You'll Love: A Practical Guide to Unlocking Your Talents and Finding Your Ideal Career.* McGraw Hill Professional (Chapter 7 'What Do You Have to Offer?' has useful exercises and a commentary on identifying your skills)

Hopson, B. and Scally, M. (2004) Build Your Own Rainbow: A Workbook for Career and Life Management. Management Books 2000 Ltd (You might use the section 'You're more skilled that you think.')

It may also be useful to read what other researchers and employers say about transferable skills and the following case studies and reports contain interesting insights from researchers and employers:

UK GRAD (2004, 2006, 2007). *'What Do PhDs Do?'*

EMPRESS – *Employer's Perceptions of Recruiting Research Staff and Students* – Claire Souter, Careers Centre, The University of Leeds (go to www.careerweb.leeds.ac.uk/ and search for Empress). Funded by Research Councils UK

Career Paths of Academic Researchers – contact your university careers service to access this set of profiles of researchers from all disciplines.

Conclusion

> Successful people rarely get where they are by following a pre-planned career – they position themselves to seize future opportunities.
>
> (Hawkins, 2005: 48)

This quote sums up why you need to value your transferable skills. The confidence you will gain from this will enable you to be in a position to seize opportunities and to clearly demonstrate how you will be able to rise to the challenges they may present.

SOURCES OF SUPPORT

It can be extremely valuable to discuss your analysis with others as self-analysts are often self-critics. Discussing your findings can help to identify a greater level of competency than was identified initially; may allow consideration of more skills and can offer an opportunity to discuss future options. Family and friends often offer friendly and informative feedback. Supervisors will appreciate meetings which are underpinned by a systematic and informed self-analysis, and may be willing to discuss your broader skill development. Remember you may need to take the initiative on this and you can use the Joint Skills Statement as a useful framework. Your supervisors are also well placed to offer advice to those seeking to develop an academic research career.

Further support is available through your University Careers Service where there will be resources on career options and opportunities for individual discussions with a Careers Adviser.

Careers services provide advice and guidance for all students and a number of services offer specialist careers advice for postgraduate researchers. All discussions with a careers adviser are confidential and impartial. An early discussion of options is advisable as there may be actions you can take that will help you to achieve your ambitions. It is not necessary for you to have specific career ideas before seeing an adviser, in fact many guidance appointments start with the words, 'I have no idea what I want to do next.' Careers advisers will be able to work from this, they will not 'match' you to a career but will help you to explore options and to take a decision which is right for you. If you do have ideas it is worth checking out how you can gain greater insights into particular careers; careers advisers can provide suggestions as to how this might be achieved. These deeper insights will assist in making career decisions and will strengthen applications.

Attending a national or local UK GRAD school will also offer an opportunity to review your skills development and to get feedback from careers specialists, mentors and tutors.

References

Arnold, J. (1997) *Managing Careers into the 21st Century*. London: Paul Chapman Publishing Company

Hawkins, P. (2005) *The Art of Building Windmills: Career Tactics for the 21st Century*. Liverpool: GIEU (Graduate into Employment Unit – an independent unit of The University of Liverpool)

The Higher Education Staff Development Agency (HESDA) and AGCAS (Association of Graduate Careers Advisory Services) *Career Paths of Academic Researchers* – case studies of the career paths of former academic researchers. See your careers service to access these case studies.

The UK GRAD Programme (2004, 2006, 2007). *What Do PhDs Do?* Available online at: www.grad.ac.uk/wdpd/ (accessed 5 October 2007) This report also contains information on the career motivations of PhD researchers, what they offer to the labour market and getting the most from a PhD.

24 Staying in Academia
Professor Wyn Grant

Introduction

Staying in academia is only one option for a successful research student and various alternatives are explored in other chapters in this book, but it is one of the most popular and attractive career routes. Completion of a postgraduate research degree provides the successful student with a range of skills that are of particular relevance to academic work. As research degrees have evolved to include a more systematically designed and implemented training programme, usually including mentored opportunities to teach, the range of skills acquired has improved substantially compared with earlier generations who followed more scholastic forms of study. The contemporary research student should therefore be better equipped to enter the academic job market than earlier generations, although the market itself has probably become more competitive.

The fact that the market is so competitive emphasises that many people continue to find an academic career highly attractive. It offers the possibility of intellectually challenging work with the opportunity to develop new theories and innovations. Teaching provides the challenge of helping students to develop intellectually and as people, while academic work still offers more choices about how you develop your career and organise your work than many professional careers. The financial rewards may not be the best available anywhere, but opportunities for real job satisfaction, in particular making a difference, are considerable. Doing work that is challenging and rewarding is more satisfying than posts that are higher paid.

This chapter reviews motivations for staying in academia and looks at the various types of posts at UK and overseas universities that are available to research postgraduates and their advantages and disadvantages, including the possibility of working abroad. It also considers the type of UK institution in which you might wish to secure a post. It provides some guidance on undertaking job search for academic posts, completing an application and being interviewed. The chapter concludes with a list of other available sources of support.

Motivations for Staying in Academia

There are many good reasons for becoming and remaining an academic, but one needs to be aware of the drawbacks of academic life, even though these are generally outweighed by the advantages. Although attempts have been made to improve academic pay, becoming an academic is never going to maximise your lifetime income. Contrary to popular belief, you will also not enjoy long holidays as your vacations will be taken up with planning and undertaking research and writing it up, preparing teaching materials for the next session and supervising postgraduates. Although it is dangerous to present academic life as a kind of secular priesthood, as it encourages the belief that job satisfaction compensates for lower pay compared with other professions, you do need some sense of vocation to become an academic. This does not mean a spirit of self-denying sacrifice, but it does mean that you need to be able derive satisfaction from developing students academically and in terms of their general life skills, from the intellectual challenges of your research and from your contribution to society through the development of new ideas or technologies.

As in any job, there are times when academic life can be frustrating. Time management can be challenging when you are expected to demonstrate excellence in teaching, research and administration. Colleagues can sometimes be difficult, although that can happen in any workplace. The increasing bureaucratisation of academic life and the need to comply with demands from managers can be a source of annoyance, but academics still enjoy more autonomy than in many careers. There is also more flexibility about how you organise your time, although you are never completely free of your job and there is always something more that could be done. Being sensible about maintaining a work–life balance is as important as in any time-intensive profession.

It is a useful exercise to sit down and write as honest a list of reasons as possible explaining why you want to pursue an academic career. Then write a list of what you think are the main difficulties you will encounter in such a career. Hopefully, the first list will be longer and more persuasive. Then compare this second list with the first one and ask whether any of these difficulties are likely to prevent you from achieving the goals you have specified in your first list and, if there are any, what you could do to overcome them. Then file the lists away and re-visit them after a long interval of time, say three years, and review how your thinking has changed.

As in any job it is possible for the immediate to drive out the long-term and from time to time you need to review your strategic goals and see how close you are to achieving them. Such goals would include the type of job you want and where you want it to be and how you want to develop intellectually both through the contribution of your work to your discipline and through your teaching. One way of thinking about this is to ask, 'what would I like to have achieved in five or ten years' time?' Academic life will give you scope for achieving a wider range of goals than many careers.

What Sort of Post?

In broad terms, there are three types of UK-based academic post that are available to the research postgraduate:

- As a research assistant in a project
- A post-doctoral fellowship
- A lectureship (often temporary).

Research Assistant in a Project

Contract research posts are more common in the natural and social sciences and engineering than in the humanities. In 2002–2003 a third (46,000) of all academics in UK universities were in research-only posts, and of these research – only posts 93 per cent were on fixed-term contracts (*Times Higher Education Supplement*, 4 February 2005). In other words, these are the classic 'research assistant or associate' posts where you work for a fixed period of time on a particular project, usually funded by a research council or a charitable foundation. The nature of these posts can vary across disciplines. In the humanities, you may be helping someone in a senior position write a book by undertaking research in archives and libraries. In the natural sciences, you may be part of a large team with a clearly defined and specified set of tasks to complete in the laboratory. In the social sciences, the team may be smaller and your role may be less clearly defined.

There are some drawbacks to making a career as a contract researcher. There is no real job security or career structure and you will always be working on someone else's project which will constrain your ability to define and develop your own academic interests and a distinctive voice. Universities may not be interested in employing more senior individuals in contract research positions, as they would cost too much money. A study by John Hockey of the University of Gloucestershire of 60 contract researchers in the social sciences found that many of them had to work free for their universities as a means of maintaining their contracts (*Times Higher Education Supplement*, 4 February 2005). Particularly in the humanities and social sciences, contract researchers may find themselves isolated from their departments as they have to spend large periods of time away from the university working in archives or undertaking field research.

Contract research posts can pose particular dilemmas for natural scientists. There are many scientists who would rather be in the laboratory or in the field doing the technical work. Many good scientists would rather be technicians and contract researchers in the natural sciences are often in effect technicians with more interesting work and status. However, this is not a good route for going higher up the career ladder. As your career in the natural sciences progresses, the emphasis will increasingly be on building research groups, applying for research funds and managing a research team. Those who are more motivated by technical work may fail to develop these key skills.

Nevertheless, a contract research post can be a very good entry position, provided that you move on to a different sort of position once you have completed at most two contracts. The research should give you the opportunity to publish and build your CV, even if only through joint publications. It will also give you the opportunity to get to know and build networks with key players in your chosen specialist sub-area of your discipline. Make sure, however, that you try and undertake some teaching while you are a contract researcher, as this will increase your attractiveness for lecturing posts.

Post-doctoral Fellowships

A position as a post-doctoral fellow might seem to have all the advantages of being a contract researcher with some additional ones as well; notably greater autonomy to pursue your own research. Teaching duties, if there are any, are usually very limited and there are rarely any administrative burdens. However, there are some important differences between the disciplines here. Post-doctoral fellowships are more common in the natural sciences and can be the typical career stage between completing a doctorate and obtaining a lecturing post. However, it is more usual to work as a member of a team than in the humanities and social sciences, reflecting the importance and particular character of laboratory work in the natural sciences. It can also be quite difficult to move to the next level because of a shortage of permanent academic jobs and hence intense competition for them. Indeed, at this stage of their careers, some natural scientists move to the commercial sector.

In the humanities and social sciences, the shortage of post-doctoral fellowships is the main problem, although increased provision has been made by the Economic and Social Research Council (ESRC). Oxford and Cambridge colleges have a number of such fellowships, but they are highly competitive. If you are fortunate to obtain one, you may become too used to a situation where all your time is available for research. Remember that all post-doctoral fellowships are time limited, often to only one year, and eventually you will have to obtain a conventional academic post. You need to be self-disciplined to make the most of a post-doctoral fellowship, not going off on interesting tangents which means that your research loses focus and is not productive in terms of publications that will help you to obtain a permanent post. As one young academic interviewed by Grant and Sherrington (2006: 28) commented:

> I think that having a post-doc is great for some people. I think that for other people it can provide a three year space where you do nothing and become very disillusioned and I have seen that happen as well.

Lectureships

Most postgraduates will eventually take up a lectureship, even if they have a contract research post or post-doctoral fellowship as an intervening stage. Indeed, a permanent lectureship is the career goal of most academics. It offers considerable security of tenure, which although to some extent eroded, is still better than most people enjoy in the private sector. It usually offers a combination of research and teaching, with the chance to develop management skills that most academics still find attractive. Teaching can inform research, while being involved in cutting-edge research can enhance your teaching. Some academics find that they have a talent for management and develop their careers in that direction.

However, for many postgraduates the only available post is a temporary lectureship which has most usually been created to provide cover for someone who has won a research grant or is on maternity leave or is away for some other reason. As a consequence, you will have little choice about what you teach and will not have usually have the opportunities to develop an option in your own research area that a permanent post provides. You may have to teach a major module in an area in which you have relatively little expertise with little choice about the content of the syllabus. For example, you may be an expert on the English Revolution and find that you have to teach a module about the Holocaust. This can be stimulating, and may even open up a new area of research, but it can also be very demanding. You may find that you are one week ahead of the students in the reading and have few opportunities to find time to write up publications from your research degree. It is also likely that you will be treated as a relatively peripheral member of a department.

Nevertheless, there are advantages to being a temporary lecturer. It does expose you to different intellectual and organisational environments, broadening and deepening your experience. It is possible that the person on leave may not return or that a new opportunity may occur in the department that is closer to your own interests. If you have done well as a temporary lecturer, there is no guarantee that you will be appointed, but you should at least make it to the short list of candidates. On the other hand, internal candidates sometimes 'complain that they are disadvantaged because the interviewers know too much about them already' (Basnett, 2004: 8).

For all its disadvantages, accepting a temporary post may be a necessary way station en route to a permanent position. As one young academic told Grant and Sherrington (2006: 30), 'I think it is quite important in the long run to show that you are willing to take a temporary post and make the necessary sacrifices if you want to end up in a permanent position.' However, at some point you need to convert a temporary post into a permanent position. A succession of temporary lectureships on your CV can send out the message that 'this person is perfectly satisfactory for stopgap teaching cover, but can't make it to the next level.'

Above all, don't get trapped in a series of part-time teaching positions or rolling contracts as a 'teaching fellow' (which is often a more accurate description of what a temporary lecturer actually does). Such individuals are not unknown in academic life and they often have a struggle with their budgets, and their academic integrity and identity. For some people, there has to come a point, difficult though such a decision is, when they need to recognise that they are not going to succeed as an academic. This should not be seen as a failure but as opening up new opportunities which may turn out to be more fulfilling and rewarding. However, you need to be conscious about the fact that you are making the break and that there is little prospect of going back. Some people enter university administration as a holding post in the hope that their academic career may revive. The risk is then re-entry to academic life may not happen and they may not make as much of a success of their career as a university administrator as they could have done.

Which University?

One important consideration is where to work, including whether one should apply for a job outside the UK. Given that around a third of postgraduate research students in the UK are from overseas, returning to one's home country may be a strong motivation in job search for a variety of reasons. The decision will be affected by a variety of factors including how strong your discipline is in your home country, what the financial rewards are there and how strongly you have become attached to life in the UK. It may be possible to combine an academic post in the UK with giving something back to your home country through research links with a university there and return visits during sabbaticals.

Sometimes there may be personal considerations other than returning to your country of origin which impel such a move. For example, someone who has a Japanese partner may consider working in Japan, particularly as some universities will permit teaching in English until the language is learnt. Japanese is a particularly difficult language to learn, but your language skills, and the ease with which you can acquire new ones, are a key consideration when thinking about taking a job abroad, even though many continental European universities are increasingly teaching in English to cater to an international market. Countries such as Australia and New Zealand, which have relatively similar higher education systems to that of the UK, are often popular destinations for British-trained academics, but the distance involved in travelling to major conferences should be borne in mind. The US is another popular destination, although obtaining immigration clearance may be less easy compared to securing immigration clearance in a Commonwealth country such as Canada.

Leaving aside special personal considerations, it is important to be clear why you want to move abroad. A particularly valid reason may be that you are a specialist in a particular area of the world and want to live and work there at least for a time, a decision which may enhance your future career prospects. It may well be that a particular speciality or school of thinking is well developed in a particular university abroad. For natural scientists, a country like the US may offer better laboratory facilities than are available in the UK; there will be opportunities to demonstrate a capacity for working well in different research groups, and gaining expertise in a broad range of research techniques that can be beneficial to your CV. Or you may simply want to work in a developing country for a while to deploy your skills to help its development.

These are all good reasons for taking a job abroad, but be more cautious about working elsewhere because you cannot obtain a job in the UK. You then seriously have to ask yourself, 'do I want to come back to the UK and how easy would it be for me to do so? How would I feel if I could never come back to an academic post there?' For overseas students returning home, this may also be a relevant question.

Some institutions overseas carry considerable prestige and will provide you with considerable facilities for your work. Others may be less well-known, will place demands on you that will not be balanced by commensurate support, and hence may hold back your career.

The choice of which type of institution to apply to in the UK will not be a completely free one, as it will depend on where jobs become available that fit your particular profile. For example, if you have completed a professional doctorate in nursing, you may find that most posts are available in the former polytechnics and other higher education institutions that were upgraded to universities in or after 1992. Nevertheless, one consequence of subsequent research-assessment exercises, and the conversion of former polytechnics and other higher education institutions into universities, is that a hierarchy of universities has developed in the UK, which has some similarities to that found in the US and is reflected to some extent in the quality of the students attracted to different institutions. This does not mean that all post-1992 universities are permanently placed below more traditional institutions. Indeed, it is clear that some of them are overtaking more established institutions, particularly in defined research niches. Post-1992 universities may also have other advantages as places to work.

Oxford and Cambridge are world-class institutions and are clearly very attractive places to work. However, they remain college-based universities, despite some changes, and one consequence is that not all colleges have equal resources. Working in a college-based system may require some adjustment for someone who is not used to a university organised in this way. Although some changes are under way, the tutorial system in Oxford and Cambridge is very labour-intensive and leads to longer contact hours than would be normal in a research-intensive university. Those who have been educated at Oxford and Cambridge are understandably keen to stay or return there as college fellows, but such adjustment could be difficult for those educated in a different environment.

The University of London is really a cluster of distinct institutions linked loosely together; indeed Imperial College is now an independent university in its own right. Most of the London institutions are world class and as a world city London itself has many attractions as a place to live. It attracts leading academics from all over the world as visitors. However, it is a very expensive place to live and because of the costs of office accommodation you may find that you have more cramped facilities than outside the capital.

A leading research university outside London that is a member of the Russell Group which organises what claim to be the major research-intensive universities in the UK (www.russellgroup.ac.uk/index1.html) might seem an attractive option and in many ways it is. Such universities are keen to encourage bright young scholars and will do their best to support their research by providing funds to attend international conferences, providing them with initial research funds and advising and guiding them on how to obtain their first research grant. However, you will be in a very competitive environment alongside other high achievers and the university will expect excellence from you in research, teaching and administration.

Many postgraduates will obtain their first post at one of the smaller or less-renowned traditional universities. Some of these are making considerable efforts to raise their game. If they succeed, you could be on a rising tide, but if they fail to meet their targets, resources could be constrained. The former chief executive of the Higher Education Funding Council (HEFC) for England, Sir Howard Newby, referred to smaller research universities as the 'squeezed middle' and they may be particularly vulnerable to cutbacks if they do not do well in the Research Assessment Exercise (RAE), a mechanism for distributing research funds from HEFC and its counterparts in Scotland, Wales and Northern Ireland (www.rae.ac.uk/).

There are a number of reasons, other than the lack of availability of suitable posts elsewhere, that may lead you to seek your first position in a post-1992 university. A particular university may have research strength in your area of interest or it may have a good reputation for developing young staff who may be encouraged to build up their own research units at an early stage in their careers. You may be motivated to join an institution that has a greater emphasis on teaching and learning, particularly in terms of creating opportunities for social groups that are often excluded from higher education. If you are interested in developing a career in academic management, you may get more opportunities to do so earlier in a post-1992 university.

It is important to be sensitive to the differences between post-1992 universities. One of the respondents interviewed by Grant and Sherrington (2006: 14–15) had moved from an institution where student numbers were declining and research was not emphasised to one where student numbers were more buoyant and there was more encouragement to undertake research. He had found it incredibly difficult and frustrating to continually adapt courses to what were perceived as new opportunities in the market place.

Relatively few young academics are fortunate enough to get their ideal post as their first appointment and factors such as location will always play a part in the decision about where to go. However, it is important to realise that a strategy of treating a position in a post-1992 university as a staging post on the way to a position in a more highly ranked university may not be viable. The workload encountered may make it difficult for you to publish sufficient work of a high-enough quality to make you attractive to a more research-intensive university. Whilst stressing that there is considerable variation between post-1992 universities, and indeed between departments in a particular university, the worst-case scenario is to find oneself trapped in an institution with intrusive management, low-quality students and a burdensome workload.

Choice of Department

So far the discussion has been about universities, but you will be joining a department, by which is meant a unit organised for teaching and research in a discipline or related set of disciplines, whatever its particular title. Strong universities can have weak departments and vice versa. You therefore need to spend some time finding out about the unit you intend to join. Ideally, it should meet three criteria. First, it should be of a reasonable size. This reduces the likelihood of an excessive workload and means that you are more likely to be confined to teaching courses that relate to your own specialist expertise. Second, it should have an active research group that is related to your own particular interests. This is of particular importance for natural scientists as it will mean that the equipment and facilities you need for your research work are likely to be available. Third, it should not be a department that is factionalised, for example, between different branches or interpretations of a discipline, or that has a reputation for poor relationships among colleagues. Tensions within a department are often exaggerated in gossip, but if someone tells you that a particular department has a reputation for poor relationships among colleagues, at least be wary and try and check the information out with others.

Getting a Job

Which Jobs to Apply for?

First, you have to decide which jobs to apply for. The completion of an application is a time-consuming task and there is no point in applying for jobs where you do not meet the specification, particularly in the case of temporary posts where a specific teaching need has to be met. However, do not be too cautious. If you meet the majority of the criteria but not all of them, do not be discouraged from applying as the other candidates may well not be a particular fit.

Written Applications

It is always important to remember that the initial sifting of applications for a post is often done by academics operating under considerable time pressure, particularly when a temporary position needs to be filled urgently. Procedures can vary from department to department and from post to post, but often the first stage is to produce a long, short list which reduces, say, 80 applicants to 20. Applicants are discarded relatively quickly because they have not completed or are not near completing their research degree, do not meet the teaching needs for the job or have insufficient publications. The RAE makes special arrangements for new entrants, but nevertheless its normal requirement of four quality publications, generally articles in well-regarded peer-reviewed journals, or in the humanities and social sciences including a research monograph, is a good target to aim at. The selection panel will make allowance for the stage of your career you have reached, but an absence of any quality publications may stop you reaching even the long, short list. This long, short list is then reduced to the number of persons to be interviewed which may be as few as three but is rarely more than six.

The initial sifting decision will made on the basis of your application form, which needs to be completed fully, and to a large extent on the basis of your CV. As Blaxter, Hughes and Tight note (1998: 39), 'Your curriculum vitae embodies a tension which will be present throughout your application – between, on the one hand, brevity and clarity, and, on the other, comprehensiveness.' Many CVs from new recruits contain too much information, much of it padding intended to make the CV look more impressive than it is. Padding of this kind does not fool experienced recruiters and it often prevents them finding the most important information quickly. Containing information about exotic outside interests may simply make you look eccentric, or raise questions about your dedication and motivation, while listing book reviews (as distinct from review articles) or presentations given to postgraduate seminars is unlikely to impress. What information is included will depend on the nature of the post so CVs need adjustment to take account of the needs of particular positions. However, in most cases, the information that is most needed is about your teaching experience and your research publications. This information needs to be clearly set out and easily found. As Blaxter, Hughes and Tight emphasise (1998: 38):

> However, you structure it, it is critical that anyone examining your curriculum vitae should be able to find their way around it quickly. So don't make it longer than necessary, include short summary sections, and lay particular emphasis on key aspects of your academic and work histories.

Interviews

When you are called for an interview, find out as much as you can about the department so that you can see how your own profile and skills can meet its particular needs. However, it is important to be yourself. 'It's counter productive to try and shape what you say and how you present yourself to what you think the other people might want to hear' (Goldsmith, Komlos and Gold, 2001: 38). Presenting a false image of oneself is stressful and ultimately unlikely to be successful. Do not dress too casually, but make sure that you are comfortable with what you are wearing.

Interviews are often preceded by a presentation to a wider audience which provides an opportunity for those making the appointment to find out more about your research and your presentation skills. In the interview itself you may be given a chance to make an opening statement which should not be too long. This also applies to answers to questions in the interview. The longer your answer is, the greater the chance of irrelevance or of saying things that concern some of the panel. It should also be remembered that interviews have a limited duration and panel members have usually agreed a schedule of questions they want to ask.

It is difficult to anticipate everything you will be asked at the presentation or interview, but it is very likely that you will be asked about your research and how you would deal with common challenges in teaching such as students who do not participate in seminars. It has to be borne in mind that there may already be a preferred candidate for a post, but that is not a reason for not doing your best. If you make a good impression, you may be favourably considered as a candidate for another post. You will usually be asked if you have any questions at the end of the interview, but don't feel obliged to ask anything, if you feel it is not appropriate.

When You Are Not Offered the Post

Relatively few applicants obtain the first post they apply for. Try not to see this as a failure on your part. It was simply that someone else better fitted the requirements for the particular post, not that you are unsuitable for a academic career. Try and see the sequence of applications and interviews as a learning process that will assist your own development. Reflect on how you could improve your presentation or interview technique. Note down if there were any particular types of question that you had difficulty with, think about whether your answers were too long or too short or whether there were any aspects of a presentation you made that did not go down well. Having identified the key areas that you found challenging, discuss these both with peers and with more senior members of your own department or experienced people you know elsewhere in your discipline. If there are shortcomings in the content of your CV, try and remedy them, although obviously that will take more time. However, if you persistently fail, you may need to review the situation with mentors and peers and think about possible alternative career options.

Building Your Career

Once you have obtained a post, you will want to build the career to open up new opportunities and in due course to obtain promotion or move to another institution. 'Networking' is of great importance in achieving such objectives. As well as what you know, who you know is important. You need to get to know other people working in your particular sub-field of the discipline so that you do not replicate the work that they are doing and cooperate with them on research projects when possible.

Most contemporary research grant applications of any size in all disciplines require a team of researchers and not necessarily all at one institution which may not be able to offer the full range of relevant expertise. Attending conferences is an important way to get to know people, not just by giving papers and contributing to discussions, but also meeting people for informal discussions that are as important for career development as the formal business of the conference.

Raising your profile in other ways is important. Publications and conference papers are of key importance here. Although you are unlikely to be offered a journal editorship at an early stage in your career, you may be offered a position as an associate editor, for example, of book reviews. Journals are centrally important to all disciplines and being involved in one is an excellent way to get to know the people who matter, both the established leaders of the discipline and the rising young stars.

Getting involved in conference or workshop organisation is also an excellent way of raising your profile. Such conferences are often run by professional associations and they are always looking for individuals to get involved in their work, as there are a number of chores that have to be undertaken on a voluntary basis and will again get you known in your discipline.

Conclusion

An academic career can be enjoyable and fulfilling. There will also be disappointing and difficult days as in any job. However, considerable satisfaction can be derived from teaching a course that develops students intellectually, from supervising a PhD to successful completion, making a breakthrough in the laboratory or having your articles and books published. An academic career is not the right choice for every research student, but it is still the best and most rewarding choice for many (see Chapter 22 which presents statistics on numbers of people with research degrees securing academic posts).

SOURCES OF SUPPORT

www.bris.ac.uk/cas/postgrads/ A very helpful site for postgraduates provided by the University of Bristol Careers Service with much useful practical advice.

www.chronicle.com/jobs/ *The Chronicle of Higher Education*, equivalent of *The Times Higher Education Supplement* with job vacancies in the US.

www.grad.ac.uk/academia Advice on launching an academic career.

www.jobs.ac.uk This is the main site for academic jobs in the UK.

www.sciencecareers.sciencemag.org/ International site on science careers.

Goldsmith, J., Komlos, J. and Gold, P.S. (2001) *The Chicago Guide to Your Academic Career*. Chicago: Chicago University Press.

Helpful introduction to how the US higher education system works from the perspective of a new entrant to an academic career.

Grant, W. and Sherrington, P. (2006) *Managing Your Academic Career*. Basingstoke: Palgrave Macmillan.

Seeks to provide a comprehensive guide for new entrants to academic life.

Lucas, C.J. and Murry, J.W. Jr (2002) *New Faculty: A Practical Guide for Academic Beginners*. New York: Palgrave.

Written for an American audience, but has wider value.

References

Basnett, S. (2004) 'The first rung' in *How to Get Promoted: A Career Guide for Academics*. London: *The Times Higher Education Supplement*, pp. 8–11.

Blaxter, L., Hughes, C. and Tight, M. (1998) *The Academic Career Handbook*. Buckingham: Open University Press.

Goldsmith, J., Komlos, J. and Gold, P.S. (2001) *The Chicago Guide to Your Academic Career*. Chicago: Chicago University Press.

Grant, W. and Sherrington, P. (2006) *Managing Your Academic Career*. Basingstoke: Palgrave Macmillan.

25 Research outside Academia
Dr Seema Sharma

Introduction

As a research student, you may be passionate about working in a research environment. After all, this is precisely what your training in academia has geared you towards to date. Now, however, you may be wondering if academic research in a university is really the career that you want. At this point in your life you will have gained a number of transferable skills that make you highly suitable for research work. These could include: data analysis; project management; problem-solving; autonomy; computer literacy; written communication; the ability to generate novel research ideas; experience of training undergraduate students; collaborating with other research groups and manual dexterity.

This chapter will focus on the diverse and rewarding research opportunities available in an environment outside academic research in universities. Such an environment will help you to continue to work in research and will also make good use of all the research skills you have developed.

The chapter aims to give you a practical insight into non-academic research environments; the opportunities available to you; how to tailor your job applications; the working conditions and the opportunities for career progression. Case studies are used to demonstrate the experiences of researchers working in the differing sectors. By the end of the chapter, you should have a clear idea of the various employers involved in research outside academia and what non-academic research entails. If you're considering a career path in this area, you should also be able to focus on which of these environments you would be most suited to.

Depending on the sector, the move into non-academic research doesn't necessarily involve a huge shift in mindset or setting. The fundamental basis of your role is still to conduct novel research and the differences in your environment may, in certain cases, be minimal. Take the example of working in the public sector, the basis of your work is still to conduct original research in your chosen discipline. In this sector, your employers are agencies, research institutes and centres funded by the government many of whom collaborate and overlap with local universities. You are required to use approaches to research which are similar to those employed in academia with a view to going on to publish.

Alternatively, the private sector contrasts more significantly to academia. Here the focus is usually on a practical solution to a problem in the form of applied research. One example would be the pharmaceutical industry – here, for example, the development of a drug for therapeutic intervention in a specific disease state would provide the solution for a problem.

Why Might You Decide to Leave Academia but Stay in Research?

After finishing a research degree the traditional academic career path often involves taking on short-term post-doctoral positions of two to three years, with a view to bolstering your publication record and technical experience. If all goes well, you will gain enough publications and knowledge to apply for a permanent lectureship.

As a masters student you may be contemplating moving on to doctoral-level studies or alternatively, moving straight into employment. As a masters-qualified graduate you have focused in depth on a particular research area and you have gained a number of research skills, which are valued by employers in research, although you may have had a lesser degree of autonomy in your research.

There is a natural attrition in the number of posts available from doctoral level to post-doctoral level, and finally to lectureship level in academia. The career opportunities are pyramidal, with relatively large numbers of research studentships at the base of the pyramid and a few lectureship posts available at the top. As a result, competition is high and some researchers refer to the period where they are having to take on a series of short-term contracts prior to their successful application for a lectureship as being in 'post-doc limbo'.

Once you obtain a lectureship or become a research fellow, your research funding is gained by the ongoing submission of grant or fellowship applications for project ideas to the relevant research councils or other funders of research.

This academic career path does not appeal to everyone. If you don't feel strongly motivated about gaining a lectureship but do enjoy research work you may want to consider the options outlined in this chapter. A beneficial approach for a healthy career path is to be aware of all of the options available to you at an early stage and find which one would suit your expectations, personality and skills the most.

The results of the *What do PhDs Do?* survey (UK GRAD, 2004, 2006, 2007) discussed at length in Chapter 22 of this volume, showed that 22% went on to a post-doctoral research position in academia. Research positions outside academia, accounted for 14% of PhD graduate destinations. Amongst other employers, this included the chemical and pharmaceutical industry.

The remaining 64% were working in diverse sectors including health and associated work, marketing, sales, engineering professionals, clinical psychologists and as commercial, and public sector managers to name a few non-research roles. This serves to emphasise that the job opportunities and options for researchers *are* numerous and diverse.

Commercial Research

Arguments for

Researchers who I have met at numerous scientific careers workshops I have organised across Europe and interviewed for this chapter cite several motivating reasons for making the move away from academia into working in research in a commercial environment. One commonly quoted reason is that the positions are permanent rather than on a short-term contractual basis. Researchers state they receive a better salary, typically earning more than their career counterparts at a similar level working in academia, and have more opportunities for promotion. They feel that there are personal benefits of working in a commercial environment, which may include personal healthcare, childcare provision and a private pension. Also, they face fewer funding restrictions on the research that can be carried out.

The research and development process in a commercial setting usually involves working in multidisciplinary groups as part of a team. Indeed, team work and communication with individuals from other disciplines and backgrounds, for example, in the business development area and senior management, is an essential part of a research role.

The individuals who thrive in commercial research feel they are involved in applied research that can be correlated more quickly to an application in society. They find this more fulfilling than blue-sky research. You may of course feel the exact opposite and like the idea of doing more 'blue-sky' research. In that case, moving away from academia may not be the right move for you to make.

PERCEIVED ADVANTAGES OF WORKING IN COMMERCIAL RESEARCH

- Better remuneration
- More personal benefits (including private healthcare, share options and childcare provision)
- Fewer funding restrictions for the research that can be carried out
- Involvement in applied rather than blue-sky research
- Shorter working hours
- Working as part of a team
- More room to be promoted and make career transitions (depending on the size of company)
- Having a permanent position.

An important point to remember is that you will not necessarily be severing all your links with academia when moving into a commercial environment. There has been an active convergence between academia and more commercial research in the past decade. Commercial research employers do collaborate with academic groups, as well as other companies. Your position may, in fact, include the supervision of research students. In a similar vein to academia, conference attendance is often seen as a key way of bringing new ideas on targets and techniques into the company and is often actively encouraged.

Arguments against

Research projects can change rapidly in a commercial environment due to changes in market demand, and team leaders state that a key skill for workers to possess is adaptability. Posts can be permanent, however, a position in commercial research does not always equate to job security as mergers and acquisitions (with associated redundancies) are common place. If a research product fails, for example, a drug in clinical trials, a cut in workforce may be a way to recoup lost profit. Researchers say that the environment is more pressured, in comparison to academia, due to the commercial nature of the process.

Some researchers who work for larger companies state that they do not have as many opportunities as they did in academia to innovate, for example, to run parallel experiments. The research is more focused on the development of products.

Another reservation that researchers cite is less opportunity to publish due to the confidential nature of the work. The publication strategy adopted by a company can vary hugely and working on confidential products does not always preclude researchers from publishing in peer-reviewed journals. Some employers actively encourage it. It is worth researching the publication output for a department prior to taking up a position.

Researchers working in smaller companies, for example, start-ups in the biotech sector, or spin-offs from academic institutes, state that they may feel a degree of job insecurity in their role. These companies are reliant on seed-funding from venture capitalists or so-called business angels and therefore are under time pressure to become profitable. Not all companies will make profit in the given time frame and as a result they can fold which results in the loss of jobs.

PERCEIVED DISADVANTAGES OF WORKING IN COMMERCIAL RESEARCH

- More pressure
- Less chance to innovate
- Less opportunity to publish due to confidential projects
- Mergers and acquisitions means posts are not always secure
- Smaller companies are often relying on venture capitalist money. If they fail to make a profit they can fold.

Research in the Public Sector

Arguments for

Researchers moving into the public sector report that they feel there is little difference in the manner in which they conduct research between the public sector and academia. Research council and charitable trust funded research institutes have an objective of advancing knowledge much akin to universities. However, some researchers working at the institutes reveal they may receive better remuneration than the equivalent in academia, although on average the salary scale is comparable. They may have access to private healthcare, life assurance, help with childcare and with some of the larger research centres, for example, the Wellcome Trust Sanger Research Centre, have onsite facilities like a gym.

Research council institutes are geared to a specific discipline area and this focus means that researchers may have access to better research equipment and facilities than they had in a prior post in academia. They also state that they have a similar degree of flexibility in their post as in universities and are able to innovate with their research.

Institutes are supported through a combination of funding sources including government departments, industry and the EU. They also may have charitable status.

The Biotechnology and Biological Sciences Research Council (BBSRC) states that their sponsored institutes have core grants from the research council. In addition, individual research grants can be applied for in the same manner as in academia. They also cite that they are characterised by having specialist facilities coupled with a clear strategy, which includes cross-disciplinary research, that fit into a clear mission for each respective institute. For more information on the BBSRC-sponsored centres, including the results of an assessment exercise visit www.bbsrc.ac.uk/about/centres/Welcome.html Similar information is available from the other research councils (see the resources at the end of the chapter).

Government agency laboratories in the UK also have access to excellent facilities. They offer good employee benefits, with options for a final salary and stakeholder pensions. Most departments and units offer flexible working hours. Performance-related bonuses are also offered, for example, the Centre for Environment, Fisheries & Aquaculture Science offers its' staff a 9% performance-related bonus in addition to standard pay. Some departments, for example, the Veterinary Laboratory Agency, also have onsite nursery care.

There is an emphasis in government labs to produce their own publications and reports. However, they also submit their research to relevant peer-reviewed journals. The Defence Science and Technology Laboratory (DSTL), for example, has published 90 peer-reviewed articles and papers over the past three years.

PERCEIVED ADVANTAGES OF WORKING IN THE PUBLIC SECTOR

- In some cases more personal benefits (including private healthcare and crèche provisions)
- Access to improved facilities due to targeted research
- Opportunities to innovate
- Similar approach to publishing as in academia.

Arguments against

The public sector research institutes generally employ early-stage researchers on temporary contracts. Government agency laboratories normally take employees on a three-year fixed contract in the first instance. This can then be extended to a full-time position. Since many researchers cite this as a reason for leaving academia, they may have similar reservations about taking up certain public sector positions.

The National Health Service (NHS) in contrast, does offer employees permanent contracts providing they have worked for a period of 12 months.

PERCEIVED DISADVANTAGES OF WORKING IN THE PUBLIC SECTOR

- Employment may be on a short term contractual basis
- A clear promotional path may not be offered
- Salary is comparable to academia but generally lower than the private sector.

An Overview of Non-academic Research Opportunities in the Private Sector

Employers in the private sector include contract research organisations, pharmaceutical industry, biotech companies, physical sciences related industry including energy and defence, engineering firms, companies involved in social and risk assessment, telecommunications, environment, cosmetics, information technology/informatics companies, and food and drink manufacturers. Some of these sectors are explored in more detail below.

For a more comprehensive list of all employment sectors in industry, readers may find the sector summaries published on the *Prospects* website useful (Graduate Prospects Ltd, 2007).

Chemical Industry

The chemical industry in the UK represents one of the largest manufacturing areas employing 214,000 individuals. According to the latest report from the Chemical Industries Association, it has grown five times faster in the last decade than the average for the rest of industry in the UK. This extent of expansion has not been seen in Germany, France and Italy where it is comparable to the rest of industry. Also, the European trend is not mirrored in the US where growth in the area is below average for industry. In the UK there is a growing trend for mergers and acquisitions by foreign, mainly US investors. The range of companies include those manufacturing and developing chemical components for pharmaceutical products (37%), soaps, toiletries and cleaning preparations (12%), organics (10%), plastics, paints, varnishes and ink (8%) amongst others.

Pharmaceutical Industry

The pharmaceutical drug development industry in the UK has grown exponentially over the last quarter of a century to be one of the most profitable in the world. The industry offers research opportunities for scientists in many disciplines, the most obvious being biology and chemistry related, which include: cellular biology; genomics and proteomics; molecular biology; protein biochemistry; assay development; electrophysiology; physiology; medicine; crystallography; toxicology; veterinarian services; analytical chemistry; medicinal and synthetic chemistry to name but a few. There are also opportunities available in other less obvious disciplines which include engineering, mathematics, statistics, bio- and chemo-informatics, IT, hardware and software design.

Qualified researchers in both pharmaceutical and chemical industries can expect to enter with a title of research or senior scientist, forming part of a project team with a starting salary of around £30,000–£35,000 which may, of course, vary between companies. Dr Jim Loftus, Discovery Recruitment Manager at Pfizer states, 'a PhD qualified researcher can expect to start on £30,000 +. This would most likely increase if you started a position after completing a postdoctoral post.' The career pathway from entry level would then take you to project team leader level where you supervise other staff within the team and then on to senior management positions.

Case Study – Biotech sector

Bik Chopra currently works as senior scientist for a small biotech company based in Cambridge, UK. His career path started with a BSc in pharmacology, which was followed by a two-year stint working in the pharmaceutical industry as a research assistant. He says, 'I enjoyed working in an industry environment, however, I felt there was a glass ceiling for the career development of researchers who were not doctorate-qualified.' As a result, he opted to return to study for a PhD at the University of Leicester on 'Molecular Mechanisms Regulating Nociceptor Excitability'.

After having completed his PhD in 2002, Bik accepted a post-doctoral position at Pittsburgh University in the US. The two-year contract enabled him to diversify his range of laboratory techniques and broaden his horizons and experience what he describes as a more 'focused' research environment in the US. Bik subsequently returned to the UK after accepting a post-doctoral position on a one-year contract at the University of York.

Bik made the transition to his current post in Biotech in December 2005. He provides several reasons for his transition. He states: 'it's a permanent position, with better pay and benefits than academia.' He indicates that in his view there are several advantages to his current position over his prior academic positions. 'It's a 9–5 position and you rarely take your work home with you. As a postdoc I was working late into the evening and weekends.' He states that 'this was partly because I felt more solely responsible for my research project, whereas now I feel I am part of a team effort.'

When asked to compare and contrast academia and his current position in biotech, he felt his current position offered: 'Increased structure [compared to academia] with clear deadlines to meet. There is definitely more communication between you and senior management.' Although, in his experience it is in fact academia that offered him more chances to innovate with his research as he states: 'my supervisors in academia often encouraged me to do things outside of my core projects.' He expresses the fact that step-by-step weekly progress reports are not requested by research funding bodies as would be the case in a commercial environment and that this promotes an innovative environment in academia. According to Bik, 'in large biotech companies and the pharmaceutical industry the emphasis is on developing products and patents. Working for a smaller biotech company like I do, there is degree of flexibility – I feel like I have the opportunity to innovate with experiments around 20% of the time.' Bik states that he doesn't believe this approach would be encouraged in larger companies.

When asked who he feels the biotech industry look to recruit he states:

My experience of recruitment in industry is that they are focused on what relevant [laboratory] techniques you have and whether you fit into the criteria outlined for the job. They are looking for someone who is driven and could fit into a corporate environment. This means an individual who is decisive and can communicate at all levels, who can present data and give talks on a regular basis.

Physical Sciences-related Industry

Multinational organisations, like Phillips, employ physical science researchers to work in diverse product development related fields. The products may vary from domestic appliances, lighting, medical devices, specialist scientific instrumentation or electronics.

Energy-related companies are involved in trading gas and oil, specialist fuels, generating electricity and developing sustainable energy resources. There has been a sharp increase in opportunities available in the sustainable energy area in the last few years in response to environmental concerns. The energy industry, for example companies like Shell, employ geologists, geophysicists, production and chemical engineers and those in related research areas.

The telecommunication industry, which includes mobile phone manufacturers like Nokia and Sony Ericsson, cable companies and internet service providers employ electronic engineers and related researchers in product development fields.

There are several companies working in the defence and security area who require electronic, mechanical and structural engineers. An example would be QinetiQ, which employs 13,500 in the UK to develop defence and security solutions for global customers and the UK government.

There are several other opportunities in the physical sciences and the engineering sectors. Please refer to resources at the end of the chapter for further information.

Contract Research Companies/Agencies

Contract Research Organisations (CROs) are companies which offer external clients a range of research services. It is a term often used in relation to pharmaceutical-related areas, for example, clinical trial administration (from pre-clinical through to phase IV). Companies offering pre-clinical and clinical services constitute a large part of the market but CROs encompass a wide range of areas including forensic analysis, information technology, computational analysis, data management, chemical formulation and many more. There has been an increasing trend to outsourcing to contract research organisations and it is favoured by companies for many reasons. Companies may lack the resources and the in-house expertise to carry out certain procedures, for example, clinical trial administration or customised software development. Alternatively, the use of a CRO may allow a company to use its resources elsewhere, reducing the time required to bring a product to the market and gaining a competitive advantage.

Researchers working within the field describe it as a fast-paced, results-oriented environment. The work you do within the company is ultimately a service provided to an external client, which must meet their needs.

Case Study Social risk assessment industry

Ellen Raphael currently works as Head of Programmes for a registered charity, 'Sense about Science'. She has a social science background, having studied for a BA in Sociology & Social Anthropology, followed by an MA in Sociology & Social Research at the University of Kent.

Ellen mentions she thought of continuing her studies with a doctorate but stated 'I wanted experiences of different fields in sociology rather than specialising with a

PhD and being confined to one.' She also did not hold an interest in the teaching element of a career in academia.

Her first non-academic research role was as an Information Officer with a charity, the British Pregnancy Advisory Service. Her research involved women's experiences of early medical abortion, and developing a database. She monitored the media and also developed material for patient care. Raphael mentions 'I really enjoyed the role and I felt passionately about the subject matter. I had been involved in pro-choice as a student.' The post was a temporary position to cover one year's maternity leave. 'The salary was around £19,000.'

Her next post was in Regester Larkin, a risk issues and crisis management company. She mentioned she met someone who worked there (now her current manager) through a mutual network. Her contact worked at the risk assessment centre at the company and had got in touch with her regarding a vacancy. As she states 'it was a really positive experience. I was really interested in the issues and my main research was putting together risk analyses for key issues in the science and technology fields.' She also mentioned her salary was 'considerably' better than in the charity sector. However, this was not her motivation for the move, since she was 'genuinely interested in the issues – like assessing the safety of mobile phone masts'. Her final move has bought her back to the charity sector.

When asked whether there have been any advantages to pursuing a career in research outside academia, Ellen states, 'I think I've had a lot more flexibility and researched a lot of different areas. The applied nature of what I am doing makes it more exciting and cutting edge, with direct relevance to the real world.' In her opinion there have been few obstacles to getting into the commercial sector with her sociology research background, since she thinks 'it is open to anyone with a real interest. There are no barriers really. Even if you did do a PhD there would also be a lot of scope.'

Skills and Recruitment

In the private sector, recruitment is more discipline specific for doctorate-qualified candidates than at masters or undergraduate level and there are therefore relatively fewer positions. The main asset and sought-after qualities are the experience and technical expertise you gained during your research degree. Industry has to respond to how its products fare in final tests and also respond to novel research findings. The relative success or failure of current products in the latter stages of the development process can also result in projects going through either a radical revamp or abandoned entirely. Market demand for products can also alter. Developments in research in the field may also require changes in the course of projects and reassignment of staff to new ones. Adaptability, therefore, is key.

Some of the key skills required to succeed in the private sector are as follows:

- Technical expertise you gained as a postgraduate
- A demonstration of flexibility is seen as a key asset for employees to possess. One way to demonstrate this is having changed disciplines or being involved in interdisciplinary projects beforehand
- Any prior industry or non-academic research or work experience is also valued. Some undergraduate university degrees actually include a year in industry, which can serve as excellent experience
- Any private sector funding you have received as a researcher will also be valued
- Your ability to work as part of a team, give presentations and communicate with peers at all levels is essential. Including an example of communication skills in your application and CV will serve to emphasise this point.

The recruitment process varies between employers but the initial screen is your CV. Ensure that if possible, this is a maximum of two pages long and clearly structured to include examples of the skills listed above. If necessary leave your referees off the end of the CV and state they are available upon request to save space.

Employers may include an initial screening interview over the phone and personality test sent to you in an electronic format. Some companies invite you to attend dinner with future colleagues prior to the interview day, which helps ascertain how you interact with peers. It is important to note that this is part of the recruitment process and should be treated accordingly.

The interview itself normally includes a technical aspect where applicants are asked about their scientific expertise and are required to give a presentation on their current postgraduate research. A well-structured and well-prepared presentation will demonstrate your communication skills effectively to the employer. Pre-empting any questions which may arise from your research and preparing answers and discussions will also stand you in good stead. Standard aptitude tests may be included as part of the process where candidates are assessed under timed conditions. Many companies also include an interview with a human resources manager and you can also expect to receive a tour of the facilities.

Vacancies are usually posted on the company website, (please see the links at the end of the chapter). The job listings in scientific journals also include vacancies in the sector. There are a number of industry-specific recruitment agencies. For further information please refer to the list of job sites and other sources of support at the end of the chapter.

For CROs, the picture is slightly different. They often advertise vacancies on their own websites in dedicated careers sections. They also actively encourage uploading speculative CVs to match to any vacancies that may arise within the company. Whilst speculative applications may be considered an ineffective way of targeting yourself to the right job when applying for jobs in other research sectors, the CRO sector lends itself to this approach. Uploaded CVs are matched by internal recruiters to vacancies. CROs also advertise in job sections in science journals both in print and on-line.

An Overview of Non-academic Research Opportunities in the Public Sector

Research in the public sector is carried out in a wide range of establishments that include government departments and agencies, the National Health Service (NHS), and independent research institutes which are funded by charitable trusts and the research councils.

The research councils are in effect independent non-departmental public bodies, financed by the government science budget. There are seven research councils:

1 Arts and Humanities Research Council (AHRC)
2 Engineering and Physical Sciences Research Council (EPSRC)
3 Biotechnology and Biological Sciences Research Council (BBSRC)
4 Economic and Social Research Council (ESRC)
5 Medical Research Council (MRC)
6 Natural Environment Research Council (NERC)
7 Science and Technology Facilities Council (SciTech) which was formed on 1 April 2007 by the merger of what was formerly known as the Particle Physics and Astronomy Research Council (PPARC) and the Council for the Central Laboratory of the Research Councils (CCLRC).

In addition to the research councils, there are specific charitable trusts which run their own research institutes. The Wellcome Trust is an example of such an organisation which runs its own independent medical research units, for example, the Wellcome Trust Sanger Institute.

The research institutes often have close collaborations with, or in some cases are housed within local universities. As a result there is generally a great deal of overlap and many researchers state that they feel that there is no major difference between the two environments.

There are several non-departmental government laboratories in the UK who employ researchers from diverse research backgrounds. These include the Central Science Laboratory (CSL), the Centre for Environment, Fisheries and Aquaculture Science (CEFAS), the Defence Science and Technology Laboratory (DSTL), the Health and Safety Laboratory (HSL), the Health Protection Agency (HPA) and the Veterinary Laboratories Agency (VLA). They all employ researchers with relevant scientific backgrounds from graduate level upwards.

From a more international perspective, the World Health Organisation (WHO), an agency of the United Nations (UN), also recruits researchers in areas related to international public health. The European headquarters of the WHO is in Copenhagen in Denmark. For more information on the research council institutes, government laboratories and the WHO visit their respective websites which are included in the public sector resources listed under 'Sources of support' at the end of the chapter.

Case Study NHS laboratory

Jo is currently employed as a non-clinical lecturer and academic fellow at City hospital in the West Midlands. Her employer is the National Health Service (NHS) and she works to run a clinical trials unit and carry out related research.

She completed a degree in Psychology at the University of Liverpool, followed by a PhD researching effects of depression and anxiety on patients following a heart attack. When asked why she chose to apply for her current role, she mentioned, 'when I was doing my PhD I collected data from patients – I liked the idea of doing hands-on clinical work. I didn't really want to do too much lecturing and the NHS was an ideal environment for the balance I wanted.'

She discussed that she viewed the position differently to academia, as she was not required to teach undergraduates and had no pastoral duties or lecturing commitments. Jo currently has a permanent contract. She mentioned, 'I am awarded a permanent position after working for a twelve-month period for the NHS and therefore I have not encountered the same problems as my counterparts in academia.'

Jo works in a relatively small department within the hospital; she says that she would most likely have access to better resources if she worked at a university-affiliated hospital. However, she states, 'we have no issues with funding and I think the salary may be better than the academic equivalent.'

Case Study Research council institutes

Graham Mckenzie currently works as Head of Translational Research at the MRC-funded Hutchison unit, based in Cambridge in the UK. Graham completed a doctorate in immunology in 1998, which involved using transgenic models to research cytokine pathways implicated in asthma and allergy. He then considered travelling to the US for a post-doctoral position. Graham said, 'Going to the US after your PhD was a recognised career path – the quality of the labs was the main appeal.' However, he chose to stay in the UK for personal reasons and applied for a post as research scientist at Novartis, a pharmaceutical company. He was drawn to the position as he viewed the research as cutting edge. He stated 'I was going to be working on *Xenopus* transplantation – it was a novel and exciting project.'

After two years he moved briefly to another pharmaceutical company but chose to leave, alongside his then manager, who was starting up his own biotech company. He started work as a lab scientist and progressed to a role as Head of Molecular Immunology. After five years, the company down-sized radically following a set back in product development.

Graham subsequently moved to another biotech company to work as a senior scientist. In hindsight he noted that there is a degree of uncertainty in working for start-up firms.

His current role at the Cambridge-based MRC unit was of particular appeal, due to 'the quality of the research underway.' When asked whether he viewed his current role in the public sector as different to work in academia, Graham stated he viewed himself as an academic scientist. He feels there is an extensive overlap between his current role and an academic position. In fact, he pointed out that he sees little, if any distinction between the two: 'I actually hold a parallel position at the University of Cambridge as part of my role at the MRC and we have close collaborations.' He viewed his recruitment process as comparable to academia and felt the remuneration was in line with an academic post.

Skills and Recruitment

The recruitment process and the skills sought by the public sector are similar, and in some cases, for example, in research council funded institutes, identical to academia. Your technical expertise, experience and publication record to date serve as your main assets in the recruitment process.

Your curriculum vitae will be used as a primary recruitment screen for public sector employers. Amongst other things, it should include your education to date, in reverse chronological order, relevant techniques and publications. In contrast to the private sector, where a curriculum vitae of a maximum of two pages is recommended, public sector applications can be extended.

Aim to include the most relevant information on the first page. For example if you have completed a PhD, the title of the thesis and institute should be included. The main subject areas can then be bulleted underneath. Using reverse chronological order for your education ensures the most recent and relevant qualification is included first. This should be followed by any work experience gained to date, again with the most relevant first. Also consider including subheadings for techniques, awards, publications (which should be formatted like a bibliography and include pending publications), teaching experience, additional skills and referees. Always include a cover letter to explain your interest in the employer, your rationale for applying for the job and your suitability to the role. Try to include any additional information which may not have been covered in your CV. The letter should be limited to a single side of A4 paper.

The second part of the recruitment process in the public sector is an interview. Most candidates are expected to give a short presentation of their former research so ensure that this is well prepared. Government jobs may also include an aptitude test.

Key Skills in the Public Sector are as follows:

- Relevant technical expertise you gained during your postgraduate studies
- Ability to plan research projects

- Communication, including written publications to date
- Ability to work as part of a research team.

Public sector bodies, charitable trusts and government labs advertise the current posts they have on their individual websites and listings for these are cited at the end of the chapter. Jobsites which cover academic job listings also include public sector work in the UK, an example of this would be www.jobs.ac.uk.

Conclusion

This chapter has provided an overview of the opportunities for researchers considering working outside academia. The real-life case studies demonstrate that there is no hard and fast rule to forging your career path. Moving out of academia is not a one-way street and researchers may return into roles in universities at a later stage. The skill set you have acquired is the most valued asset by your employers.

A comprehensive list of all the possible roles is beyond the scope of a single chapter and there are many opportunities above and beyond those listed here. Individuals who make successful career transitions have a proactive approach to job-seeking. They have usually gained some experience or shown a solid interest in the field that they are making a transition into. When making their application they have presented the relevant transferable skills required clearly to an employer. It is important to remember that these skills can be drawn upon from your extracurricular activities by reframing what you have done, if you have no direct employment experience. For example, if the job requires negotiation skills, you could use the example of having gained commercial sponsorship for an event you were organising or receiving discounted prices for laboratory equipment. Finally, successful candidates present a strong rationale for choosing to apply for a position to the employer.

An additional factor in finding employment is using your existing networks of friends and colleagues. Any contact you can make with potential employers using networks or by attending professional society events, conferences, meetings and job fairs may provide you with insights into upcoming recruitment. Communicating directly with employers can help you gain a competitive edge over those seeking employment by answering advertisements. This approach can also help you gain valuable information about the working environment and whether it would suit you.

It may be beneficial to arrange a short informational phone interview with a current employee at a company to help gain an indication of what it is like to work there. A useful approach is to speak to someone who is two years ahead of you in their career path. They can then still relate to your position, and also comment on the progress they have made. They may also offer you a unique insight into the working environment. It does not have to be lengthy, in fact if prepared with a series of succinct questions, requesting to speak to an employee for five to fifteen minutes can help you gain an overview of a sector.

An important factor for career well-being is to ensure that your work environment is a suitable match for your skills, expectations and lifestyle. This can be achieved by adopting a proactive approach to ensure you research several careers and potential employers thoroughly. One of the first steps is to become aware of your skills and specific strengths. If you are finding this hard, use feedback from trusted colleagues and friends or even personality tests, and have a look at Chapter 23 in this volume. In addition to this, listing which of your skills you most like using may be helpful. Not all points you list as skills are things you necessarily enjoy. For example, you may be excellent at data analysis but you may find it tedious to exercise this skill. Most individuals find their work more fulfilling if they are using their 'favourite' skills.

It is essential to establish what working conditions would most suit your personality and lifestyle. You may, for example, require flexible working hours, onsite childcare, or be willing to offset a high salary against long working hours – aim for an employer who would meet your needs and matches your ethos best.

Finally, awareness of the many options available to you as a researcher is essential for helping you make an informed decision for your career. There are several resources available to you, some of which are listed at the end of this chapter. The resources and this chapter serve to highlight that, contrary to what you may have been told to date, the opportunities in research outside academia are numerous and the transition to a non-academic role can be a rewarding one.

SOURCES OF SUPPORT

Public Sector

AHRC www.ahrc.ac.uk/about/ahrc_structure.asp
BBSRC www.bbsrc.ac.uk
Cancer Research UK www.cancerresearchuk.org/
EMBL European Molecular Biology Laboratory www.embl-heidelberg.de/
ESRC www.esrc.ac.uk

Government Laboratories

Central Science Laboratory www.csl.gov.uk/
Defence Science and Technology Laboratory (MoD) www.dstl.gov.uk/careers/index.php
Environment Agency (EA) www.environment-agency.gov.uk
Centre for Environment, Fisheries & Aquaculture Science (Cefas) www.cefas.co.uk/
The Forensic Science Service www.forensic.gov.uk/forensic_t/inside/career/opp_1.htm
Met Office www.metoffice.com
National Institute for Biological Standards and Control (NIBSC) www.nibsc.ac.uk/

NHS Health Protection Agency www.hpa.org.uk/careers/
The Health and Safety Laboratory (HSL) www.hsl.gov.uk/about-us/index.htm
Veterinary Laboratories Agency (VLA) www.defra.gov.uk/corporate/vla/
MRC www.mrc.ac.uk/index.htm
NERC www.nerc.ac.uk
SciTech www.scitech.ac.uk/
Wellcome Trust www.wellcome.ac.uk/
World Health Organisation www.who.int/employment/vacancies/en/
European World Health Organisation HQ www.euro.who.int/

Private Sector

Chemical Industry

Chemical Industries Association www.cia.org.uk
Eastman Chemical Company http://www.eastman.com/Company/
Huntsman http://huntsman.com/
ICI http://www.ici.com/

Contract Research Organisations

Charles River Laboratories http://www.criver.com/about_charles_river/careers/
Covance http://www.covance.com/
IT Contract Research Job listings www.cwjobs.co.uk/
LGC Forensics http://www.lgc.co.uk/vacancies.asp
Paraxel International http://www.paraxel.com/
Quintiles Transnational Corp. http://www.qtrn.com/Careers/Fin

Crisis Management

Regester Larkin www.regesterlarkin.com/

Defence

European Aeronautics, Defence & Space Agency www.eads.com/1024/en/career/
    career.html
QinetiQ www.qinetiq.com/home/careers.html

Engineering and Construction

Aker Kvaerner Careers www.akerkvaerner.com/Internet/CareerOld/default.htm
Alstom Careers & Vacancies www.alstom.com/home/Careers/JOBS/
British Nuclear Group www.britishnucleargroup.com/careers.php?pageID=25
Nokia Careers & Vacancies www.nokia.com/A4126302
Schlumberger www.slb.com/content/careers/index.asp?entry=careers&

Pharmaceutical Industry

Association of British Pharmaceutical Industry (includes job listing from all UK
    employers) www.abpi.org.uk

Astra Zeneca Careers & Vacancies www.astrazeneca.com/article/11238.aspx
Eli Lilly Careers &Vacancies www.lilly.co.uk/Nitro/newTemplates/general/Content_
    IT_LBCT.jsp?page=1155
GSK Careers & Vacancies www.gsk.com/careers/uk_careers.htm
Novartis Careers & Vacancies www.novartis.co.uk/careers/index.shtml
Pfizer Careers & Vacancies www.pfizer.co.uk/template4.asp?pageid=3
Roche Careers & Vacancies www.roche.com/home/careers.htm

Sources of Pharmaceutical Industry – Vacancies and Jobs

www.pharmiweb.com/
www.inpharm.com/

Physical Sciences and Related Areas

British Petroleum (BP) www.bp.com/careers
Phillips Careers & Vacancies www.philips.com/about/careers/index.html
Shell Group www.shell.com

Recruitment for Oil and Gas industry

www.oilcareers.com/worldwide/

Other Sources of Support

www.jobs.ac.uk Academic jobs including at research council institutes
www.naturejobs.com Career advice and jobs from *Nature*
www.newscientist.co.uk Career advice and jobs from *New Scientist*
www.physicsweb.org/jobs Physics-related jobs
www.sciencecareers.org Career development advice and jobs from *Science* magazine

References

Graduate Prospects Ltd (2007) *Explore Job Sectors* www.prospects.ac.uk/cms/ShowPage/
    Home_page/Explore_job_sectors/p!ebfklk (accessed 5 October 2007)
The UK GRAD Programme (2004, 2006, 2007). *What Do PhDs Do?* Available on-line
    at: www.grad.ac.uk/wdpd/ (accessed 5 October 2007)

Further Reading

Bolles, R.N. (ed.) (2000) *What Colour Is Your Parachute?* Berkeley, Ten Speed Press.
Rosen, S. and Paul, C. (1997) *Career Renewal for Technical Professionals.* San Diego,
    Academic Press.

26 Leaving Academia and Research
Sarah Musson

Introduction

This chapter is aimed at research students considering a career outside academia and research. The chapter is divided into five sections:

1 Some reasons people leave academia and research
2 Approaches to choosing an appropriate career
3 Guidance on where to get information about careers
4 Advice on successful applications
5 Sources of support.

Deciding what you want to do in your career can be complex. No one exercise or idea discussed here will tell you what the answer is for you, but each will contribute to a picture which will help you come to a decision.

Some Reasons People Leave Academia and Research

There are many reasons that people choose to leave academia after a research degree:

- The research degree means they can return to their previous career with improved prospects
- They have discovered that they just don't enjoy day-to-day research
- They have identified the parts of the role they enjoy most and decide to seek a job where they focus on those parts
- They thought they were going to 'make a difference' but became aware that this was unrealistic
- They want to stay in a particular location because their friend(s)/house/ partner is there (researchers often need mobility to be successful in academia)

- Job security – many researchers are concerned about the insecurity of short-term funding (of course there are no guarantees against redundancy in a job outside academia)
- They don't think they're good enough. This can be the result of some very good researchers inappropriately comparing themselves with their supervisor who is one of the best in the world. It is advisable to check your opinion with others.

These are all personal points of view that will depend on your preferences, skills and lifestyle. In order to make a wise decision about your future you need to understand yourself. What do you like? What are you good at? You may reply by saying 'But that's just it, I don't know!' the next section titled 'Approaches to choosing an appropriate career' will help you understand yourself better.

Before you take your next step, be sure you know what you are leaving behind. If you are leaving because of something you haven't liked, are you sure it applies to other research groups/departments/institutions? Might there be a way of continuing in academia and avoiding the part you don't like? To check, speak to colleagues, peers, senior staff and people in research outside academia to compare experiences.

Case Study George

After doing two degrees in psychology and working as a research assistant for two years I decided to leave academia. I was fed up with short-term contracts, and the last university position I held was stressful and unproductive in terms of publications. Work was making me feel unhappy and unwell: I decided that I had to leave, even with no job to go to. I knew I wanted to work in the voluntary sector as a researcher. I scoured the job section of the local newspaper and also searched the *Guardian* job site on the web. I found a permanent position of Research Officer in a cancer charity specialising in complementary therapies for cancer. I met a very helpful academic who gave me background information about the new research arena I was entering which helped me get the job and haven't looked back! I've used my research skills to great effect, learning and developing my knowledge base of complementary therapies for cancer, expert literature search techniques and also taking part in the wider activities of the charity. My only regret is that I didn't leave the university sooner than I did! My advice to you is to recognise your impressive set of skills and know that work outside academia can be stimulating, rewarding and exciting.

Approaches to Choosing an Appropriate Career

Some people start their job search by looking in newspapers and journals as indicated in the case study above. However if you find yourself dispirited by the lack of jobs which interest you there is still another way to get more leads. This approach involves understanding yourself, generating career ideas that suit you and then doing research to find opportunities. You need to understand the following:

- Your skills
- Your values
- Your interests and motivators
- Your preferred work/life balance.

This section guides you through this analysis by giving you ways to explore your life so far. Your past, for example, contains a wealth of information which can help you navigate the future.

Skills

Re-visit Chapters 14 and 23 of this volume to assess your transferable skills. You may also find the skills guide on the UK GRAD website helpful: www. grad.ac.uk/evaluateskills

Remember to ask yourself which skills you want to use as well as those skills you are good at; just because you are good at something doesn't mean you necessarily need to keep doing it.

Your Values

EXERCISE 1 – VALUES AND PRIORITIES

Recognising the values by which you live your life will help you to choose a role and an organisation in which you will feel comfortable. If you get this right you will be able to go to work each day and be yourself, rather than hiding the 'real you' or trying to fit in with a culture that clashes with your values.

Table 26.1 lists a number of work and non-work values, needs and priorities. Think about how important each value is to you. Rate each one using the scale shown at the foot of the table.

TABLE 26.1   Work and non-work values and priorities

	Value category (See key)	Your rating 1–7 (See below)
I To have the company of other people	SO	
2 To belong to a group	SO	
3 To be involved actively in family life	SO	
4 To be sought out for advice	SO	
5 To do something useful for society	ALT	
6 To enjoy assisting others, with or without reward	ALT	

TABLE 26.1 Continued

	Value category (See key)	Your rating 1–7 (See below)
7 To make a great deal of money for myself and others	EC	
8 To be free of concern over my economic needs	SEC	
9 To have security of employment	SEC	
10 To accomplish important things	ACH	
11 To take risks	ACH	
12 To have considerable responsibility	ACH	
13 To use skill and judgement	ACH	
14 To develop existing skills	ACH	
15 To have competition	ACH	
16 To have considerable authority or power	P	
17 To be well known	P	
18 To lead other people	P	
19 To influence the thoughts and actions of others	P	
20 To be recognised as an expert	P	
21 To seek knowledge	L	
22 To learn new skills	L	
23 To have change and variety of people	V	
24 To have change and variety of activity	V	
25 To have change and variety of scene	V	
26 To have a great deal of discretion	IND	
27 To be my own boss	IND	
28 To work alone	IND	
29 To work at my own pace	IND	
30 To develop and create new ideas	C	
31 To develop and create new devices	C	
32 To develop artistic creations	C	
33 To live simply, away from crowds and sophistication	LS	
34 To live the 'good life': theatres, restaurants…	LS	
35 To be busy most of the time	LS	
36 To be free of pressures and expectations	LS	

1 of no importance
2 of very little importance
3 of little importance
4 of some importance
5 of considerable importance
6 of a great deal of importance
7 of the utmost importance

Category Key

SO	Social: enjoying the company of other people
ALT	Altruistic; helping others, being involved with good causes
EC	Economic; earning a lot of money, emphasising material wealth
SE	Security: having a secure job
ACH	Achievement: meeting challenges successfully
P	Power: having control and influence over others
L	Learning; seeking knowledge, acquiring new skills
V	Variety; having a change of people, activity
IND	Independence; doing things your own way, being your own boss
C	Creativity; developing new ideas, products, artistic creations
LS	Lifestyle; leading an active, quiet or sophisticated life

Source: © Career Counselling Services.

Take a separate sheet of paper and list those values by which you have scored 7 points. Then list those you have scored 6 points and so on.

- Are your main values where you would have expected them to be?
- Are you currently meeting your most important values at work?
- If these are not being met at work, are you finding an outlet for your values in your leisure, home or community life?

This exercise has been reproduced with the kind permission of Robert Nathan of Career Counselling Services (Nathan and Hill, 2005).

Your Interests and Motivators

Matching a career to your interests and things that motivate you will ensure that you are enthusiastic about your work.

EXERCISE 2 – ENJOYABLE EVENTS

Think back over your life and pick out the events that you have really enjoyed. These can be from any aspect of your life and could be as diverse as getting your degree, climbing a mountain, organising a birthday party or learning to play the trumpet. Write each one down.

- What was it about each of these events that you loved? Write this down next to each event.
- When you have finished look over them all. Are there any themes?

EXAMPLE

Duke of Edinburgh Gold award

Team work – really helping to pull each other through
Realising I had something to offer others
Pushing myself physically, mentally, emotionally
Discovering my stamina
Sense of achievement – really need to see results to be satisfied
Variety – physical, social, environmental

Work/Life Balance

EXERCISE 3 – MY WORLD AS IT IS NOW

- Take a piece of flipchart paper and turn it on its side.
- Using coloured pens draw a picture or diagram, no words allowed, of your world as it is now. This does not have to be beautifully drawn – you can use stick people and symbols.
- What do you notice when you look at it?
- What is striking about it?
- What feels most important to you about it – what do you most want to keep?
- What do you most want to change?

EXERCISE 4 – MY WORLD AS I WOULD LIKE IT TO BE

- Repeat the exercise but this time think 5 years into the future, to allow enough time for your dreams to come to fruition.
- What do you notice when you look at it?
- What is striking about it?
- What is different to your world as it is now?
- What feels most important to you about it – what do you most want to achieve?
- What are the first steps to making this dream reality?
- You may wish to talk this through with someone you trust: a partner, close friend or colleague.

Summarise your findings

By now you should have built up quite a dossier of information on yourself. Stop and construct a summary.

- Note down the key words that have appeared.
- What patterns do you notice?
- What are the elements that you really want to have in a new job?

Your summary may look something like this:

Characteristics	Key descriptors
Key skills	Creative, using hands, producing tangible results
	Attention to detail
Main values	Independence – would like to be my own boss
	Creativity – again!
	Lifestyle – countryside

Interests and motivators	Aesthetic objects – surrounding myself with beauty
	I love learning new skills
	Much happier when I am working alone
	All my happiest times have involved artistic work of some kind
	When I have been happiest in academia is when I have been
	designing projects – it is still the creative element coming out
Work/life balance	Two parts of life blending together, maybe working from home
	Really want to be away from the city
	Want to have a family
	Finances might be difficult but it's not the most important thing

Case Study Laura

At the end of my PhD I chose to leave academia and move into industry. This decision was based on a number of factors, the most important being a desire to leave research and move into an area which I perceived to have a greater impact on society. My PhD research was based on model systems which were relevant to current industrial processes but the results were not directly applicable. The idea of working on, and improving, existing products and processes really appealed to me, especially in a fast moving customer-focused environment. I was also swayed by the prospect of a better salary package and the greater flexibility industry offered in terms of my future career. I have no regrets about the decision to leave academia. When I first moved into industry my job as a development chemist gave me a breadth of experience from small-scale lab work to manufacture on a plant scale, plus lots of customer contact. After five years in a technical role I was ready for another challenge and moved internally within the company to a position as market analyst, looking at the use of precious metals throughout the world. My advice is to find out as much as you can about the job or post you have applied for by asking questions before or during the interview. Be realistic about what the job involves and what level you will enter at. Having a PhD does not guarantee you the highest-level jobs and many new starters find that the work can, at times, be more routine than they had envisaged. Cultural differences between industry and academia are also worth bearing in mind. I have found industry faster and more structured. Finally, as a customer- (and ultimately profit-) driven business, there can be less freedom over the direction your work takes than you may have experienced in academia.

Generating Job Ideas

Having compiled your summary, ask a friend to help you brainstorm some ideas.

- Carefully read over the results of the exercises and the summary
- Make sure your friend understands all that you have written

- Take a piece of flipchart paper and a pen
- Give yourself 10 minutes in which both of you call out as many different jobs as you can think of
- Don't edit them. Write down everything each of you says
- Come up with silly suggestions as well as sensible ones
- At the end of the 10 minutes, circle the three ideas that interest you most.

This gives you a starting point for your research. Find out more about each of three you have circled.

You may well not choose to follow one of these three in the end, but in the course of your research they will lead you to further ideas.

This is one of many ways of generating ideas. Alternatively you can ask friends, family and colleagues what they think you would be good at or you can find out what other people from your lab have gone on to do. The next section explains how you can find out more about each idea.

Guidance on Where to Get Information about Careers

Imagine you are interested in finding out more about being a patent attorney. You will need to find out the following:

QUESTIONS TO CONSIDER

- What are the entry requirements?
- What is a typical patent attorney day like?
- Who are the potential employers?
- What could you be paid?
- Will your PhD improve your chances or your salary?
- Where are jobs advertised and are direct applications without an advert possible?
- Does this career match well against your summary of who you are?

You will probably have more questions you can add to this list. There are several sources of information for your research.

Books and the Internet

Use the information centre of your careers service or public libraries in your area. They will have books on how to make a career choice as well as books about potential careers together with more information on how to get into them. See the suggestions at the end of the chapter for starting points with books and the internet.

People

People are one of the most useful and most overlooked sources of information. The information they can give you may be different to that in books or websites:

- Real life rather than theoretical
- Up to date
- Subjective because it comes from one person's experience
- Can lead to more contacts.

There is a list of suggested questions for information interviews on the grad website at www.grad.ac.uk/networking

Case Study Alison

Alison was considering being a chiropractor. She didn't yet know much about the career so she phoned a chiropractor who agreed to meet her. They spent several hours together with Alison finding out what the training was like, what the pros and cons of the job were, what the pay was like, what kind of person you needed to be to love it, where the growth areas are. The chiropractor put Alison in touch with three of her colleagues who practised in different ways. Alison got up-to-date information from a real chiropractor, saw the work environment, heard the enthusiasm with which one person works and was put in touch with more people.

When you are seeking advice approach as many people as you can. Don't ask one person and follow their advice blindly. If you don't know anyone who works in the field you are exploring, ask everyone you know in order to get more information and eventually find the right person.

EXERCISE – MINDMAP

Take a blank sheet of paper and start to map out all the people that you know. You might want to make it into a mindmap as shown in Figure 26.1 or if you prefer, lists as shown in Table 26.2.

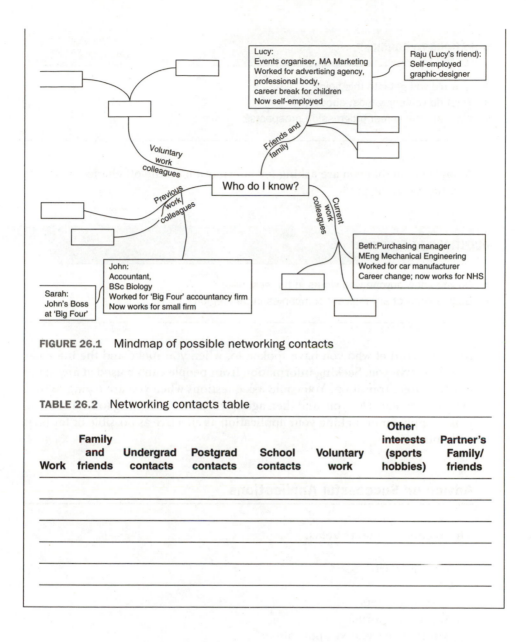

FIGURE 26.1   Mindmap of possible networking contacts

TABLE 26.2   Networking contacts table

Work	Family and friends	Undergrad contacts	Postgrad contacts	School contacts	Voluntary work	Other interests (sports hobbies)	Partner's Family/ friends

Some of these people might be obvious choices to ask for the information that you are looking for. Others might seem at first sight as if they would be no use. Try them, you never know who they met last week, what article they have just read, a programme they heard or saw. Once you have your paper full of names, work out the right questions to ask different categories of people. Someone with specialist knowledge might be asked:

QUESTIONS TO CONSIDER

- How did you get into this field?
- What do you enjoy most about it?
- What are the career progression prospects?

A 'lay' person that you are asking for information on the off chance that they may be able to help:

QUESTIONS TO CONSIDER

- Do you know anyone who works in the sector?
- Do you know of any relevant companies in this region?

Keep a record of who you have spoken to, when you spoke and the information they gave you. Seeking information from people can be used at any stage in your career transition. You could ask questions when you are trying to find out if this career is for you, and then again when you are trying to find specific jobs to apply for or making your application as effective as possible or for help with interviews.

Advice on Successful Applications

This section covers six areas:

1 Your mindset
2 CVs
3 Covering letters
4 Application forms
5 Direct or speculative applications
6 Interviews.

Your Mindset

One way of thinking about the process of applying for a job is to think of yourself as a product that you are selling to a buyer. They are going to part with money to buy your time, skills, experience, knowledge and attitude (salary, pension, space and equipment costs, and training). They need to be told why you are worth that money. You need to work out the following:

There is no one absolute, 'true' you. There can never be one CV that is an authoritative statement that captures the essence of you. You have different facets, skills, approaches and styles that you will draw on in different situations. For every job you apply for, you will want to subtly change your 'advert' to appeal to this buyer. See CV section below.

What Are They Looking for?

If you are responding to an advert you have seen, make a note of all the requirements that have been mentioned both in the advert and in the application pack. Highlight key words and phrases. If you are making a speculative application, you will need to glean this information through your contacts, your web searches etc.

How Do You Fit Their Needs and Wants?

You may find Table 26.3 reproduced from the UK GRAD website helpful as a way of recording your skills against the needs of the employer.

TABLE 26.3   Employer needs and evidence

Employer needs	My evidence
Excellent academic record	Research degree, undergraduate prizes
Strong technical skills	Experience with relevant equipment
Communication skills	Conferences, demonstrating
Initiative	Finding funding to attend conference
Leadership	Postgraduate rep and president of student society
Good command of English	Written skills: articles and publications
	Oral skills: presentations, teaching, spoken at conferences
Other languages	No evidence
Commercial awareness	Attendance at GRADschool, membership of Student Industrial Society, part-time work

The Right Pitch

Look back at Chapter 23. Make sure you are aware of how to sell the skills you have in a language that suits the employer, rather than using academic language. Make sure you are showing them that side of your skills set which they want to see.

CVs

A CV is a written summary of your career. It is often used as a way of choosing which applicants to invite to interview.

Content

- Contact details such as address
- Employment history
- Education
- Interests where they show skills or motivators that fit with the job.

Format

A CV may get a few seconds of an employer's time on first reading. Doing the following would enhance your presentation and thus gain better attention from your prospective employer.

- Put the most important information at the top of the CV. Use the first half page to sell your key points
- Limit it to two sides of A4
- Ideally use 12-point font
- Match the font to suit the culture of the organisation – a modern font for a modern company
- Clearly signpost different sections, to help the reader navigate around it
- Use a consistent style for your sub-headings.

Seek Feedback

Once you have a document you are fairly happy with, seek feedback. All sorts of people could be useful here, especially anyone who is used to the following:

- A person who is used to recruiting staff and reading CVs
- A person who is within the industry you are aiming for
- Careers advisers or consultants who have seen lots of CVs.

For example CVs see: www.grad.ac.uk/cvs

Covering Letters

You need to send a letter with your CV. This should cover the following, in one side of A4:

KEY POINTS

- What you are applying for
- Why you are interested in the role
- Why you are interested in the organisation
- Why you will be suited to the role.

You will want to refer to aspects of your CV in order to support your claims. However, do not repeat sections of your CV word for word. An employer might have concerns about why you are leaving academia so give your reasons for leaving, ensuring that they are positive, with an explanation of how that background fits this new direction.

Application Forms

Many large organisations use application forms as a way of standardising the information they receive. You will have less control over the way you present yourself because of the prescribed order and questions they require you to answer. Many forms use one main question such as 'describe how your skills and experience suit you to this job'. Sell the transferable skills you have identified and give them context by using examples of your experience to demonstrate why you suit this career. You may wish to use sub-headings and pick out key skills in bold in order to make this long section easy to follow.

Direct or Speculative Applications

Many positions are found by applying directly to an organisation. If it is possible to get a new employee without the considerable cost and time of advertising, short-listing and selecting then many companies will do so. Use the resources listed in the previous section to help you research opportunities. Key points to remember in making direct or speculative applications are:

- Avoid sending identical letters and CVs to lots of organisations, rather send a small number of targeted applications.
- Research the organisation – what developments are under way that will need your skills?

- Explain what you have to offer them before you tell them what you are seeking.

Interviews

Congratulations! If you are at interview stage your CV or application form has worked. You have got the employer interested, and you may be one of a very small group of people to get through to this stage. There is plenty of preparation that you can do which will put you in a strong position for your interview.

- Research the organisation – what are their latest projects? Who are their competitors? Use the internet and read the relevant sections of appropriate newspapers and journals.
- Research the role – why is this role vacant? Is it new and if so why? Understand what they really want you to do. You can find this out by using the contacts you have found or by phoning the organisation directly.
- What questions do you have left unanswered that you might ask in the interview?

Anticipate questions by putting yourself into the employer's shoes. Imagine you have to recruit for this role:

QUESTIONS TO CONSIDER

- What would you be looking for?
- How would you test whether the applicant had what you were looking for?
- What questions would you ask?

Prepare by focusing on you:

QUESTIONS TO CONSIDER

- What is unique about you? What sets you apart from other potential candidates?
- What do you really have to offer?
- Be very clear on your key strengths and skills and the evidence that you have to demonstrate them.
- What 3 key points do you need to convey by the end of the interview?
- What questions are you most dreading being asked? Prepare answers to them

---

Practicalities:

QUESTIONS TO CONSIDER

- How are you going to get to the interview?
- What are you going to wear?

Conclusion

Choosing a career can be both exciting and daunting. Most people find discussing their ideas with friends, families or careers advisers helpful so make the most of the people around you. Don't, however, let them decide your actual career for you: this is a decision you need to make for yourself. Many people change careers several times in their life so don't feel that the decision you make now is the one you need to stick to forever.

Case Study Ben

When I tell people that I spent four years as a PhD student counting ducks most people just laugh. When they've stopped laughing and realise that I'm not joking, they start to think I must be slightly odd. I'm now co-founder of an award-winning magazine and far more interested in business than research, but what led me to go from Donald Duck to Donald Trump? I naively went into my PhD thinking I was going to save the world (albeit from ducks) but it soon became apparent that very few people actually cared about what I was doing. I witnessed brilliant young scientists, who I greatly respected, struggling to secure a future and I soon decided that for me, academia was a sinking ship. A hair-brained idea in the pub and a university business plan competition offered me a fresh opportunity and I've not looked back. I don't regret my time in academia because it taught me so much about communication of ideas and dealing with a multitude of situations. A professor once told me that life is all about running through brick walls but sometimes you just have to know when to run round them.

SOURCES OF SUPPORT

- University Careers Service – your institution might have a specific careers advisor for research students and you might be eligible to use the service after you've left.
- UK GRAD website and GRADschools – www.grad.ac.uk
- External consultancy if you are prepared to pay. Ask colleagues, friends and careers advisers for recommendations.

Career Management

Ali, L. and Graham, B. (2000) *Moving On in Your Career: A Guide for Postgraduates and Research Staff*. London, Routledge Falmer

Bolles, R. (2006) *What Colour is Your Parachute?* Berkeley, CA: Ten Speed Press.

Fagan, A. (2003) *Brilliant Job Hunter's Manual*. London: Prentice Hall.

Lees, J. (2005) *How to Get a Job You'll Love*. London: McGraw Hill.

London Career Group (2005) *How to Change Your Career*. London: The Careers Group, University of London.

Nathan, R. and Hill, L. (2005) *Career Counselling* (2nd edition). London: Sage.

Information on Different Careers

Basalla, S. and Debelius, M. (2007) *So What Are You Going to Do with That? Finding Careers outside Academia*. Chicago, IL: University Of Chicago Press.

DeLuca, M. and Lees, J. (2004) *Job Interviews: Top Answers to Tough Questions*. London: McGraw Hill.

Faust, B. and Faust, M. (2006) *Pitch Yourself: The CV and Interview Masterclass*. Harlow: Pearson Prentice Hall Business.

Leach, J. (ed.) (2005) *The Guardian Guide to Careers*. London: Guardian Books.

Robbins-Roth, C. (ed.) (2006) *Alternative Careers in Science: Leaving the Ivory Tower*. London: Elsevier Academic Press.

Secrist, J. and Fitzpatrick, J. (2000) *What Else You Can Do with a PhD?* Thousand Oaks, CA: Sage (CV and interview advice).

Website List

www.doctorjob.com/ Information on particular sectors and careers

www.hobsons.com/ Information on particular sectors and careers

www.prospects.ac.uk/ Information on particular sectors and careers

www.sciencecareers.sciencemag.org/ Articles written by people who have left academia

27 Entrepreneurship
Dr Richard Lilley

Introduction

The budding entrepreneurs among you will doubtless have a large number of questions in mind that you hope the following pages will answer. To avoid disappointment, the main points covered here are as follows:

- The potential for commercialising your research and research skills
- Understanding the principles of business
- Where to get advice and help.

This chapter will provide you with the means to assess your great idea sensibly, draw up a plan to turn the dream into reality and find help and support to avoid joining the alarming 50% of businesses that fail in their first three years (see the National *Business Link* website at www.businesslink.gov.uk click on *Starting Up, Considering Starting Up,* then *Common Mistakes*).

Key points and exercises are highlighted at the end of each section, allowing you to shape your plan of action. Where possible, exercises are also included, which are drawn from the source material listed in the bibliography.

The Potential for Commercialising Your Research and Research Skills

You may have a great idea, but people don't buy ideas, they buy goods and services. Some ideas are a long way from the market; they still require research and development. A piece of machinery to do a particular job would be an example; you can prove a design in principle, but manufacturing it on a commercial scale, to the correct standards, is a long way off. In contrast, a piece of software that already works may need less development, although it would still need to be rigorously tested. If your product is a service of some sort no development may be needed, but refinement of its delivery would be likely. To start with you'll need to assess (and get good advice about) the potential market for whatever you plan to offer and how far you are from it. The questions you're trying to answer include the following:

- Is there a market for this?
- How big is the market? How long will it last?
- What will it take to get my idea into a form that can be sold?
- Is it really my idea, or is the intellectual property shared?

You should first turn to your immediate colleagues. If they fall about laughing, stifle a petulant response and assess the flaws they suggest rationally. There is an alarming tendency among academics to hit on an idea, fall in love with it and assume everyone will do the same. This tendency is often retained when such a person sets up in business. I have watched in dismay while a product was developed at great cost for a customer with a misplaced confidence it would be first of many. The product actually turned out to be quite unique!

If, on the other hand, your colleagues think your idea is fantastic (both in the pub and in the cold light of day the next morning) then you may have a potential success on your hands. Your next step should be to define what you plan to offer clearly and succinctly. Get this definition assessed by as many trusted people as you can, so there is no doubt you know what it is you've got to offer. Most universities have specialist staff whose remit is to support the commercialisation of research (see 'Sources of Support' later in this chapter. After that, you need to decide how valuable your idea is. There is a scale of value to the potential customer that runs in decreasing order as follows:

- The product does something in a new way that saves time, or money, or both
- The product works in an established way and saves time, or money, or both
- The product does not save time or money, but is more reliable
- The product comes with better service (service and support)
- The product is cheaper.

(inspired by Southon and West, 2005).

It is vital to constantly put yourself in your would-be customers' shoes. Who are your buyers and why would they buy what you have to offer? How many are there of them? How much would they pay? Answering these sort of questions begins to turn your idea into a viable proposition.

KEY POINTS AND EXERCISES

Define the product(s) or service(s) that will be offered, for example, a software company might have the aim 'to help everyone benefit from the potential of personal computing'
Exercise:

- Summarise what will be delivered in a way that makes it irresistible to its target market.
- Assess whether people will actually want what is on offer. Where is the need?

Exercise:

- Consider the *Features* your product has and how these *Benefit* the potential customer. For example, a software product may have a new user interface that is easier to use (feature) and as a result users can get their work done quicker and more accurately (benefit); a complete 'course on personal development', for example, may have good ideas for improving a client's lifestyle (feature) which will only work if they put them into practice (benefit).
- What still needs doing before the idea is in a form that someone will buy? For example, have you got a working prototype that does something useful, or do you have an idea that you have yet to turn into a physical reality? If your idea is more of a service than a product, is it already a complete package you can offer to a customer?

Exercise:

- If someone asked you for your product next week, what could you give them?

Exercise:

- Test the idea. Make a prototype, ask colleagues and potential customers for their views on functionality, quality and cost.

Understanding the Principles of Business

Now that you have a fantastic idea, which cannot possibly fail to make you rich and famous, its time to face the cold, clammy reality that is 'business planning'. Entrepreneurs are not necessarily that keen on this aspect, but fortunately one of your considerations will be who else is joining your great venture. To begin with you'll need a provisional plan of action. This will be your very first 'business plan' and will shape how your great idea is brought to the masses (excited yet?!).

The initial business plan consists of the following:

- A punchy statement of what you offer
- Support for your plan : mentor and core staff
- Funding and material matters
- Learning to sell: your first customer
- How much of an entrepreneur are you?

A Punchy Statement of What You Offer

This requires the definition of what you offer in a way that is easy to communicate to a wide range of people, especially potential customers and financiers. It is more than the simple definition you'll have come up with if you did the exercise in the previous section. It still needs to be concise, but should also be exciting so the reader is keen to know more. Without wishing to labour the point don't keep this to yourself – everything you come up with should be assessed by trusted colleagues for feedback and constructive criticism.

By now some of you will have a particular question in mind: 'If I tell people what I am planning, won't they steal my idea?' At this stage all you have is an idea – there is so much involved in bringing this to market that there is virtually no risk that someone will drop everything and try to get ahead. Later on you may worry about industrial espionage, patents and litigation. Avoid all of this by being the best at whatever it is you are planning to do. There will always be competition whatever the product or service you provide. Indeed, if you're honest, somebody may already be thinking on the same lines. Have you got the determination to push your idea through to market? Or will you be saying in a year's time: 'Hey, here's someone selling the product (or service) I thought of!'

Support for Your Plan: Mentor and Core Staff

Depending on which entrepreneurial guide you read, the value of a mentor varies from negligible to vital. Personally, I think embarking on your grand plan without one is needlessly reckless. There are various definitions of 'mentor', but mainly such people act as a critical friend, challenging, supporting and helping you to learn in a variety of ways. Typically they will be more knowledgeable and experienced and therefore a source of good advice, and they will have a network of contacts that they can help you access. They should understand your business and be enthusiastic about it. Importantly, you must like your mentor and vice versa. The role is very much like that of your supervisor. Reflect for a moment on how hard your studies would have been without all that support, knowledge and guidance.

Naturally, finding a mentor might be difficult, so here are a few ideas on how and where to look for one. Your mentor will probably be someone you know, or is a friend of someone you know well. Remember, you are looking for a person who clearly has a background and experience in the sort of business area you want to move into. If your immediate professional or personal pool of people offers scant choice, your local Chamber of Commerce or The Princes Trust (if you are aged 30 or under) can help. If you join a course or club for entrepreneurs, this may include a mentoring scheme.

If you already know who you'd like to talk to, but they are well-known and difficult to contact, make your approach with care. An effective strategy is to make very cordial contact with their Personal Assistant or Secretary first and ask for their help. Most people are amenable to polite requests and if you are rudely refused then your prospective mentor was probably the wrong choice anyway. On the other hand, successful business people are busy and you shouldn't be offended if someone can't find the time to help you.

With your mentor in place you can now think of assembling the immediate team who will develop your business. The chances are you are part of a small group already unless your revelation came to you in an isolated moment of inspiration. A successful business is normally built around

- an entrepreneur (you of course!)
- an innovator (the brains behind the product or service)
- a delivery specialist (to get things done to schedule)
- a sales specialist (obviously!)
- a financial manager (to deal with credit providers and accountants etc.).

These are best found among people you know or your mentor knows. Together they form the nucleus of your business. As it expands each will become the head of their own department. Assembling this team of support will take time and effort, but it will be invaluable if you get your choices right. But where on earth are you, a researcher in a university, going to find people like this? Even if you wanted to, employing four specialists full-time even for a year would cost over a 100,000 pounds. It's more likely that your team will be partners in the business, and you may all have to multi-task in the early days. So where do you find them? Many universities, especially those with business schools, have Enterprise Societies, where budding entrepreneurs get together to learn and form business alliances. Through such societies you may, for example, meet a marketing specialist who is also looking for an opportunity like yours. You can also find people through a business incubator unit, through events at a local Chamber of Commerce, or through enterprise courses run by colleges. Above all, aim to keep expanding and maintaining your networks, as somebody will know a colleague or friend who may be able to help.

Funding and Material Matters

Without an excellent business plan it is unlikely you will be able to extract funding from third parties such as banks and venture capitalists. Even with a solid plan in place, you may be required to provide good evidence that your product or service will be successful (say through a market research exercise). Furthermore, it is likely that any investor will need to see projected returns on their investment over the short- and long-term. This process may take far longer than you imagine and you should be prepared to be patient. You should also accept that your proposals may be turned down a number of times before you are successful.

Financial support for your business, in descending order of preference, can come from the following sources:

- Your own money
- Money from family and friends
- A grant
- Revenue
- A loan from your mentor
- A loan from the bank or
- Venture capital.

There is much more that could be said of financial management; indeed many large books are dedicated to the subject (see Bibliography). A succinct summary would be; don't spend what you don't have, have a good financial manager in-house, don't mess with them and hire an accountant to keep the Inland Revenue at bay. Tax is so terribly complicated for the non-specialist that a competent accountant will easily repay their fee in the tax efficiencies they will gain for you.

Having established your solvency, you need to think about what this money is used for. Do you need equipment and premises? You will certainly need stationery, advertising and a database to manage your customers and leads. There is nothing more likely to focus your attention to detail than knowing your money could be wasted if you don't do a thorough job; so work with your mentor and supporting team to reduce the chances of error.

Learning to Sell: Your First Customer

The final part of the journey from great idea to product is when someone *gives you money for what you are selling.* If you have not experienced this before, it does make all the hard work worthwhile!

Your first customer will certainly be someone you know or someone your mentor knows. It's time to do your research again, so make sure you know exactly why that person should buy what you offer and prepare for your meeting with them exactly like you would for a vital job interview.

Working with your sales specialist, develop a tailored story that clearly shows your customer the value of buying what you offer. If you've done your homework you should be in a position to overcome any criticisms.

Above all *listen* to your customer. At this moment your customer is the most important person in the world, so respond to what they say rather than supplying prepared answers. The objective is to leave this meeting with the customer's commitment to trial your product, such that your second meeting secures the sale.

How Much of an Entrepreneur Are You?

Finally, we come to the crux of this section. At some point the initial excitement is going to wear off. When it does you need to be sure that the life you've chosen is what you want. So how can you tell? Here's a typical set of characteristics associated with entrepreneurs: confident, charismatic, energetic, workaholic, ambitious, opportunity seeker, future-oriented, market-driven and customer-oriented, resilient and decisive, arrogant, manipulative, starter, not a finisher, prone to a loss of focus.

If you've chatted to entrepreneurs as part of your research into whether to join them you'll probably agree with most of the list. Obviously, no one person has all of these attributes (and I am sure you can see which ones are undesirable anyway). The key point here is not to force you into psychoanalysis, but to ask you the following question:

> Do I understand what is required to become an entrepreneur and do I want to dedicate the vast majority of my waking hours to this occupation?

If the answer is a tentative 'yes' then you need to consider what your role as 'figurehead' is and what the demands are. If you are already uncomfortable with the characteristics I've listed ask yourself 'why?'. Are you perhaps an innovator, not an entrepreneur? Would you be better off as a so-called *intrapreneur*, developing products in a larger organisation?

If you are not sure then we're back to doing what you do best – research. I am often flabbergasted by how rarely people talk to those in the job(s) they would like to do themselves. If you are about to commit a good chunk of your life and income to this venture of yours you need to be as sure as possible that it is for you.

KEY POINTS AND EXERCISES

Come up with a short statement that quickly conveys what you can offer and why it is desirable. Composing an 'elevator pitch', such that if you find yourself in an elevator with someone you could convince them they could benefit your business during the ride. What will you say?

Find a business mentor who is appropriate for your business, has 'signed-on' to the idea and with whom you share a mutual respect. Make finding a mentor a priority. Finding a mentor is not impossible and may take valuable time, but will pay dividends if you get your choice right.

- Assemble a business team.
- Get your finances sorted early on. Spend time working out how much money is needed and how it is to be deployed. Constantly review this!
- Make a sale! If you fail with the first few customers make absolutely sure you know why it happened – and put it right.
- Be clear on why you are doing this and whether it suits your personality and circumstances.

Where to Get Advice and Help

This section is divided into three parts: 'Sources of support', 'Do's and don'ts' and 'Bibliography'.

SOURCES OF SUPPORT

Commercialising Your Research

If you work within a university then this is the best place to start. Many Universities have dedicated staff or departments that help fledgling companies 'spin-out'. Find yours and go and see them as soon as possible. First of all you will have to deal with the notion of 'Intellectual Property'. Is the idea really yours to sell? If it has arisen as part of your research degree, for example, it is unlikely that you hold all the rights to commercialisation. This is a complex legal area and you must establish your IP rights at the outset. Universities now have consistent, fair terms for sharing the proceeds between you, the university and the rest of your team if research done in the university has a commercial outcome. Don't try to escape this obligation: you'll be in legal difficulties later if you try. See Chapter 13 in this volume for further information.

Part of this process will also bring you into contact with people who have successfully pursued the path you are trying to take. Such people are often vital when you are building up your network. They may be able to advise on whether an idea is truly commercial. They may also have experience of good ideas that failed in the market place for reasons you have not considered. There are other options for realising the commercial value of your ideas besides forming a company. It may be easier and more profitable in the long run to look into patents and licensing, for example.

A lot of universities and local business-support organisations have 'business incubator units'. These are office facilities where fledgling companies can have dedicated office space, but share the support-structure like communications, secretarial support and administration. They usually also have business advisers onsite and are, of course, excellent places to make contacts.

If your idea doesn't stem from your university work, the business-support function will probably still be able to give you initial advice and point you at the sources of help in the wider world.

Finding a Mentor

The Princes Trust provides funding and support for young entrepreneurs. You need to be aged between 18–30 and the Trust aims to support the most needy of applicants. You'll have spotted that 'needy' wasn't a personal characteristic I've listed for the typical entrepreneur, so you'll want to show how your limited means could be improved so much by their help. Contact them via the web www.princes-trust.org.uk/ or on 0800 842842 to see if you qualify.

Courses and Training

Local colleges and university community programmes are increasingly running courses in entrepreneurship and business start-up. Such courses include everything covered in this chapter and more besides and will help you to work up a business plan. If you find the right course, you may also work with mentors and advisors that you would never otherwise have met. Such courses can be a very fast and cost-effective way of learning about business

Do's and Don'ts

Take care of the following or you may find yourself needing to fill your working hours some other way.

Cash Flow

Income won't start to flow in until you are making sales (and even then there is an inevitable 'lag'). Make sure you have enough capital behind you to get started and sustain things until the money is flowing in regularly.

Hand-in-hand with this, make sure you spend sensibly. Sort out budgets early on and stick to them. You can be hopeful and optimistic about the prospects for your business, but financial decisions should as far as possible be based on realism and hard facts.

Business Planning, or Lack Thereof

Within the scope of this chapter we've only discussed a provisional business plan. The full version will contain marketing, finance, sales and promotional plans, as well as detailed breakdowns of costs and profit predictions. Even if such a plan is created, if you don't stick to it it's worthless. Keep good records, monitor sales (and prospective sales) constantly. This is good for your blood pressure day-to-day and also allows you to plan for the future.

No Clear Objectives

From the outset all the work you have been doing should fall within and contribute to what is often referred to as your 'mission statement'. This is what your business is about and if you plan radical changes they must be carefully managed and communicated to everyone who needs to know.

Poor Management

If your management skills are weak or non-existent do something about it! Either hire someone who know what they are doing or learn yourself. In the latter case there are plenty of courses around to help small businesses get on their feet. Failure to do either will probably be fatal to your business.

Location and Communications

This needs to be good for your employees, big enough to accommodate your business as it grows, easy enough for suppliers and customers to find, and fully equipped with the hardware to support good communication with the outside world. It needs to be cost-effective too. Business incubators are an ideal option if you can find one.

(Un)happy Staff

Why do the people who work for you choose to do so? Check regularly and certainly don't assume this happy state requires no maintenance.

I am My Job

Finally, make no mistake that this *will* take over your life. You will rarely be able to switch your phone off and there will be lots of sleepless nights before profits are made. You will need to take calculated risks and respond positively to rejection and failure.

Conclusion

Setting up a business is potentially one of the most rewarding experiences of your professional life. Whether you will be offering products, services or a mixture of both, you will find considerable satisfaction from having happy customers reward you – verbally and financially!

The process of making a successful business work can be challenging, but much of the associated stress can be alleviated through careful planning and having a strong team of supporters around you who have a vested interest in the success of your venture.

Following the steps outlined in this chapter, being mindful of the potential problems that have been highlighted and making use of some of the recommended texts listed at the end should make the likelihood of your success that much greater.

Bibliography

Southon, M. and West, C. (2005) *The Beermat Entrepreneur*. Pearson. 160pp. www. beermat.biz (5 January 2008)

Financial Management

Dickerson, B.D., Campsey, B.J. and Brigham, E.F. (1994) *Introduction to Financial Management*. Harcourt. 800pp.

Martin, J.D., Petty, J., Scott, D.F. and Keown, A.J. (2004) *Financial Management: Principles and Applications*. Prentice Hall, 880pp.

Other General Texts

Ashton, R. (2004) *The Entrepreneur's Book of Checklists: 1000 Tips to Help You Start and Grow Your Business*. Prentice Hall. 224pp.

Excellent reference

Harper, S.C. (2003) The McGraw-Hill Guide to Starting Your Own Business. Harper. 254pp.

Good, but not as accessible as Beermat

Lang, J. (2002) The High-Tech Entrepreneurs Handbook. Pearson Education. 405pp.

A little impenetrable, but very relevant if it covers your would-be area.

Appendix 1: Code of Practice for the Assurance of Academic Quality and Standards in Higher Education – Postgraduate Research Programmes

This extract from the Code of Practice includes the context to the reforms of the first published draft with respect to research degree programmes and the actual precepts institutions are required to address. The full code of practice can be accessed via the QAA website www.qaa.ac.uk/academicinfrastructure/codeofPractice/section1/postgrad2004.pdf

Foreword

1   This document is the second edition of a code of practice for postgraduate research programmes provided in UK higher education institutions. It is one of a suite of inter-related documents which forms an overall Code of Practice for the assurance of academic quality and standards in higher education (the Code) for the guidance of higher education institutions subscribing to the Quality Assurance Agency (QAA) for Higher Education.

2   The overall Code and its 10 constituent sections were originally prepared by QAA between 1998 and 2001 in response to the reports of the National Committee of Inquiry into Higher Education and its Scottish Committee (the Dearing and Garrick Reports). The Code supports the national arrangements within the UK for quality assurance in higher education. The Code identifies a comprehensive series of system-wide principles (precepts) covering matters relating to the management of academic quality and standards in higher education. It provides an authoritative reference point for institutions as they consciously, actively and systematically assure the academic quality and standards of their programmes, awards and qualifications.

3   The Code assumes that, taking into account principles and practices agreed UK-wide, each institution has its own systems for independent verification both of its quality and standards and of the effectiveness of its

quality assurance systems. In developing the Code, extensive advice has been sought from a range of knowledgeable practitioners.

4   The Code does not incorporate statutory requirements relating to relevant legislation, for example, the Special Educational Needs and Disability Act 2001. It assumes that institutions have an overriding obligation in all such cases to ensure that they meet the requirements of legislation. However, where a section of the Code is related to legislative or similar obligations, efforts have been made to ensure compatibility between them.

5   Since 2001, a number of developments in UK higher education have encouraged QAA to begin a revision of individual sections of the Code. In undertaking this task QAA has also decided to review the structure of the sections and, in particular, to replace the original 'precepts and guidance' format with a 'precepts and explanation' approach, using the explanations to make clear why the precepts are considered important and reducing opportunities for a 'checklist' approach to the Code. In doing so QAA has sought to meet Recommendation 4 (part 4) of the Better Regulation Task Force in its interim report 'Higher Education: Easing the Burden, July 2002'.

6   Revised sections of the Code are therefore now structured into a series of precepts and accompanying explanations. The precepts express key matters of principle that the higher education community has identified as important for the assurance of quality and academic standards. Individual institutions should be able to demonstrate they are addressing the matters tackled by the precepts effectively, through their own management and organisational processes, taking account of institutional needs, traditions, culture and decision-making. The accompanying explanations show why the precepts are important.

7   The Code is a statement of good practice that has been endorsed by the higher education community. As such it is useful in QAA's audit and review processes that consider the extent to which an institution, in developing and implementing its own policies, has taken account of the Code and its precepts.

8   Institutions may find the explanations useful for developing their own policy and for allowing some flexibility of practice at subject level, depending on local needs. It is important to emphasise that the explanations do not form part of QAA's expectations of institutional practice when its teams are conducting audits and reviews.

9   Academic staff in departments and schools do not necessarily need to be aware of the detail of the various sections of the Code, although they might well be expected to be familiar with the institutional policies it informs and any parts which are particularly relevant to their own responsibilities.

10 To assist users, the precepts are listed, without the accompanying explanations in Appendix 1 of this section of the Code.

11 The first version of this section of the Code was published in January 1999. The publication of this second version follows consultation with staff in institutions, who have helped to update the Code to take account

of institutions' practical experience of using the guidance contained in its predecessor.

Context

12   This section of the Code is written in a firmer style than some other sections, especially the precepts, to give institutions clear guidance on the expectations of funding councils, research councils and QAA in respect of the management, quality and academic standards of research programmes. Institutions' use of the Code is monitored through the QAA audit and review processes (see paragraph 7 above). In the case of this section, the outputs of these review processes will be used by other agencies, including the UK funding councils, for monitoring purposes.

13   This section of the Code is also designed to guide institutions on the development of institutional codes of practice in the area of postgraduate research programmes (see Precept 3 below).

The precepts

Institutional arrangements

1   Institutions will put in place effective arrangements to maintain appropriate academic standards and enhance the quality of postgraduate research programmes.

2   Institutional regulations for postgraduate research degree programmes will be clear and readily available to students and staff. Where appropriate, regulations will be supplemented by similarly accessible, subject-specific guidance at the level of the faculty, school or department.

3   Institutions will develop, implement and keep under review a code or codes of practice applicable across the institution, which include(s) the areas covered by this document. The code(s) should be readily available to all students and staff involved in postgraduate research programmes.

4   Institutions will monitor the success of their postgraduate research programmes against appropriate internal and/or external indicators and targets.

The research environment

5   Institutions will only accept research students into an environment that provides support for doing and learning about research and where high-quality research is occurring.

Selection, admission and induction of students

6   Admissions procedures will be clear, consistently applied and will demonstrate equality of opportunity.

7   Only appropriately qualified and prepared students will be admitted to research programmes.

8   Admissions decisions will involve at least two members of the institution's staff who will have received instruction, advice and guidance in respect of selection and admissions procedures. The decision-making process will enable the institution to assure itself that balanced and independent admissions decisions have been made, that support its admissions policy.

9   The entitlements and responsibilities of a research student undertaking a postgraduate research programme will be defined and communicated clearly.

10 Institutions will provide research students with sufficient information to enable them to begin their studies with an understanding of the academic and social environment in which they will be working.

Supervision

11 Institutions will appoint supervisors who have the appropriate skills and subject knowledge to support, encourage and monitor research students effectively.

12 Each research student will have a minimum of one main supervisor. He or she will normally be part of a supervisory team. There must always be one clearly identified point of contact for the student.

13 Institutions will ensure that the responsibilities of all research student supervisors are clearly communicated to supervisors and students through written guidance.

14 Institutions will ensure that the quality of supervision is not put at risk as a result of an excessive volume and range of responsibilities assigned to individual supervisors.

Progress and review arrangements

15 Institutions will put in place and bring to the attention of students and relevant staff clearly defined mechanisms for monitoring and supporting student progress.

16 Institutions will put in place and bring to the attention of students and relevant staff clearly defined mechanisms for formal reviews of student progress, including explicit review stages.

17 Institutions will provide guidance to students, supervisors and others involved in progress monitoring and review processes about the importance of keeping appropriate records of the outcomes of meetings and related activities.

Development of research and other skills

18   Institutions will provide research students with appropriate opportunities
      for personal and professional development.
19   Each student's development needs will be identified and agreed jointly by
      the student and appropriate academic staff, initially during the student's
      induction period; they will be regularly reviewed during the research
      programme and amended as appropriate.
20   Institutions will provide opportunities for research students to maintain a
      record of personal progress, which includes reference to the development
      of research and other skills.

Feedback mechanisms

21   Institutions will put in place mechanisms to collect, review and, where
      appropriate, respond to feedback from all concerned with postgraduate
      research programmes. They will make arrangements for feedback to be
      considered openly and constructively and for the results to be communi-
      cated appropriately.

Assessment

22   Institutions will use criteria for assessing research degrees that enable
      them to define the academic standards of different research programmes
      and the achievements of their graduates. The criteria used to assess
      research degrees must be clear and readily available to students, staff and
      external examiners.
23   Research degree assessment procedures must be clear; they must be
      operated rigorously, fairly and consistently; include input from an
      external examiner; and carried out to a reasonable timescale.
24   Institutions will communicate their assessment procedures clearly to all the
      parties involved, that is the students, the supervisor(s) and the examiners.

Student representations

25   Institutions will put in place and publicise procedures for dealing with
      student representations that are fair, clear to all concerned, robust and
      applied consistently. Such procedures will allow all students access to rel-
      evant information and an opportunity to present their case.

Complaints

26 Independent and formal procedures will exist to resolve effectively complaints from research students about the quality of the institution's learning and support provision.

Appeals

27 Institutions will put in place formal procedures to deal with any appeals made by research students. The acceptable grounds for appeals will be clearly defined.

Acknowledgements

Appendix 1 is reproduced with permission, from the *Code of Practice for the Assurance of Academic Quality and Standards in Higher Education, Section 1: Postgraduate Research Programmes* © The Quality Assurance Agency for Higher Education, 2004.

Appendix 2: Skills Training Requirements for Research Students – Joint Statement by the Research Councils/AHRB (Issued in 2001)

See www.grad.ac.uk/jss
(reproduced with kind permission from the Research Councils)

The Joint Skills Statement forms Annex 3 of the **QAA Code of Practice for the Assurance of Academic Quality and Standards in Higher Education:** Postgraduate Research Programmes (see www.qaa.ac.uk/academicinfrastructure/codeOfPractice/section1/postgrad2004.pdf)

Introduction

The Research Councils play an important role in setting standards and identifying best practice in research training. This document sets out a joint statement of the skills that doctoral research students funded by the Research Councils would be expected to develop during their research training.

These skills may be present on commencement, explicitly taught, or developed during the course of the research. It is expected that different mechanisms will be used to support learning as appropriate, including self-direction, supervisor support and mentoring, departmental support, workshops, conferences, elective training courses, formally assessed courses and informal opportunities.

The Research Councils would also want to re-emphasise their belief that training in research skills and techniques is the key element in the development of a research student, and that PhD students are expected to make a substantial, original contribution to knowledge in their area, normally leading to published work. The development of wider employment-related skills should not detract from that core objective.

The purpose of this statement is to give a common view of the skills and experience of a typical research student thereby providing universities with a clear and consistent message aimed at helping them to ensure that all research training was of the highest standard, across all disciplines. It is not the intention of this document to provide assessment criteria for research training.

It is expected that each Council will have additional requirements specific to their field of interest and will continue to have their own measures for the evaluation of research training within institutions.

A) Research Skills and Techniques – to be able to demonstrate:

- the ability to recognise and validate problems
- original, independent and critical thinking, and the ability to develop theoretical concepts
- a knowledge of recent advances within one's field and in related areas
- an understanding of relevant research methodologies and techniques and their appropriate application within one's research field
- the ability to critically analyse and evaluate one's findings and those of others
- an ability to summarise, document, report and reflect on progress

B) Research Environment – to be able to:

- show a broad understanding of the context, at the national and international level, in which research takes place
- demonstrate awareness of issues relating to the rights of other researchers, of research subjects, and of others who may be affected by the research, for example, confidentiality, ethical issues, attribution, copyright, malpractice, ownership of data and the requirements of the Data Protection Act
- demonstrate appreciation of standards of good research practice in their institution and/or discipline
- understand relevant health and safety issues and demonstrate responsible working practices
- understand the processes for funding and evaluation of research
- justify the principles and experimental techniques used in one's own research
- understand the process of academic or commercial exploitation of research results

C) Research Management – to be able to:

- apply effective project management through the setting of research goals, intermediate milestones and prioritisation of activities

- design and execute systems for the acquisition and collation of information through the effective use of appropriate resources and equipment
- identify and access appropriate bibliographical resources, archives, and other sources of relevant information
- use information technology appropriately for database management, recording and presenting information

D)   Personal Effectiveness – to be able to:

- demonstrate a willingness and ability to learn and acquire knowledge
- be creative, innovative and original in one's approach to research
- demonstrate flexibility and open-mindedness
- demonstrate self-awareness and the ability to identify own training needs
- demonstrate self-discipline, motivation, and thoroughness
- recognise boundaries and draw upon/use sources of support as appropriate
- show initiative, work independently and be self-reliant

E)   Communication Skills – to be able to:

- write clearly and in a style appropriate to purpose, e.g. progress reports, published documents, thesis
- construct coherent arguments and articulate ideas clearly to a range of audiences, formally and informally through a variety of techniques
- constructively defend research outcomes at seminars and viva examination
- contribute to promoting the public understanding of one's research field
- effectively support the learning of others when involved in teaching, mentoring or demonstrating activities

F)   Networking and Teamworking – to be able to:

- develop and maintain co-operative networks and working relationships with supervisors, colleagues and peers, within the institution and the wider research community
- understand one's behaviours and impact on others when working in and contributing to the success of formal and informal teams
- listen, give and receive feedback and respond perceptively to others

G)   Career Management – to be able to:

- appreciate the need for and show commitment to continued professional development

- take ownership for and manage one's career progression, set realistic and achievable career goals, and identify and develop ways to improve employability
- demonstrate an insight into the transferable nature of research skills to other work environments and the range of career opportunities within and outside academia
- present one's skills, personal attributes and experiences through effective CVs, applications and interviews

Glossary

Doctoral-level Qualification/Doctorate

This is the highest level of study in the UK. It includes all varieties of PhDs, the Doctor of Medicine, Practice-based doctorates, European doctorates, Taught doctorates and Professional doctorates.

Department for Employment and Learning (DELNI or DEL)

A government department in the Northern Ireland Executive responsible for distributing public money for higher education in Northern Ireland. Visit their website at: www.delni.gov.uk

Framework for Higher Education Qualifications (FHEQ)

Published in 2001 by the Quality Assurance Agency (QAA) (visit their website given below). The framework includes formal definitions of qualifications including doctorates for England, Wales and Northern Ireland. www.qaa.ac.uk/academicinfrastructure/FHEQ/EWNI/default.asp

Higher Education Funding Council for England (HEFCE)

HEFCE is the funding council for postgraduate research degree programmes in England. There are different funding councils for Scotland, Wales and Northern Ireland as well. To know more, visit HEFCE's website at: www. hefce.ac.uk/Higher Education Funding Council for Wales (HEFCW)
This is the funding council for postgraduate research for Wales region. To know more visit their website at: www.hefcw.ac.uk/

Higher Education Institution (HEI or sometimes simply 'institution')

Higher Education Institution; another term for an institution that has degree-conferring powers.

Higher Education Statistics Agency (HESA)

HESA is the official agency for the collection, analysis and dissemination of quantitative information about higher education (www.hesa.ac.uk)

Joint Statement of Skills Training Requirements of Research Postgraduates (JSS)

This is a joint statement released by the Research Councils and AHRB in 2001 (seewww.grad.ac.uk/jss). It captures the skills that can be demonstrated after the completion of a research degree. Appendix 2 to this volume reproduces the statement.

National Postgraduate Committee (NPC)

NPC was formed in the 1980s and became a 'charitable' organisation in 2002. It seeks to advance postgraduate education in the UK. To know more about the role played by NPC visit their website at: www.npc.org.uk/

Personal Development Programme (PDP)

A process that produces a plan to support individuals in identifying their key skills and development activities to enhance these skills.

Postgraduate Research (Student) (PGR)

A postgraduate student undertaking a postgraduate degree that is predominantly research-based.

Postgraduate Taught (Student) (PGT)

A postgraduate student undertaking a postgraduate degree that is predominantly taught rather than research-based.

Quality Assurance Agency for Higher Education (QAA)

QAA safeguards and helps to improve the academic standards and quality of higher education in the UK. Established in 1997, QAA is an independent body funded by subscriptions from UK universities and colleges of higher education, and through contracts with the main UK higher education funding bodies. www.qaa.ac.uk/

Research Councils UK (RCUK)

Research Councils UK. The strategic partnership of the UK's seven Research Councils. www.rcuk.ac.uk/

Research Council

The seven research councils (Medical Research Council, Arts and Humanities Research Council, Biotechnology and Biological Sciences Research Council, Engineering and Physical Sciences Research Council, Economic and Social Research Council, Natural Environment Research Council, Science and Technology Facilities Council) are the UK's main government agencies for funding research. They are funded by the government through the Department for Innovation, Universities and Skills (DIUS) www.dti.gov.uk/science/index.html

Research Degree

A qualification whose process is predominantly based around research. Some of these degrees can lead to a doctoral level award and some to a masters level award.

Research Student

Another term for Postgraduate Research (Student) PGR see above.

The Scottish Funding Council (SFC)

SFC distributes funds to Scotland's colleges and universities for teaching and learning, research and other activities in support of Scottish government priorities. www.sfc.ac.uk/index.htm

Standing Conference of Principals (SCOP)

The representative body for higher education colleges in England and Northern Ireland. www.scop.ac.uk/Scop.asp

UK

United Kingdom, made up of the countries of England, Scotland, Wales and Northern Ireland.

UK Council for Graduate Education (UKCGE)

Established for the public benefit to advance graduate education in all academic disciplines throughout the UK (provides workshops, conferences and discussion forums for academics and professionals).

The UK GRAD Programme

The Programme supports the academic sector to embed personal and professional skills development into research degree programmes. www.grad.ac.uk/

Universities UK (UUK)

UUK is a representative body of UK universities with 131 universities to its membership. www.universitiesuk.ac.uk/

Index